Hymns to the Mystic Fire

D1453831

Sri Aurobindo

Hymns to the Mystic Fire

With Sanskrit text, English translation and commentary

LOTUS LIGHT PUBLICATIONS
Box 325, Twin Lakes, WI 53181
USA

This edition is published and distributed in the United States by Lotus Light Publications, PO Box 325, Twin Lakes, WI 53181 by arrangement with Sri Aurobindo Ashram Trust, Publication Department, Pondicherry 605002 India.

First U.S. Edition
ISBN 0-914955-22-5
Library of Congress Catalog Card No. 96-75800

Printed at Sri Aurobindo Ashram Press
Pondicherry, India

Printed in India.

CONTENTS

CONTENTS

Foreword

IN ANCIENT times the Veda was revered as a sacred book of wisdom, a great mass of inspired poetry, the work of Rishis, seers and sages, who received in their illumined minds rather than mentally constructed a great universal, eternal and impersonal Truth which they embodied in Mantras, revealed verses of power, not of an ordinary but of a divine inspiration and source. The name given to these sages was Kavi, which afterwards came to mean any poet, but at the time had the sense of a seer of truth, — the Veda itself describes them as *kavayah satyaśrutah*, "seers who are hearers of the Truth" and the Veda itself was called, *śruti*, a word which came to mean "revealed Scripture". The seers of the Upanishad had the same idea about the Veda and frequently appealed to its authority for the truths they themselves announced and these too afterwards came to be regarded as Sruti, revealed Scripture, and were included in the sacred Canon.

This tradition persevered in the Brahmanas and continued to maintain itself in spite of the efforts of the ritualistic commentators, Yajnikas, to explain everything as myth and rite and the division made by the Pandits distinguishing the section of works, Karmakanda, and the section of Knowledge, Jnanakanda, identifying the former with the hymns and the latter with the Upanishads. This drowning of the parts of Knowledge by the parts of ceremonial works was strongly criticised in one of the Upanishads and in the Gita, but both look on the Veda as a Book of Knowledge. Even, the Sruti including both Veda and Upanishad was regarded as the supreme authority for spiritual knowledge and infallible.

Is this all legend and moonshine, or a groundless and even nonsensical tradition? Or is it the fact that there is only a scanty element of higher ideas in some later hymns which started this theory? Did the writers of the Upanishads foist upon the Riks a meaning which was not there but read into it by their imagination

or a fanciful interpretation? Modern European scholarship insists on having it so. And it has persuaded the mind of modern
India. In favour of this view is the fact that the Rishis of the Veda
were not only seers but singers and priests of sacrifice, that their
chants were written to be sung at public sacrifices and refer constantly to the customary ritual and seem to call for the outward
objects of these ceremonies, wealth, prosperity, victory over enemies. Sayana, the great commentator, gives us a ritualistic and
where necessary a tentatively mythical or historical sense to the
Riks, very rarely does he put forward any higher meaning though
sometimes he lets a higher sense come through or puts it as an
alternative as if in despair of finding out some ritualistic or
mythical interpretation. But still he does not reject the spiritual
authority of the Veda or deny that there is a higher truth contained in the Riks. This last development was left to our own
times and popularised by occidental scholars.

The European scholars took up the ritualistic tradition, but
for the rest they dropped Sayana overboard and went on to make
their own etymological explanation of the words, or build up
their own conjectural meanings of the Vedic verses and gave a
new presentation often arbitrary and imaginative. What they
sought for in the Veda was the early history of India, its society,
institutions, customs, a civilisation-picture of the times. They
invented the theory based on the difference of languages of an
Aryan invasion from the north, an invasion of a Dravidian India
of which the Indians themselves had no memory or tradition
and of which there is no record in their epic or classical literature.
The Vedic religion was in this account only a worship of Nature-
Gods full of solar myths and consecrated by sacrifices and a sacrificial liturgy primitive enough in its ideas and contents, and it is
these barbaric prayers that are the much vaunted, haloed and
apotheosized Veda.

There can be no doubt that in the beginning there was a
worship of the Powers of the physical world, the Sun, Moon,
Heaven and Earth, Wind, Rain and Storm etc., the Sacred Rivers
and a number of Gods who presided over the workings of Nature.
That was the general aspect of the ancient worship in Greece,
Rome, India and among other ancient peoples. But in all these

countires these gods began to assume a higher, a psychological function; Pallas Athene who may have been originally a Dawn-Goddess springing in flames from the head of Zeus, the Sky-God, Dyaus of the Veda, has in classical Greece a higher function and was identified by the Romans with their Minerva, the Goddess of learning and wisdom; similarly, Saraswati, a River Goddess, becomes in India the goddess of wisdom, learning and the arts and crafts: all the Greek deities have undergone a change in this direction — Apollo, the Sun-God, has become a god of poetry and prophecy, Hephaestus the Fire-God a divine smith, god of labour. In India the process was arrested half-way, and the Vedic Gods developed their psychological functions but retained more fixedly their external character and for higher purposes gave place to a new pantheon. They had to give precedence to Puranic deities who developed out of the early company but assumed larger cosmic functions, Vishnu, Rudra, Brahma, — developing from the Vedic Brihaspati, or Brahmanaspati, — Shiva, Lakshmi, Durga. Thus in India the change in the gods was less complete, the earlier deities became the inferior divinities of the Puranic pantheon and this was largely due to the survival of the Rig-veda in which their psychological and their external functions co-existed and are both given a powerful emphasis; there was no such early literary record to maintain the original features of the Gods of Greece and Rome.

This change was evidently due to a cultural development in these early peoples who became progressively more mentalised and less engrossed in the physical life as they advanced in civilisation and needed to read into their religion and their deities finer and subtler aspects which would support their more highly mentalised concepts and interests and find for them a true spiritual being or some celestial figure as their support and sanction. But the largest part in determining and deepening this inward turn must be attributed to the Mystics who had an enormous influence on these early civilisations; there was indeed almost everywhere an age of the Mysteries in which men of a deeper knowledge and self-knowledge established their practices, significant rites, symbols, secret lore within or on the border of the more primitive exterior religions. This took different forms in different countries; in Greece there were the Orphic and Eleusinian Mysteries, in Egypt and Chaldea the priests and their occult lore and magic, in Persia the Magi, in India the Rishis. The preoccupation of the Mystics was with self-knowledge and a profounder world-knowledge; they found out that in man there was a deeper self and inner being behind the surface of the outward physical man, which it was his highest business to discover and know. "Know thyself" was their great precept, just as in India to know the Self, the Atman became the great spiritual need, the highest thing for the human being. They found also a Truth, a Reality behind the outward aspects of the universe and to discover, follow, realise this Truth was their great aspiration. They discovered secrets and powers of Nature which were not those of the physical world but which could bring occult mastery over the physical world and physical things and to systematise this occult knowledge and power was also one of their strong preoccupations. But all this could only be safely done by a difficult and careful training, discipline, purification of the nature; it could not be done by the ordinary man. If men entered into these things without a severe test and training it would be dangerous to themselves and others; this knowledge, these powers could be misused, misinterpreted, turned from truth to falsehood, from good to evil. A strict secrecy was therefore maintained, the knowledge handed down behind a veil from master to disciple. A veil of symbols was created behind which these mysteries could shelter, formulas of speech also which could be understood by the initiated but were either not known by others or were taken by them in an outward sense which carefully covered their true meaning and secret. This was the substance of Mysticism everywhere.

It has been the tradition in India from the earliest times that the Rishis, the poet-seers of the Veda, were men of this type, men with a great spiritual and occult knowledge not shared by ordinary human beings, men who handed down this knowledge and their powers by a secret initiation to their descendant and chosen disciples. It is a gratuitous assumption to suppose that this tradition was wholly unfounded, a superstition that arose suddenly or slowly formed in a void, with nothing whatever to support it; some foundation there must have been however

small or however swelled by legend and the accretions of centu-
ries. But if it is true, then inevitably the poet-seers must have
expressed something of their secret knowledge, their mystic lore
in their writings and such an element must be present, however
well-concealed by an occult language or behind a technique of
symbols, and if it is there it must be to some extent discoverable.
It is true that an antique language, obsolete words, — Yaska
counts more than four hundred of which he did not know the
meaning, — and often a difficult and out-of-date diction helped
to obscure their meaning; the loss of the sense of their symbols,
the glossary of which they kept to themselves, made them unin-
telligible to later generations; even in the time of the Upanishads
the spiritual seekers of the age had to resort to initiation and
meditation to penetrate into their secret knowledge, while the
scholars afterwards were at sea and had to resort to conjecture
and to concentrate on a mental interpretation or to explain by
myths, by the legends of the Brahmanas themselves often symbolic and obscure. But still to make this discovery will be the sole
way of getting at the true sense and the true value of the Veda.
We must take seriously the hint of Yaska, accept the Rishi's description of the Veda's contents as "seer-wisdoms, seer-words",
and look for whatever clue we can find to this ancient wisdom.
Otherwise the Veda must remain for ever a sealed book; grammarians, etymologists, scholastic conjectures will not open to us
the sealed chamber.

For it is a fact that the tradition of a secret meaning and a
mystic wisdom couched in the Riks of the ancient Veda was as
old as the Veda itself. The Vedic Rishis believed that their
Mantras were inspired from higher hidden planes of consciousness
and contained this secret knowledge. The words of the Veda
could only be known in their true meaning by one who was himself a seer or mystic; from others the verses withheld their hidden
knowledge. In one of Vamadeva's hymns in the fourth Mandala
(IV.3.16) the Rishi describes himself as one illumined expressing
through his thought and speech words of guidance, "secret
words" — *ninyā vacāṁsi* — "seer-wisdoms that utter their inner
meaning to the seer" — *kāvyāni kavaye nivacanā*. The Rishi
Dirghatamas speaks of the Riks, the Mantras of the Veda, as

existing "in a supreme ether, imperishable and immutable in which all the gods are seated", and he adds "one who knows not That what shall he do with the Rik?" (I.164.39) He further alludes to four planes from which the speech issues, three of them hidden in the secrecy while the fourth is human, and from there comes the ordinary word; but the word and thought of the Veda belongs to the higher planes (I.164.46). Elsewhere in the Riks the Vedic Word is described (X.71) as that which is supreme and the topmost height of speech, the best and the most faultless. It is something that is hidden in secrecy and from there comes out and is manifested. It has entered into the truth-seers, the Rishis, and it is found by following the track of their speech. But all cannot enter into its secret meaning. Those who do not know the inner sense are as men who seeing see not, hearing hear not, only to one here and there the Word desiring him like a beautifully robed wife to a husband lays open her body. Others unable to drink steadily of the milk of the Word, the Vedic cow, move with it as with one that gives no milk, to him the Word is a tree without flowers or fruits. This is quite clear and precise; it results from it beyond doubt that even then while the Rig-veda was being written the Riks were regarded as having a secret sense which was not open to all. There was an occult and spiritual knowledge in the sacred hymns and by this knowledge alone, it is said, one can know the truth and rise to a higher existence. This belief was not a later tradition but held, probably, by all and evidently by some of the greatest Rishis such as Dirghatamas and Vamadeva.

The tradition, then, was there and it was prolonged after the Vedic times. Yaska speaks of several schools of interpretation of the Veda. There was a sacrificial or ritualistic interpretation, the historical or rather mythological explanation, an explanation by the grammarians and etymologists, by the logicians, a spiritual interpretation. Yaska himself declares that there is a triple knowledge and therefore a triple meaning of the Vedic hymns, a sacrificial or ritualistic knowledge, a knowledge of the gods and finally a spiritual knowledge; but the last is the true sense and when one gets it the others drop or are cut away. It is this spiritual sense that saves and the rest is outward and subordinate. He says further that "the Rishis saw the truth, the true law of things, directly by an inner vision"; afterwards the knowledge and the inner sense of the Veda were almost lost and the Rishis who still knew had to save it by handing it down through initiation to disciples and at a last stage outward and mental means had to be used for finding the sense such as Nirukta and other Vedangas. But even then, he says, "the true sense of the Veda can be recovered directly by meditation and tapasya", those who can use these means need no outward aids for this knowledge. This also is sufficiently clear and positive.

The tradition of a mystic element in the Veda as a source of Indian civilisation, its religion, its philosophy, its culture is more in consonance with historical fact than the European scouting of this idea. The nineteenth century European scholarship writing in a period of materialistic rationalism regarded the history of the race as a development out of primitive barbarism or semi-barbarism, a crude social life and religion and a mass of superstitions, by the growth of outward civilised institutions, manners and habits through the development of intellect and reason, art, philosophy and science and a clearer and sounder, more matter-of-fact intelligence. The ancient idea about the Veda could not fit into this picture; it was regarded as rather a part of ancient superstitious ideas and a primitive error. But we can now form a more accurate idea of the development of the race. The ancient more primitive civilisations held in themselves the elements of the later growth but their early wise men were not scientists and philosophers or men of high intellectual reason but mystics and even mystery-men, occultists, religious seekers; they were seekers after a veiled truth behind things and not of an outward knowledge. The scientists and philosophers came afterwards; they were preceded by the mystics and often like Pythagoras and Plato were to some extent mystics themselves or drew many of their ideas from the mystics. In India philosophy grew out of the seeking of the mystics and retained and developed their spiritual aims and kept something of their methods in later Indian spiritual discipline and Yoga. The Vedic tradition, the fact of a mystical element in the Veda fits in perfectly with this historical truth and takes its place in the history of Indian culture.

The tradition of the Veda as the bed-rock of Indian civilisation — not merely a barbaric sacrificial liturgy — is more than a tradition, it is an actual fact of history.

But even if an element of high spiritual knowledge, or passages full of high ideas were found in the hymns, it might be supposed that those are perhaps only a small factor, while the rest is a sacrificial liturgy, formulas of prayer and praise to the Gods meant to induce them to shower on the sacrificers material blessings such as plenty of cows, horses, fighting men, sons, food, wealth of all kinds, protection, victory in battle, or to bring down rain from heaven, recover the sun from clouds or from the grip of Night, the free flowing of the seven rivers, recovery of cattle from the Dasyus (or the Dravidians) and the other boons which on the surface seem to be the object of this ritual worship. The Rishis would then be men with some spiritual or mystic knowledge but otherwise dominated by all the popular ideas proper to their times. These two elements they would then mix up intimately in their hymns and this would account at least in part for the obscurity and the rather strange and sometimes grotesque jumble which the traditional interpretation offers us. But if, on the other hand, a considerable body of high thinking clearly appears, if there is a large mass of verses or whole hymns which admit only of a mystic character and significance, and if finally, the ritualistic and external details are found to take frequently the appearance of symbols such as were always used by the mystics, and if there are many clear indications, even some explicit statements in the hymns themselves of such a meaning, then all changes. We are in the presence of a great scripture of the mystics with a double significance, one exoteric the other esoteric, the symbols themselves have a meaning which makes them a part of the esoteric significance, an element in the secret teaching and knowledge. The whole of the Rig-veda, a small number of hymns perhaps excepted, becomes in its inner sense such a Scripture. At the same time the exoteric sense need not be merely a mask; the Riks may have been regarded by their authors as words of power, powerful not only for internal but for external things. A purely spiritual scripture would concern itself with only spiritual significances, but the ancient mystics were also what we would call occultists, men who believed that by inner means outer as well as inner results could be produced, that thought and words could be so used as to bring about realisations of every kind, — in the phrase common in the Veda itself, — both the human and the divine.

But where is this body of esoteric meaning in the Veda? It is only discoverable if we give a constant and straightforward meaning to the words and formulas employed by the Rishis, especially to the key-words which bear as keystones the whole structure of their doctrine. One such word is the great word, Ritam, Truth; Truth was the central object of the seeking of the Mystics, a spiritual or inner Truth, a truth of ourselves, a truth of things, a truth of the world and of the gods, a truth behind all we are and all that things are. In the ritualistic interpretation this master word of the Vedic knowledge has been interpreted in all kinds of senses according to the convenience or fancy of the interpreter, "truth", "sacrifice", "water", "one who has gone", even "food", not to speak of a number of other meanings; if we do that, there can be no certitude in our dealings with the Veda. But let us consistently give it the same master sense and a strange but clear result emerges. If we apply the same treatment to other standing terms of the Veda, if we give them their ordinary, natural and straightforward meaning and give it constantly and consistently not monkeying about with their sense or turning them into purely ritualistic expressions, if we allow to certain important words, such as *śravas*, *kratu*, the psychological meaning of which they are capable and which they undoubtedly bear in certain passages as when the Veda describes Agni as *kratur hṛdi*, then this result becomes all the more clear, extended, pervasive. If, in addition, we follow the indications which abound, sometimes the explicit statement of the Rishis about the inner sense of their symbols, interpret in the same sense the significant legends and figures on which they constantly return, the conquest over Vritra and the battle with the Vritras, his powers, the recovery of the Sun, the Waters, the Cows from the Panis or other Dasyus, the whole Rig-veda reveals itself as a body of doctrine and practice, esoteric, occult, spiritual, such as might have been given by the mystics in any ancient country but which

2

actually survives for us only in the Veda. It is there deliberately hidden by a veil, but the veil is not so thick as we first imagine; we have only to use our eyes and the veil vanishes; the body of the Word, the Truth stands out before us.

Many of the lines, many whole hymns even of the Veda bear on their face a mystic meaning; they are evidently an occult form of speech, have an inner meaning. When the seer speaks of Agni as "the luminous guardian of the Truth shining out in his own home", or of Mitra and Varuna or other gods as "in touch with the Truth and making the Truth grow" or as "born in the Truth", these are words of a mystic poet, who is thinking of that inner Truth behind things of which the early sages were the seekers. He is not thinking of the Nature-Power presiding over the outer element of fire or of the fire of the ceremonial sacrifice. Or he speaks of Saraswati as one who impels the words of Truth and awakes to right thinkings or as one opulent with the thought: Saraswati awakes to consciousness or makes us conscious of the "Great Ocean and illumines all our thoughts". It is surely not the River Goddess whom he is thus hymning but the Power, the River if you will, of inspiration, the word of the Truth, bringing its light into our thoughts, building up in us that Truth, an inner knowledge. The Gods constantly stand out in their psychological functions; the sacrifice is the outer symbol of an inner work, an inner interchange between the gods and men, — man giving what he has, the gods giving in return the horses of power, the herds of light, the heroes of Strength to be his retinue, winning for him victory in his battle with the hosts of Darkness, Vritras, Dasyus, Panis. When the Rishi says, "Let us become conscious whether by the War-Horse or by the Word of a Strength beyond men", his words have either a mystic significance or they have no co-herent meaning at all. In the portions translated in this book we have many mystic verses and whole hymns which, however mystic, tear the veil off the outer sacrificial images covering the real sense of the Veda. "Thought," says the Rishi, "has nou-rished for us human things in the Immortals, in the Great Hea-vens; it is the milch-cow which milks of itself the wealth of many forms" — the many kinds of wealth, cows, horses and the rest for which the sacrificer prays; evidently this is no material wealth, it is something which Thought, the Thought embodied in the Mantra, can give and it is the result of the same Thought that nourishes our human things in the Immortals, in the Great Heavens. A process of divinisation, and of a bringing down of great and luminous riches, treasures won from the Gods by the inner work of sacrifice, is hinted at in terms necessarily covert but still for one who knows how to read these secret words, *niṇyā vacāṁsi,* sufficiently expressive, *kavaye nivacanā.* Again, Night and Dawn the eternal sisters are like "joyful weaving women weaving the weft of our perfected works into the form of a sacrifice". Again, words with a mystic form and meaning, but there could hardly be a more positive statement of the psychological character of the Sacrifice, the real meaning of the Cow, of the riches sought for, the plenitudes of the Great Treasure.

Under pressure of the necessity to mask their meaning with symbols and symbolic words — for secrecy must be observed — the Rishis resorted to fix double meanings, a device easily manageable in the Sanskrit language where one word often bears several different meanings, but not easy to render in an English translation and very often impossible. Thus the word for cow, *go,* meant also light or a ray of light; this appears in the names of some of the Rishis, Gotama, most radiant, Gavishthira, steadfast in the Light. The cows of the Veda were the Herds of the Sun, familiar in Greek myth and mystery, the rays of the Sun of Truth and Light and Knowledge; this meaning which comes out in some passages can be consistently applied everywhere yielding a coherent sense. The word *ghṛta* means ghee or clarified butter and this was one of the chief elements of the sacrificial rite; but *ghṛta* could also mean light, from the root *ghṛ* to shine and it is used in this sense in many passages. Thus the horses of Indra, the Lord of Heaven, are described as dripping with light, *ghṛta-snū*[1] — it certainly does not mean that ghee dripped from them as they ran, although that seems to be the sense of the same epithet as applied to the grain of which Indra's horses are invited to

---

[1] Sayana, though in several passages he takes *ghṛta* in the sense of light, renders it here by 'water'; he seems to think that the divine horses were very tired and perspiring profusely! A Naturalistic interpreter might as well argue that as Indra is a God of the sky, the primitive poet might well believe that rain was the perspiration of Indra's horses.

partake when they come to the sacrifice. Evidently this sense of light doubles with that of clarified butter in the symbolism of the sacrifice. The thought or the word expressing the thought is compared to pure clarified butter, expressions like *dhiyaṁ ghr̥tācīm*, the luminous thought or understanding occur. There is a curious passage in one of the hymns translated in this book calling on Fire as priest of the sacrifice to flood the offering with a mind pouring ghrita, *ghr̥tapruṣā manasā* and so manifest the Seats ("places, or planes"), the three heavens each of them and manifest the Gods.[1] But what is a ghee-pouring mind, and how by pouring ghee can a priest manifest the Gods and the triple heavens? But admit the mystical and esoteric meaning and the sense becomes clear. What the Rishi means is a "mind pouring the light", a labour of the clarity of an enlightened or illumined mind; it is not a human priest or a sacrificial fire, but the inner Flame, the mystic seer-will, *kavikratu*, and that can certainly manifest by this process the Gods and the worlds and all planes of the being. The Rishis, it must be remembered, were seers as well as sages, they were men of vision who saw things in their meditation in images, often symbolic images which might precede or accompany an experience and put it in a concrete form, might predict or give an occult body to it: so it would be quite possible for him to see at once the inner experience and in image its symbolic happening, the flow of clarifying light and the priest god pouring this clarified butter on the inner self-offering which brought the experience. This might seem strange to a Western mind, but to an Indian mind accustomed to the Indian tradition or capable of meditation and occult vision it would be perfectly intelligible. The mystics were and normally are symbolists, they can even see all physical things and happenings as symbols of inner truths and realities, even their outer selves, the outer happenings of their life and all around them. That would make their identification or else an association of the thing and its symbol easy, its habit possible.

Other standing words and symbols of the Veda invite a similar interpretation of their sense. As the Vedic "cow" is the symbol of light, so the Vedic "horse" is a symbol of power,

---

[1] This is Sayana's rendering of the passage and rises directly from the words.

spiritual strength, force of tapasya. When the Rishi asks Agni for a "horse-form cow-in-front gift" he is not asking really for a number of horses forming a body of the gift with some cows walking in front, he is asking for a great body of spiritual power led by the light or, as we may translate it, "with the Ray-Cow walking in its front."[1] As one hymn describes the recovery from the Panis of the mass of the rays (the cows, — the shining herds, *gavyam*), so another hymn asks Agni for a mass of abundance or power of the horse — *aśvyam*. So too the Rishi asks sometimes for the heroes or fighting men as his retinue, sometimes in more abstract language and without symbol for a complete hero-force — *suvīryam*; sometimes he combines the symbol and the thing. So too the Rishis ask for a son or sons or offspring, *apatyam*, as an element of the wealth for which they pray to the Gods, but here too an esoteric sense can be seen, for in certain passages the son born to us is clearly an image of some inner birth: Agni himself is our son, the child of our works, the child who as the Universal Fire is the father of his fathers, and it is by setting the steps on things that have fair offspring that we create or discover a path to the higher world of Truth. Again, "water" in the Veda is used as a symbol. It speaks of the inconscient ocean, *salilam apraketam*, in which the Godhead is involved and out of which he is born by his greatness; it speaks also of the great ocean, *maho arṇaḥ*, the upper waters which, as one hymn says, Saraswati makes conscious for us or of which she makes us conscious by the ray of intuition — *pra cetayati ketunā*. The seven rivers seem to be the rivers of Northern India but the Veda speaks of the seven Mighty Ones of Heaven who flow down from Heaven; they are waters that know, knowers of the Truth — *ṛtajña* — and when they are released they discover for us the road to the great Heavens. So, too, Parashara speaks of Knowledge and universal Life, "in the house of the waters". Indra releases the rain by slaying Vritra, but this rain too is the rain of Heaven and sets the rivers flowing. Thus the legend of the release of the waters which takes so large a place in the Veda puts on the aspect of a symbolic myth. Along with it comes the other symbolic

---

[1] Compare the expression which describes the Aryan, the noble people as led by the light — *jyotir-agrāḥ*.

legend of the discovery and rescue, from the dark cave in the mountain, of the Sun, the cows or herds of the Sun, or the Sun-world — *svar* — by the Gods and the Angiras Rishis. The symbol of the Sun is constantly associated with the higher Light and the Truth: it is in the Truth concealed by an inferior Truth that are unyoked the horses of the Sun, it is the Sun in its highest light that is called upon in the great Gayatri Mantra to impel our thoughts. So, too, the enemies in the Veda are spoken of as robbers, *dasyus*, who steal the cows, or Vritras and are taken literally as human enemies in the ordinary interpretation, but Vritra is a demon who covers and holds back the Light and the waters and the Vritras are his forces fulfilling that function. The Dasyus, robbers or destroyers, are the powers of darkness, adversaries of the seekers of Light and the Truth. Always there are indications that lead us from the outward and exoteric to an inner and esoteric sense.

In connection with the symbol of the Sun a notable and most significant verse in a hymn of the fifth Mandala may here be mentioned; for it shows not only the profound mystic symbolism of the Vedic poets, but also how the writers of the Upanishads understood the Rig-veda and justifies their belief in the inspired knowledge of their forerunners. "There is a Truth covered by a Truth", runs the Vedic passage, "where they unyoke the horses of the Sun; the ten hundreds stood together, there was That One;[1] I saw the greatest (best, most glorious) of the embodied gods."[2] Then mark how the seer of the Upanishad translates this thought or this mystic experience into his own later style, keeping the central symbol of the Sun but without any secrecy in the sense. Thus runs the passage in the Upanishad, "The face of the Truth is covered with a golden lid. O Pushan, that remove for the vision of the law of the Truth.[3] O Pushan (fosterer), sole seer, O Yama, O Sun, O Child of the Father of beings, marshal and gather together thy rays; I see the Light which is that fairest (most auspicious) form of thee; he who is this Purusha, He am I." The golden lid is meant to be the same as the inferior covering

---

[1] Or, That (the supreme Truth) was one;

[2] Or, it means, "I saw the greatest (best) of the bodies of the gods."

[3] Or, for the law of the Truth, for vision.

truth, *ṛtam*, spoken of in the Vedic verse; the "best of the bodies of the Gods" is equivalent to the "fairest form of the Sun", it is the supreme Light which is other and greater than all outer light; the great formula of the Upanishad, "He am I", corresponds to That One, *tad ekam*, of the Rig-vedic verse; the "standing together of the ten hundreds" (the rays of the Sun, says Sayana, and that is evidently the meaning) is reproduced in the prayer to the Sun "to marshal and mass his rays" so that the supreme form may be seen. The Sun in both the passages, as constantly in the Veda and frequently in the Upanishad, is the Godhead of the supreme Truth and Knowledge and his rays are the light emanating from that supreme Truth and Knowledge. It is clear from this instance — and there are others — that the seer of the Upanishad had a truer sense of the meaning of the ancient Veda than the mediaeval ritualistic commentator with his gigantic learning, much truer than the modern and very different mind of the European scholars.

There are certain psychological terms which have to be taken consistently in their true sense if we are to find the inner or esoteric meaning. Apart from the Truth, Ritam, we have to take always in the sense of "thought" the word *dhī* which constantly recurs in the hymns. This is the natural meaning of *dhī* which corresponds to the later word Buddhi; it means thought, understanding, intelligence and in the plural 'thoughts', *dhiyaḥ*. It is given in the ordinary interpretation all kinds of meanings; "water", "work", "sacrifice", "food", etc. as well as thought. But in our search we have to take it consistently in its ordinary and natural significance and see what is the result. The word *ketu* means very ordinarily "ray" but it also bears the meaning of intellect, judgment or an intellectual perception. If we compare the passages in the Veda in which it occurs we can come to the conclusion that it meant a ray of perception or intuition, as for instance, it is by the ray of intuition, *ketunā*, that Saraswati makes us conscious of the great waters; that too probably is the meaning of the rays which come from the Supreme foundation above and are directed downwards; these are the intuitions of knowledge as the rays of the Sun of Truth and Light. The word *kratu* means ordinarily work or sacrifice but it also means intelligence, power or resolution and especially the power of the intelligence that determines the work, the will. It is in this latter sense that we can interpret it in the esoteric rendering of the Veda. Agni is a seer-will, *kavikratu*, he is the "will in the heart", *kratur hṛdi*. Finally the word *śravas* which is constantly in use in the Veda means fame, it is also taken by the commentators in the sense of food, but these significances cannot be fitted in everywhere and very ordinarily lack all point and apposite force. But *śravas* comes from the root *śru* to hear and is used in the sense of ear itself or of hymn or prayer — a sense which Sayana accepts — and from this we can infer that it means the "thing heard" or its result knowledge that comes to us through hearing. The Rishis speak of themselves as hearers of the Truth, *satyaśrutaḥ*, and the knowledge received by this hearing as Sruti. It is in this sense of inspiration or inspired knowledge that we can take it in the esoteric meaning of the Veda and we find that it fits in with a perfect appositeness; thus when the Rishi speaks of *śravāṁsi* as being brought through upward and brought through downward, this cannot be applied to food or fame but is perfectly apposite and significant if he is speaking of inspirations which rise up to the Truth above or bring down the Truth to us. This is the method we can apply everywhere, but we cannot pursue the subject any further here. In the brief limits of this Foreword these slight indications must suffice; they are meant only to give the reader an initial insight into the esoteric method of interpretation of the Veda.

But what then is the secret meaning, the esoteric sense, which emerges by this way of understanding the Veda? It is what we would expect from the nature of the seeking of the mystics everywhere. It is also, as we should expect from the actual course of the development of Indian culture, an early form of the spiritual truth which found its culmination in the Upanishads; the secret knowledge of the Veda is the seed which is evolved later on into the Vedanta. The thought around which all is centred is the seeking after Truth, Light, Immortality. There is a Truth deeper and higher than the truth of outward existence, a Light greater and higher than the light of human understanding which comes by revelation and inspiration, an immortality towards which the soul has to rise. We have to find our way to that, to get into touch with this Truth and Immortality, *sapanta ṛtam amṛtam,*[1] to be born into the Truth, to grow in it, to ascend in spirit into the world of Truth and to live in it. To do so is to unite ourselves with the Godhead and to pass from mortality into immortality. This is the first and the central teaching of the Vedic mystics. The Platonists, developing their doctrine from the early mystics, held that we live in relation to two worlds, — a world of higher truth which might be called the spiritual world and that in which we live, the world of the embodied soul which is derived from the higher but also degraded from it into an inferior truth and inferior consciousness. The Vedic mystics held this doctrine in a more concrete and pragmatic form, for they had the experience of these two worlds. There is the inferior truth here of this world mixed as it is with much falsehood and error, *anṛtasya bhūreḥ,*[2] and there is a world or home of Truth, *sadanam ṛtasya,*[3] the Truth, the Right, the Vast, *satyam ṛtaṁ bṛhat,*[4] where all is Truth-Conscious, *ṛtaciṭ*[5]. There are many worlds between up to the triple heavens and their lights but this is the world of the highest Light — the world of the Sun of Truth, *svar,* or the Great Heaven. We have to find the path to this Great Heaven, the path of Truth, *ṛtasya panthāḥ,*[6] or as it is sometimes called the way of the gods. This is the second mystic doctrine. The third is that our life is a battle between the powers of Light and Truth, the Gods who are the Immortals and the powers of Darkness. These are spoken of under various names as Vritra and Vritras, Vala and the Panis, the Dasyus and their kings. We have to call in the aid of the Gods to destroy the opposition of these powers of Darkness who conceal the Light from us or rob us of it, who obstruct the flowing of the streams of Truth, *ṛtasya dhārāḥ,*[7] the streams of Heaven and obstruct in every way the soul's ascent. We have to invoke the Gods by the inner sacrifice, and by the Word call them into us, — that is the specific power of the Mantra, — to offer to them the gifts of the sacrifice and by that giving secure their gifts, so that by this process we may build the way of our

---

[1] I.68.2. [2] VII.60.5. [3] I.164.47; also IV.21.3. [4] Atharva XII.1.1. [5] IV.3.4.
[6] III.12.7; also VII.66.3. [7] V.12.2; also VII.43.4.

ascent to the goal. The elements of the outer sacrifice in the
Veda are used as symbols of the inner sacrifice and self-offering;
we give what we are and what we have in order that the riches of
the divine Truth and Light may descend into our life and become
the elements of our inner birth into the Truth, — a right thinking, a right understanding, a right action must develop in us
which is the thinking, impulsion and action of that higher Truth,
ṛtasya preṣā, ṛtasya dhītiḥ,[1] and by this we must build up ourselves
in that Truth. Our sacrifice is a journey, a pilgrimage and a
battle, — a travel towards the Gods and we also make that journey with Agni, the inner Flame, as our path-finder and leader.
Our human things are raised up by the mystic Fire into the immortal being, into the Great Heaven, and the things divine come
down into us. As the doctrine of the Rig-veda is the seed of the
teaching of the Vedanta, so is its inner practice and discipline a
seed of the later practice and discipline of Yoga. Finally, as
the summit of the teaching of the Vedic mystics comes the secret
of the one Reality, *ekaṁ sat*,[2] or *tad ekam*,[3] which became the
central word of the Upanishads. The Gods, the powers of Light
and Truth are powers and names of the One, each God is himself all the Gods or carries them in him: there is the one Truth,
tat satyam,[4] and one bliss to which we must rise. But in the
Veda this looks out still mostly from behind the veil. There is
much else but this is the kernel of the doctrine.

The interpretation I have put forward was set out at length
in a series of articles with the title "The Secret of the Veda" in
the monthly philosophical magazine, *Arya*, some thirty years
ago; written in serial form while still developing the theory and
not quite complete in its scope or composed on a preconceived
and well-ordered plan it was not published in book-form and is
therefore not yet available to the reading public. It was accompanied by a number of renderings of the hymns of the Rig-veda
which were rather interpretations than translations and to these
there was an introduction explanatory of the "Doctrine of the
Mystics". Subsequently there was planned a complete translation of all the hymns to Agni in the ten Mandalas which kept
close to the text; the renderings of those hymns in the second

---

[1] I.68.3. [2] I.164.46. [3] X.129.2. [4] III.39.5; also IV.54.4 and VIII.45.27.

and sixth Mandalas are now published in this book for the first time as well as a few from the first Mandala. But to establish on a scholastic basis the conclusions of the hypothesis it would have been necessary to prepare an edition of the Rig-veda or of a large part of it with a word by word construing in Sanskrit and English, notes explanatory of important points in the text and justifying the interpretation both of separate words and of whole verses and also elaborate appendices to fix firmly the rendering of key-words like *ṛta, śravas, kratu, ketu,* etc. essential to the esoteric interpretation. This also was planned, but meanwhile greater preoccupations of a permanent nature intervened and no time was left to proceed with such a considerable undertaking. For the benefit of the reader of these translations who might otherwise be at a loss, this Foreword has been written and some passages[1] from the unpublished "Doctrine of the Mystics" have been included. The text of the Veda has been given for use by those who can read the original Sanskrit. These translations however are not intended to be a scholastic work meant to justify a hypothesis; the object of this publication is only to present them in a permanent form for disciples and those who are inclined to see more in the Vedas than a superficial liturgy and would be interested in knowing what might be the esoteric sense of this ancient Scripture.

This is a literary and not a strictly literal translation. But a fidelity to the meaning, the sense of the words and the structure of the thought, has been preserved: in fact the method has been to start with a bare and scrupulously exact rendering of the actual language and adhere to that as the basis of the interpretation; for it is only so that we can find out the actual thoughts of these ancient mystics. But any rendering of such great poetry as the hymns of the Rig-veda, magnificent in their colouring and images, noble and beautiful in rhythm, perfect in their diction, must, if it is not to be a merely dead scholastic work, bring at least a faint echo of their poetic force, — more cannot be done in a prose translation and in so different a language. The turn of phrase and the syntax of English and Vedic Sanskrit are poles asunder; to achieve some sense of style and natural writing

---

[1] In the present edition the entire essay has been reproduced. - Ed.

one has constantly to turn the concentrated speech of the Veda into a looser, more diluted English form. Another stumbling-block for the translator is the ubiquitous *double entendre* marking in one word the symbol and the thing symbolised, Ray and Cow, clear light of the mind and clarified butter, horses and spiritual power; one has to invent phrases like the "herds of the light" or "the shining herds" or to use devices such as writing the word horse with a capital H to indicate that it is a symbolic horse that is meant and not the common physical animal; but very often the symbol has to be dropped, or else the symbol has to be kept and the inner meaning left to be understood;[1] I have not always used the same phrase though always keeping the same sense, but varied the translation according to the needs of the passage. Often I have been unable to find an adequate English word which will convey the full connotation or colour of the original text; I have used two words instead of one or a phrase or resorted to some other device to give the exact and complete meaning. Besides, there is often a use of antique words or turns of language of which the sense is not really known and can only be conjectured or else different renderings are equally possible. In many passages I have had to leave a provisional rendering; it was intended to keep the final decision on the point until the time when a more considerable body of the hymns had been translated and were ready for publication; but this time has not yet come.

---

[1] The Rishis sometimes seem to combine two different meanings in the same word; I have occasionally tried to render this double sense.

The Doctrine of the Mystics

THE Veda possesses the high spiritual substance of the Upanishads, but lacks their phraseology; it is an inspired knowledge as yet insufficiently equipped with intellectual and philosophical terms. We find a language of poets and illuminates to whom all experience is real, vivid, sensible, even concrete, not yet of thinkers and systematisers to whom the realities of the mind and soul have become abstractions. Yet a system, a doctrine there is; but its structure is supple, its terms are concrete, the cast of its thought is practical and experimental, but in the accomplished type of an old and sure experience, not of one that is crude and uncertain because yet in the making. Here we have the ancient psychological science and the art of spiritual living of which the Upanishads are the philosophical outcome and modification and Vedanta, Sankhya and Yoga the late intellectual result and logical dogma. But like all life, like all science that is still vital, it is free from the armoured rigidities of the reasoning intellect; in spite of its established symbols and sacred formulae it is still large, free, flexible, fluid, supple and subtle. It has the movement of life and the large breath of the soul. And while the later Philosophies are books of Knowledge and make liberation the one supreme good, the Veda is a Book of Works and the hope for which it spurns our present bonds and littleness is perfection, self-achievement, immortality.

The doctrine of the Mystics recognises an Unknowable, Timeless and Unnameable behind and above all things and not seizable by the studious pursuit of the mind. Impersonally, it is That, the One Existence; to the pursuit of our personality it reveals itself out of the secrecy of things as the God or Deva, — nameless though he has many names, immeasurable and beyond description though he holds in himself all description of name and knowledge and all measures of form and substance, force and activity.

The Deva or Godhead is both the original cause and the final result. Divine Existent, builder of the worlds, lord and begetter of all things, Male and Female, Being and Consciousness, Father and Mother of the Worlds and their inhabitants, he is also their Son and ours: for he is the Divine Child born into the Worlds who manifests himself in the growth of the creature. He is Rudra and Vishnu, Prajapati and Hiranyagarbha, Surya, Agni, Indra, Vayu, Soma, Brihaspati, — Varuna and Mitra and Bhaga and Aryaman, all the gods. He is the wise, mighty and liberating Son born from our works and our sacrifice, the Hero in our warfare and Seer of our knowledge, the White Steed in the front of our days who gallops towards the upper Ocean.

The soul of man soars as the Bird, the Hansa, past the shining firmaments of physical and mental consciousness, climbs as the traveller and fighter beyond earth of body and heaven of mind by the ascending path of the Truth to find this Godhead waiting for us, leaning down to us from the secrecy of the highest supreme where it is seated in the triple divine Principle and the source of the Beatitude. The Deva is indeed, whether attracting and exalted there or here helpful to us in the person of the greater Gods, always the Friend and Lover of man, the pastoral Master of the Herds who gives us the sweet milk and the clarified butter from the udder of the shining Cow of the infinitude. He is the source and outpourer of the ambrosial Wine of divine delight and we drink it drawn from the sevenfold waters of existence or pressed out from the luminous plant on the hill of being and uplifted by its raptures we become immortal.

Such are some of the images of this ancient mystic adoration.

The Godhead has built this universe in a complex system of worlds which we find both within us and without, subjectively cognised and objectively sensed. It is a rising tier of earths and heavens; it is a stream of diverse waters; it is a Light of seven rays, or of eight or nine or ten; it is a Hill of many plateaus. The seers often image it in a series of trios; there are three earths and three heavens. More, there is a triple world below, — Heaven, Earth and the intervening mid-region; a triple world between, the shining heavens of the Sun; a triple world above, the supreme and rapturous abodes of the Godhead.

But other principles intervene and make the order of the worlds yet more complex. These principles are psychological; for since all creation is a formation of the Spirit, every external system of worlds must in each of its planes be in material correspondence with some power or rising degree of consciousness of which it is the objective symbol and must house a kindred internal order of things. To understand the Veda we must seize this Vedic parallelism and distinguish the cosmic gradations to which it leads. We rediscover the same system behind the later Puranic symbols and it is thence that we can derive its tabulated series most simply and clearly. For there are seven principles of existence and the seven Puranic worlds correspond to them with sufficient precision, thus:

Principle	*World*
1. Pure Existence — Sat	World of the highest truth of being (Satyaloka)
2. Pure Consciousness — Chit	World of infinite Will or conscious force (Tapoloka)
3. Pure Bliss — Ananda	World of creative delight of existence (Janaloka)
4. Knowledge or Truth — Vijnana	World of the Vastness (Maharloka)
5. Mind	World of light (Swar)
6. Life (nervous being)	World of various becoming (Bhuvar)
7. Matter	The material world (Bhur)

Now this system which in the Purana is simple enough, is a good deal more intricate in the Veda. There the three highest worlds are classed together as the triple divine Principle, — for they dwell always together in a Trinity; infinity is their scope, bliss is their foundation. They are supported by the vast regions of the Truth whence a divine Light radiates out towards our mentality in the three heavenly luminous worlds of Swar, the domain of Indra. Below is ranked the triple system in which we live.

We have the same cosmic gradations as in the Puranas but

they are differently grouped, — seven worlds in principle, five in
practice, three in their general groupings:

1.	The Supreme Sat-Chit- Ananda	The Triple divine worlds
2.	The Link-World Super- mind	The Truth, Right, Vast, manifested in Swar, with its three luminous heavens
3.	The triple lower world Pure Mind Life-force Matter	Heaven (Dyaus, the three heavens) The Mid-Region (Antariksha) Earth (the three earths)

And as each principle can be modified by the subordinate
manifestation of the others within it, each world is divisible into
several provinces according to different arrangements and self-
orderings of its creative light of consciousness. Into this frame-
work, then, we must place all the complexities of the subtle vision
and the fertile imagery of the seers down to the hundred cities
which are now in the possession of the hostile kings, the Lords of
division and evil. But the gods shall break them open and give
them for his free possession to the Aryan worshipper!

But where are these worlds and whence are they created?
Here we have one of the profoundest ideas of the Vedic sages.
Man dwells in the bosom of the Earth-Mother and is aware of
this world of mortality only; but there is a superconscient high
beyond where the divine worlds are seated in a luminous secrecy;
there is a subconscient or inconscient below his surface waking
impressions and from that pregnant Night the worlds as he sees
them are born. And these other worlds between the luminous
upper and the tenebrous lower ocean? They are here. Man draws
from the life-world his vital being, from the mind-world his mentality; he is ever in secret communication with them; he can con-
sciously enter into them, be born into them, if he will. Even into
the solar worlds of the Truth he can rise, enter the portals of the
Superconscient, cross the threshold of the Supreme. The divine
doors shall swing open to his increasing soul.

This human ascension is possible because every being really

holds in himself all that his outward vision perceives as if external to him. We have subjective faculties hidden in us which correspond to all the tiers and strata of the objective cosmic system and these form for us so many planes of our possible existence. This material life and our narrowly limited consciousness of the physical world are far from being the sole experience permitted to man, — be he a thousand times the Son of Earth. If maternal Earth bore him and retains him in her arms, yet is Heaven also one of his parents and has a claim on his being. It is open to him to become awake to profounder depths and higher heights within and such awakening is his intended progress. And as he mounts thus to higher and ever higher planes of himself, new worlds open to his life and his vision and become the field of his experience and the home of his spirit. He lives in contact and union with their powers and godheads and remoulds himself in their image. Each ascent is thus a new birth of the soul, and the Veda calls the worlds "births" as well as seats and dwelling-places.

For as the Gods have built the series of the cosmic worlds, even so they labour to build up the same series of ordered states and ascending degrees in man's consciousness from the mortal condition to the crowning immortality. They raise him from the limited material state of being in which our lowest manhood dwells contented and subject to the Lords of Division, give him a life rich and abundant with the many and rapid shocks and impulsions from the dynamic worlds of Life and Desire where the Gods battle with the demons and raise him yet higher from those troubled rapidities and intensities into the steadfast purity and clarity of the high mental existence. For pure thought and feeling are man's sky, his heaven; this whole vitalistic existence of emotion, passions, affections of which desire is the pivot, forms for him a mid-world; body and material living are his earth.

But pure thought and pure psychic state are not the highest height of the human ascension. The home of the Gods is an absolute Truth which lives in solar glories beyond mind. Man ascending thither strives no longer as the thinker but is victoriously the seer; he is no longer this mental creature but a divine being. His will, life, thought, emotion, sense, act are all transformed into values of an all-puissant Truth and remain no longer an embarrassed or a helpless tangle of mixed truth and false-hood. He moves lamely no more in our narrow and grudging limits but ranges in the unobstructed Vast; toils and zigzags no longer amid these crookednesses, but follows a swift and con-quering straightness; feeds no longer on broken fragments, but is suckled by the teats of Infinity. Therefore he has to break through and out beyond these firmaments of earth and heaven; conquering firm possession of the solar worlds, entering on to his highest Height he has to learn how to dwell in the triple principle of Immortality.

This contrast of the mortality we are and the immortal condition to which we can aspire is the key of the Vedic thought and practice. Veda is the earliest gospel we have of man's immor-tality and these ancient stanzas conceal the primitive discipline of its inspired discoverers.

Substance of being, light of consciousness, active force and possessive delight are the constituent principles of existence; but their combination in us may be either limited, divided, hurt, broken and obscure or infinite, enlightened, vast, whole and un-hurt. Limited and divided being is ignorance; it is darkness and weakness, it is grief and pain; in the Vast, in the integral, in the infinite we must seek for the desirable riches of substance, light, force and joy. Limitation is mortality; immortality comes to us as an accomplished self-possession in the infinite and the power to live and move in firm vastnesses. Therefore it is in proportion as he widens and on condition that he increases constantly in substance of his being, brightens an ever loftier flame of will and vaster light of knowledge, advances the boundaries of his con-sciousness, raises the degrees and enlarges the breadth of his power, force and strength, confirms an intenser beatitude of joy and liberates his soul into immeasurable peace that man becomes capable of immortality.

To widen is to acquire new births. The aspiring material creature becomes the straining vital man; he in turn transmutes himself into the subtle mental and psychical being; this subtle thinker grows into the wide, multiple and cosmic man open on all sides of him to all the multitudinous inflowings of the Truth;

the cosmic soul rising in attainment strives as the spiritual man for a higher peace, joy and harmony. These are the five Aryan types, each of them a great people occupying its own province or state of the total human nature. But there is also the absolute Aryan who would conquer and pass beyond these states to the transcendental harmony of them all.

It is the supramental Truth that is the instrument of this great inner transfiguration. That replaces mentality by luminous vision and the eye of the gods, mortal life by breath and force of the infinite existence, obscure and death-possessed substance by the free and immortal conscious-being. The progress of man must be therefore, first, his self-expanding into a puissant vitality capable of sustaining all vibrations of action and experience and a clear mental and psychical purity; secondly, an outgrowing of this human light and power and its transmutation into an infinite Truth and an immortal Will.

Our normal life and consciousness are a dark or at best a starlit Night. Dawn comes by the arising of the Sun of that higher Truth and with Dawn there comes the effective sacrifice. By the sacrifice the Dawn itself and the lost Sun are constantly conquered out of the returning Night and the luminous herds rescued from the darkling cave of the Panis; by the sacrifice the rain of the abundance of heaven is poured out for us and the sevenfold waters of the higher existence descend impetuously upon our earth because the coils of the obscuring Python, the all-enfolding and all-withholding Vritra, have been cloven asunder by the God-Mind's flashing lightnings; in the sacrifice the Soma-wine is distilled and uplifts us on the stream of its immortalising ecstasy to the highest heavens.

Our sacrifice is the offering of all our gains and works to the powers of the higher existence. The whole world is a dumb and helpless sacrifice in which the soul is bound as a victim self-offered to unseen Gods. The liberating Word must be found, the illuminating hymn must be framed in the heart and mind of man and his life must be turned into a conscious and voluntary offering in which the soul is no longer the victim, but the master of the sacrifice. By right sacrifice and by the all-creative and all-expressive Word that shall arise out of his depths as a sublime hymn to the Gods man can achieve all things. He shall conquer his perfection; Nature shall come to him as a willing and longing bride; he shall become her seer and rule her as her King.

By the hymn of prayer and God-attraction, by the hymn of praise and God-affirmation, by the hymn of God-attainment and self-expression man can house in himself the Gods, build in this gated house of his being the living image of their deity, grow into divine births, form within himself vast and luminous worlds for his soul to inhabit. By the word of the Truth the all-engendering Surya creates; by that rhythm Brahmanaspati evokes the worlds and Twashtri fashions them; finding the all-puissant Word in his intuitive heart, shaping it in his mind the human thinker, the mortal creature can create in himself all the forms, all the states and conditions he desires and, achieving, can conquer for himself all wealth of being, light, strength and enjoyment. He builds up his integral being and aids his gods to destroy the evil armies; the hosts of his spiritual enemies are slain who have divided, torn and afflicted his nature.

The image of this sacrifice is sometimes that of a journey or voyage; for it travels, it ascends; it has a goal — the vastness, the true existence, the light, the felicity — and it is called upon to discover and keep the good, the straight and the happy path to the goal, the arduous, yet joyful road of the Truth. It has to climb, led by the flaming strength of the divine Will, from plateau to plateau as of a mountain, it has to cross as in a ship the waters of existence, traverse its rivers, overcome their deep pits and rapid currents; its aim is to arrive at the far-off ocean of light and infinity.

And this is no easy or peaceful march; it is for long seasons a fierce and relentless battle. Constantly the Aryan man has to labour and to fight and conquer; he must be a tireless toiler and traveller and a stern warrior, he must force open and storm and sack city after city, win kingdom after kingdom, overthrow and tread down ruthlessly enemy after enemy. His whole progress is a warring of Gods and Titans, Gods and Giants, Indra and the Python, Aryan and Dasyu. Aryan adversaries even he has to face in the open field; for old friends and helpers turn into enemies; the kings of Aryan states he would conquer and overpass join themselves to the Dasyus and are leagued against him in supreme battle to prevent his free and utter passing on.

But the Dasyu is the natural enemy. These dividers, plunderers, harmful powers, these Danavas, sons of the Mother of division, are spoken of by the Rishis under many general appellations. There are Rakshasas; there are Eaters and Devourers, Wolves and Tearers; there are hurters and haters; there are dualisers; there are confiners or censurers. But we are given also many specific names. Vritra, the Serpent, is the grand Adversary; for he obstructs with his coils of darkness all possibility of divine existence and divine action. And even when Vritra is slain by the light, fiercer enemies arise out of him. Shushna afflicts us with his impure and ineffective force, Namuchi fights man by his weaknesses, and others too assail, each with his proper evil. Then there are Vala and the Panis, miser traffickers in the sense-life, stealers and concealers of the higher Light and its illuminations which they can only darken and misuse, — an impious host who are jealous of their store and will not offer sacrifice to the Gods. These and other personalities, — they are much more than personifications, — of our ignorance, evil, weakness and many limitations make constant war upon man; they encircle him from near or they shoot their arrows at him from afar or even dwell in his gated house in the place of the Gods and with their shapeless stammering mouths and their insufficient breath of force mar his self-expression. They must be expelled, overpowered, slain, thrust down into their nether darkness by the aid of the mighty and helpful deities.

The Vedic deities are names, powers, personalities of the universal Godhead and they represent each some essential puissance of the Divine Being. They manifest the cosmos and are manifest in it. Children of Light, Sons of the Infinite, they recognise in the soul of man their brother and ally and desire to help and increase him by themselves increasing in him so as to possess his world with their light, strength and beauty. The Gods call man to a divine companionship and alliance; they attract and uplift him to their luminous fraternity, invite his aid and offer theirs against the Sons of Darkness and Division. Man in return calls the Gods to his sacrifice, offers to them his swiftnesses and his strengths, his clarities and his sweetnesses, — milk and butter of the shining Cow, distilled juices of the Plant of Joy, the Horse of the Sacrifice, the cake and the wine, the grain for the God-Mind's radiant coursers. He receives them into his being and their gifts into his life, increases them by the hymn and the wine and forms perfectly, — as a smith forges iron, says the Veda, — their great and luminous godheads.

All this Vedic imagery is easy to understand when once we have the key, but it must not be mistaken for mere imagery. The Gods are not simply poetical personifications of abstract ideas or of psychological and physical functions of Nature. To the Vedic seers they are living realities; the vicissitudes of the human soul represent a cosmic struggle not merely of principles and tendencies but of the cosmic Powers which support and embody them. These are the Gods and the Demons. On the world-stage and in the individual soul the same real drama with the same personages is enacted.

To what gods shall the sacrifice be offered? Who shall be invoked to manifest and protect in the human being this increasing godhead?

Agni first, for without him the sacrificial flame cannot burn on the altar of the soul. That flame of Agni is the seven-tongued power of the Will, a Force of God instinct with knowledge. This conscious and forceful will is the immortal guest in our mortality, a pure priest and a divine worker, the mediator between earth and heaven. It carries what we offer to the higher Powers and brings back in return their force and light and joy into our humanity.

Indra, the Puissant next, who is the power of pure Existence self-manifested as the Divine Mind. As Agni is one pole of Force instinct with knowledge that sends its current upward from earth to heaven, so Indra is the other pole of Light instinct with force which descends from heaven to earth. He comes down into our world as the Hero with the shining horses and slays darkness and division with his lightnings, pours down the life-giving heavenly waters, finds in the trace of the hound, Intuition, the lost or hidden illuminations, makes the Sun of Truth mount high in the heaven of our mentality.

Surya, the Sun, is the master of that supreme Truth, — truth of being, truth of knowledge, truth of process and act and movement and functioning. He is therefore the creator or rather the manifester of all things, — for creation is outbringing, expression by the Truth and Will, — and the father, fosterer, enlightener of our souls. The illuminations we seek are the herds of this Sun who comes to us in the track of the divine Dawn and releases and reveals in us night-hidden world after world up to the highest Beatitude.

Of that beatitude Soma is the representative deity. The wine of his ecstasy is concealed in the growths of earth, in the waters of existence; even here in our physical being are his immortalising juices and they have to be pressed out and offered to all the gods; for in that strength these shall increase and conquer.

Each of these primary deities has others associated with him who fulfil functions that arise from his own. For if the truth of Surya is to be established firmly in our mortal nature, there are previous conditions that are indispensable; a vast purity and clear wideness destructive of all sin and crooked falsehood, — and this is Varuna; a luminous power of love and comprehension leading and forming into harmony all our thoughts, acts and impulses, — this is Mitra; an immortal puissance of clear-discerning aspiration and endeavour, — this is Aryaman; a happy spontaneity of the right enjoyment of all things dispelling the evil dream of sin and error and suffering, — this is Bhaga. These four are powers of the Truth of Surya.

For the whole bliss of Soma to be established perfectly in our nature a happy and enlightened and unmaimed condition of mind, vitality and body are necessary. This condition is given to us by the twin Ashwins; wedded to the daughter of Light, drinkers of honey, bringers of perfect satisfactions, healers of maim and malady they occupy our parts of knowledge and parts of action and prepare our mental, vital and physical being for an easy and victorious ascension.

Indra, the Divine Mind, as the shaper of mental forms has

for his assistants, his artisans, the Ribhus, human powers who by the work of sacrifice and their brilliant ascension to the high dwelling-place of the Sun have attained to immortality and help mankind to repeat their achievement. They shape by the mind Indra's horses, the Ashwins' chariot, the weapons of the Gods, all the means of the journey and the battle. But as giver of the Light of truth and as Vritra-slayer Indra is aided by the Maruts, who are powers of will and nervous or vital Force that have attained to the light of thought and the voice of self-expression. They are behind all thought and speech as its impellers and they battle towards the Light, Truth and Bliss of the supreme Consciousness.

There are also female energies; for the Deva is both Male and Female and the gods also are either activising souls or passively executive and methodising energies. Aditi, infinite Mother of the gods, comes first; and there are besides five powers of the Truth-Consciousness, — Mahi or Bharati, the vast Word that brings us all things out of the divine source; Ila, the strong primal word of the Truth who gives us its active vision; Saraswati, its streaming current and the word of its inspiration; Sarama, the Intuition, hound of heaven who descends into the cavern of the subconscient and finds there the concealed illuminations; Dakshina, whose function is to discern rightly, dispose the action and the offering and distribute in the sacrifice to each godhead its portion. Each god, too, has his female energy.

All this action and struggle and ascension is supported by Heaven our Father and Earth our Mother, Parents of the Gods, who sustain respectively the purely mental and psychic and the physical consciousness. Their large and free scope is the condition of our achievement. Vayu, Master of life, links them together by the mid-air, the region of vital force. And there are other deities, — Parjanya, giver of the rain of heaven; Dadhikravan, the divine war-horse, a power of Agni; the mystic Dragon of the Foundations; Trita Aptya who on the third plane of existence consummates our triple being; and more besides.

The development of all these godheads is necessary to our

perfection. And that perfection must be attained on all our levels, — in the wideness of earth, our physical being and consciousness; in the full force of vital speed and action and enjoyment and nervous vibration, typified as the Horse which must be brought forward to upbear our endeavour; in the perfect gladness of the heart of emotion and a brilliant heat and clarity of the mind throughout our intellectual and psychical being; in the coming of the supramental Light, the Dawn and the Sun and the shining Mother of the herds, to transform all our existence; for so comes to us the possession of the Truth, by the Truth the admirable surge of the Bliss, in the Bliss infinite Consciousness of absolute being.

Three great Gods, origin of the Puranic Trinity, largest puissances of the supreme Godhead, make possible this development and upward evolution; they support in its grand lines and fundamental energies all these complexities of the cosmos. Brahmanaspati is the Creator; by the word, by his cry he creates, — that is to say, he expresses, he brings out all existence and conscious knowledge and movement of life and eventual forms from the darkness of the Inconscient. Rudra, the Violent and Merciful, the Mighty One, presides over the struggle of life to affirm itself; he is the armed, wrathful and beneficent Power of God who lifts forcibly the creation upward, smites all that opposes, scourges all that errs and resists, heals all that is wounded and suffers and complains and submits. Vishnu of the vast pervading motion holds in his triple stride all these worlds; it is he that makes a wide room for the action of Indra in our limited mortality; it is by him and with him that we rise into his highest seats where we find waiting for us the Friend, the Beloved, the Beatific Godhead.

Our earth shaped out of the dark inconscient ocean of existence lifts its high formations and ascending peaks heavenward; heaven of mind has its own formations, clouds that give out their lightnings and their waters of life; the streams of the clarity and the honey ascend out of the subconscient ocean below and seek the superconscient ocean above; and from above that ocean sends downward its rivers of the light and truth and bliss even into our physical being. Thus in images of physical Nature the

Vedic poets sing the hymn of our spiritual ascension.

That ascension has already been effected by the Ancients, the human forefathers, and the spirits of these great Ancestors still assist their offspring; for the new dawns repeat the old and lean forward in light to join the dawns of the future. Kanwa, Kutsa, Atri, Kakshiwan, Gotama, Shunahshepa have become types of certain spiritual victories which tend to be constantly repeated in the experience of humanity. The seven sages, the Angirasas, are waiting still and always, ready to chant the word, to rend the cavern, to find the lost herds, to recover the hidden Sun. Thus the soul is a battlefield full of helpers and hurters, friends and enemies. All this lives, teems, is personal, is conscious, is active. We create for ourselves by the sacrifice and by the word shining seers, heroes to fight for us, children of our works. The Rishis and the Gods find for us our luminous herds; the Ribhus fashion by the mind the chariots of the gods and their horses and their shining weapons. Our life is a horse that neighing and galloping bears us onward and upward; its forces are swift-hooved steeds, the liberated powers of the mind are wide-winging birds; this mental being or this soul is the upsoaring Swan or the Falcon that breaks out from a hundred iron walls and wrests from the jealous guardians of felicity the wine of the Soma. Every shining godward Thought that arises from the secret abysses of the heart is a priest and a creator and chants a divine hymn of luminous realisation and puissant fulfilment. We seek for the shining gold of the Truth; we lust after a heavenly treasure.

The soul of man is a world full of beings, a kingdom in which armies clash to help or hinder a supreme conquest, a house where the gods are our guests and which the demons strive to possess; the fullness of its energies and wideness of its being make a seat of sacrifice spread, arranged and purified for a celestial session.

Such are some of the principal images of the Veda and a very brief and insufficient outline of the teaching of the Forefathers. So understood the Rig-veda ceases to be an obscure, confused and barbarous hymnal; it becomes the high-aspiring

Song of Humanity; its chants are episodes of the lyrical epic of the soul in its immortal ascension.

This at least; what more there may be in the Veda of ancient science, lost knowledge, old psycho-physical tradition remains yet to be discovered.

MANDALA ONE

MADHUCHCHHANDAS VAISHWAMITRA

SUKTA 1

अग्निमीळे पुरोहितं यज्ञस्य देवमृत्विजम् ।
होतारं रत्नधातमम् ॥१॥

1. I adore the Flame, the vicar, the divine Ritwik of the Sacrifice, the summoner who most founds the ecstasy.

अग्निः पूर्वेभिर्ऋषिभिरीड्यो नूतनैरुत ।
स देवाँ एह वक्षति ॥२॥

2. The Flame adorable by the ancient sages is adorable too by the new. He brings here the Gods.

अग्निना रयिमश्नवत् पोषमेव दिवेदिवे ।
यशसं वीरवत्तमम् ॥३॥

3. By the Flame one enjoys a treasure that verily increases day by day, glorious, most full of hero-power.

अग्ने यं यज्ञमध्वरं विश्वतः परिभूरसि ।
स इद् देवेषु गच्छति ॥४॥

4. O Flame! the pilgrim-sacrifice on every side of which thou art with the environing being, that truly goes among the Gods.

अग्निर्होता कविक्रतुः सत्यश्चित्रश्रवस्तमः ।
देवो देवेभिरा गमत् ॥५॥

5. The Flame, the summoner, the Seer-Will, true and most full of richly varied listenings, may he come a God with the Gods.

यदङ्ग दाशुषे त्वमग्ने भद्रं करिष्यसि ।
तवेत् तत् सत्यमङ्गिरः ॥६॥

6. O Flame! the happy good which thou shalt create for the
    giver is that Truth and verily thine, O Angiras!

उप त्वाग्ने दिवेदिवे दोषावस्तर्धिया वयम् ।
नमो भरन्त एमसि ॥७॥

7. To thee, O Flame! we day by day, in the night and in the
    light, come, carrying by our thought the obeisance.

राजन्तमध्वराणां गोपामृतस्य दीदिविम् ।
वर्धमानं स्वे दमे ॥८॥

8. To thee, who reignest over our pilgrim-sacrifices, luminous
    guardian of the Truth, increasing in thy own home.

स नः पितेव सूनवेऽग्ने सूपायनो भव ।
सचस्वा नः स्वस्तये ॥९॥

9. Therefore, be easy of access to us as a father unto his son,
    cling to us for our happy state.

MEDHATITHI KANWA

SUKTA 12

अग्निं दूतं वृणीमहे होतारं विश्ववेदसम् ।
अस्य यज्ञस्य सुक्रतुम् ॥१॥

1. We choose Agni, the summoner, the all-knowing, the
    messenger, the will effective of this sacrifice.

अग्निमग्निं हवीमभिः सदा हवन्त विश्पतिम् ।
हव्यवाहं पुरुप्रियम् ॥२॥

2. To the Lord of the creatures, the bearer of our offerings, the beloved of Many, to every flame the sacrificers ever call with hymns that summon the Gods, One in whom are many dear things.

अग्ने देवाँ इहा वह जज्ञानो वृक्तबर्हिषे ।
असि होता न ईड्यः ॥३॥

3. O Fire, thou being born hither bear the Gods for the sacrificer who spreads the holy seat, thou art our desirable summoning priest.

ताँ उशतो वि बोधय यदग्ने यासि दूत्यम् ।
देवेरा सत्सि बर्हिषि ॥४॥

4. O Fire, when thou goest as our envoy, awaken them up who desire our offerings. Take thy seat with the Gods on the holy grass.

घृताहवन वीदिवः प्रति ष्म रिषतो दह ।
अग्ने त्वं रक्षस्विनः ॥५॥

5. O Fire, thou who art called by the offerings of clarity, thou shining one, do thou oppose and burn down the haters that confine.

अग्निनाग्निः समिध्यते कविगृहपतिर्युवा ।
हव्यवाड् जुह्वास्यः ॥६॥

6. By the Fire is the fire perfectly kindled, the seer, the lord of the house, the youth, the bearer of offering whose mouth receives the offerings.

कविमग्निमुप स्तुहि सत्यधर्माणमध्वरे ।
देवममीवचातनम् ॥७॥

7. To the divine Flame, the seer, him whose law of being is the Truth, the shining one, the destroyer of all evils, approach

4

and chant the hymn of praise.

यस्त्वामग्ने हविष्पतिर्दूतं देव सपर्यति ।
तस्य स्म प्राविता भव ॥८॥

8. O Flame, O divine messenger, the lord of the offerings who waits on thee, of him become the protector.

यो अग्निं देववीतये हविष्माँ आविवासति ।
तस्मै पावक मृळय ॥९॥

9. He who with the offerings approaches the divine force, for the Birth of the Gods, O Purifier, on him have grace.

स नः पावक दीदिवोऽग्ने देवाँ इहा वह ।
उप यज्ञं हविश्च नः ॥१०॥

10. O shining Flame, thou who purifiest, hither bear the Gods to our offerings and to our sacrifice.

स नः स्तवान आ भर गायत्रेण नवीयसा ।
रयिं वीरवतीमिषम् ॥११॥

11. Thou adored by our fresh Gayatri rhythms bring for us the felicity and force full of hero's strength.

अग्ने शुक्रेण शोचिषा विश्ववाभिर्वेहूतिभिः ।
इमं स्तोमं जुषस्व नः ॥१२॥

12. O Fire, with thy lustres white, and all thy divine hymns that summon the Gods, come and accept this hymn that we affirm.

Sukta 13

सुसमिद्धो न आ वह देवाँ अग्ने हविष्मते ।
होतः पावक यक्षि च ॥१॥

1. O Fire! perfectly kindled, bear the gods to him who has the offerings, O Thou who purifiest! Thou summoner! sacrifice to the gods.

मधुमन्तं तनूनपाद् यज्ञं देवेषु नः कवे ।
अद्या कृणुहि वीतये ॥२॥

2. O Son of the body! Now make the sacrifice honied for the gods (or full of honey among the gods) for their enjoyment, O seer.

नराशंसमिह प्रियमस्मिन् यज्ञ उप ह्वये ।
मधुजिह्वं हविष्कृतम् ॥३॥

3. Him, the beloved, I call hither to this sacrifice, he who creates the offerings, possessed of honied tongue.

अग्ने सुखतमे रथे देवाँ ईळित आ वह ।
असि होता मनुर्हितः ॥४॥

4. O Fire! Thou who art adored, bring here the gods in thy happiest car; (for) thou art the summoner established by man.

स्तृणीत बर्हिरानुषग् घृतपृष्ठं मनीषिणः ।
यत्रामृतस्य चक्षणम् ॥५॥

5. O Thinkers! spread you the holy seat continuous and true in order, sprinkled with clear offerings (of clarified butter), to where is the vision of immortality.

SUKTA 14

ऐभिरग्ने दुवो गिरो विश्वेभिः सोमपीतये ।
देवेभिर्याहि यक्षि च ॥१॥

1. With all these gods, O Agni, thou who art the activity of

speech, arrive and do thy work.

आ त्वा कण्वा अह्वयत गृणन्ति विप्र ते धियः ।
देवेभिरग्न आ गहि ॥२॥

2. On thee, O Agni, the Kanwas have called, for thee, O master
of wisdom, their movements of understanding become arti-
culate; arrive, O Agni, with the gods.

इन्द्रवायू बृहस्पतिं मित्राग्निं पूषणं भगम् ।
आदित्यान् मारुतं गणम् ॥३॥

3. On Indra and Vayu, Brihaspati, on Mitra and Agni, Pushan, Bhaga, the Adityas and the Marut host.

प्र वो भ्रियन्त इन्दवो मत्सरा मादयिष्णवः ।
द्रप्सा मध्वश्चमूषदः ॥४॥

4. For you the nectar streams are filled in, rapturous and mad-
dening, dripping sweetness, into their vessel they settle down.

ईळते त्वामवस्यवः कण्वासो वृक्तबर्हिषः ।
हविष्मन्तो अरंकृतः ॥५॥

5. Thee the Kanwas protected adore, when they have manifested the Flame, hold the offering and have set their array.

घृतपृष्ठा मनोयुजो ये त्वा वहन्ति वह्नयः ।
आ देवान्त्सोमपीतये ॥६॥

6. Shining of flank, yoked to the mind, the bearers that bear
thee and bear to us the gods to drink the Soma-wine,

तान् यजत्राँ ऋतावृधोऽग्ने पत्नीवतस्कृधि ।
मध्वः सुजिह्व पायय ॥७॥

7. make them active to the Yajna, O Agni, they increase by
truth, they have with them their female powers; make them
drink the sweetnesses, O keen of tongue.

ये यजत्रा य ईंडघास् ते ते पिबन्तु जिह्वया ।
मधोरग्ने वषट्कृति ॥८॥

8. Those that are active to Yajna, those that are adorable, let
both of them drink with thy tongue, O Agni, the heady
sweetness of the wine.

आकीं सूर्यस्य रोचनाद् विश्वान्देवाँ उषर्बुधः ।
विप्रो होतेह् वक्षति ॥९॥

9. From the world of the lustre of the sun the seer, the priest
of the offering bringeth the gods that wake to the dawn.

विश्वेभिः सोम्यं मध्वऽग्न इन्द्रेण वायुना ।
पिबा मित्रस्य धामभिः ॥१०॥

10. With all of them, O Agni, drink thou the sweetness of the
Soma-wine, with Indra and Vayu and Mitra's lustres.

त्वं होता मनुर्हितोऽग्ने यज्ञेषु सीदसि ।
सेमं नो अध्वरं यज ॥११॥

11. Thou, the priest of the oblation, thinker and friend, sittest,
O Agni, at the Yajnas, therefore do thou set thyself to this
action of sacrifice of ours.

युक्ष्वा ह्यरुषी रथे हरितो देव रोहितः ।
ताभिर्देवाँ इहा वह ॥१२॥

12. Yoking, O God, in thy chariot the rosy and the green and
the crimson, by these bear hither the gods.

KANWA GHAURA

SUKTA 36

प्र वो यह्वं पुरूणां विशां देवयतीनाम् ।
अग्निं सूक्तेभिर्वचोभिरीमहे यं सीमिदन्य ईळते ॥१॥

1. The master of many peoples who labour towards the godhead, we seek for you with words of perfect expression,
Agni whom others also everywhere desire.

जनासो अग्निं दधिरे सहोवृधं हविष्मन्तो विधेम ते ।
स त्वं नो अद्य सुमना इहाविता भवा वाजेषु सन्त्य ॥२॥

2. Men hold Agni in them as the increaser of strength. With
offerings we dispose the sacrifice for thee, do thou then become today to us perfect-minded and our keeper here in our
havings, O thou who art of the truth of being.

प्र त्वा दूतं वृणीमहे होतारं विश्ववेदसम् ।
महस्ते सतो वि चरन्त्यर्चयो दिवि स्पृशन्ति भानवः ॥३॥

3. Thee we choose out for our messenger, the priest of offering
who hast universal knowledge; when thou art greatened in
thy being thy flames range wide, thy lustres touch the
heavens.

देवासस्त्वा वरुणो मित्रो अर्यमा सं दूतं प्रत्नमिन्धते ।
विश्वं सो अग्ने जयति त्वया धनं यस्ते ददाश मर्त्यः ॥४॥

4. The gods even Varuna and Mitra and Aryaman light thee
utterly, the ancient messenger; all wealth that mortal
conquers by thee, O Agni, who to thee has given.

मन्द्रो होता गृहपतिरग्ने दूतो विशामसि ।
त्वे विश्वा संगतानि व्रता ध्रुवा यानि देवा अकृण्वत ॥५॥

5. Thou art the rapturous priest of the sacrifice and master of
this house and the envoy of creatures; in thee are met
together all the steadfast laws of action which the gods have
made.

त्वे इदग्ने सुभगे यविष्ठ्य विश्वमा हूयते हविः ।
स त्वं नो अद्य सुमना उतापरं यक्षि देवान्त्सुवीर्या ॥६॥

6. It is in thee, O Agni, young and mighty, because thou art rich in joy that every offering is cast, therefore do thou today and hereafter, perfect of mind, offer to the gods perfected energies.

तं घेमित्था नमस्विन उप स्वराजमासते ।
होत्राभिरर्गिन मनुष: समिन्धते तितिर्वांसो अति स्निध: ॥७॥

7. He it is, whom as the self-ruler men who have attained submission adore; by the greatness of the oblation men light entirely Agni when they have broken through their opposers.

घ्नन्तो वृत्रमतरन् रोदसी अप उरु क्षयाय चक्रिरे ।
भुवत् कण्वे वृषा द्युम्न्याहुत: क्रन्ददश्वो गविष्टिषु ॥८॥

8. They smite Vritra the coverer and pass beyond the two firmaments, and they make the wide kingdom their home. May the mighty One become in Kanwa a luminous energy fed with the offerings, the Steed of Life neighing in the pastures (stations) of the kine.

सं सीदस्व महाँ असि शोचस्व देववीतम: ।
वि धूममग्ने अरुषं मियेध्य सृज प्रशस्त दर्शतम् ॥९॥

9. Take thy established seat; wide art thou, shine in thy purity revealing utterly the godhead; pour forth, O thou of the sacrifice, thy red active smoke of passion, thou wide-manifested, that full of vision.

यं त्वा देवासो मनवे दधुरिह यजिष्ठं हव्यवाहन ।
यं कण्वो मेध्यातिथिर्धनस्पृतं यं वृषा यमुपस्तुत: ॥१०॥

10. Even thou whom the gods have set here for man most strong for the sacrifice, O bearer of the offering, whom Kanwa Medhyatithi has established as a seizer for him of his desired wealth, whom the mighty Indra and all who establish him by the song of praise;

यमग्निं मेध्यातिथिः कण्व ईध ऋतादधि ।
तस्य प्रेषो दीदियुस्तमिमा ऋचस्तमग्निं वर्धयामसि ॥११॥

11. even that Agni whom Medhyatithi Kanwa has kindled high
upon the Truth, may his impulses blaze forth, him may these
fulfilling Words, him, even Agni, may we increase.

रायस्पूर्धि स्वधावोऽस्ति हि तेऽग्ने देवेष्वाप्यम् ।
त्वं वाजस्य श्रुत्यस्य राजसि स नो मृळ महाँ असि ॥१२॥

12. Complete our felicities, O thou who hast the self-fixity; for
with thee, O Agni, is effectivity in the gods; thou rulest over
the wealth of inspired knowledge. Show thou then favour
to us, great art thou.

ऊर्ध्व ऊ षु ण ऊतये तिष्ठा देवो न सविता ।
ऊर्ध्वो वाजस्य सनिता यदञ्जिभिर्वाघद्भिर्विह्वयामहे ॥१३॥

13. Utterly high uplifted stand for our growth, like the god
Savitri; it is from these heights that thou becomest the sa-
viour of our store when we call on thee...

ऊर्ध्वो नः पाह्यंहसो नि केतुना विश्वं समत्रिणं दह ।
कृधी न ऊर्ध्वाञ्चरथाय जीवसे विदा देवेषु नो दुवः ॥१४॥

14. High-raised protect us from the evil by the perceiving mind,
burn utterly every eater of our being; raise us too on high
for action, for life; distribute among the gods our activity.

पाहि नो अग्ने रक्षसः पाहि धूर्तेरराण्णः ।
पाहि रीषत उत वा जिघांसतो बृहद्भानो यविष्ठ्य ॥१५॥

15. Protect us, O Agni, from the Rakshasa, protect us from the
harm of the undelighting, protect us from him who assails
and him who would slay us, O Vast of lustres, O mighty
and young.

घनेव विष्वग्वि जह्यराव्णस्तपुर्जंभ यो अस्मध्रुक् ।
यो मर्त्यः शिशीते अत्यक्तुभिर्मा नः स रिपुरीशत ॥१६॥

16. As with thick falling blows scatter utterly (or scatter like clouds to every side) all the powers of undelight, O devourer of their force (or destroyer of affliction), and him who would do us harm; whatsoever mortal being exceeds us by the keenness of his actions, may he not as our enemy have mastery over us.

अग्निर्वळ्ने सुवीर्यमग्निः कण्वाय सौभगम् ।
अग्निः प्रावन् मित्रोत मेध्यातिथिमग्निः साता उपस्तुतम् ॥१७॥

17. Agni has won perfected energy for Kanwa and has won perfected enjoyment; Agni protects for him all friendly things, Agni keeps ever in safe being Medhyatithi who has confirmed him by the song of praise.

अग्निना तुर्वशं यदुं परावत उग्रादेवं हवामहे ।
अग्निनयप्रववास्त्वं बृहद्रथं तुर्वीतिं दस्यवे सहः ॥१८॥

18. By Agni we call Turvasha and Yadu from the upper kingdoms; Agni has led to a new dwelling Brihadratha and Turviti (or Turviti of wide delight), a power against the foe.

नि त्वामग्ने मनुर्दधे ज्योतिर्जनाय शश्वते ।
दीदेथ कण्व ऋतजात उक्षितो यं नमस्यन्ति कृष्टयः ॥१९॥

19. Man establisheth thee within, O Agni, as a light for the eternal birth; mayest thou burn brightly in Kanwa manifested in the Truth and increased in being, thou to whom the doers of action bow down.

त्वेषासो अग्नेरमवन्तो अर्चयो भीमासो न प्रतीतये ।
रक्षस्विनः सदमिद् यातुमावतो विश्वं समत्रिणं दह ॥२०॥

20. Impetuous, O Agni, and forceful are thy flames, terrible and not to be approached; always thou do burn utterly the powers who detain and the powers who are vessels of suffering, yea, every devourer.

NODHAS GAUTAMA

SUKTA 59

A HYMN OF THE UNIVERSAL DIVINE FORCE AND WILL

वया इदग्ने अग्नयस्ते अन्ये त्वे विश्वे अमृता मादयन्ते ।
वैश्वानर नाभिरसि क्षितीनां स्थूणेव जनाँ उपमिद् ययन्थ ॥१॥

1. Other flames are only branches of thy stock, O Fire. All the
   immortals take in thee their rapturous joy. O universal
   Godhead, thou art the navel-knot of the earths and their
   inhabitants; all men born thou controllest and supportest
   like a pillar.

मूर्धा दिवो नाभिरग्निः पृथिव्या अथाभवदरती रोदस्योः ।
तं त्वा देवासोऽजनयन्त देवं वैश्वानर ज्योतिरिदार्याय ॥२॥

2. The Flame is the head of heaven and the navel of the earth
   and he is the power that moves at work in the two worlds.
   O Vaishwanara, the gods brought thee to birth a god to be a
   light to Aryan man.

आ सूर्ये न रश्मयो ध्रुवासो वैश्वानरे दधिरेऽग्ना वसूनि ।
या पर्वतेष्वोषधीष्वप्सु या मानुषेष्वसि तस्य राजा ॥३॥

3. As the firm rays sit steadfast in the Sun, all treasures have
   been placed in the universal godhead and flame. King art
   thou of all the riches that are in the growths of the earth and
   the hills and the waters and all the riches that are in men.

बृहती इव सूनवे रोदसी गिरो होता मनुष्यो न दक्षः ।
स्ववते सत्यशुष्माय पूर्वीर्वैश्वानराय नृतमाय यह्वीः ॥४॥

4. Heaven and Earth grow as if vaster worlds to the Son. He
   is the priest of our sacrifice and sings our words even as
   might a man of discerning skill. To Vaishwanara, for this
   most strong god who brings with him the light of the

sun-world, its many mighty waters because his strength is of the truth.

दिवश्चित् ते बृहतो जातवेदो वैश्वानर प्र रिरिचे महित्वम् ।
राजा कृष्टीनामसि मानुषीणां युधा देवेभ्यो वरिवश्चकर्थ ॥५॥

5. O universal godhead, O knower of all things born, thy excess of greatness overflows even the Great Heaven. Thou art the king of the toiling human peoples and by battle madest the supreme good for the gods.

वैश्वानरो महिम्ना विश्वकृष्टिभिरद्वाजेषु यजतो विभावा ।
शातवनेये शतिनीभिररनिः पुरुणीये जरते सूनृतावान् ॥७॥

7. This is the universal godhead who by his greatness labours in all the peoples, the lustrous master of sacrifice, the Flame with his hundred treasures. This is he who has the word of the Truth.

PARASHARA SHAKTYA

SUKTA 65

पश्वा न तायुं गुहा चतन्तं नमो युजानं नमो वहन्तम् ।
सजोषा धीराः पदैरनु ग्मन्नुप त्वा सीदन्विश्वे यजत्राः ॥१॥

1. He hides himself like a thief with the cow of vision in the secret cavern, he takes to himself our adoration, and thither he carries it.[1] The thinkers take a common joy in him, they follow him by his footprints; all the Masters of sacrifice come to thee, O Flame, in the secrecy.

ऋतस्य देवा अनु व्रता गुर्भुवत्परिष्टिर्द्यौर्न भूम ।
वर्धन्तीमापः पन्वा सुशिश्विमृतस्य योना गर्भे सुजातम् ॥२॥

2. The Gods follow after him the law of the workings of Truth. He stands encompassing all as heaven the earth. The Waters

---

[1] Or better, he takes to himself our surrender, he carries with him our surrender.

make him grow increasing in his bulk by their toil,[1] the
Flame well-born in their womb, in the abode of the Truth.

पुष्टिनं रण्वा क्षितिनं पृथ्वी गिरिनं भुज्म क्षोदो न शंभु ।
अत्यो नाज्मन्त्सर्गप्रतक्तः सिन्धुनं क्षोदः क ईं वराते ॥३॥

3.　He is as if a delightful thriving, he is like the earth our wide
dwelling-place. He is enjoyable like a hill and bliss-giving
like fast-running water. He is like a charger in the battle
rushing to the gallop and like a flowing river;[2] who shall
hedge in his course?

जामिः सिन्धूनां भ्रातेव स्वस्राभिर्भ्यात्र राजा वनान्यत्ति ।
यद्वातजूतो वना व्यस्थादग्निनर्हं दाति रोमा पृथिव्याः ॥४॥

4.　He is the close comrade of the Rivers as is a brother of his
sisters. He devours the earth's forests as a king his enemies.
When driven by the breath of the wind he ranges around the
forests, the Flame tears asunder the hairs of Earth's body.

श्वसित्यप्सु हंसो न सीदन् कृत्वा चेतिष्ठो विशामुषर्भुत् ।
सोमो न वेधा ऋतप्रजातः पशुनं शिश्वा विभुर्दूरेभाः ॥५॥

5.　He breathes in the Waters like a seated swan. Waking in the
dawn he has power by the will of his works to give knowledge to the peoples. He is like the God of the Wine, born of
the Truth and a creator. He is like a cow with her new-
born. He is wide-spreading and his light is seen from afar.

SUKTA 66

रयिनं चित्रा सुरो न संदृगायुनं प्राणो नित्यो न सूनुः ।
तक्वा न भूर्णिवंना सिषक्ति पयो न धेनुः शुचिविभावा ॥१॥

1.　He is like a wealth richly diverse and like the all-seeing of
the Sun. He is as if life and the breath of our existence, he

---

[1] Or, by their chant,　[2] Or, like a sea in its motion,

is as if our eternal child. He is like a galloper bearing us. He clings to the forests: he is like a cow with her milk. He is pure-bright and wide is his lustre.

दाधार क्षेममोको न रण्वो यवो न पक्वो जेता जनानाम् ।
ऋषिनं स्तुभ्वा विक्षु प्रशस्तो वाजी न प्रीतो वयो दधाति ॥२॥

2. He holds all our good like a pleasant home; he is like ripe corn. He is a conqueror of men and like a chanting Rishi; there is word of him among the folk: he is as if our exultant steed of swiftness; he upholds our growth.

दुरोकशोचि: ऋतुर्नं नित्यो जायेव योनावरं विश्वस्मै ।
चित्रो यदभ्राट् छ्वेतो न विक्षु रथो न रुक्मी त्वेष: समत्सु ॥३॥

3. He is light in a house difficult to inhabit;[1] he is as a will ever active in us; he is like a wife in our abode and sufficient to every man. When he blazes wonderfully manifold, he is like one white in the peoples: he is like a golden chariot; he is a splendour in our battles.

सेनेव सृष्टामं दधात्यस्तुर्नं दिद्युत्त्वेषप्रतीका ।
यमो ह जातो यमो जनित्वं जार: कनीनां पतिर्जनीनाम् ॥४॥

4. He is like an army running to the charge and puts strength in us: he is like the flaming shaft of the Archer with its keen burning front. A twin he is born, a twin he is that which is to be born: he is the lover of the virgins and the husband of the mothers.

तं वश्चराथा वयं वसत्यास्तं न गावो नक्षन्त इद्धम् ।
सिन्धुर्नं क्षोद: प्र नीचीरैनोन्नवन्त गाव: स्वदृंशीके ॥५॥

5. We by your movement, we by your staying, come to him when his light is kindled as the cows come home to their stall. He is like a river running in its channel and sends in his front the descending Waters: the Ray-Cows move to him in the manifesting of the world of the Sun.[2]

---

[1] Or, he is a light difficult to kindle; [2] Or, when the Sun appears.

SUKTA 67

वनेषु जायुर्मर्तेषु मित्रो वृणीते श्रुष्टिं राजेवाजुर्यम् ।
क्षेमो न साधुः क्रतुर्न भद्रो भुवत्स्वाधीर्होता हव्यवाट् ॥१॥

1. He is the conqueror in the forests; in mortals he is a friend:
   he chooses inspiration as a king an unaging councillor. He
   is as if our perfect welfare;[1] he is like a happy will just in its
   thinking and becomes to us our Priest of the call and the
   bearer of our offerings.

हस्ते दधानो नृम्णा विश्वान्यमे देवान्धाद् गुहा निषीदन् ।
विदन्तीमत्र नरो धियंधा हृदा यत्तष्टान्मन्त्राँ अशंसन् ॥२॥

2. He holds in his hands all mights: sitting in the secret cave
   he upholds[2] the gods in his strength. Here men who hold in
   themselves the Thought come to know him when they have
   uttered the Mantras formed by the heart.

अजो न क्षां दाधार पृथिवीं तस्तम्भ द्यां मन्त्रेभिः सत्यैः ।
प्रिया पदानि पश्वो नि पाहि विश्वायुरग्ने गुहा गुहं गाः ॥३॥

3. As the unborn he has held the wide earth, he has up-pillared
   heaven with his Mantras of truth. Guard the cherished footprints of the Cow of vision; O Fire, thou art universal life,
   enter into the secrecy of secrecies.[3]

य ईं चिकेत गुहा भवन्तमा यः ससाद धारामृतस्य ।
वि ये चृतन्त्युता सपन्त आदिद्वसूनि प्र ववाचास्मै ॥४॥

4. He who has perceived him when he is in the secret cave, he
   who has come to the stream of the Truth, those who touch
   the things of the Truth and kindle him, — to such a one he
   gives word of the Riches.

वि यो वीरुत्सु रोधन्महित्वोत प्रजा उत प्रसूष्वन्तः ।
चित्तिरपां दमे विश्वायुः सद्येव धीराः संमाय चक्रुः ॥५॥

---

[1] Or, a perfecting good;   [2] Or, establishes   [3] Or, the secrecy of the secret Cave.

5. He who in the growths of earth holds up his greatnesses, both the progeny born and what is in the mothers, he is Knowledge in the house of the Waters, and life universal; the thinkers have measured and constructed him like a mansion.

SUKTA 68

श्रीणन्नुप स्थादि्दवं भुरण्युः स्थातुश्चरथमक्तृन्व्यूर्णोत् ।
परि यदेषामेको विश्वेषां भुवद्देवो देवानां महित्वा ॥१॥

1. The carrier, burning, he reaches heaven. He unravels the nights and uncovers the stable and the moving; for this is the one God who envelops with himself the grandeurs of all the Gods.

आदित्ते विश्वे क्रतुं जुषन्त शुष्काद्यद्देव जीवो जनिष्ठाः ।
भजन्त विश्वे देवत्वं नाम ऋतं सपन्तो अमृतमेवैः ॥२॥

2. All cleave to[1] thy will of works when, O God, thou art born a living being from dry matter. All enjoy the Name, the Godhead; by thy movements they touch Truth and Immortality.

ऋतस्य प्रेषा ऋतस्य धीतिर्विश्वायुर्विश्वे अपांसि चक्रुः ।
यस्तुभ्यं दाशाद्यो वा ते शिक्षात्तस्मै चिकित्वान्रयिं दयस्व ॥३॥

3. He is the urgings of the Truth, the thinking of the Truth, the universal life by whom all do the works. He who gives to thee, he who gains from thee,[2] to him, for thou knowest, give the Riches.

होता निषत्तो मनोरपत्ये स चिन्न्वासां पती रयीणाम् ।
इच्छन्त रेतो मियस्तनूषु सं जानत स्वैर्दक्षैरमूराः ॥४॥

4. He is the priest of the sacrifice seated in the son of Man: he

---

[1] Or, take joy in   [2] Or, learns from thee,

verily is the lord of these riches. They desire the seed mu-
tually in their bodies; the wise by their own discernings come
wholly to know.

पितुर्न पुत्रः ऋतुं जुषन्त श्रोषन्ये अस्य शासं तुरासः ।
वि राय और्णोद् दुरः पुरुक्षुः पिपेश नाकं स्तृभिर्दमूनाः ॥५॥

5. Those who listen to his teaching, those who are swift to the
journey, serve gladly his will as sons the will of a father. He
houses a multitude of riches and flings wide the doors of the
Treasure. He is the dweller within who has formed heaven
with its stars.

SUKTA 69

शुक्रः शुशुक्वाँ उषो न जारः पप्रा समीची दिवो न ज्योतिः ।
परि प्रजातः ऋत्वा बभूथ भुवो देवानां पिता पुत्रः सन् ॥१॥

1. Blazing out brilliant as the lover of the Dawn, filling the two
equal worlds[1] like the Light of Heaven, thou art born by our
will and comest into being all around us; thou hast become
the father of the Gods, thou who art the Son.

वेधा अदृप्तो अग्निर्विजानन्नूधर्न गोनां स्वाद्मा पितूनाम् ।
जने न शेव आहूर्यः सन्मध्ये निषत्तो रण्वो दुरोणे ॥२॥

2. The Fire having the knowledge is a creator[2] without proud
rashness; he is as if the teat of the Cows of Light, the sweet-
ener[3] of the draughts of the Wine. He is as one blissful in a
man, one whom we must call in; he is seated rapturous in
the middle of the house.

पुत्रो न जातो रण्वो दुरोणे वाजी न प्रीतो विशो वि तारीत् ।
विशो यदह्वे नृभिः सनीळा अग्निर्देवत्वा विश्वान्यद्या ॥३॥

3. He is born to us as if a son rapturous in our house; like a

---

[1] Or, the two companions [2] Or, ordainer of things [3] Or, taster of all foods

glad horse of swiftness he carries safe through their battle
the peoples: when I call to the beings who dwell in one abode
with the Gods,[1] the Flame attains all godheads.

नकिष्ट एता व्रता मिनन्ति नृभ्यो यदेभ्यः श्रुष्टि चकर्थ ।
तत्सु ते बंसो यदहन्त्समानेनंनृभिर्यंयुक्तो विवे रपांसि ॥४॥

4. None can impair the ways of thy workings when for these
gods[2] thou hast created inspired knowledge. This is thy
work that yoked with the Gods, thy equals, thou hast
smitten,[3] that thou hast scattered the powers of evil.

उषो न जारो विभावोल्मः संज्ञातरूपश्चिकेतदस्मे ।
त्मना बहन्तो दुरो व्यृण्वन्नवन्त विश्वे स्वर्दृशीके ॥५॥

5. Very bright and lustrous is he like the lover of Dawn. May
his form be known and may he wake to knowledge for this
human being, may all bear him in themselves, part wide
the Doors and move into the vision of the world of the
Sun.[4]

SUKTA 70

वनेम पूर्वीरर्यो मनीषा अग्निः सुश्रोको विश्वान्यश्याः ।
आ दैव्यानि व्रता चिकित्वाना मानुषस्य जनस्य जन्म ॥१॥

1. May we win the many Riches, may the Fire, flaming high
with his light, master by the thinking mind, take possession
of all things that are, he who knows the laws of the divine
workings and knows the birth of the human being.

गर्भो यो अपां गर्भो वनानां गर्भश्च स्थातां गर्भश्चरथाम् ।
अद्रौ चिदस्मा अन्तर्दुरोणे विशां न विश्वो अमृतः स्वाधीः ॥२॥

---

[1] Or, with men, [2] Or, these men [3] Or, that thou hast slain,
[4] Or, come to the seeing of the Sun.

2. He is the child of the waters, the child of the forests, the
    child of things stable and the child of things that move.
    Even in the stone he is there for man, he is there in the
    middle of his house, — he is as one universal in creatures;
    he is the Immortal, the perfect thinker.

स हि क्षपावाँ अग्नी रयीणां दाशद्यो अस्मा अरं सूक्तैः ।
एता चिकित्वो भूमा नि पाहि देवानां जन्म मर्ताँश्च विद्वान् ॥३॥

3. The Fire is a master of the nights, he gives of the Riches to
    him who prepares for him the sacrifice with the perfect
    words. O thou who art conscious, guard, as the knower,
    these worlds, and the birth of the Gods, and mortal men.

वर्धान्यं पूर्वीः क्षपो विरूपाः स्थातुश्चरथमृतप्रवीतम् ।
अराधि होता स्वनिषत्तः कृण्वन्विश्वान्यपांसि सत्या ॥४॥

4. Many nights of different forms have increased him, the
    Fire who came forth from the Truth, who is the stable and
    the moving: the Priest of the call, he is achieved for us, seated
    in the sun-world,[1] making true all our works.

गोषु प्रशस्तिं वनेषु धिषे भरन्त विश्वे बलि स्वर्णः ।
वि त्वा नरः पुरुत्रा सपर्यन्नितुनं जिन्वैरि वेदो भरन्त ॥५॥

5. Thou establishest word of thee in the Ray-Cow and in the
    forests; it is as if all were bringing the sun-world as offering.
    Men in many parts serve thee and gather in knowledge as
    from a long-lived father.

साधुर्नं गृध्नुरस्तेव शूरो यातेव भीमस्त्वेषः समत्सु ॥६॥

6. He is like one efficient in works and hungry to seize, heroic
    like one shooting arrows, terrible like an assailant charging,
    he is a splendour in our battles.

---

[1] Or, the sun,

SUKTA 71

उप प्र जिन्वन्नुशतीरिशन्तं पर्ति न नित्यं जनयः सनीळाः ।
स्वसारः श्यावीमरुषीमजुष्रञ्चित्रमुच्छन्तीमुषसं न गावः ॥१॥

1. The Mothers who dwell in one abode, desiring came to him
who desired them and gave him pleasure as to their eternal
spouse: the sisters took joy in him as the Ray-Cows in the
Dawn when she comes dusky, flushing red, then shining out
in rich hues.

वीळु चिद् दृळ्हा पितरो न उक्थैरद्रिं रुजन्नङ्गिरसो रवेण ।
चक्रुर्दिवो बृहतो गातुमस्मे अहः स्वर्विविदुः केतुमुस्राः ॥२॥

2. Our fathers by their words broke the strong and stubborn
places, the Angiras seers shattered the mountain rock with
their cry; they made in us a path to the Great Heaven, they
discovered the Day and the sun-world and the intuitive ray
and the shining herds.

दधन्नृतं धनयन्नस्य धीतिमादिद्दर्यो दिधिष्वो विभृत्राः ।
अतृष्यन्तीरपसो यन्त्यच्छा देवाञ्जन्म प्रयसा वर्धयन्तीः ॥३॥

3. They held the Truth, they enriched the thought of this human being; then, indeed, had they mastery and understanding bearing wide the Flame, the powers at work go towards
the gods making the Birth to grow by delight.

मथीद्यदीं विभृतो मातरिश्वा गृहेगृहे श्येतो जेन्यो भूत् ।
आदीं राज्ञे न सहीयसे सचा सन्ना दूत्यं भृगवाणो विवाय ॥४॥

4. When the Life-Breath borne pervadingly within has churned
him out in house and house he becomes white and a conqueror. Then, indeed, he becomes the Flaming Seer and
companioning us goes on an embassy as for a powerful
king.

महे यत्पित्र ईं रसं दिवे करव त्सरत्पृशन्यश्चिकित्वान् ।
सृजदस्ता धृषता दिद्युमस्मे स्वायां देवो दुहितरि त्विषिं धात् ॥५॥

5. When he had made this sap of essence for the great Father
   Heaven, he came slipping downward, one close in touch,
   having knowledge. The Archer loosed violently on him his
   arrow of lightning, but the god set the flaming energy in his
   own daughter.

स्व आ यस्तुभ्यं दम आ विभाति नमो वा दाशादुशतो अनु द्यून् ।
वर्धो अग्ने वयो अस्य द्विबर्हा यासद्राया सरथं यं जुनासि ॥६॥

6. He who kindles the light for thee in thy own home and
   offers obeisance of surrender day by day and thy desire is
   towards him, mayst thou in thy twofold mass, increase his
   growth, he whom thou speedest in one car with thee, may he
   travel with the riches.

अग्निं विश्वा अभि पृक्षः सचन्ते समुद्रं न स्रवतः सप्त यह्वीः ।
न जामिभिर्वि चिकिते वयो नो विदा देवेषु प्रमतिं चिकित्वान् ॥७॥

7. All satisfactions cleave to the Fire as the seven mighty rivers
   join the ocean. Our growth of being has not been perceived
   by thy companions, but thou who hast perceived, impart
   to the gods thy knowledge.[1]

आ यदिषे नृपतिं तेज आनट् छुचि रेतो निषिक्तं द्यौरभीके ।
अग्निः शर्धमनवद्यं युवानं स्वाध्यं जनयत्सूदयच्च ॥८॥

8. When a flame of energy came to this King of men for impelling force, when in their meeting Heaven was cast in him
   like pure seed, the Fire gave birth to a might,[2] young and
   faultless and perfect in thought and sped it on its way.

मनो न योऽध्वनः सद्य एत्येकः सत्रा सूरो वस्व ईशे ।
राजाना मित्रावरुणा सुपाणी गोषु प्रियममृतं रक्षमाणा ॥९॥

---

[1] Or, gain for us knowledge in the Gods.
[2] Or, a host. It may mean the army of the life-gods, *marutām śardhaḥ*.

9. He who travels the paths suddenly like the mind, the Sun, ever sole is the master of the treasure: Mitra and Varuna, the Kings with beautiful hands, are there guarding in the Rays[1] delight and immortality.

मा नो अग्ने सख्या पित्र्याणि प्र मर्षिष्ठा अभि विदुष्कविः सन् ।
नभो न रूपं जरिमा मिनाति पुरा तस्या अभिशस्तेरधीहि ॥१०॥

10. O Fire, mayst thou not forget[2] ancient friendships, thou who art turned towards us as the knower and seer. As a mist dims a form, age diminishes us; before that hurt falls upon us, arrive.[3]

SUKTA 72

नि काव्या वेधसः शश्वतस्कर्हस्ते दधानो नर्या पुरूणि ।
अग्निर्भुवद्रयिपती रयीणां सत्रा चक्राणो अमृतानि विश्वा ॥१॥

1. He forms within us the seer-wisdoms of the eternal Creator holding in his hand many powers[4] of the godheads. May Fire become the treasure-master of the riches, ever fashioning all immortal things.[5]

अस्मे वत्सं परि षन्तं न विन्दन्निच्छन्तो विश्वे अमृता अमूराः ।
श्रमयुवः पदव्यो धियंधास्तस्युः पदे परमे चार्वग्नेः ॥२॥

2. All the immortals, the wise ones, desired but found not in us the Child who is all around; turning to toil on his track, upholding the Thought, they stood in the supreme plane, they reached the beauty of the Flame.

तिस्रो यदग्ने शरदस्त्वामिच्छुचिं घृतेन शुचयः सपर्यान् ।
नामानि चिद्दधिरे यज्ञियान्यसूदयन्त तन्वः सुजाताः ॥३॥

---

[1] *Goṣu*, in the Ray-Cows, the shining herds of the Sun [2] Or, neglect or wipe out
[3] Or, give heed, before that assault comes upon us. [4] Or, many Strengths
[5] Or, fashioning together all immortal things.

3. When for three years, O Fire, they worshipped thee, the pure
    ones thee the pure, with the clarity of the light, they held too
    the sacrificial Names, their bodies came to perfect birth and
    they sped them on the way.

आ रोदसी बृहती वेविदानाः प्र रुद्रिया जभ्रिरे यज्ञियासः ।
विदन्मर्तो नेमधिता चिकित्वानग्निं पदे परमे तस्थिवांसम् ॥४॥

4. The masters of sacrifice discovered and in their impetuous
    might bore the Vast Earth and Heaven, then the mortal
    knew them and by his holding of the upper[1] hemisphere per-
    ceived the Fire, standing in the supreme plane.

संजानाना उप सीदन्नभिज्ञु पत्नीवन्तो नमस्यं नमस्यन् ।
रिरिक्वांसस्तन्वः कृण्वत स्वाः सखा सख्युर्निमिषि रक्षमाणाः ॥५॥

5. Utterly knowing him they with their wives came and knelt
    before him and adored with obeisance the adorable. They
    made themselves empty and formed their own bodies
    guarded in his gaze, friend in the gaze of friend.

त्रिः सप्त यद् गुह्यानि त्वे इत्पदाविदन्निहिता यज्ञियासः ।
तेभी रक्षन्ते अमृतं सजोषाः पशूञ्च स्थातॄञ्चरथं च पाहि ॥६॥

6. When the masters of sacrifice have found hidden in thee
    the thrice seven secret planes, by them they guard with one
    mind of acceptance Immortality. Protect the Herds, those
    that stand and that which is mobile.

विद्वाँ अग्ने वयुनानि क्षितीनां व्यानुषक्छुरुधो जीवसे धाः ।
अन्तर्विद्वाँ अध्वनो देवयानानतन्द्रो दूतो अभवो हविर्वाट् ॥७॥

7. O Fire, thou art the knower of our knowings, ordain for
    the people an unbroken succession of strengths that they
    may live. The knower within of the paths of the journey
    of the gods, thou hast become a sleepless messenger and

---

[1] *Nema*, the half, referring apparently to the Great Heaven, "*brhad dyauḥ*", the upper
half beyond which is the supreme plane.

the carrier of the offerings.

स्वाध्यो दिव आ सप्त यह्वी रायो दुरो व्यृतज्ञा अजानन् ।
विदद् गव्यं सरमा दृळहमूर्वं येना नु कं मानुषी भोजते विट् ॥८॥

8. The seven mighty Rivers from Heaven, deep-thinking, knowers of the Truth, knew the doors of the treasure; Sarama discovered the mass of the Ray-Cow, the strong place, the wideness, and now by that the human creature enjoys bliss.

आ ये विश्वा स्वपत्यानि तस्थुः कृष्वानासो अमृतत्वाय गातुम् ।
मह्ना महद्भिः पृथिवी वि तस्थे माता पुत्रैरदितिर्धयिसे वेः ॥९॥

9. These are they who set their steps on all things that have fair issue, making a path towards immortality. Earth stood wide in greatness by the Great Ones, the Mother infinite with her sons came to uphold her.

अधि श्रियं नि दधुश्चारुमस्मिन्दिवो यदक्षी अमृता अकृण्वन् ।
अध क्षरन्ति सिन्धवो न सृष्टाः प्र नीचीरग्ने अरुषीरजानन् ॥१०॥

10. When the immortals made the two eyes of Heaven, they set in him the splendour and the beauty. Then there flow as if rivers loosed to their course; downward they ran, his ruddy mares, and knew, O Fire.

SUKTA 73

रयिं यः पितृवित्तो वयोधाः सुप्रणीतिश्चिकितुषो न शासुः ।
स्योनशीरतिथिर्न प्रीणानो होतेव सद्म विधतो वि तारीत् ॥१॥

1. He is like an ancestral wealth that founds our strength, perfect in his leading like the command[1] of one who knows, he is like a guest lying happily well-pleased, he is like a priest of invocation and increases the house of his worshipper.

[1] Or, the teaching

देवो न यः सविता सत्यमन्मा ऋत्वा निपाति वृजनानि विश्वा ।
पुरुप्रशस्तो अमतिनं सत्य आत्मेव श्रेबो दिधिषाय्यो भूत् ॥२॥

2. He is like the divine Sun true in his thoughts and guards by
his will all our strong places; he is like a splendour manifoldly expressed, he is like a blissful self and our support.[1]

देवो न यः पृथिवीं विश्वधाया उपक्षेति हितमित्रो न राजा ।
पुरःसवः शर्मसवो न वीरा अनवद्या पतिजुष्टेव नारी ॥ ३ ॥

3. He is like a God upholding the world and he inhabits earth
like a good and friendly king: he is like a company of heroes
sitting in our front, dwelling in our house; he is as if a
blameless wife beloved of her lord.

तं त्वा नरो दम आ नित्यमिद्धमग्ने सचन्त क्षितिषु ध्रुवासु ।
अधि द्युम्नं नि दधुर्भूर्यस्मिन्भवा विश्वायुर्धरुणो रयीणाम् ॥४॥

4. Such art thou, O Fire, to whom men cleave, kindled eternal
in the house in the abiding worlds of thy habitation. They
have founded within upon thee a great light; become a universal life holder of the riches.

वि पृक्षो अग्ने मधवानो अश्युर्वि सूरयो ददतो विश्वमायुः ।
सनेम वाजं समिथेष्वर्यो भागं देवेषु श्रवसे दधानाः ॥५॥

5. O Fire, may the masters of wealth enjoy thy satisfactions,
the illumined wise Ones givers of the whole of life: may
we conquer the plenitude from the foe in our battles[2] holding
our part in the Gods for inspired knowledge.

ऋतस्य हि धेनवो वावशानाः स्मदूध्नीः पीपयन्त द्युभक्ताः ।
परावतः सुमतिं भिक्षमाणा वि सिन्धवः समया सस्रुरद्रिम् ॥६॥

6. The milch-cows of the Truth, enjoyed in heaven,[3] full-

---

[1] Or, he is one to be meditated on (upheld in thought), blissful like the self.
[2] Or, warriors in the battles may we conquer the plenitude
[3] Or, shared by heaven,

uddered, desiring us, have fed us with their milk: praying for right-thinking from the Beyond the Rivers flowed wide over the Mountain.

त्वे अग्ने सुमतिं भिक्षमाणा दिवि श्रवो दधिरे यज्ञियासः ।
नक्ता च चक्रुरुषसा विरूपे कृष्णं च वर्णमरुणं च सं धुः ॥७॥

7. O Fire, in thee praying for right-thinking, the masters of sacrifice set inspired knowledge in heaven: they made night and dawn of different forms and joined together the black and the rosy hue.

यान्राये मर्तान्त्सुषूदो अग्ने ते स्याम मघवानो वयं च ।
छायेव विश्वं भुवनं सिसक्ष्यापप्रिवान् रोदसी अन्तरिक्षम् ॥८॥

8. The mortals whom thou speedest to the Treasure, may we be of them, the lords of riches and we. Filling earth and heaven and mid-air thou clingest to the whole world like a shadow.

अर्वद्भिरग्ने अर्वतो नृभिर्नॄन्वीरैर्वीरान्वनुयामा त्वोताः ।
ईशानासः पितृवित्तस्य रायो वि सूरयः शतहिमा नो अश्युः ॥९॥

9. O Fire, safeguarded[1] by thee may we conquer the war-horses by our war-horses, the strong men by our strong men, the heroes by our heroes; may our illumined wise ones become masters of the treasure gained by the fathers, and possess them living a hundred winters.

एता ते अग्न उच्चथानि वेधो जुष्टानि सन्तु मनसे हृदे च ।
शकेम रायः सुधुरो यमं तेऽधि श्रवो देवभक्तं दधानाः ॥१०॥

10. O ordainer of things, O Fire, may these utterances be acceptable to thee, to the mind and to the heart; may we have strength to control with firm yoke thy riches, holding in thee the inspired knowledge enjoyed by the gods.[2]

---

[1] Or, upheld   [2] Or, distributed by the gods.

KUTSA ANGIRASA

Sukta 94

इमं स्तोममर्हते जातवेदसे रथमिव सं महेमा मनीषया ।
भद्रा हि नः प्रमतिरस्य संसद्यग्ने सख्ये मा रिषामा वयं तव ॥१॥

1. This is the omniscient who knows the law of our being
   and is sufficient to his works; let us build the song of his
   truth by our thought and make it as if a chariot on which
   he shall mount. When he dwells with us, then a happy
   wisdom becomes ours. With him for friend we cannot
   come to harm.

यस्मै त्वमायजसे स साधत्यनर्वा क्षेति दधते सुवीर्यम् ।
स तूताव नैनमश्नोत्यंहतिरग्ने सख्ये मा रिषामा वयं तव ॥२॥

2. Whosoever makes him his priest of the sacrifice, reaches the
   perfection that is the fruit of his striving, a home on a
   height of being where there is no warring and no enemies;
   he confirms in himself an ample energy; he is safe in his
   strength, evil cannot lay its hand upon him.

शकेम त्वा समिधं साधया धियस्त्वे देवा हविरदन्त्याहुतम् ।
त्वमादित्यां आ वह तान् हृपुरमस्यग्ने सख्ये मा रिषामा वयं तव ॥३॥

3. This is the fire of our sacrifice! May we have strength to
   kindle it to its height, may it perfect our thoughts. In
   this all that we give must be thrown that it may become a
   food for the gods; this shall bring to us the godheads
   of the infinite consciousness who are our desire.

भरामेध्मं कृणवामा हवींषि ते चितयन्तः पर्वणापर्वणा वयम् ।
जीवातवे प्रतरं साधया धियोऽग्ने सख्ये मा रिषामा वयं तव ॥४॥

4. Let us gather fuel for it, let us prepare for it offerings, let us
   make ourselves conscious of the jointings of its times and
   its seasons. It shall so perfect our thoughts that they shall

extend our being and create for us a larger life.

विशां गोपा अस्य चरन्ति जन्तवो द्विपच्च यदुत चतुष्पदक्तुभिः ।
चित्रः प्रकेत उषसो महाँ अस्यग्ने सख्ये मा रिषामा वयं तव ॥५॥

5. This is the guardian of the world and its peoples, the shep-
   herd of all these herds; all that is born moves by his rays
   and is compelled by his flame, both the two-footed and the
   four-footed creatures. This is the rich and great thought-
   awakening of the Dawn within.

त्वमध्वर्युरुत होतासि पूर्व्यः प्रशास्ता पोता जनुषा पुरोहितः ।
विश्वा विद्वाँ आर्त्विज्या धीर पुष्यस्यग्ने सख्ये मा रिषामा वयं तव ॥६॥

6. This is the priest who guides the march of the sacrifice, the
   first and ancient who calls to the gods and gives the
   offerings; his is the command and his the purification;
   from his birth he stands in front the vicar of our sacrifice.
   He knows all the works of this divine priesthood, for he is
   the Thinker who increases in us.

यो विश्वतः सुप्रतीकः सदृङ्ङसि दूरे चित् सन्तळिदिवाति रोचसे ।
रात्र्याश्चिदन्धो अति देव पश्यस्यग्ने सख्ये मा रिषामा वयं तव ॥७॥

7. The faces of this God are everywhere and he fronts all things
   perfectly; he has the eye and the vision: when we see him
   from afar, yet he seems near to us, so brilliantly he shines
   across the gulfs. He sees beyond the darkness of our
   night, for his vision is divine.

पूर्वो देवा भवतु सुन्वतो रथोऽस्माकं शंसो अभ्यस्तु दूढ्यः ।
तदा जानीतोत पुष्यता वचोऽग्ने सख्ये मा रिषामा वयं तव ॥८॥

8. O you godheads, let our chariot be always in front, let our
   clear and strong word overcome all that thinks the falsehood. O you godheads, know for us, know in us that Truth,
   increase the speech that finds and utters it.

वर्घदुःशंसाँ अप दूढ्घो जहि दूरे वा ये अन्ति वा के चिद्त्रिणः ।
अथा यज्ञाय गृणते सुगं कृध्यग्ने सख्ये मा रिषामा वयं तव ॥९॥

9. With blows that slay cast from our path, O thou Flame, the
   powers that stammer in the speech and stumble in the
   thought, the devourers of our power and our knowledge
   who leap at us from near and shoot at us from afar. Make
   the path of the sacrifice a clear and happy journeying.

यदयुक्था अरुषा रोहिता रथे वातजूता वृषभस्येव ते रवः ।
आदिन्वसि वनिनो धूमकेतुनाऽग्ने सख्ये मा रिषामा वयं तव ॥१०॥

10. Thou hast bright red horses for thy chariot, O Will divine,
    who are driven by the storm-wind of thy passion; thou roar-
    est like a bull, thou rushest upon the forests of life, on its
    pleasant trees that encumber thy path, with the smoke of
    thy passion in which there is the thought and the sight.

अध स्वनादुत बिभ्युः पतत्रिणो द्रप्सा यत् ते यवसादो व्यस्थिरन् ।
सुगं तत् ते ताबकेभ्यो रथेभ्योऽग्ने सख्ये मा रिषामा वयं तव ॥११॥

11. At the noise of thy coming even they that wing in the skies
    are afraid, when thy eaters of the pasture go abroad in their
    haste. So thou makest clear thy path to thy kingdom that
    thy chariots may run towards it easily.

अयं मित्रस्य वरुणस्य धायसेऽवयातां मरुतां हेळो अद्भुतः ।
मृळा सु नो भूत्वेषां मनः पुनरग्ने सख्ये मा रिषामा वयं तव ॥१२॥

12. This dread and tumult of thee, is it not the wonderful and
    exceeding wrath of the gods of the Life rushing down on
    us to found here the purity of the Infinite, the harmony of
    the Lover? Be gracious, O thou fierce Fire, let their minds
    be again sweet to us and pleasant.

देवो देवानामसि मित्रो अद्भुतो वसुर्वसूनामसि चारुरध्वरे ।
शर्मन्त्स्याम तव सप्रथस्तमेऽग्ने सख्ये मा रिषामा वयं तव ॥१३॥

13. God art thou of the gods, for thou art the lover and friend;
    richest art thou of the masters of the Treasure, the founders
    of the home, for thou art very bright and pleasant in the
    pilgrimage and the sacrifice. Very wide and far-extending
    is the peace of thy beatitude; may that be the home of our
    abiding!

तत् ते भद्रं यत् समिद्धः स्वे दमे सोमाहुतो जरसे मृळयत्तमः ।
दधासि रत्नं द्रविणं च दाशुषेऽग्ने सख्ये मा रिषामा वयं तव ॥१४॥

14. That is the bliss of him and the happiness; for then is this
    Will very gracious and joy-giving when in its own divine
    house, lit into its high and perfect flame, it is adored by
    our thoughts and satisfied with the wine of our delight.
    Then it lavishes its deliciousness, then it returns in treasure
    and substance all that we have given into its hands.

यस्मै त्वं सुद्रविणो ददाशोऽनागास्त्वमदिते सर्वताता ।
यं भद्रेण शवसा चोदयासि प्रजावता राधसा ते स्याम ॥१५॥

15. O thou infinite and indivisible Being, it is thou ever that
    formest the sinless universalities of the spirit by our sacri-
    fice; thou compellest and inspirest thy favourites by thy
    happy and luminous forcefulness, by the fruitful riches of
    thy joy. Among them may we be numbered.

स त्वमग्ने सौभगत्वस्य विद्वानस्माकमायुः प्र तिरेह देव ।
तन्नो मित्रो वरुणो मामहन्तामदितिः सिन्धुः पृथिवी उत द्यौः ॥१६॥

16. Thou art the knower of felicity and the increaser here of our
    life and advancer of our being! Thou art the godhead!...

SUKTA 97

अप नः शोशुचदघमग्ने शुशुग्ध्या रयिम् ।
अप नः शोशुचदघम् ॥१॥

1. Burn away from us the sin, flame out on us the bliss. Burn away from us the sin!

सुक्षेत्रिया सुगातुया वसूया च यजामहे ।
अप नः शोशुचदघम् ॥२॥

2. For the perfect path to the happy field, for the exceeding treasure when we would do sacrifice, — burn away from us the sin!

प्र यद् भन्दिष्ठ एषां प्रास्माकासश्च सूरयः ।
अप नः शोशुचदघम् ॥३॥

3. That the happiest of all these many godheads may be born in us, that the seers who see in our thought may multiply, — burn away from us the sin!

प्र यत् ते अग्ने सूरयो जायेमहि प्र ते वयम् ।
अप नः शोशुचदघम् ॥४॥

4. That thy seers, O Flame divine, may multiply and we be new-born as thine, — burn away from us the sin!

प्र यदग्नेः सहस्वतो विश्वतो यन्ति भानवः ।
अप नः शोशुचदघम् ॥५॥

5. When the flaming rays of thy might rush abroad on every side violently, — burn away from us the sin!

त्वं हि विश्वतोमुख विश्वतः परिभूरसि ।
अप नः शोशुचदघम् ॥६॥

6. God, thy faces are everywhere! thou besiegest us on every side with thy being. Burn away from us the sin!

द्विषो नो विश्वतोमुखाति नावेव पारय ।
अप नः शोशुचदघम् ॥७॥

7. Let thy face front the Enemy wherever he turns; bear us in thy ship over the dangerous waters. Burn away from us the sin!

स नः सिन्धुमिव नाबयाति पर्षा स्वस्तये ।
अप नः शोशुचदघम् ॥८॥

8. As in a ship over the ocean, bear us over into thy felicity. Burn away from us the sin!

PARUCHCHHEPA DAIVODASI

SUKTA 127

अग्निं होतारं मन्ये दास्वन्तं
वसुं सूनुं सहसो जातवेदसं विप्रं न जातवेदसम् ।
य ऊर्ध्वया स्वध्वरो देवो देवाच्या कृपा ।
घृतस्य विभ्राष्टिमनु वष्टि शोचिषाऽऽजुह्वानस्य सर्पिषः ॥१॥

1. I meditate on the Fire, the priest of the call, the giver of the Treasure, the son of force, who knows all things born, the Fire who is like one illumined and knowing all things born.

    The Fire who perfect in the pilgrim-sacrifice, a God with his high-lifted longing[1] hungers with his flame for the blaze of the offering of light, for its current poured on him as an oblation.

यजिष्ठं त्वा यजमाना हुवेम
ज्येष्ठमङ्गिरसां विप्र मन्मभि विप्रेभिः शुक्र मन्मभिः ।
परिज्मानमिव द्यां होतारं चर्षणीनाम् ।
शोचिष्केशं वृषणं यमिमा विशः प्रावन्तु जूतये विशः ॥२॥

2. Thee most powerful for sacrifice, as givers of sacrifice may we call, the eldest of the Angiras, the Illumined One, call thee with our thoughts, O Brilliant Fire, with our illumined

[1] Or, high-uplifted lustre seeking for the Gods

thoughts, men's priest of the call,[1] who encircles all like
heaven, the Male with hair of flaming-light whom may these
peoples cherish for his urge.

स हि पुरू चिदोजसा विरुक्मता
दीद्यानो भवति द्रुहंतरः परशुर्न द्रुहंतरः ।
वीळु चिद्यस्य समृतौ श्रुवद्वनेव यत्स्थिरम् ।
निष्षहमाणो यमते नायते धन्वासहा नायते ॥३॥

3. Many things illumining with his wide-shining energy he
    becomes one who cleaves through those who would hurt
    us, like a battle-axe he cleaves through those who would
    hurt us, he in whose shock even that which is strong falls
    asunder, even what is firmly fixed falls like trees; over-
    whelming with his force he toils on and goes not back, like
    warriors with the bow from the battle he goes not back.

दृळ्हा चिदस्मा अनु दुर्यथा विदे
तेजिष्ठाभिररणिभिर्दाष्टचवसेऽनये दाष्टचवसे ।
प्र यः पुरूणि गाहते तक्षद्वनेव शोचिषा ।
स्थिरा चिदन्ना नि रिणात्योजसा नि स्थिराणि चिदोजसा ॥४॥

4. Even things strongly built they give to him as to one who
    knows: one gives for safeguarding by his movements of
    flaming-power, gives to the Fire that he may guard us. Into
    many things he enters and hews them with his flaming light
    like trees, even things firmly fixed he tears by his energy
    and makes his food by his energy even things firmly fixed.

तमस्य पृक्षमुपरासु धीमहि
नक्तं यः सुदर्शतरो दिवातरादप्रायुषे दिवातरात् ।
आदस्यायुर्ग्रभणवद् वीळु शर्म न सूनवे ।
भक्तमभक्तमवो व्यन्तो अजरा अग्नयो व्यन्तो अजराः ॥५॥

5. We meditate on[2] that fullness of him on the upper levels,
    this Fire the vision of whom is brighter in the night than in

---

[1] Or, the priest of the call for men who see,   [2] or, we hold

the day, for his undeparting life brighter than in the day.
Then does his life grasp and support us like a strong house
of refuge for the Son, — ageless fires moving towards the
happiness enjoyed and that not yet enjoyed, moving his
ageless fires.

स हि शर्धो न मारूतं तुविष्वणि-
रप्नस्वतीवूर्वरास्विष्टनिरार्तनास्विष्टनिः ।
आदद्ध्यान्याददि यंज्ञस्य केतुरर्हणा ।
अध स्मास्य हर्षतो
हृषीवतो विश्वे जुषन्त पन्यां नरः शुभे न पन्थाम् ॥६॥

6. He is many-noised like the army of the storm-winds hurrying over the fertile lands full of our labour, hurrying over the
waste lands.[1] He takes and devours the offerings, he is the
eye of intuition of the sacrifice in its due action; so all men
follow with pleasure the path of this joyful and joy-giving
Fire, as on a path leading to happiness.

द्विता यदीं कीस्तासो अभिद्यवो
नमस्यन्त उपवोचन्त भृगवो मध्नन्तो दाशा भृगवः ।
अग्निरीशे वसूनां शुचिर्यो धर्णिरेषाम् ।
प्रियाँ अपिधीँर्वनिषीष्ट मेधिर आ वनिषीष्ट मेधिरः ॥७॥

7. When in his twofold strength, bards with illumination upon
them, the Bhrigu-flame-seers have made obeisance and spoken to him the word, when they have churned him out by
their worship, — the Flame-Seers, the Fire becomes master
of the riches, he who in his purity holds them within him,
wise he enjoys the things laid upon him and they are pleasant
to him, he takes joy of them in his wisdom.

विश्वासां त्वा विशां पतिं हवामहे
सर्वासां समानं दम्पतिं भुजे सत्यगिर्वाहसं भुजे ।
अतिथिं मानुषाणां पितुं यस्यासया ।
अमी च विश्वे अमृतास आ वयो हव्या देवेष्वा वयः ॥८॥

---

[1] Or, in the esoteric sense, the army of the Life-Powers moving with fertilising rain over
our tilled and our waste lands.

8. We call to thee, the Lord of all creatures, the master of the house common to them all for the enjoying, the carrier of the true words for the enjoying, — to the Guest of men in whose presence stand as in the presence of a father, all these Immortals and make our offerings their food — in the Gods they become their food.

त्वमग्ने सहसा सहन्तमः
शुष्मिन्तमो जायसे देवतातये रयिं देवतातये ।
शुष्मिन्तमो हि ते मदो द्युम्निन्तम उत क्रतुः ।
अध स्मा ते परि चरन्त्यजर श्रुष्टीवानो नाजर ॥९॥

9. O Fire, thou art overwhelming in thy strength, thou art born most forceful for the forming of the Gods, as if a wealth for the forming of the Gods; most forceful is thy rapture, most luminous thy will. So they serve thee, O Ageless Fire, who hear thy word serve thee, O Ageless Fire!

प्र वो महे सहसा सहस्वत
उषर्बुधे पशुषे नाग्नये स्तोमो बभूत्वग्नये ।
प्रति यदीं हविष्मान् विश्वासु क्षासु जोगुवे ।
अग्ने रेभो न जरत ऋषूणां जूर्णिर्होत ऋषूणाम् ॥१०॥

10. To the Great One, the Strong in his force, the waker in the Dawn, to Fire as to one who has vision, let your hymn arise. When the giver of the offering cries towards him in all the planes, in the front of the wise he chants our adoration, the priest of the call of the wise who chants their adoration.

स नो नेदिष्ठं ददृशान आ भरा-
ग्ने देवेभिः सचनाः सुचेतुना महो रायः सुचेतुना ।
महि शविष्ठ नस्कृधि संचक्षे भुजे अस्यै ।
महि स्तोतृभ्यो मघवन्त्सुवीर्यं मथीरुग्रो न शवसा ॥११॥

11. So, becoming visible, most near to us bring, O Fire, by thy perfect consciousness, the Riches that ever accompany the Gods, by thy perfect consciousness the Great Riches. O most strong Fire, create for us that which is great for vision,

for the enjoying; for those who hymn thee, O Lord of plenty, churn out a great hero-strength as one puissant by his force.

DIRGHATAMAS AUCHATHYA

SUKTA 140

वेदिषदे प्रियधामाय सुद्युते धासिमिव प्र भरा योनिमग्नये ।
वस्त्रेणेव वासया मन्मना शुचिं ज्योतीरथं शुक्रवर्णं तमोहनम् ॥१॥

1. Offer like a secure seat that womb to Agni the utterly bright who sits upon the altar and his abode is bliss; clothe with thought as with a robe the slayer of the darkness who is pure and charioted in light and pure bright[1] of hue.

अभि द्विजन्मा त्रिवृदन्नमृज्यते संवत्सरे वावृधे जग्धमी पुनः ।
अन्यस्यासा जिह्वया जेन्यो वृषा न्यन्येन वनिनो मृष्ट वारणः ॥२॥

2. The twice-born Agni moves (intense) about his triple food; it is eaten and with the year it has grown again; with the tongue and mouth of the one[2] he is the strong master and enjoyer, with the other he engirdles and crushes in his embrace[3] his delightful things.

कृष्णप्रुतौ वेविजे अस्य सक्षिता उभा तरेते अभि मातरा शिशुम् ।
प्राचाजिह्वं ध्वसयन्तं तृषुच्युतमा साच्यं कृपयं वर्धनं पितुः ॥३॥

3. He gives energy of movement to both his mothers on their dark path, in their common dwelling and both make their way through to their child[4] for his tongue is lifted upward, he destroys and rushes swiftly through and should be chosen, increasing his father.[5]

---

[1] Or, white; *śukra*, a white brightness.
[2] Or, with his tongue in the presence of the one
[3] *Mṛś* is used of the sexual contact; *vāraṇaḥ* from *vṛ* to cover, surround.
[4] Or, following their child
[5] Expl. Heaven and Earth, Mind and Body dwelling together in one frame or in one

मुमुक्ष्वो मनवे मानवस्यते रघुद्रुवः कृष्णसीतास ऊ जुवः ।
असमना आंजिरासो रघुष्यदो वातजूता उप युज्यन्त आशवः ॥४॥

4. For the thinker becoming man his swift hastening impulsions dark and bright desire freedom; active, rapid, quivering, they are yoked to their works, swift steeds and driven
forward by the Breath of things.

आदस्य ते ध्वसयन्तो वृथेरते कृष्णमभ्वं महि वर्पः करिक्रतः ।
यत् सीं महीमर्वंनि प्राभि मर्मृशदभिश्वसन् स्तनयन्नेति नानदत् ॥५॥

5. They for him destroy and speed lightly on[1] creating his dark
being of thickness and his mighty form of light; when reaching forward he touches the Vast of Being, he pants towards
it and, thundering, cries aloud.[2]

भूषन् न योऽधि बभ्रूषु नम्नते वृषेव पत्नीरभ्येति रोरुवत् ।
ओजायमानस्तन्वश्च शुम्भते भीमो न शृङ्गा दविधाव दुर्गृभिः ॥६॥

6. He who when he would become in the tawny ones, bends
down and goes to them bellowing as the male to its mates,
— putting out his forces he gives joy to their bodies[3] and like
a fierce beast hard to seize he tosses his horns.[4]

स संस्तिरो विष्टिरः सं गृभायति जानन्नेव जानतीरनित्य आ शये ।
पुनर्वर्धन्ते अपि यन्ति देव्यमन्यद् वर्पः पित्रोः कृण्वते सचा ॥७॥

7. He whether contracted in being or wide-extended seizes on
them utterly; he knowing, they knowing the eternal Agni
enjoys[5] them, then again they increase and go to the state

---

material world move in the darkness of ignorance, they pass through it by following the divine
Force which is born to their activities. *Kupaya* is of doubtful significance. The father is the
Purusha or else Heaven in the sense of the higher spiritual being.

[1] Or, speed and pervade

[2] *Mahimavanim* might mean the vast earth, but *avani* and even *prthivi* are not used in the
Veda invariably, the former not usually, to mean earth, but stray or return to their original
sense — *sapta avanayah.*

[3] Or, he makes blissful the forms of things

[4] *Babhrūṣu*, the cows, *aruṇayah* of a later verse — knowledge in the mortal mind.

[5] Or, lies with

divine; uniting, another form they make for the Father and Mother.

तमग्रुवः केशिनीः सं हि रेभिर ऊर्ध्वास्तस्थुर्मन्नुषीः प्रायबे पुनः ।
तासां जरां प्रमुञ्चन्तेति नानददसुं परं जनयञ्जीवमस्तृतम् ॥८॥

8. Bright with their flowing tresses they take utter delight of him, they who were about to perish, stand upon high once more for his coming;[1] for he loosens from them their decay and goes to them shouting high, he creates supreme force and unconquerable life.

अधीवासं परि मातू रिहन्नह तुविग्रेभिः सत्वभिर्याति वि ज्रयः ।
वयो दधत् पद्यते रेरिहत् सदाऽनु श्येनी सचते वर्तनीरह ॥९॥

9. Tearing about her the robe that conceals the other he moves on utterly to the Delight with the creatures of pure Being who manifest the Force; he establishes the wideness, he breaks through to the goal for this traveller, even though swift-rushing, he cleaves always to the paths.[2]

अस्माकमग्ने मघवत्सु दीदिह्यध श्वसीवान् वृषभो दमूनाः ।
अवास्या शिशुमतीरदीदेर्वर्मेव युत्सु परिजर्भुराणः ॥१०॥

10. Burn bright for us, O Agni, in our fullnesses, henceforth be the strong master and inhabit in us with the sisters; casting away from thee those of them that are infant minds thou shouldst burn bright encompassing us all about like a cuirass in our battles.[3]

इदमग्ने सुधितं दुर्धितादधि प्रियादु चिन्मन्मनः प्रेयो अस्तु ते ।
यत् ते शुक्रं तन्वो रोचते शुचि तेनास्मभ्यं वनसे रत्नमा त्वम् ॥११॥

11. This, O Agni, is that which is well-established upon the ill-

[1] *Mamruṣiḥ* is uncertain. It may be dead or dying. *Rebhire* = delight, is here perfectly proved.

[2] *Rihan, rerihat* are uncertain.

[3] *Śvasi* is the Greek *Kasis* and an old variant of *svasṛ* wife or sister. Therefore it is ıpled with *vṛṣā* like *patni.*

placed; even out of this blissful mentality may there be born
to thee that greater bliss. By that which shines bright and
pure from thy body, thou winnest for us the delight.

रथाय नावमुत नो गृहाय नित्यारित्रां पद्वतीं रास्यग्ने ।
अस्माकं वीरां उत नो मघोनो जनांश्च या पारयाच्छर्म या च ॥१२॥

12. Thou givest us, O Agni, for chariot and for home a ship
travelling with eternal progress of motion that shall carry
our strong spirits and our spirits of fullness across the births
and cross the peace.

अभी नो अग्न उक्थमिज्जुगुर्या द्यावाक्षामा सिन्धवश्च स्वगूर्ताः ।
गव्यं यव्यं यन्तो दीर्घहिषं वरमरुण्यो वरन्त ॥१३॥

13. Mayest thou, O Agni, about our Word for thy pivot bring
to light for us Heaven and Earth and the rivers that are
self-revealed; may the Red Ones reach to knowledge and
strength and long days of light, may they choose the force
and the supreme good.

MANDALA TWO

GRITSAMADA BHARGAVA

SUKTA 1

त्वमग्ने द्युभिस्त्वमाशुशुक्षणिस्त्वमद्भ्यस्त्वमश्मनस्परि ।
त्वं वनेभ्यस्त्वमोषधीभ्यस्त्वं नृणां नृपते जायसे शुचिः ॥१॥

1. O Fire, thou art born with thy lights, flaming out on us in
   thy effulgence; thou art born from the waters and around
   the stone, thou art born from the forests and born from the
   plants of the earth. Pure art thou in thy birth, O Master of
   man and his race.

तवाग्ने होत्रं तव पोत्रमृत्वियं तव नेष्ट्रं त्वमग्निदृतायतः ।
तव प्रशास्त्रं त्वमध्वरीयसि ब्रह्मा चासि गृहपतिश्च नो दमे ॥२॥

2. O Fire, thine are the call and the offering, thine the purification and the order of the sacrifice, thine the lustration; thou
   art the fire-bringer for the seeker of the Truth. The annunciation is thine, thou becomest the pilgrim-rite:[1] thou art
   the priest of the Word and the master of the house in our
   home.

त्वमग्न इन्द्रो वृषभः सतामसि त्वं विष्णुरुरुगायो नमस्यः ।
त्वं ब्रह्मा रयिविद् ब्रह्मणस्पते त्वं विधर्तः सचसे पुरन्ध्या ॥३॥

3. O Fire, thou art Indra the Bull of all that are and thou art
   wide-moving[2] Vishnu, one to be worshipped with obeisance.
   O Master of the Word, thou art Brahma, the finder of the
   Riches: O Fire, who sustainest each and all, closely thou
   companionest the Goddess of the many thoughts.[3]

त्वमग्ने राजा वरुणो धृतव्रतस्त्वं मित्रो भवसि दस्म ईड्यः ।
त्वमर्यमा सत्पतिर्यस्य संभुजं त्वमंशो विदथे देव भाजयुः ॥४॥

4. O Fire, thou art Varuna the king who holds in his hands the

---

[1] Or, thou art the priest of the pilgrim-rite: [2] Or, wide-sung
[3] Or, the Goddess tenant of the city.

law of all workings and thou art Mitra the potent and desirable Godhead. Thou art Aryaman, master of beings, with
whom is complete enjoying; O Godhead, thou art Ansha
who gives us our portion in the winning of the knowledge.

त्वमग्ने त्वष्टा विधते सुवीर्यं तव ग्नावो मित्रमहः सजात्यम् ।
त्वमाशुहेमा ररिषे स्वश्व्यं त्वं नरां शर्धो असि पूरूवसुः ॥५॥

5. O Fire, thou art Twashtri and fashionest fullness of force
for thy worshipper; thine, O friendly Light, are the goddess-
Energies and all oneness of natural kind. Thou art the swift
galloper and lavishest good power of the Horse; thou art
the host of the gods and great is the multitude of thy riches.

त्वमग्ने रुद्रो असुरो महो दिवस्त्वं शर्धो मारुतं पृक्ष ईशिषे ।
त्वं वातैररुणैर्यासि शंगयस्त्वं पूषा विधतः पासि नु त्मना ॥६॥

6. O Fire, thou art Rudra, the mighty one of the great Heaven
and thou art the army of the Life-Gods and hast power over
all that fills desire. Thou journeyest with dawn-red winds
to bear thee and thine is the house of bliss; thou art Pushan
and thou guardest with thyself thy worshippers.

त्वमग्ने द्रविणोदा अरंकृते त्वं देवः सविता रत्नधा असि ।
त्वं भगो नृपते वस्व ईशिषे त्वं पायुर्दमे यस्तेऽविधत् ॥७॥

7. O Fire, to one who makes ready and sufficient his works thou
art the giver of the treasure; thou art divine Savitri and a
founder of the ecstasy. O Master of man, thou art Bhaga
and hast power for the riches; thou art the guardian in the
house for one who worships thee with his works.

त्वामग्ने दम आ विश्पतिं विशस्त्वां राजानं सुविदत्रमृञ्जते ।
त्वं विश्वानि स्वनीक पत्यसे त्वं सहस्राणि शता दश प्रति ॥८॥

8. O Fire, men turn to thee the master of the human being in
his house; thee they crown, the king perfect in knowledge.
O strong force of Fire, thou masterest all things; thou

movest to the thousands and the hundreds and the tens.

त्वामग्ने पितरमिष्टिभिर्नरस्त्वां भ्रात्राय शम्या तनूरुचम् ।
त्वं पुत्रो भवसि यस्तेऽविधत् त्वं सखा सुशेवः पास्याधृषः ॥९॥

9. O Fire, men worship thee with their sacrifices as a father and
    thee that thou mayst be their brother by their achievement
    of works when thou illuminest the body with thy light.
    Thou becomest a son to the man who worships thee; thou
    art his blissful friend and guardest him from the violence
    of the adversary.

त्वमग्न ऋभुराके नमस्यस्त्वं वाजस्य क्षुमतो राय ईशिषे ।
त्वं वि भास्यनु दक्षि दावने त्वं विशिक्षुरसि यज्ञमातनिः ॥१०॥

10. O Fire, thou art the craftsman Ribhu, near to us and to be
    worshipped with obeisance of surrender; thou hast mastery
    over the store of the plenitude and the riches. All thy wide
    shining of light and onward burning is for the gift of the
    treasure; thou art our instructor in wisdom and our builder
    of sacrifice.

त्वमग्ने अदितिर्देव दाशुषे त्वं होत्रा भारती वर्धसे गिरा ।
त्वमिळा शतहिमासि दक्षसे त्वं वृत्रहा वसुपते सरस्वती ॥११॥

11. O Divine Fire, thou art Aditi, the indivisible Mother to the
    giver of the sacrifice; thou art Bharati, voice of the offering,
    and thou growest by the word. Thou art Ila of the hundred
    winters wise to discern; O Master of the Treasure, thou art
    Saraswati who slays the python adversary.

त्वमग्ने सुभृत उत्तमं वयस्तव स्पार्हे वर्ण आ संदृशि श्रियः ।
त्वं वाजः प्रतरणो बृहन्नसि त्वं रयिर्बहुलो विश्वतस्पृथुः ॥१२॥

12. O Fire, when thou art well borne by us thou becomest the
    supreme growth and expansion of our being, all glory and
    beauty are in thy desirable hue and thy perfect vision. O
    Vastness, thou art the plenitude that carries us to the end of

our way; thou art a multitude of riches spread out on every side.

त्वामग्न आदित्यास आस्यं त्वां जिह्वां शुचयश्चक्रिरे कवे ।
त्वां रातिषाचो अध्वरेषु सश्चिरे त्वे देवा हविरदन्त्याहुतम् ॥१३॥

13. O Fire, the sons of the indivisible Mother made thee their mouth, the pure Gods made thee their tongue; O Seer, they who are ever close to our giving are constant to thee in the rites of the Path; the Gods eat in thee the offering cast before them.

त्वे अग्ने विश्वे अमृतासो अद्रुह आसा देवा हविरदन्त्याहुतम् ।
त्वया मर्तासः स्वदन्त आसुतिं त्वं गर्भो वीरुधां जज्ञिषे शुचिः ॥१४॥

14. O Fire, all the Gods, the Immortals unhurtful to man, eat in thee and by thy mouth the offering cast before them; by thee mortal men taste of the libation. Pure art thou born, a child of the growths of the earth.

त्वं तान्त्सं च प्रति चासि मज्मनाग्ने सुजात प्र च देव रिच्यसे ।
पृक्षो यदत्र महिना वि ते भुवदनु द्यावापृथिवी रोदसी उभे ॥१५॥

15. O Fire that hast come to perfect birth, thou art with the Gods and thou frontest them in thy might and thou exceedest them too, O God, when here the satisfying fullness of thee becomes all-pervading in its greatness along both the continents, Earth and Heaven.

ये स्तोतृभ्यो गोअग्रामश्वपेशसमग्ने रातिमुपसृजन्ति सूरयः ।
अस्माञ्च तांश्च प्र हि नेषि वस्य आ बृहद् वदेम विदथे सुवीराः ॥१६॥

16. When to those who chant thee, the luminous Wise Ones set free thy gift, O Fire, the wealth in whose front the Ray-Cow walks and its form is the Horse, thou leadest us on and leadest them to a world of greater riches. Strong with the strength of the heroes, may we voice the Vast in the coming of knowledge.

SUKTA 2

यज्ञेन वर्धत जातवेदसमग्निं यजध्वं हविषा तना गिरा ।
समिधानं सुप्रयसं स्वर्णरं द्युक्षं होतारं वृजनेषु धूर्षदम् ॥१॥

1. Make the Fire that knows all things born to grow by your
   sacrifice; worship him with thy offering and thy body and
   thy speech. Worship in his kindling Fire with whom are his
   strong delights, the male of the sun-world, the Priest of the
   Call, the inhabitant of Heaven[1] who sits at the chariot yoke
   in our battles.

अभि त्वा नक्तीरुषसो ववाशिरेऽग्ने वत्सं न स्वसरेषु धेनवः ।
दिव इवेदरतिर्मानुषा युगा क्षपो भासि पुरुवार संयतः ॥२॥

2. The Nights and the Dawns have lowed to thee as the milch-
   cows low towards a calf in their lairs of rest. O Fire of
   many blessings, thou art the traveller of Heaven through
   the ages of man and thou shinest self-gathered through his
   nights.[2]

तं देवा बुध्ने रजसः सुदंससं दिवस्पृथिव्योररतिं न्येरिरे ।
रथमिव वेद्यं शुक्रशोचिषमग्निं मित्रं न क्षितिषु प्रशंस्यम् ॥३॥

3. The Gods have sent into the foundation of the middle
   world this great worker and pilgrim of earth and of heaven,
   whom we must know, like our chariot of white-flaming light,
   Fire whom we must voice with our lauds like a friend in the
   peoples.

तमुक्षमाणं रजसि स्व आ दमे चन्द्रमिव सुरुचं ह्वार आ दधुः ।
पृश्न्याः पतरं चितयन्तमक्षभिः पाथो न पायुं जनसी उभे अनु ॥४॥

4. They have set in the crookedness, set pouring his rain like
   gold in the beauty of his light,[3] in the middle world and in
   his own home, the guardian of the dappled mother who

---

[1] Or, who dwells in the Light   [2] Or, self-gathered thou illuminest his nights.
[3] Or, like a thing of delight in his shining beauty,

awakens us to knowledge with his eyes of vision, the protector of our path along either birth.

स होता विश्वं परि भूत्वध्वरं तमु हव्यैर्मनुष ऋञ्जते गिरा।
हिरिशिप्रो वृधसानासु जर्भुरद् द्यौनं स्तृभिश्चितयद्रोदसी अनु ॥५॥

5. Let Fire be the priest of your call, let his presence be around every pilgrim-rite; this is he whom men crown with the word and the offering. He shall play in his growing fires wearing his tiara of golden light; like heaven with its stars he shall give us knowledge of our steps along both the continent-worlds.

स नो रेवत्समिधानः स्वस्तये संददस्वान् रयिमस्मासु वीदिहि।
आ नः कृणुष्व सुविताय रोदसी अग्ने हव्या मनुषो देव वीतये ॥६॥

6. O Fire, opulently kindling for our peace, let thy light arise in us and bring its gift of riches. Make Earth and Heaven ways for our happy journeying and the offerings of man a means for the coming of the Gods.

दा नो अग्ने बृहतो दाः सहस्रिणो तुरो न वाजं श्रुत्या अपा वृधि।
प्राची द्यावापृथिवी ब्रह्मणा कृधि स्वर्णं शुक्रमुषसो वि दिद्युतुः ॥७॥

7. O Fire, give us the vast possessions, the thousandfold riches; open to inspiration like gates the plenitude; make Earth and Heaven turned to the Beyond by the Word. The Dawns have broken into splendour as if there shone the brilliant world of the Sun.

स इधान उषसो राम्या अनु स्वर्णं वीदेदरुषेण भानुना।
होत्राभिरग्निर्मनुषः स्वध्वरो राजा विशामतिथिश्चारुरायवे ॥८॥

8. Kindled in the procession of the beautiful Dawns, he shall break into roseate splendour like the world of the Sun. O Fire, making effective the pilgrim-rite by man's voices of offering, thou art the King of the peoples and the Guest delightful to the human being.

एवा नो अग्ने अमृतेषु पूर्व्य धीष्पीपाय बृहद्दिवेषु मानुषा ।
दुहाना घेनुर्वृजनेषु कारवे त्मना शतिनं पुरुरूपमिषणि ॥९॥

9. O pristine Fire, even thus the Thought has nourished our human things in the immortals, in the great Heavens. The Thought is our milch-cow, of herself she milks for the doer of works in his battles and in his speed to the journey the many forms and the hundreds of the Treasure.

वयमग्ने अर्वता वा सुवीर्यं ब्रह्मणा वा चितयेमा जनाँ अति ।
अस्माकं द्युम्नमधि पञ्च कृष्टिषूच्चा स्वर्ण शुशुचीत दुष्टरम् ॥१०॥

10. O Fire, let us conquer a hero-strength by the War-Horse, or let us awake to knowledge beyond men by the Word;[1] let our light shine out in the Five Nations high and inviolable like the world of the Sun.

स नो बोधि सहस्य प्रशंस्यो यस्मिन्त्सुजाता इषयन्त सूरयः ।
यमग्ने यज्ञमुपयन्ति वाजिनो नित्ये तोके दीदिवांसं स्वे दमे ॥११॥

11. Awake, O forceful Fire, one to be voiced by our lauds; for thou art he in whom the luminous seers come to perfect birth and speed on their way. O Fire, thou art the sacrifice and to thee the Horses of swiftness come there where thou shinest with light in the eternal son and in thy own home.

उभयासो जातवेदः स्याम ते स्तोतारो अग्ने सूरयश्च शर्मणि ।
वस्वो रायः पुरुश्चन्द्रस्य भूयसः प्रजावतः स्वपत्यस्य शग्धि नः ॥१२॥

12. O Fire, O God who knowest all things born, may we both abide in thy peace, those who hymn thee and the luminous seers. Be forceful for the opulence of the Treasure with the multitude of its riches and its many delights and its issue and the offspring of the Treasure.

---

[1] Or, wake in ourselves a strength of heroes beyond men's scope by the power of the War-Horse or by the Word;

ये स्तोतृभ्यो गोअग्रामश्वपेशसमग्ने रातिमृपसृजन्ति सूरयः ।
अस्माञ्च तांश्च प्र हि नेषि वस्य आ बृहद् वदेम विदथे सुवीराः ॥१३॥

13. When to those who hymn thee the luminous Wise set free,
     O Fire, the gift in whose front the Ray-Cow walks and
     whose form is the Horse, thou leadest us on and leadest them
     to a world of greater riches. Strong with the strength of the
     Heroes, may we voice the Vast in the coming of the know-
     ledge.

SUKTA 3

समिद्धो अग्निर्निहितः पृथिव्यां प्रत्यङ् विश्वानि भुवनान्यस्थात् ।
होता पावकः प्रदिवः सुमेधा देवो देवान् यजत्वग्निरर्हन् ॥१॥

1.   The Fire that was set inward in the earth is kindled and
     has arisen fronting all the worlds. He has arisen, the puri-
     fying Flame, the priest of the call, the wise of understanding,
     the Ancient of Days. Today let the Fire in the fullness of
     his powers, a god to the gods, do sacrifice.

नराशंसः प्रति धामान्यञ्जन् तिस्रो दिवः प्रति मह्ना स्वर्चिः ।
घृतप्रुषा मनसा हव्यमुन्दन् मूर्धन् यज्ञस्य समनक्तु देवान् ॥२॥

2.   Fire who voices the godhead, shines revealing the planes,
     each and each; high of ray he reveals, each and each, the
     triple heavens by his greatness. Let him flood the oblation
     with a mind that diffuses the light and manifest the gods on
     the head of the sacrifice.

ईळितो अग्ने मनसा नो अहन् देवान् यक्षि मानुषात् पूर्वो अद्य ।
स आ वह मरुतां शर्धो अच्युतमिन्द्रं नरो बर्हिषदं यजध्वम् ॥३॥

3.   O Fire, aspired to by our mind, putting forth today thy
     power do sacrifice to the gods, O thou who wast of old
     before aught that is human. Bring to us the unfallen host
     of the Life-Gods; and you, O Powers, sacrifice to Indra
     where he sits on the seat of our altar.

देव बर्हिर्वधमानं सुवीरं स्तीर्णं राये सुभरं वेदस्याम् ।
घृतेनाक्तं वसवः सीदतेदं विश्वे देवा आदित्या यज्ञियासः ॥४॥

4. O Godhead, strewn is the seat on this altar, the hero-guarded seat that ever grows, the seat well-packed for the riches,[1] anointed with the Light. O all Gods, sit on this altar-seat, sons of the indivisible Mother, princes of the treasure, kings of sacrifice.

वि श्रयन्तामुर्विया हूयमाना द्वारो देवीः सुप्रायणा नमोभिः ।
व्यचस्वतीर्वि प्रयन्तामजुर्या वर्णं पुनाना यशसं सुवीरम् ॥५॥

5. May the divine Doors swing open, wide to our call, easy of approach with our prostrations of surrender; may they stretch wide opening into vastnesses, the imperishable Doors purifying the glorious and heroic kind.

साध्वपांसि सनता न उक्षिते उषासानक्ता वय्येव रण्विते ।
तन्तुं ततं संवयन्ती समीची यज्ञस्य पेशः सुदुघे पयस्वती ॥६॥

6. Milch-cows, good milkers, pouring out on us may Night and Dawn, the eternal and equal sisters, come like weaving women full of gladness, weaving out the weft that is spun, the weft of our perfected works into a shape of sacrifice.

दैव्या होतारा प्रथमा विदुष्टर ऋजु यक्षतः समृचा वपुष्टरा ।
देवान्यजन्तावृतुथा समञ्जतो नाभा पृथिव्या अधि सानुषु त्रिषु ॥७॥

7. The two divine Priests of the call, the first, the full in wisdom and stature, offer by the illumining Word the straight things in us; sacrificing to the Gods in season, they reveal them in light in the navel of the Earth and on the three peaks of Heaven.

सरस्वती साधयन्ती धियं न इळा देवी भारती विश्वतूर्तिः ।
तिस्रो देवीः स्वधया बर्हिरेदमच्छिद्रं पान्तु शरणं निषद्य ॥८॥

8. May Saraswati effecting our thought and goddess Ila and

---

[1] Or, made strong to bear for the riches,

Bharati who carries all to their goal, the three goddesses, sit
on our altar-seat and guard by the self-law of things our
gapless house of refuge.

पिशङ्गरूपः सुभरो वयोधाः श्रुष्टी बीरो जायते देवकामः ।
प्रजां त्वष्टा वि ष्यतु नाभिमस्मे अथ देवानामप्येतु पाथः ॥९॥

9. Soon there is born a Hero of golden-red form, an aspirant to
the Godheads, a mighty bringer of riches and founder of our
growth to wideness. Let the Maker of forms loosen the knot
of the navel in us, let him set free the issue of our works;
then let him walk on the way of the Gods.[1]

वनस्पतिरवसृजन्नुप स्वादवग्निर्हविः सूवयाति प्र धीभिः ।
त्रिधा समक्तं नयतु प्रजानन्देवेभ्यो दैव्यः शमितोप हव्यम् ॥१०॥

10. The Plant is with us streaming out the Wine. Fire speeds the
oblation by our thoughts. Let the divine Achiever of works,
understanding, lead the offering triply revealed[2] in his light
on its way to the Godheads.

घृतं मिमिक्षे घृतमस्य योनिर्घृते श्रितो घृतम्वस्य धाम ।
अनुष्वधमा वह मादयस्व स्वाहाकृतं वृषभ वक्षि हव्यम् ॥११॥

11. I pour on him the running light; for the light is his native
lair, he is lodged in the light, the light is his plane. According to thy self-nature, bring the Gods and fill them with rapture. O Male of the herd, carry to them our offering blessed
with *svāhā*.[3]

SOMAHUTI BHARGAVA

SUKTA 4

हुवे वः सुद्योतमानं सुवृक्तिं विशामग्निमतिथिं सुप्रयसम् ।
मित्र इव यो दिधिषाय्यो भूद्देव आदेवे जने जातवेदाः ॥१॥

---

[1] Or, let the way of the Gods come to us.   [2] Or, triply anointed   [3] Or, made into *svāhā*.

1. I call to you the Fire with his strong delights and his splendours of light, Fire who strips all sin from us, the guest of the peoples. He becomes like a supporting friend, he becomes the God who knows all things born in the man with whom are the Gods.[1]

इमं विधन्तो अपां सधस्थे द्विताददुर्भृगवो विश्ववायोः ।
एष विश्वान्यभ्यस्तु भूमा देवानामग्निररतिर्जीराश्वः ॥२॥

2. The Bhrigus worshipping in the session of the Waters set him a twofold Light in the peoples of Man. May he master all planes prevailing vastly, Fire the traveller of the Gods with his rapid horses.

अग्ने देवासो मानुषीषु विक्षु प्रियं धुः क्षेष्यन्तो न मित्रम् ।
स दीदयदुशतीरूर्म्या आ दक्षाय्यो यो दास्वते दम आ ॥३॥

3. As men who would settle in a home bring into it a beloved friend, the Gods have set the Fire in these human peoples. Let him illumine the desire of the billowing nights, let him be one full of discerning mind in the house for the giver of sacrifice.

अस्य रण्वा स्वस्येव पुष्टिः संदृष्टिरस्य हियानस्य दक्षोः ।
वि यो भरिभ्रदोषधीषु जिह्वामत्यो न रथ्यो दोधवीति वारान् ॥४॥

4. Delightful is his growth as if one's own increase, rapturous is his vision as he gallops burning on his way. He darts about his tongue mid the growths of the forest and tosses his mane like a chariot courser.

आ यन्मे अभ्वं वनदः पनन्तोशिग्भ्यो नामिमीत वर्णम् ।
स चित्रेण चिकिते रंसु भासा जुजुर्वा यो मुहुरा युवा भूत् ॥५॥

5. When my thoughts enjoying him chant his mightiness, he shapes hue of kind as if to our desire. He awakes to knowledge in men that have the ecstasy by the rich diversity of his

---

[1] Or, in all from men to the Gods.

light; old and outworn he grows young again and again.

आ यो वना तातृषाणो न भाति वार्णं पथा रथ्येव स्वानीत् ।
कृष्णाध्वा तपू रण्वश्चिकेत द्यौरिव स्मयमानो नमोभिः ॥६॥

6. Like one who thirsts he lifts his light on the forests; his roar
is like the cry of waters on their path, he neighs like a chariot war-horse. Black is his trail, burning his heat; he is full
of rapture and awakes to knowledge: he is like Father
Heaven smiling with his starry spaces.

स यो व्यस्थादभि दक्षदुर्वीं पशुर्नेति स्वयुरगोपाः ।
अग्निः शोचिष्मां अतसान्युष्णन् कृष्णव्यथिरस्वदयन्न भूम ॥७॥

7. He starts on his journey to burn through all wide earth and
moves like a beast that wanders at will and has no keeper;
Fire with his blazing light and his black affliction assails the
dry trunks with his heat as if he tasted the vastness.

नू ते पूर्वस्यावसो अधीतौ तृतीये विदथे मन्म शंसि ।
अस्मे अग्ने संयद्वीरं बृहन्तं क्षुमन्तं वाजं स्वपत्यं रयिं दाः ॥८॥

8. Now in our mind's return on thy former safe-guarding, our
thought has been spoken in the third session of the knowledge. O Fire, give us the treasure with its children; give us
a vast and opulent plenitude where the heroes assemble.

त्वया यथा गृत्समदासो अग्ने गुहा वन्वन्त उपरां अभि ष्युः ।
सुवीरासो अभिमातिषाहः स्मत्सूरिभ्यो गृणते तद्वयो धाः ॥९॥

9. To the luminous Wise Ones and to him who voices thee, O
Fire, be the founder of their growth and expansion, that the
Gritsamadas strong with the strength of the Heroes and
overcoming the hostile forces may conquer the higher worlds
by thy force and take delight of[1] the secret inner spaces.

---

[1] Or, win

SUKTA 5

होताजनिष्ट चेतन: पिता पितृभ्य ऊतये ।
प्रयक्षञ्जेन्यं वसु शकेम वाजिनो यमम् ॥१॥

1. A conscious Priest of the call is born to us; a father is born to
   his fathers for their safeguard. May we avail to achieve by
   sacrifice the wealth that is for the victor,[1] and to rein the
   Horse of swiftness.

आ यस्मिन्त्सप्त रश्मयस्तता यज्ञस्य नेतरि ।
मनुष्वद्दैव्यमष्टमं पोता विश्वं तदिन्वति ॥२॥

2. The seven rays are extended in this leader of sacrifice; there
   is a divine eighth that carries with it the human. The Priest
   of the purification takes possession of[2] That All.

दधन्वे वा यदीमनु वोचद् ब्रह्माणि वेरु तत् ।
परि विश्वानि काव्या नेमिश्चक्रमिवाभवत् ॥३॥

3. When a man has firmly established this Fire, he echoes the
   Words of knowledge and comes to[3] That: for he embraces
   all seer-wisdoms as the rim surrounds a wheel.

साकं हि शुचिना शुचि: प्रशास्ता क्रतुनाजनि ।
विद्वाँ अस्य व्रता ध्रुवा वया इवानु रोहते ॥४॥

4. Pure, the Priest of the annunciation is born along with the
   pure will. The man who knows the laws of his workings that
   are steadfast for ever, climbs them one by one like branches.

ता अस्य वर्णमायुवो नेष्टु: सचन्त धेनव: ।
कुविल्सिसृभ्य आ वरं स्वसारो या इदं ययु: ॥५॥

5. The milch-cows come to and cleave to the hue of Light[4] of
   this Priest of the lustration, the Sisters who have gone once

---

[1] Or, the wealth that has to be conquered,   [2] Or, travels to (reaches)
[3] Or, and comes to know   [4] Or, the hue of kind

and again to that Supreme over the three.[1]

यदी मातुरुप स्वसा घृतं भरत्यस्थित ।
तासामध्वर्युरागतौ यवो वृष्टीव मोदते ॥६॥

6. When the sister of the Mother comes to him bringing the
   yield of the Light, the Priest of the pilgrim-sacrifice rejoices
   in her advent as a field of barley revels in the rain.

स्वः स्वाय धायसे कृणुतामृत्विगृत्विजम् ।
स्तोमं यज्ञं चादरं वनेमा ररिमा वयम् ॥७॥

7. Himself for his own confirming let the Priest of the rite create
   the Priest; let us take joy of the laud and the sacrifice, for
   then it is complete,[2] what we have given.[3]

यथा विद्वाँ अरं करद्विश्वेभ्यो यजतेभ्यः ।
अयमग्ने त्वे अपि यं यज्ञं चकृमा वयम् ॥८॥

8. Even as one who has the knowledge let him work out the
   rite for all the lords of the sacrifice. On thee, O Fire, is this
   sacrifice that we have made.

SUKTA 6

इमां मे अग्ने समिधमिमामुपसदं वनेः ।
इमा उ षु श्रुषी गिरः ॥१॥

1. O Fire, mayst thou rejoice in the fuel I bring thee, rejoice in
   my session of sacrifice. Deeply lend ear to my words.

अया ते अग्ने विधेमोर्जो नपादश्वमिष्टे ।
एना सूक्तेन सुजात ॥२॥

2. O Fire, who art brought to perfect birth, Child of Energy,

---

[1] The fourth world, Turiyam above the three, so called in the Rig-veda, *turiyam svid.*
[2] Or, for then it is complete, we have moved (on the way),
[3] Or, let us take full joy of the laud and the sacrifice; for we have given.

Impeller of the Horse, we would worship thee with this oblation, we would worship thee with this Word well-spoken.

तं त्वा गीर्भिर्गिर्वणसं द्रविणस्युं द्रविणोदः ।
सपर्येम सपर्यवः ॥३॥

3. We would wait with our Words on thy joy in the Word; O Treasure-giver, we would wait on the seeker of the Treasure. Let us serve thee, all whose desire is thy service.

स बोधि सूरिर्मघवा वसुपते वसुदावन् ।
युयोध्यस्मद् द्वेषांसि ॥४॥

4. O Wealth-Lord, Wealth-giver, awake, a seer and a Master of Treasures; put away from us the things that are hostile.

स नो वृष्टि दिवस्परि स नो वाजमनर्वाणम् ।
स नः सहस्रिणीरिषः ॥५॥

5. For us, O Fire, the Rain of Heaven around us; for us, O Fire, the wealth immovable;[1] for us, O Fire, the impulsions that bring their thousands!

ईळानायावस्यवे यविष्ठ दूत नो गिरा ।
यजिष्ठ होतरा गहि ॥६॥

6. O Messenger, O youngest Power, come at our word for him who aspires to thee and craves for thy safeguard; arrive, O Priest of the call, strong for sacrifice.

अन्तह्यग्न ईयसे विद्वान् जन्मोभया कवे ।
दूतो जन्येव मित्र्यः ॥७॥

7. O Fire, O seer, thou movest within having knowledge of both the Births;[2] thou art like a messenger from a friendly people.[3]

---

[1] Or, free from all littleness;   [2] Or, as one who has knowledge between both Births;
[3] Or, like a friendly universal messenger.

स विद्वाँ आ च पिप्रयो यक्षि चिकित्व आनुषक् ।
आ चास्मिन्त्सत्सि बर्हिषि ॥८॥

8. Come with thy knowledge, O Conscious Fire, and fill us;
   perform the unbroken order of the sacrifice. Take thy seat
   on the sacred grass of our altar.

SUKTA 7

श्रेष्ठं यविष्ठ भारताग्ने द्युमन्तमा भर ।
वसो पुरुस्पृहं रयिम् ॥१॥

1. O Fire, O Youngest Power! Fire of the Bringers, Prince of
   the Treasure, bring to us a wealth, the best, made all of
   light and packed with our many desires.

मा नो अरातिरीशत देवस्य मर्त्यस्य च ।
पर्षि तस्या उत द्विषः ॥२॥

2. Let not the Force that wars against us master the God and
   the mortal;[1] carry us beyond that hostile power.

विश्वा उत त्वया वयं धारा उदन्या इव ।
अति गाहेमहि द्विषः ॥३॥

3. And so by thee may we plunge and pass beyond all hostile
   forces as through streams of rushing water.

शुचिः पावक वन्द्योऽग्ने बृहद्धि रोचसे ।
त्वं घृतेभिराहुतः ॥४॥

4. O cleansing Fire, thou art pure and adorable; vast is the
   beauty of thy light fed with the clarities.

त्वं नो असि भारताग्ने वशाभिरुक्षभिः ।
अष्टापदीभिराहुतः ॥५॥

---

[1] Or, against us, God and mortal, overmaster us;

5. O Fire of the Bringers, thou art called by[1] our bulls and our heifers and by our eight-footed Kine.[2]

द्रन्नः सर्पिरासुतिः प्रत्नो होता वरेण्यः ।
सहसस्पुत्रो अद्भुतः ॥६॥

6. This is the eater of the Tree for whom is poured the running butter of the Light; this is the Desirable, the ancient, the Priest of the call, the Wonderful, the son of Force.

GRITSAMADA BHARGAVA

SUKTA 8

वाजयन्निव नू रथान् योगाँ अग्नेरुप स्तुहि ।
यशस्तमस्य मीळ्हुषः ॥१॥

1. As if to replenish[3] him chant now the chariots of Fire and his yokings, Fire the lavish and glorious Godhead.

यः सुनीथो ददाशुषेऽज्जुर्यो जरयन्नरिम् ।
चारुप्रतीक आहुतः ॥२॥

2. He brings his perfect leading to the man who has given; he is invulnerable and wears out with wounds the foe. Fair is the front of him fed with the offerings.

य उ श्रिया दमेष्वा दोषोषसि प्रशस्यते ।
यस्य व्रतं न मीयते ॥३॥

3. He is voiced in his glory and beauty at dusk and dawn in our homes. Never impaired is the law of his working.

आ यः स्वर्णं भानुना चित्रो विभात्यर्चिषा ।
अञ्जानो अजरैरभि ॥४॥

---

[1] Or, fed with
[2] Or, by our bulls and by our barren and pregnant kine. *Aṣṭāpadī*, literally eight-footed.
[3] Or, as one seeking for plenitude

4. He shines rich with diverse lustres like the heavens of the
    Sun[1] in his illumining splendour, shines wide with his ray,
    putting forth on us a revealing light with his ageless fires.

अत्रिमनु स्वराज्यमग्निमुक्थानि वावृधुः ।
विश्वा अधि श्रियो दधे ॥५॥

5. Our words have made the Fire to grow, made the Traveller
    to grow in the way of self-empire; he holds in himself all
    glory and beauty.

अग्नेरिन्द्रस्य सोमस्य देवानामूतिभिर्वयम् ।
अरिष्यन्तः सचेमह्लाभि व्याम पूतन्यतः ॥६॥

6. May we cleave to the safeguardings of the Fire and Soma
    and Indra and of the Gods, meeting with no hurt overcome
    those that are embattled against us.

SUKTA 9

नि होता होतृषदने विदानस्त्वेषो दीदिवाँ असदत्सुदक्षः ।
अदब्धव्रतप्रमतिर्वसिष्ठः सहस्रंभरः शुचिजिह्लो अग्निः ॥१॥

1. The Priest of the call has taken his seat in the house of his
    priesthood; he is ablaze with light and vivid in radiance, he
    is full of knowledge and perfect in judgment. He has a mind
    of wisdom whose workings are invincible and is most rich
    in treasures: Fire with his tongue of purity is a bringer of
    the thousand.

त्वं दूतस्त्वमु नः परस्पास्त्वं वस्य आ वृषभ प्रणेता ।
अग्ने तोकस्य नस्तने तनूनामप्रयुच्छन्दीद्यद्धोषि गोपाः ॥२॥

2. Thou art the Messenger, thou art our protector who takest
    us to the other side; O Bull of the herds, thou art our leader
    on the way to a world of greater riches. For the shaping of

---
[1] Or, like the Sun

the Son and the building of the bodies[1] awake in thy light,
a guardian, and turn not from thy work, O Fire.

विधेम ते परमे जन्मन्नग्ने विधेम स्तोमैरवरे सधस्थे ।
यस्माद्योनेरुदारिथा यजे तं प्र त्वे हवींषि जुहुरे समिद्धे ॥३॥

3. May we worship thee in thy supreme Birth, O Fire; may we
   worship thee with our chants in the world of thy lower
   session: I adore with sacrifice thy native lair from which
   thou hast arisen. The offerings have been cast into thee
   when thou wert kindled and ablaze.

अग्ने यजस्व हविषा यजीयाञ्छ्रुष्टी देष्णमभि गृणीहि राधः ।
त्वं ह्यसि रयिपती रयीणां त्वं शुक्रस्य वचसो मनोता ॥४॥

4. O Fire, be strong for sacrifice, do worship with my oblation;
   swiftly voice my thought towards the gift of the Treasure.
   For thou art the wealth-master who hast power over the
   riches, thou art the thinker of the brilliant Word.

उभयं ते न क्षीयते वसव्यं दिवेदिवे जायमानस्य दस्म ।
कृधि क्षुमन्तं जरितारमग्ने कृधि पतिं स्वपत्यस्य रायः ॥५॥

5. Both kinds of wealth are thine, O potent Godhead and
   because thou art born from day to day, neither can waste
   and perish. O Fire, make thy adorer one full of possessions;
   make him a master of the Treasure and of wealth rich in
   progeny.

सैनानीकेन सुविदत्रो अस्मे यष्टा देवाँ आयजिष्ठः स्वस्ति ।
अदब्धो गोपा उत नः परस्पा अग्ने द्युमत्रेवदिदीहि ॥६॥

6. O Fire, shine forth with this force[2] of thine in us, one perfect in knowledge, one who worships the Gods and is strong
   for sacrifice. Be our indomitable guardian and our protector
   to take us to the other side; flame in us with thy light, flame
   in us with thy opulence.

---

[1] Or, in the offspring of the son of our bodies   [2] Or, form

SUKTA 10

जोहूत्रो अग्निः प्रथमः पितेवेळस्पदे मनुषा यत्समिद्धः ।
श्रियं वसानो अमृतो विचेता मर्मृजेन्यः श्रवस्यः स वाजी ॥१॥

1. Fire is to us as our first father and to him must rise our call
   when he is kindled by man in the seat of his aspiration. He
   puts on glory and beauty like a robe; he is our Horse of
   swiftness full of inspiration to be groomed by us, he is the
   immortal wide in knowledge.

श्रूया अग्निश्चित्रभानुर्हवं मे विश्वाभिर्गीर्भिरमृतो विचेताः ।
श्यावा रथं वहतो रोहिता वोतारुषाह चक्रे विभृत्रः ॥२॥

2. May Fire in the rich diversity of his lights, the immortal wide
   in knowledge, hearken to my cry in all its words. Two
   tawny horses bear him or two that are red or ruddy in glow:
   Oh, one widely borne has been created.

उत्तानायामजनयन्त्सुषूतं भुवदग्निः पुरुपेशासु गर्भः ।
शिरिणायां चिदक्तुना महोभिरपरीवृतो वसति प्रचेताः ॥३॥

3. They have given him birth in one laid supine who with
   happy delivery bore him; the Fire became a child in mothers
   of many forms. This thinker and knower by the greatness
   of his lights dwells[1] even in the destroying Night unenveloped
   by the darkness.

जिघर्म्यग्निं हविषा घृतेन प्रतिक्षियन्तं भुवनानि विश्वा ।
पृथुं तिरश्चा वयसा बृहन्तं व्यचिष्ठमन्नं रभसं दृशानम् ॥४॥

4. I anoint the Fire with my oblation of light, where he dwells
   fronting all the worlds; wide in his horizontal expansion
   and vast, he is most open and manifest by all he has fed on,
   seen in the impetuosity of his force.[2]

---

[1] Or, shines　　[2] Or, in the violence of his rapture.

आ विश्वतः प्रत्यञ्चं जिघर्म्यरक्षसा मनसा तज्जुषेत ।
मर्यश्रीः स्पृहयद्वर्णो अग्निनर्नाभिमृशे तन्वा जर्भुराणः ॥५॥

5. I anoint him where he moves fronting all things on every
   side; let him rejoice in That with a mind that withholds not
   the riches.[1] None can touch the body of the Fire where he
   plays in his desire of the hues of light,[2] in his strong and
   glorious beauty.

ज्ञेया भागं सहसानो वरेण त्वादूतासो मनुवद्देम ।
अनूनमग्नि जुह्वा वचस्या मधुपृचं धनसा जोहवीमि ॥६॥

6. Mayst thou take knowledge of thy portion putting forth thy
   force with thy supreme flame; may we speak as the thinking
   human being with thee for Messenger. I am one who would
   conquer the Treasure and I call to the Fire with my power
   of speech and my flame of offering, Fire in whom is no in-
   sufficiency, and he brings to us the touch of the sweetness.[3]

---

[1] Or, with a mind without the will to injure.   [2] Or, with his desire-waking hue,
[3] Or, he fills us with the wine of sweetness.

MANDALA THREE

GATHINA VISHWAMITRA

SUKTA 1

सोमस्य मा तवसं वक्ष्यग्ने वर्हि चकर्थं विदये यजध्यै ।
देवाँ अच्छा दीद्यद् युञ्जे अद्रि शमाये अग्ने तन्वं जुषस्व ॥१॥

1. Bear me that I may be strong to hold the wine, O Fire, for thou hast made me a carrier flame of sacrifice in the getting of knowledge: I shine towards the gods, I put the stone to its work, I accomplish the labour;[1] O Fire, take delight in my body.

प्राञ्चं यज्ञं चक्रम वर्धतां गीः समिद्भिरग्निं नमसा दुवस्यन् ।
दिवः शशासुर्विदथा कवीनां गृत्साय चित् तवसे गातुमीषुः ॥२॥

2. We have made the sacrifice with its forward movement, may the word increase in us; with the fuel, with the obeisance they have set the Fire to its work. The heavens have declared the discoveries of knowledge of the seers and they have willed a path for the strong and wise.

मयो दधे मेधिरः पूतदक्षो दिवः सुबन्धुर्जनुषा पृथिव्याः ।
अविन्दन्नु दर्शतमप्स्वन्तर्देवासो अग्निमपसि स्वसॄणाम् ॥३॥

3. Full of understanding, pure in discernment, close kin from his birth to earth and heaven he has founded the Bliss. The gods discovered the seeing Fire within in the waters, in the work of the sisters.

अवर्धयन् सुभगं सप्त यह्वीः श्वेतं जज्ञानमरुषं महित्वा ।
शिशुं न जातमभ्याररूदवा देवासो अग्निं जनिमन् वपुष्यन् ॥४॥

4. The seven mighty rivers increased the blissful flame,[2] white in his birth, ruddy glowing in his mightiness: the Mares went up to him as to a new-born child; the gods gave body to Agni in his birth.

---
[1] Or, I attain to the peace;   [2] Or, increased him in his beauty,

8

शुक्रेभिरङ्गे रज आततन्वान् ऋतुं पुनानः कविभिः पवित्रैः ।
शोचिर्वसानः पर्यायुरपां श्रियो मिमीते बृहतीरनूनाः ॥५॥

5. With his bright limbs he has built wide the mid-world purifying the will by his pure seer-powers; wearing light like a
robe around the life of the waters he forms his glories vast
and ample.

वव्राजा सीमनवतीरदब्धा दिवो यह्वीरवसाना अनग्नाः ।
सना अत्र युवतयः सयोनीरेकं गर्भं दधिरे सप्त वाणीः ॥६॥

6. He moved all round the seven mighty Ones of heaven:
undevouring, inviolate, neither were they clothed nor were
they naked: here young and eternal in one native home the
seven Voices held in their womb the one Child.

स्तीर्णा अस्य संहतो विश्वरूपा घृतस्य योनौ स्रवथे मधूनाम् ।
अस्थुरत्र धेनवः पिन्वमाना मही दस्मस्य मातरा समीची ॥७॥

7. Wide-strewn, compact, taking universal forms are his
energies in the womb of the light, in the streaming of the
sweetnesses: here the milch-cows stand nourished and
growing; two great and equal companions[1] are the mothers
of the Doer of works.

बभ्राणः सूनो सहसो व्यद्यौद् दधानः शुक्रा रभसा वपूंषि ।
श्चोतन्ति धारा मधुनो घृतस्य वृषा यत्र वावृधे काव्येन ॥८॥

8. Upborne, O Son of Force, thou shinest out wide holding
thy bright and rapturous bodies; there drip down streams
of the light and the sweetness, there where the Bull has grown
by the seer-wisdom.

पितुश्चिदूधर्जनुषा विवेद व्यस्य धारा असृजद् वि धेनाः ।
गुहा चरन्तं सखिभिः शिवेभिर्दिवो यह्वीभिर्न गुहा बभूव ॥९॥

9. At his birth he discovered the teat of abundance of the
Father, he loosed forth wide his streams, wide his nourish-

---

[1] Or, vast and whole

ing rivers;[1] he discovered him moving in the secrecy with his helpful comrades, with the mighty Rivers of Heaven, but himself became not secret in the cave.

पितुश्च गर्भं जनितुश्च बभ्रे पूर्वीरेको अधयत्पीप्यानाः ।
वृष्णे सपत्नी शुचये सबन्धू उभे अस्मे मनुष्ये नि पाहि ॥१०॥

10. He carried the child of the father who begot him; one, he sucked the milk of many who nourished him with their overflowing. Two who have one lord and kinsman, for this pure male of the herds guard both in the human being.

उरौ महाँ अनिबाधे ववर्धाऽऽपो अग्निं यशसः सं हि पूर्वीः ।
ऋतस्य योनावशयद् दमूना जामीनामग्निरपसि स्वसृणाम् ॥११॥

11. Vast was he in the unobstructed wideness and grew, for the waters many and glorious fed the flame; in the native seat of the Truth the Fire lay down and made his home, in the work of the companions, the sisters.

अको न बभ्रिः समिथे महीनां दिदृक्षेयः सूनवे भाऋजीकः ।
उद्‌लियर्या जनिता यो जजानाऽपां गर्भो नृतमो यह्वो अग्निः ॥१२॥

12. Like a height upbearing all[2] in the meeting of the great waters, eager for vision for the Son, straight in his lustres, he is the Father who begot the shining Ray-herds, the child of the Waters, the most strong and mighty Fire.

अपां गर्भं दर्शतमोषधीनां वना जजान सुभगा विरूपम् ।
देवासश्चिन्मनसा सं हि जग्मुः पनिष्ठं जातं तवसं दुवस्यन् ॥१३॥

13. One desirable and blissful gave birth to him in many forms, a visioned child of the waters and a child of the growths of earth: the gods too met with the Mind the Fire, strong at his birth and powerful to act[3] and set him to his work.

---

[1] Or, he loosed forth the milch-cows; [2] Or, like one moving and upbearing all
[3] Or, most admirable

बृहन्त इद् भानवो भ्राज्रजीकमग्निं सचन्त विद्युतो न शुक्राः ।
गुहेव वृद्धं सदसि स्वे अन्तरपार ऊर्वे अमृतं दुहानाः ॥१४॥

14. Vast sun-blazings cleave like brilliant lightnings to this Fire,
straight in his lustres, growing as in a secret cave within
in his own home in the shoreless wideness, and they draw
the milk of immortality.

ईळे च त्वा यजमानो हर्विभिरीळे सखित्वं सुमतिं निकामः ।
देवैरवो मिर्मीहि सं जरित्रे रक्षा च नो दम्येभिरनीकैः ॥१५॥

15. Making sacrifice with my offerings for thee I pray, and pray
for thy friendship and true-mindedness with an utter desire.
Fashion with the Gods protection for thy adorer and guard
us with thy flame-forces that dwell in the house.

उपक्षेतारस्तव सुप्रणीतेऽग्ने विश्वानि धन्या दधानाः ।
सुरेतसा श्रवसा तुञ्जमाना अभि ष्याम पृतनायूँरदेवान् ॥१६॥

16. We who come to thee to dwell with thee in thy home, O
perfect leader of the way, holding all opulent things, may
we, overflowing[1] them with the full stream of inspiration,
overwhelm the hostile army of the undivine powers.

आ देवानामभवः केतुरग्ने मन्द्रो विश्वानि काव्यानि विद्वान् ।
प्रति मर्तां अवासयो दमूना अनु देवान् रथिरो यासि साधन् ॥१७॥

17. O Fire, thou becomest in us the rapturous ray of intuition
of the gods that knows all seer-wisdoms; established in thy
home thou settlest mortals in that dwelling-place, as their
charioteer achieving their aim thou journeyest in the wake
of the gods.

नि दुरोणे अमृतो मर्त्यानां राजा ससाद विदथानि साधन् ।
घृतप्रतीक उर्विया व्यद्यौदर्निर्गिबश्वानि काव्यानि विद्वान् ॥१८॥

18. In the gated house of mortals the immortal sat as King

---

[1] Or, smiting

accomplishing the things of knowledge: the Fire shone out in his wideness with his luminous front, knower of all seer-wisdoms.

आ नो गहि सख्येभिः शिवेभिर्महान् महीभिरूतिभिः सरण्यन् ।
अस्मे रयिं बहुलं संतरुत्रं सुवाचं भागं यशसं कृधी नः ॥१९॥

19. Come to us in a rapid approach with thy happy befriendings, mighty, come with thy mighty protectings; in us the abundance of the delivering riches, for us our glorious high-worded portion create.

एता ते अग्ने जनिमा सनानि प्र पूर्व्याय नूतनानि वोचम् ।
महान्ति वृष्णे सवना कृतेमा जन्मन्जन्मन् निहितो जातवेदाः ॥२०॥

20. O Fire, these are thy eternal births which I have declared to thee, ever new births for the ancient flame: great are the offerings of the Wine we have made for the mighty one. He is the knower of all births set within in birth and birth.

जन्मन्जन्मन् निहितो जातवेदा विश्वामित्रेभिरिध्यते अजस्रः ।
तस्य वयं सुमतौ यज्ञियस्याऽपि भद्रे सौमनसे स्याम ॥२१॥

21. The knower of all births set within in birth and birth is kindled by Vishwamitra, an unceasing flame; in the true thinking of this lord of sacrifice, in a happy right-mindedness may we abide.

इमं यज्ञं सहसावन् त्वं नो देवत्रा धेहि सुक्रतो रराणः ।
प्र यंसि होतर्बृहतीरिषो नोऽग्ने महि द्रविणमा यजस्व ॥२२॥

22. O forceful God, O strong Will, establish this sacrifice of ours in the gods and take in it thy delight: O Priest of the call, extend to us the vast impulsions; O Fire, bring to us by sacrifice the great Treasure.

इळामग्ने पुरुदंसं सनिं गोः शश्वत्तमं हवमानाय साध ।
स्यान्नः सूनुस्तनयो विजावाऽग्ने सा ते सुमतिर्भूत्वस्मे ॥२३॥

23.   O Fire, achieve at my call the Revealing Speech, the many-
       actioned, the lasting conquest of the Light. May there
       be for us a Son of our begetting pervading in his birth;[1] O
       Fire, may there be created in us that true thinking of thine.

SUKTA 2

वैश्वानराय धिषणामृतावृधे घृतं न पूतमग्नये जनामसि ।
द्विता होतारं मनुषश्च वाघतो धिया रथं न कुलिशः समृण्वति ॥१॥

1.   We create an understanding like pure light for the Fire that
       makes the Truth to grow, for the universal godhead. The
       priests of the word fashion twofold by the thought of the
       human being[2] this priest of the call, as the saw carves a cha-
       riot, and join him into a whole.

स रोचयज्जनुषा रोदसी उभे स मात्रोरभवत् पुत्र ईड्यः ।
हव्यवाळग्निरजरश्चनोहितो दूळभो विशामतिथिर्विभावसुः ॥२॥

2.   He from his birth illumined both the firmaments, he became
       the desirable son of the Father and Mother. The ageless
       and inviolable Fire, firmly founded in bliss, with his riches
       of the Light, is the carrier of offering and the guest of the
       peoples.

कृत्वा दक्षस्य तरुषो विधर्मणि देवासो अग्निं जनयन्त चित्तिभिः ।
रुरुचानं भानुना ज्योतिषा महामत्यं न वाजं सनिष्यन्नुप ब्रुवे ॥३॥

3.   By the will, in the order and law of a delivering discernment,
       the gods brought the Fire into being by their perceptions of
       the Knowledge. In his greatness shining forth with his blaz-
       ing light I invoke him as the Horse so that I may conquer
       the plenitude.

आ मन्द्रस्य सनिष्यन्तो वरेण्यं वृणीमहे अह्रयं वाजमग्मियम् ।
रातिं भृगूणामुशिजं कविक्रतुमग्निं राजन्तं दिव्येन शोचिषा ॥४॥

_____

[1] Or, himself a begetter   [2] Or, the human priest of the word by their thought

4. To conquer the supreme bliss of the rapturous godhead, the undeviating plenitude full of the word of illumination, we accept the gift of the Flame-Seers,[1] the Fire that aspires, the Seer-Will shining with heavenly light.

अग्निं सुम्नाय दधिरे पुरो जना वाजश्रवसमिह वृक्तबर्हिषः ।
यतस्रुचः सुरुचं विश्ववेद्यं रुद्रं यज्ञानां साधदिष्टिमपसाम् ॥५॥

5. Having gathered the sacred grass, stretching out the ladle of offering, men have set here in their front the Fire for the happiness, in his plenitude of inspiration, the Violent, the universal in godhead, the bright and beautiful, one who accomplishes the seekings of sacrifice of the doers of the works.

पावकशोचे तव हि क्षयं परि होतर्यज्ञेषु वृक्तबर्हिषो नरः ।
अग्ने दुव इच्छमानास आप्यमुपासते द्रविणं धेहि तेभ्यः ॥६॥

6. O Fire, O purifying light, O Priest of the call, men in their sacrifices having gathered the sacred grass, desiring the work, sit around thy house which we must obtain as ours; found for them the Treasure.

आ रोदसी अपृणदा स्वर्महञ्जातं यदेनमपसो अधारयन् ।
सो अध्वराय परि णीयते कविरत्यो न वाजसातये चनोहितः ॥७॥

7. He filled the two firmaments, he filled the vast sun-world, when he was born and held by the doers of the work. He is led around for the pilgrim-sacrifice, the Seer founded in the Bliss, as the Horse for the conquest of the plenitude.

नमस्यत हव्यदातिं स्वध्वरं दुवस्यत दम्यं जातवेदसम् ।
रयीर्ऋतस्य बृहतो विचर्षणिरग्निर्देवानामभवत् पुरोहितः ॥८॥

8. Bow down to the giver of the offering, set to his work the perfect in the pilgrim-rite, the knower of all the births who dwells in the house: for he is the all-seeing charioteer of the

---

[1] Or, the Bhrigus,

vast Truth, the Fire has become the priest of the gods set in front.

तिस्रो यद्धव्य समिधः परिज्मनोऽग्नेरपुनन्नृशिजो अमृत्यवः ।
तासामेकामदधुर्मत्र्ये भुजमु लोकमु द्वे उप जामिमीयतुः ॥९॥

9. Triple is the fuel of the mighty and pervading Fire purified by the aspiring immortals; one of three they have set in the mortal, the fuel of the enjoyment, two have gone to that companion world.

विशां कविं विश्पतिं मानुषीरिषः सं सीमक्रण्वन् त्वधिर्तिं न तेजसे ।
स उद्वतो निवतो याति वेविषत् स गर्भमेषु भुवनेषु दीधरत् ॥१०॥

10. This seer and lord of creatures human impulsions have perfected everywhere like an axe for sharpness. He goes overrunning the high and the low places; he holds the child born in these worlds.

स जिन्वते जठरेषु प्रजज्ञिवान् वृषा चित्रेषु नानदन्न सिंहः ।
वैश्वानरः पृथुपाजा अमर्त्यो वसु रत्ना दयमानो वि दाशुषे ॥११॥

11. The male of the herds has been born in different wombs and he stirs abroad like a roaring lion, the universal godhead, the immortal wide in his might bestowing the riches and the ecstasies on the offerer of sacrifice.

वैश्वानरः प्रत्नथा नाकमारुह्द् दिवस्पृष्ठं भन्दमानः सुमन्मभिः ।
स पूर्ववज्जनयञ्जन्तवे धनं समानमज्मं पर्येति जागृविः ॥१२॥

12. Universal godhead as in the ancient days has ascended glad by high thoughts to the firmament, to the back of heaven, even as of old he creates the riches for the creature born; wakeful he travels ever over the same field of movement.

ऋतावानं यज्ञियं विप्रमुक्थ्यमा यं दधे मातरिश्वा दिवि क्षयम् ।
तं चित्रयामं हरिकेशमीमहे सुदीतिमग्निं सुविताय नव्यसे ॥१३॥

13. The sacrificial Fire whose home is in heaven and who possesses the Truth, the illumined seer with his utterance of the word whom life that grows here in the mother has set, him with his diverse journeying, his tawny hair of flame we desire, the deep thinking Fire for a new and happy movement.

शुचि न यामन्निषिरं स्ववृशं केतुं दिवो रोचनस्थामुषर्बुधम् ।
अग्निं मूर्धानं दिवो अप्रतिष्कुतं तमीमहे नमसा वाजिनं बृहत् ॥१४॥

14. Pure-bright, rapid of impulsion in his journeying, Fire that looks upon the sun-world, heaven's ray of intuition, standing in the luminous planes, waking in the Dawn, Fire, head of heaven, whom no darkness can cover, him we desire with obeisance of surrender, the Fire of the plenitudes who is the Vast.

मन्द्रं होतारं शुचिमद्वयाविनं दमूनसमुक्थ्यं विश्वचर्षणिम् ।
रथं न चित्रं वपुषाय दर्शतं मनुर्हितं सदमिद् राय ईमहे ॥१५॥

15. The pure and rapturous Priest of the call in whom is no duality, the dweller in the house, the speaker of the word, the all-seeing, the visioned Fire set in the thinking human being who is like a many-hued chariot in his embodiment, him ever we desire and his riches.

SUKTA 3

वैश्वानराय पृथुपाजसे विपो रत्ना विघन्त धरुणेषु गातवे ।
अग्निर्हि देवाँ अमृतो दुवस्यत्यथा धर्माणि सनता न दूदुषत् ॥१॥

1. For the universal godhead, wide in his might, his illuminations[1] create the ecstasies to make a path on the foundations of things: because the immortal Fire sets the gods to their work none can corrupt the eternal Laws.

[1] Or, the illumined Ones

अन्तर्दूतो रोदसी दस्म ईयते होता निषत्तो मनुषः पुरोहितः ।
क्षयं बृहन्तं परि भूषति द्युभिर्देवेभिरग्निरिरिवितो धियावसुः ॥२॥

2. He travels as the Messenger between earth and heaven, the
    doer of works, man's Priest of the call, seated within him,
    the vicar set in his front; with his light he envelops the Vast
    Home, the Fire missioned by the gods, rich with the
    Thought.

केतुं यज्ञानां विदथस्य साधनं विप्रासो अग्निं महयन्त चित्तिभिः ।
अपांसि यस्मिन्नधि संदधुर्गिरस्तस्मिन्त्सुम्नानि यजमान आ चके ॥३॥

3. Ray of intuition of their sacrifices, effective means of the
    finding of knowledge, the illumined seers greatened the
    Fire by their awakenings to Wisdom; the Fire in whom
    his words have built into a harmony his works, in him the
    doer of sacrifice desires the things of his happiness.

पिता यज्ञानामसुरो विपश्चितां विमानमग्निर्विबयुनं च वाघताम् ।
आ विवेश रोदसी भूरिवर्पसा पुरुप्रियो भन्दते धामभिः कविः ॥४॥

4. The Fire is the father of sacrifice, the Mighty Lord of the
    wise, he is the measure and the manifestation of knowledge
    for the priests of the word: he enters into earth and heaven
    with his manifold shape, many delightful things are in him,
    he is the seer who has gladness of all the planes.

चन्द्रमग्निं चन्द्ररथं हरिव्रतं वैश्वानरमप्सुषदं स्वर्विदम् ।
विगाहं तूर्णिं तविषीभिरावृतं भूरिणि देवास इह सुश्रियं दधुः ॥५॥

5. The gods have set in this world in his beauty and glory the
    delightful Fire, with his chariot of delight, luminous in the
    way of his workings, the universal godhead, who is seated
    in the waters, who is the discoverer of the sun-world, who
    enters into the depths and is swift to cross beyond, who is
    rapt in his mights, who bears in himself all things.

अग्निर्देवेभिर्मनुषश्च जन्तुभिस्तन्वानो यज्ञं पुरुपेशसं धिया ।
रथीरन्तरीयते साधदिष्टिभिर्जिरो वमूना अभिशस्तिचातनः ॥६॥

6. The Fire with the gods and creatures born builds by the
thought of man the sacrifice in its many forms, he moves
between earth and heaven as their charioteer bearing them
to the achievement of their desires; he is the swift in motion
and he is a dweller in the house who drives off every assailant.

अग्ने जरस्व स्वपत्य आयुन्यूर्जा पिन्वस्व समिषो दिदीहि नः ।
वयांसि जिन्व बृहतश्च जागृव उशिग्देवानामसि सुक्रतुर्विपाम् ॥७॥

7. O Fire, come near to us in a life rich with offspring, nourish
us with energy, illumine our impulsions, animate in us the
expanding powers of the Vast, O wakeful Flame; thou art
the aspirant strong in will for the gods and the illumined
seers.

विश्पतिं यह्वमतिथिं नरः सदा यन्तारं धीनामुशिजं च वाघताम् ।
अध्वराणां चेतनं जातवेदसं प्र शंसन्ति नमसा जूतिभिर्वृधे ॥८॥

8. Men ever with obeisance, with swift urgings, give expression
for their growth, to the knower of all births, the mighty one,
the lord of the peoples, the Guest, the driver of our thoughts,
the aspirant in those who speak the word, the wakener to
consciousness in the pilgrim-sacrifice.

विभावा देवः सुरणः परि क्षितीरग्निर्बभूव शवसा सुमद्रथः ।
तस्य व्रतानि भूरिपोषिणो वयमुप भूषेम दम आ सुवृक्तिभिः ॥९॥

9. Fire, the wide-shining godhead, joyful in his happy chariot,
has enveloped in his might our abodes;[1] with complete
purification may we obey[2] in the house the laws of work of
this giver of our manifold increase.

वैश्वानर तव धामान्या चके येभिः स्वर्विदभवो विचक्षण ।
जात आपृणो भुवनानि रोदसी अग्ने ता विश्वा परिभूरसि त्मना ॥१०॥

---

[1] Or, the worlds of our habitation;   [2] Or, may we approach with reverence

10.   O universal godhead, I desire thy lights[1] by which thou
       becomest, O all-seeing,[2] the knower of the sun-world: born,
       thou hast filled the worlds and earth and heaven, thou art
       there enveloping them all with thyself, O Fire.

वैश्वानरस्य दंसनाभ्यो बृहदरिणादेकः स्वपस्यया कविः ।
उभा पितरा महयन्नजायतान्निर्द्यावापृथिवी भूरिरेतसा ॥११॥

11.   Fire the One Seer by his seeking for perfect works[3] released
       out of the actions[4] of the universal godhead, the Vast: the
       Fire greatening both the parents, earth and heaven, was born
       from a mighty seed.[5]

SUKTA 4

समित्समित् सुमना बोध्यस्मे शुचाशुचा सुमतिं रासि वस्वः ।
आ देव देवान् यजथाय वक्षि सखा सखीन् त्सुमना यक्ष्यग्ने ॥१॥

1.   Aflame and again aflame in us awake with thy truth of
       mind, with light upon light grant us right understanding
       from the shining One. A god, bring the gods for the sacri-
       fice; right-minded, a friend do sacrifice to the friends, O
       Fire.

यं देवासस्त्रिरहन्नायजन्ते दिवेदिवे वरुणो मित्रो अग्निः ।
सेमं यज्ञं मधुमन्तं कृधी नस्तनूनपाद् घृतयोनिं विधन्तम् ॥२॥

2.   O thou whom the gods, even Varuna, Mitra and the Fire,
       thrice in the day worship with sacrifice from day to day, O
       Son of the body, make this sacrifice of ours full of the sweet-
       ness, so that it may create the native seat of the light.

प्र दीधितिर्विश्ववारा जिगाति होतारमिळः प्रथमं यजध्यै ।
अच्छा नमोभिर्वृषभं वन्दध्यै स देवान् यक्षदिषितो यजीयान् ॥३॥

---

[1] Or, seats or planes   [2] Or, clear-seeing,   [3] Or, by his skill in works
[4] Or, detached from the actions
[5] Or, the Fire was born greatening both the parents, earth and heaven, with his mighty
stream.

3. The Thought in which are all desirable things comes to this first and supreme Priest of the call to offer our aspirations as a sacrifice, towards the mighty one to adore him with our prostrations; missioned, strong to sacrifice, may he do worship to the gods.

ऊर्ध्वो वां गातुरध्वरे अकार्यूर्ध्वा शोचींषि प्रस्थिता रजांसि ।
दिवो वा नाभा न्यसादि होता स्तृणीमहि देवव्यचा वि बर्हिः ॥४॥

4. In the pilgrim-sacrifice a high path for you both has been made which departs to the high lustres, the mid-worlds; the Priest of the call has taken his seat in the navel-centre of heaven. We spread wide the sacred grass, a space of wideness of the gods.

सप्त होत्राणि मनसा वृणाना इन्वन्तो विश्वं प्रति यन्नृतेन ।
नृपेशसो विदथेषु प्र जाता अभीमं यज्ञं वि चरन्त पूर्वीः ॥५॥

5. Accepting with the mind the seven invocations, taking possession of all that is by the Truth, they went towards their goal. Many powers born in the finding of knowledge and wearing the forms of gods move abroad to this sacrifice.

आ भन्दमाने उषसा उपाके उत स्मयेते तन्वा विरूपे ।
यथा नो मित्रो वरुणो जुजोषदिन्द्रो मरुत्वां उत वा महोभिः ॥६॥

6. May night and dawn differently formed in their body be joined close and smile upon us in their gladness, so that Mitra may take pleasure in us and Varuna or with his greatness Indra too with the life-gods.[1]

दैव्या होतारा प्रथमा न्यृञ्जे सप्त पृक्षासः स्वधया मदन्ति ।
ऋतं शंसन्त ऋतमित् त आहुरनु व्रतं व्रतपा दीध्यानाः ॥७॥

7. I crown the two supreme Priests of the invocation. The

---

[1] Or, may they so shine with their lights that Mitra may take pleasure in us and Varuna and Indra with the life-gods.

seven pleasures take their rapture by the self-law of their
nature; the Truth they express, the Truth only they speak,
guardians of the law of its action according to that law they
shine.

आ भारती भारतीभिः सजोषा इळा देवैर्मनुष्येभिरग्निः ।
सरस्वती सारस्वतेभिरर्वाक् तिस्रो देवीर्बर्हिरेदं सदन्तु ॥८॥

8. In unison may Bharati with her Muses of invocation, Ila
with gods and men and Fire, Saraswati with her powers of
inspiration come down to us, the three goddesses sit upon
this seat of sacrifice.

तन्नस्तुरीपमध पोषयित्नु देव त्वष्टर्वि रराणः स्यस्व ।
यतो वीरः कर्मण्यः सुदक्षो युक्तग्रावा जायते देवकामः ॥९॥

9. O divine maker of forms who hast the utter rapture, cast
upon us that supreme transcendence cause of our growth,
from which is born in us the hero ever active with wise discernment, the seeker of the gods who sets to work the stone
of the wine-pressing.

वनस्पतेऽव सृजोप देवानग्निर्हविः शमिता सूदयाति ।
सेदु होता सत्यतरो यजाति यथा देवानां जनिमानि वेद ॥१०॥

10. O tree, release thy yield to the gods; Fire the achiever of the
work speeds the offering on its way. It is he who does worship as the Priest of the call, the more true in his act because
he knows the birth of the gods.

आ याह्यग्ने समिधानो अर्वाङिन्द्रेण देवैः सरथं तुरेभिः ।
बर्हिन आस्तामदितिः सुपुत्रा स्वाहा देवा अमृता मादयन्ताम् ॥११॥

11. Come down to us, O Fire, high-kindled, in one chariot with
Indra and swiftly journeying gods; let Aditi, mother of
mighty sons, sit on the sacred grass, let the gods, the immortals, take rapture in *svāhā*.

SUKTA 5

प्रत्यग्निरुषसश्चेकितानोऽबोधि विप्रः पदवीः कबीनाम् ।
पृथुपाजा देवयद्भिः समिद्धोऽग्न द्वारा तमसो वह्निरावः ॥१॥

1. The Fire is awake fronting the dawns; one illumined, he becomes aware of the paths of the seers: kindled into a wide might by the seekers of godhead, the upbearing flame opens the gates of the Darkness.

प्रेद्वग्निर्वावृधे स्तोमेभिर्गीर्भिः स्तोतॄणां नमस्य उक्थैः ।
पूर्वीर्ऋतस्य संदृशश्चकानः सं दूतो अद्यौदुषसो विरोके ॥२॥

2. Ever the Fire increases by the lauds, the words of those who hymn him by their utterances, one to be adored with prostrations; the Messenger who desires the many seeings of the Truth has shone out in the wide flaming of the Dawn.

अधाय्यग्निर्मानुषीषु विक्ष्वपां गर्भो मित्र ऋतेन साधन् ।
आ हर्यतो यजतः सान्वस्थादभूद् विप्रो हव्यो मतीनाम् ॥३॥

3. The Fire has been set in the human peoples, child of the Waters, the Friend who achieves by the Truth; luminous,[1] a power for sacrifice, he has risen to the summits; he has become the illumined seer who must be called by our thoughts.

मित्रो अग्निर्भवति यत् समिद्धो मित्रो होता वरुणो जातवेदाः ।
मित्रो अध्वर्युरिषिरो दमूना मित्रः सिन्धूनामुत पर्वतानाम् ॥४॥

4. The Fire when he has been kindled high becomes Mitra, the Friend — Mitra the Priest of the call, Varuna, the knower of the births, Mitra, the Friend, the Priest of the pilgrim-sacrifice, one rapid in his impulsions, the dweller in the house, the friend of the Rivers, the friend of the Mountains.

---

[1] Or, beloved and adorable,

पाति प्रियं रिपो अग्रं पदं वे: पाति यह्वश्चरणं सूर्यस्य ।
पाति नाभा सप्तशीर्षाणमग्नि: पाति देवानामुपमादमृष्व: ॥५॥

5. He guards from hurt the beloved[1] summit-seat of the being,
   mighty, he guards the course[2] of the Sun; Fire guards in the
   navel-centre the seven-headed thought, sublime, he guards
   the ecstasy of the gods.

ऋभुश्चक्र ईडचं चारु नाम विश्वानि देवो वयुनानि विद्वान् ।
ससस्य चर्म घृतवत् पदं वेस्तदिदग्नी रक्षत्यप्रयुच्छन् ॥६॥

6. A skilful craftsman, a god knowing all the manifestations of
   knowledge, he forms the beautiful and desirable Name, the
   luminous seat of the being in the movement of the peace;
   that the Fire guards, not deviating from his work.

आ योनिमग्निर्घृतवन्तमस्यात् पृथुप्रगाणमुशन्तमुशान: ।
दीद्यान: शुचिऋ्ङ्त्व: पावक: पुन:पुनर्मातरा नव्यसी क: ॥७॥

7. Desiring it as it desired him, the Fire entered into that
   luminous native abode wide in its approach; shining forth,
   pure, purifying, sublime, again and again he makes new
   the father and the mother.

सद्यो जात ओषधीभिर्ववक्षे यदी वर्धन्ति प्रस्वो घृतेन ।
आप इव प्रवता शुम्भमाना उरुष्यदग्नि: पित्रोरुपस्थे ॥८॥

8. Suddenly born he is carried by the growths of the earth when
   the mothers who bore him make him grow by the light.
   The Fire in the lap of the father and the mother is as one
   who defends the waters gliding happily[3] down a slope.

उदु ष्टुत: समिधा यह्वो अद्यौद् वर्ष्मन् दिवो अधि नाभा पृथिव्या: ।
मित्रो अग्निरीडघो मातरिश्वाऽऽदूतो वक्षद् यजथाय देवान् ॥९॥

9. Lauded by us mighty he shone with his high flaming in the
   largeness[4] of heaven, in the navel-centre of earth. The Fire

---

[1] Or, delightful   [2] Or, movement   [3] Or, gliding brightly   [4] Or, height

is Mitra the Friend, the desirable one, he is life growing in the mother;[1] may he as our messenger bring the gods for the sacrifice.

उदस्तम्भीत् समिधा नाकमृष्वोऽग्निर्भवन्नुत्तमो रोचनानाम् ।
यदी भृगुभ्यः परि मातरिश्वा गुहा सन्तं हव्यवाहं समीधे ॥१०॥

10. The Fire with his high flaming up-pillared, sublime, the firmament and became the highest of the luminous kingdoms,[2] when for the flame-seers life, that grows in the mother, kindled all around the carrier of the offerings who was hidden in the Secrecy.

इळामग्ने पुरुदंसं सनिं गोः शश्वत्तमं हवमानाय साध ।
स्यान्नः सूनुस्तनयो विजावाऽग्ने सा ते सुमतिर्भूत्वस्मे ॥११॥

11. O Fire, achieve at my call the Revealing Speech the many-actioned, the lasting conquest of the Light. May there be for us a Son of our begetting pervading in his birth;[3] O Fire, may there be created in us that true thinking of thine.

SUKTA 6

प्र कारवो मनना वच्यमाना देवद्रीचीं नयत देवयन्तः ।
दक्षिणावाड् वाजिनी प्राच्येति हविर्भरन्त्यग्नये घृताची ॥१॥

1. The Doers of the work, seekers of godhead, who find expression by the thought, lead it on turned godwards; full of the plenitude, luminous, carrying the Understanding, it journeys moving forwards, bringing the offering to the Fire.

आ रोदसी अपृणा जायमान उत प्र रिक्था अध नु प्रयज्यो ।
दिवश्चिदग्ने महिना पृथिव्या वच्यन्तां ते वह्नयः सप्तजिह्वाः ॥२॥

2. Even in thy birth thou hast filled earth and heaven, and now

---

[1] Or, life that breathes in the mother; [2] Or, highest of all lights,
[3] Or, himself a begetter;

thou hast exceeded them, O Flame that carriest on the sacrifice; by the greatness of earth and heaven may thy seven tongues find utterance, carriers of the word, O Fire.

द्यौश्च त्वा पृथिवी यज्ञियासो नि होतारं सादयन्ते दमाय ।
यदी विशो मानुषीर्देवयन्तीः प्रयस्वतीरीळते शुक्रमर्चिः ॥३॥

3. Heaven and earth and the lords of sacrifice set thee within as the Priest of the call for the house when human beings, seeking godhead, having the delight, ask for the resplendent Ray.

महान् त्सधस्ये ध्रुव आ निषत्तोऽन्तर्द्यावा माहिने हर्यमाणः ।
आस्क्रे सपत्नी अजरे अमृक्ते सबर्दुघे उरुगायस्य धेनू ॥४॥

4. Mighty, he is seated steadfast in the world of his session, rejoicing between the two mightinesses of earth and heaven, the united wives of one wide moving lord, ageless and inviolate, the two milch-cows giving their rich yield of milk.

व्रता ते अग्ने महतो महानि तव क्रत्वा रोदसी आ ततन्थ ।
त्वं दूतो अभवो जायमानस्त्वं नेता वृषभ चर्षणीनाम् ॥५॥

5. Great art thou, O Fire, and great the law of thy workings, by thy will thou hast built out earth and heaven; in thy very birth thou becamest the Messenger, O mighty lord, and, thou the leader of men that see.

ऋतस्य वा केशिना योग्याभिर्घृतस्नुवा रोहिता धुरि धिष्व ।
अथा वह देवान् देव विश्वान्त्स्वध्वरा कृणुहि जातवेदः ॥६॥

6. Set under the yoke with the straps of the yoking the two maned steeds of the Truth red of hue, dripping Light: thou, O God, bring all the gods; O knower of the births, make perfect the ways of the pilgrim-sacrifice.

दिवश्चिदा ते रुचयन्त रोका उषो विभातीरनु भासि पूर्वीः ।
अपो यदग्न उशधग्वनेषु होतुर्मन्द्रस्य पनयन्त देवाः ॥७॥

7. From heaven itself thy lights blazed forth, thou shinest in the wake of many outshinings of the Dawn[1] when, O Fire, passionately burning[2] in the woods, the gods set the waters[3] to their work for the rapturous Priest of the call.

उरौ वा ये अन्तरिक्षे मदन्ति दिवो वा ये रोचने सन्ति देवाः ।
ऊमा वा ये सुहवासो यजत्रा आयेमिरे रथ्यो अग्ने अश्वाः ॥८॥

8. The gods who take their rapture in the wide mid-world, or those who are in the luminous world of heaven, or those lords of sacrifice who are helpful and ready to the call, them thy chariot-horses have borne towards us.

ऐभिरग्ने सरथं याह्यर्वाङ् नानारथं वा विभवो ह्यश्वाः ।
पत्नीवतस्त्रिंशतं त्रींश्च देवाननुष्वधमा वह मादयस्व ॥९॥

9. Come down to us with them in one chariot or in many chariots for thy horses pervade and are everywhere; according to thy self-law bring here with their wives the gods thirty and three and give them to drink of the rapture.

स होता यस्य रोदसी चिदुर्वी यज्ञंयज्ञमभि वृधे गृणीतः ।
प्राची अध्वरेव तस्थतुः सुमेके ऋतावरी ऋतजातस्य सत्ये ॥१०॥

10. He is the Priest of the call for whose growing even wide earth and heaven speak the word at sacrifice on sacrifice; facing each other, fixed like two ends of the pilgrim-way, the Truth they keep in his truth who from the Truth was born.

इळामग्ने पुरुदंसं सनि गोः शश्वत्तमं हवमानाय साध ।
स्यान्नः सूनुस्तनयो विजावाग्ने सा ते सुमतिर्भूत्वस्मे ॥११॥

11. O Fire, achieve at my call the Revealing Speech the many-actioned, the lasting conquest of the Light. May there be for us a Son of our begetting pervading in his birth;[4] O Fire, may there be created in us that true thinking of thine.

---

[1] Or, in the wake of many wide-shining Dawns   [2] Or, flaming as dawn
[3] *Apas*, work, would make a clearer sense; it would then mean "set in action the work of the rapturous Priest of the call".
[4] Or, himself a begetter;

SUKTA 7

प्र य आरुः शितिपृष्ठस्य धासेरा मातरा विविशुः सप्त वाणीः ।
परिक्षिता पितरा सं चरेते प्र सर्स्राते दीर्घमायुः प्रयक्षे ॥१॥

1. They who have climbed from the dark-backed foundation
   have entered the Father and Mother, have entered into the
   seven voices. The Father and Mother who dwell encompassing all move abroad and go forward to give by sacrifice
   long-extended the Life.

दिवक्षसो घेनवो वृष्णो अश्वा देवीरा तस्थौ मधुमद् वहन्तीः ।
ऋतस्य त्वा सदसि क्षेमयन्तं पर्येका चरति वर्तनिं गौः ॥२॥

2. He reached the milch-cows that dwell in heaven, the Mares
   of the male, the divine rivers that carry in their flow the
   sweetness. The one Light moves on the way around thee
   when thou seekest thy dwelling in the house of the Truth.

आ सीमरोहत् सुयमा भवन्तीः पतिश्चिकित्वान् रयिविद् रयीणाम् ।
प्र नीलपृष्ठो अतसस्य धासेस्ता अवासयत् पुरुधप्रतीकः ॥३॥

3. On every side he ascends them and they become easy to
   control, he awakes to knowledge and is the lord and discoverer of the riches. Fire with his blue back and many
   diverse faces brings them from the ever-moving foundation
   to a settled dwelling.

महि त्वाष्ट्रमूर्जयन्तीरजुर्यं स्तभूयमानं वहतो वहन्ति ।
व्यङ्गेभिर्विद्द्युतानः सधस्य एकामिव रोदसी आ विवेश ॥४॥

4. The rivers energised and bear his mighty force of formation
   firmly fixed and undecaying; he shines out wide with his
   limbs in the world of his session and has entered earth and
   heaven as if they were one.

जानन्ति वृष्णो अरुषस्य शेवमुत ब्रध्नस्य शासने रणन्ति ।
दिवोरुचः सुरुचो रोचमाना इळा येषां गण्या माहिना गीः ॥५॥

5. They knew the bliss of the ruddy-shining bull and they rejoice in the rule of the Great One; they are the lights of heaven luminously blazing and the Word of Revelation is their mighty common speech.

उतो पितृभ्यां प्रविदानु घोषं महो महूद्रूघामनयन्त शूषम् ।
उक्षा ह यत्र परि धानमक्तोरनु स्वं धाम जरितुर्ववक्ष ॥६॥

6. And great by the knowledge of the great Father and Mother they led his strength in the wake of its proclaiming call, where the bull bears his worshipper round the hold of night towards its own seat.

अध्वर्युभि: पञ्चभि: सप्त विप्रा: प्रियं रक्षन्ते निहितं पदं वे: ।
प्राञ्चो मदन्त्युक्षणो अजुर्या देशा देवानामनु हि व्रता गु: ॥७॥

7. Seven illumined seers guard by the five priests of the pilgrim-rite the beloved[1] seat of the being that is set within: moving forward the imperishable bulls take joy; the gods move according to the law of the workings of the gods.

वैव्या होतारा प्रथमा न्यृञ्जे सप्त पृक्षास: स्वधया मदन्ति ।
ऋतं शंसन्त ऋतमित् त आहुरनु व्रतं व्रतपा दीध्यानाः ॥८॥

8. I crown the two supreme Priests of the invocation. The seven pleasures take their rapture by the self-law of their nature; the Truth they express, the Truth only they speak, guardians of the law of its action according to that law they shine.

वृषायन्ते महे अत्याय पूर्वीर्वृष्णे चित्राय रश्मय: सुयामाः ।
देव होतर्मन्द्रतरश्चिकित्वान् महो देवान् रोदसी एह वक्षि ॥९॥

9. The many Rays well governed in their course, grow passionate for the great Horse, the many-hued Bull. O divine Priest of the call, rapturous, awaking to knowledge, bring here the great gods and earth and heaven.

[1] Or, delightful

पृक्षप्रयजो द्रविणः सुवाचः सुकेतव उषसो रेवदूषुः ।
उतो चिदग्ने महिना पृथिव्याः कृतं चिदेनः सं महे दशस्य ॥१०॥

10. The swift-running dawns have shone opulently bringing us
our satisfactions, with their true speech, their rays of intuition. And do thou, O Fire, by the greatness of the earth cut
away for the Vast even the sin that has been done.

इळामग्ने पुरुदंसं सनि गोः शश्वत्तमं हवमानाय साध ।
स्यान्नः सूनुस्तनयो विजावाग्ने सा ते सुमतिर्भूत्वस्मे ॥११॥

11. O Fire, achieve at my call the Revealing Speech, the many-
actioned, the lasting conquest of the Light. May there be
for us a Son of our begetting pervading in his birth;[1] O
Fire, may there be created in us that true thinking of thine.

SUKTA 9

सखायस्त्वा ववृमहे देवं मर्तास ऊतये ।
अपां नपातं सुभगं सुदीदिति सुप्रतूर्तिमनेहसम् ॥१॥

1. Mortals we have chosen thee, a god, for our comrade to
protect us, the Child of the Waters, full of happiness and
light, victorious,[2] to whom no hurt can come.

कायमानो वना त्वं यन्मातुर्जगन्नपः ।
न तत् ते अग्ने प्रमृषे निवर्तनं यद् दूरे सन्निहाभवः ॥२॥

2. When leaving the woods thou goest to thy mother waters,
that retreat turns not to oblivion of thee,[3] O Fire, for even
though thou art far thou hast come into being here.

अति तृष्टं ववक्षिथाथैव सुमना असि ।
प्रप्रान्ये यन्ति पर्यन्य आसते येषां सख्ये असि श्रितः ॥३॥

3. When thou hast carried beyond the rough ground[4] then

---

[1] Or, himself a begetter;   [2] Or, strong to break through,   [3] Or, to thy destruction,
[4] Or, beyond thirst

hast thou truth of mind: some depart,[1] others remain seated around thee in whose comradeship thou art lodged.

ईयिवांसमति खिधः शश्वतीरति सश्चतः ।
अन्वीमविन्दन् निचिरासो अद्रुहोऽप्सु सिंहमिव श्रितम् ॥४॥

4. When he has passed beyond the forces that make to err, beyond those that cling perpetual, the long-lasting who have no hurt have followed and found him like a lion who has taken refuge in the Waters.

ससृवांसमिव त्मनाऽग्निमित्था तिरोहितम् ।
ऐनं नयन्मातरिश्वा परावतो देवेभ्यो मथितं परि ॥५॥

5. As if one who of himself has sped away and utterly disappeared, this Fire Life growing in the mother led from the Beyond, churned out on every side, for the gods.

तं त्वा मर्ता अगृभ्णत देवेभ्यो हव्यवाहन ।
विश्वान् यद् यज्ञाँ अभिपासि मानुष तव क्रत्वा यविष्ठय ॥६॥

6. This is thou upon whom mortals have seized for the gods, O carrier of the offerings, because thou guardest all sacrifices by thy will, O Flame in man, O most youthful god!

तद् भद्रं तव दंसना पाकाय चिच्छदयति ।
त्वां यदग्ने पशवः समासते समिद्धमपिशर्वरे ॥७॥

7. O Fire, thy action covers That Bliss from the ignorant when the Animals sit together around thee, kindled against the night.

आ जुहोता स्वध्वरं शीरं पावकशोचिषम् ।
आशुं दूतमजिरं प्रत्नमीडयं श्रुष्टी देवं सपर्यत ॥८॥

8. Offer the oblation to the Fire intense with its purifying light, who does perfectly the pilgrim-rite, the swift messenger,

---

[1] Or, move forward,

with his rapid pace; wait soon upon the ancient and desirable godhead.

त्रीणि शता त्री सहस्राण्यग्निं त्रिशच्च देवा नव चासपर्यन् ।
औक्षन् घृतैरस्तृणन् बर्हिरस्मा आदिद्धोतारं न्यसादयन्त ॥९॥

9. Gods three thousand and three hundred and thirty and nine waited upon the Fire. They anointed him with streams of the clarity, they spread for him the seat of sacrifice, and seated him within as Priest of the call.

Sukta 10

त्वामग्ने मनीषिणः सम्राजं चर्षणीनाम् ।
देवं मर्तास इन्धते समध्वरे ॥१॥

1. Thee, O Fire, men who have the thinking mind kindle in the sacrifice, an emperor over those who see, mortals set alight a godhead.

त्वां यज्ञेष्वृत्विजमग्ने होतारमीळते ।
गोपा ऋतस्य दीदिहि स्वे दमे ॥२॥

2. Thee, O Fire, they pray in the sacrifices as the sacrificant of the rite, the Priest of the call; shine out the guardian of the Truth in thy own home.

स घा यस्ते ददाशति समिधा जातवेदसे ।
सो अग्ने धत्ते सुवीर्यं स पुष्यति ॥३॥

3. He who gives to thee with the fuel, to the knower of the births, holds the hero-energy, he ever grows.

स केतुरध्वराणामग्निर्देवेभिरा गमत् ।
अञ्जानः सप्त होतृभिर्हविष्मते ॥४॥

4. He is the ray of intuition in the sacrifices; may he, the Fire, come with the gods, anointed by the seven priests of oblation,

to him who holds the offerings.

प्र होत्रे पूर्व्यं वचोऽग्नये भरता बृहत् ।
विपां ज्योतींषि बिभ्रते न वेधसे ॥५॥

5. Bring forward for the Fire, for the Priest of the call, the vast and supreme word[1] as for the creator and me who bring the lights of illuminations.

अग्ने वर्धन्तु नो गिरो यतो जायत उक्थ्यः ।
महे वाजाय द्रविणाय दर्शतः ॥६॥

6. May our words make the Fire to grow when he is born, the Fire that carries the utterance, visioned for the great plenitude, for the treasure.

अग्ने यजिष्ठो अध्वरे देवान् देवयते यज ।
होता मन्द्रो वि राजस्यति स्रिधः ॥७॥

7. O Fire, most strong to sacrifice in the pilgrim-rite, worship the gods for the seeker of the godhead; as the rapturous Priest of the call thou shinest wide, beyond the forces that make us err.

स नः पावक दीदिहि द्युमदस्मे सुवीर्यम् ।
भवा स्तोतृभ्यो अन्तमः स्वस्तये ॥८॥

8. So, do thou, O purifying Flame, kindle in us the luminous hero-energy, to those who laud thee become most close for their weal.

तं त्वा विप्रा विपन्यवो जागृवांसः समिन्धते ।
हव्यवाहममर्त्यं सहोवृधम् ॥९॥

9. This is thou whom the illumined seers who have the light, ever wakeful, kindle, the immortal bearer of the offering, increaser of our force.

---

[1] Or, ancient word

अग्निर्होता पुरोहितोऽध्वरस्य विचर्षणिः ।
स वेद यज्ञमानुषक् ॥१॥

1. Fire is our all-seeing Priest of the call, our vicar set in front
   in the pilgrim-rite; he knows the uninterrupted course of the
   sacrifice.

स हव्यवाळमर्त्यं उशिग्दूतश्चनोहितः ।
अग्निर्धिया समृण्वति ॥२॥

2. He is the immortal, the carrier of the offering, the aspirant,
   the messenger settled in the rapture; the Fire joins with our
   Thought.

अग्निर्धिया स चेतति केतुर्यज्ञस्य पूर्व्यः ।
अर्थं ह्यस्य तरणि ॥३॥

3. Agni wakes to knowledge companioning our Thought, he is
   the supreme[1] ray of intuition in the sacrifice; it is he who
   crosses through to man's goal.

अग्निं सूनुं सनश्रुतं सहसो जातवेदसम् ।
वर्हि देवा अकृण्वत ॥४॥

4. Fire, the Son of Force, who hears the things that are eternal,[2]
   knower of the births, the gods created as a carrier flame.

अदाभ्यः पुरएता विशामग्निर्मानुषीणाम् ।
तूर्णी रथः सदा नवः ॥५॥

5. The inviolable who goes in front of the human peoples the
   Fire is a swift chariot that is ever new.

साह्वान् विश्वा अभियुजः ऋतुर्देवानाममृक्तः ।
अग्निस्तुविश्रवस्तमः ॥६॥

---

[1] Or, ancient   [2] Or, who has the inspired konwledge of things eternal,

6. Overpowering all assailants the Fire is the will of the gods never crushed, filled with the multitude of his inspirations.

अग्नि प्रयांसि वाहसा दाशवाँ अश्नोति मर्त्यः ।
क्षयं पावकशोचिषः ॥७॥

7. By this bringer of delights the mortal who gives, reaches and possesses the house of the purifying light.

परि विश्वानि सुधिताग्नेरश्याम मन्मभिः ।
विप्रासो जातवेदसः ॥८॥

8. May we by our thought possess around us well-established all the things of the Fire, may we be illumined seers who know all things born.[1]

अग्ने विश्वानि वार्या वाजेषु सनिषामहे ।
त्वे देवास एरिरे ॥९॥

9. O Fire, we shall win all desirable things in thy plenitudes, in thee have moved towards us the gods.

SUKTA 12

इन्द्राग्नी आ गतं सुतं गीर्भिर्नभो वरेण्यम् ।
अस्य पातं धियेषिता ॥१॥

1. O Indra, O Fire, come to the offering of the wine, by our words, your supreme desirable ether; drink of it you who are missioned by the Thought.

इन्द्राग्नी जरितुः सचा यज्ञो जिगाति चेतनः ।
अया पातमिमं सुतम् ॥२॥

2. O Indra, O Fire, the conscious sacrifice journeys taking with it the worshipper: by this word drink of this offered wine.

---

[1] Or, in whom knowledge is born.

इन्द्रमग्निं कविच्छदा यज्ञस्य जूत्या वृणे ।
ता सोमस्येह तृम्पताम् ॥३॥

3. I choose by the swift impulse of the sacrifice Indra and the
    Fire whose pleasure is in the seer; take here your content of
    the Soma-wine.

तोशा वृत्रहणा हुवे सजित्वानापराजिता ।
इन्द्राग्नी वाजसातमा ॥४॥

4. The smiters, the slayers of the coverer I call, the unvan-
    quished, the companions in victory, Indra and the Fire,
    most strong to win the plenitudes.

प्र वामर्चन्त्युकिथनो नीथाविदो जरितारः ।
इन्द्राग्नी इष आ वृणे ॥५॥

5. Your adorers, speakers of the word, they who know the
    ways of the guidance hymn you: O Indra, O Fire, I accept
    your impulsions.

इन्द्राग्नी नवतिं पुरो दासपत्नीरधूनुतम् ।
साकमेकेन कर्मणा ॥६॥

6. Indra and Fire shook down the ninety cities possessed by
    the destroyers, together by one deed.

इन्द्राग्नी अपसस्पर्युप प्र यन्ति धीतयः ।
ऋतस्य पथ्या अनु ॥७॥

7. O Indra, O Fire, all around our work our thoughts go for-
    ward towards you along the paths of the Truth.

इन्द्राग्नी तविषाणि वां सधस्थानि प्रयांसि च ।
युवोरप्तूर्यं हितम् ॥८॥

8. O Indra, O Fire, your mights are companions and your
    delights; in you is founded all swiftness in the work.

इन्द्राग्नी रोचना दिव: परि वाजेषु भूषथ: ।
तव् वां चेति प्र वीर्यम् ॥९॥

9. O Indra, O Fire, you encompass the luminous kingdom of
heaven in the plenitudes; it is your strength that is manifested there.[1]

RISHABHA VAISHWAMITRA

SUKTA 13

प्र वो देवायाग्नये बर्हिष्ठमर्चास्मै ।
गमद् देवेभिरा स नो यजिष्ठो बर्हिरा सदत् ॥१॥

1. Sing out some mightiest hymn to this divine Fire; may he
come to us with the gods and, strong to sacrifice, sit upon
the sacred grass.

ऋतावा यस्य रोदसी दक्षं सचन्त ऊतय: ।
हविष्मन्तस्तमीळते तं सनिष्यन्तोऽवसे ॥२॥

2. He is the possessor of the Truth to whom belong earth and
heaven and their guardings accompany his mind of discernment; for him the givers of the oblation pray, for him for
their protection when they would win the riches.

स यन्ता विप्र एषां स यज्ञानामथा हि य: ।
अग्निं तं वो दुवस्यत दाता यो वनिता मघम् ॥३॥

3. He is the illumined seer and regent of these sacrifices, he and
always he; that Fire set to his work who shall win and give
the plenitude.

स न: शर्माणि वीतयेऽग्निर्यच्छतु शंतमा ।
यतो न: प्रुष्णवद् वसु दिवि क्षितिभ्यो अप्स्वा ॥४॥

---

[1] Or, that is your strength which wakes to knowledge.

4. May he, the Fire, give us all happy peace for our journeying there whence are rained the riches in heaven, from all the planes, in the Waters.

वीदिवांसमपूर्व्यं वस्वीभिरस्य धीतिभिः ।
ऋक्वाणो अग्निमिन्धते होतारं विश्पतिं विशाम् ॥५॥

5. Men who have the light kindle into his flaming, incomparable, by the opulent thinkings of this being Fire, the Priest of the call, the lord of all the peoples.

उत नो ब्रह्मन्नविष उक्थेषु देवहूतमः ।
शं नः शोचा मरुद्वृधोग्ने सहस्रसातमः ॥६॥

6. Do thou, strong to call the gods, protect us in the Word, in all our utterances; increasing the life-powers powerful to win the thousands. Flame out blissfully for us, O Fire.

नू नो रास्व सहस्रवत् तोकवत् पुष्टिमद् वसु ।
द्युमदग्ने सुवीर्यं वर्षिष्ठमनुपक्षितम् ॥७॥

7. Now give us a thousandfold riches bringing the Son, bringing our growth, luminous, a hero-strength, abundant, inexhaustible.

SUKTA 14

आ होता मन्द्रो विदथान्यस्थात् सत्यो यज्वा कवितमः स वेधाः ।
विद्युद्रथः सहसस्पुत्रो अग्निः शोचिष्केशः पृथिव्यां पाजो अश्रेत् ॥१॥

1. The rapturous Priest of the call has reached the things of knowledge; he is the true, doer of sacrifice, a great seer, a creator. Fire the son of force, with his chariot of lightning and his hair of flaming light has attained to a massive strength on the earth.

अयामि ते नमउवित जुषस्व ऋतावस्तुभ्यं चेतते सहस्वः ।
विद्वां आ वक्षि विदुषो नि षत्सि मध्य आ बर्हिरूतये यजत्र ॥२॥

2. I come to thee, accept my word of obeisance, O master of
Truth and strength, to thee who givest knowledge. As the
knower, bring those who know and sit in the midst on the
sacred grass, O lord of sacrifice.

द्रवतां त उषसा वाजयन्ती अग्ने वातस्य पथ्याभिरच्छ ।
यत् सीमञ्जन्ति पूर्व्यं हविर्भिरा वन्धुरेव तस्यतुर्दुरोणे ॥३॥

3. Let dawn and night full of their plenitude come running towards thee on paths of the wind, O Fire, when all around
they anoint with oblation thee the first and supreme, as if
two sides of a chariot-front they enter into the gated house.

मित्रश्च तुभ्यं वरुणः सहस्वोऽग्ने विश्वे मरुतः सुम्नमर्चन् ।
यच्छोचिषा सहसस्पुत्र तिष्ठा अभि क्षितीः प्रथयन् त्सूर्यो नॄन् ॥४॥

4. To thee, O Forceful Fire, Mitra and Varuna and all the
life-powers chant a hymn of bliss, when with thy flame of
light, O son of Force, thou standest as the sun above the
peoples shining wide upon men.

वयं ते अद्य ररिमा हि काममुत्तानहस्ता नमसोपसद्य ।
यजिष्ठेन मनसा यक्षि देवानस्रेधता मन्मना विप्रो अग्ने ॥५॥

5. Today we give to thee thy desire, approaching thee with
outstretched hands and with obeisance; worship the gods
with a mind strong for sacrifice, an illumined seer, with thy
unerring thought, O Fire.

त्वद्धि पुत्र सहसो वि पूर्वीर्देवस्य यन्त्यूतयो वि वाजाः ।
त्वं देहि सहस्रिणं रयिं नोऽद्रोघेण वचसा सत्यमग्ने ॥६॥

6. For, from thee, O son of Force, go forth the many protections of the godhead, and his plenitudes. Do thou give us
the thousandfold treasure, give by the word that betrays not
the truth, O Fire.

तुभ्यं दक्ष कविक्रतो यानीमा देव मर्तासो अध्वरे अकर्म ।
त्वं विश्वस्य सुरथस्य बोधि सर्वं तदग्ने अमृत स्वदेह ॥७॥

7. O understanding mind, O Seer-Will! now that all these things we who are mortals have done for thee, O god, in the pilgrim-sacrifice, do thou awake to the whole well-charioted action and taste all That here, O immortal Fire.

UTKILA KATYA

SUKTA 15

वि पाजसा पृथुना शोशुचानो बाधस्व द्विषो रक्षसो अमीवाः ।
सुशर्मणो बृहतः शर्मणि स्यामग्नेरहं सुहवस्य प्रणीतौ ॥१॥

1. Flaming out in a wide mass of strength press back the hostile powers that hurt and afflict. May I abide in the bliss of the all-blissful Vast, in the leading of the Fire who is swift to our call.

त्वं नो अस्या उषसो व्युष्टौ त्वं सूर उदिते बोधि गोपाः ।
जन्मेव नित्यं तनयं जुषस्व स्तोमं मे अग्ने तन्वा सुजात ॥२॥

2. Thou in the dawning of this dawn, thou when the Sun has arisen wake for us and be our protector. Take pleasure in the Son as if in an eternal birth. Accept my affirmation of thee, O Fire, perfectly born in thy body.

त्वं नृचक्षा वृषभानु पूर्वीः कृष्णास्वग्ने अरुषो वि भाहि ।
वसो नेषि च पर्षि चात्यंहः कृधी नो राय उशिजो यविष्ठ ॥३॥

3. Thou art the male with the divine vision, in the wake of many dawns shine out luminous in the black nights, O Fire. O prince of the riches, lead and carry us over beyond the evil; O youthful god, make us aspirants for the treasure.

अषाळ्हो अग्ने वृषभो दिदीहि पुरो विश्वाः सौभगा संजिगीवान् ।
यज्ञस्य नेता प्रथमस्य पायोर्जातवेदो बृहतः सुप्रणीते ॥४॥

4. Shine out, O Fire, the invincible male, conquering all the
   cities, all the felicities; thou art the knower of the births,
   O perfect guide on the way, thou art the leader of the first,
   the Vast all-protecting sacrifice.

अच्छिद्रा शर्म जरितः पुरूणि देवाँ अच्छा दीद्यानः सुमेधाः ।
रथो न सस्निरभि वक्षि वाजमग्ने त्वं रोदसी नः सुमेके ॥५॥

5. O Fire of worship, towards homes of bliss many and without
   a gap, towards the gods shining out wise in understanding,
   like a conquering chariot bring the plenitude; O Fire, do
   thou make earth and heaven firmly established for us.

प्र पीपय वृषभ जिन्व वाजानग्ने त्वं रोदसी नः सुदोघे ।
देवेभिर्देव सुरुचा रुचानो मा नो मर्तस्य दुर्मतिः परिष्ठात् ॥६॥

6. O Bull of the herds, nourish us, move towards us with plenitudes, make heaven and earth good milk-cows for us, O Fire;
   O god, come with the gods glowing in the beauty of thy
   splendour. Let not the evil mind of mortal besiege us.

इळामग्ने पुरुदंसं सनिं गोः शश्वत्तमं हवमानाय साध ।
स्यान्नः सूनुस्तनयो विजावाग्ने सा ते सुमतिर्भूत्वस्मे ॥७॥

7. O Fire, achieve at my call the Revealing Speech the many-
   actioned, the lasting conquest of the Light. May there be
   for us a Son of our begetting pervading in his birth;[1] O Fire,
   may there be created in us that true thinking of thine.

SUKTA 16

अयमग्निः सुवीर्यस्येशे महः सौभगस्य ।
राय ईशे स्वपत्यस्य गोमत ईशे वृत्रहथानाम् ॥१॥

1. This is the Fire that is lord of the hero-energy and the great
   felicity, lord of the wealth of the shining herds, and of good

---
[1] Or, himself a begetter;

progeny who has power for the slaying of the coverers.

इमं नरो मरुतः सश्चता वृधं यस्मिन् रायः श्रेवृधासः ।
अभि ये सन्ति पृतनासु दूढचो विश्वाहा शत्रुमादभुः ॥२॥

2. O gods, O life-powers, you cleave to this Fire of increase, in
whom are the treasures that make our happiness to grow.
Through all the days they have destroyed the enemies, the
evil-thoughted who attack us in our battles.

स त्वं नो रायः शिशीहि मीढ्वो अग्ने सुवीर्यस्य ।
तुविद्युम्न वर्षिष्ठस्य प्रजावतोऽनमीवस्य शुष्मिणः ॥३॥

3. So do thou, O bounteous Fire, with thy many lights bestow
on us the greatest and griefless wealth, full of the hero-
strength, of progeny and of force.

चक्रियो विश्वा भुवनाभि सासहिश्चक्रिर्वेश्वा दुवः ।
आ देवेषु यतत आ सुवीर्य आ शंस उत नृणाम् ॥४॥

4. He who puts forth his force and is the doer in all the worlds,
he who is the doer of works in the gods, labours in the gods
and in all mights and in the self-expression of men.

मा नो अग्नेऽमतये मावीरतायै रीरधः ।
मागोतायै सहसस्पुत्र मा निदेऽप द्वेषांस्या कृधि ॥५॥

5. O Fire, deliver us not to unconsciousness, nor to the lack of
the strength of the hero, nor to the absence of the Light,[1]
nor to the bondage,[2] O son of force, put away from us the
hostile powers.

शग्धि वाजस्य सुभग प्रजावतोऽग्ने बृहतो अध्वरे ।
सं राया भूयसा सृज मयोभुना तुविद्युम्न यशस्वता ॥६॥

6. O felicitous Fire, have power in the pilgrim-rite for the
fruitful plenitude, for the Vast; O thou of the many lights,

---

[1] Literally, "the Cow",   [2] Or, to the Censurer,

join us to the large and glorious riches that create the Bliss.

KATA VAISHWAMITRA

Sukta 17

समिध्यमानः प्रथमानु धर्मा समक्तुभिरज्यते विश्ववारः ।
शोचिष्केशो घृतनिर्णिक् पावकः सुयज्ञो अग्निर्यजथाय देवान् ॥१॥

1. He is kindled and blazes out according to the first and supreme laws and is united with the Rays, he in whom are all desirable things, Fire with his tresses of flame and his raiment of light, the purifier, perfect in sacrifice, for sacrifice to the gods.

यथायजो होत्रमग्ने पृथिव्या यथा दिवो जातवेदश्चिकित्वान् ।
एवानेन हविषा यक्षि देवान् मनुष्वद् यज्ञं प्र तिरेममद्य ॥२॥

2. O Fire, as thou hast accomplished in sacrifice thy priesthood for the earth, awaking to knowledge, O knower of the births, as thou hast accomplished it for heaven,[1] so with this oblation do sacrifice to the gods, carry yet further beyond the sacrifice with the human being today.

त्रीण्यायूंषि तव जातवेदस्तिस्र आजानीरुषसस्ते अग्ने ।
ताभिर्देवानामवो यक्षि विद्वानथा भव यजमानाय शं योः ॥३॥

3. Three are thy lives, O knower of all things born, three are the dawns that are thy births, O Fire;[2] by them win through sacrifice the protection of the gods, thou as the knower become for the doer of sacrifice the peace and the movement.

अग्निं सुवीर्ति सुदृशं गृणन्तो नमस्यामस्त्वेडचं जातवेदः ।
त्वां दूतमरति हव्यवाहं देवा अकृण्वन्नमृतस्य नाभिम् ॥४॥

---

[1] Or, as thou hast offered in sacrifice the oblation of the earth, as thou hast offered the oblation of heaven,

[2] Or, that gave thee birth, O Fire;

4. We hymn thee by our words, O knower of all things born, as the Fire perfect in light, perfect in vision, the object of our prayer and offer to thee our obeisance; thee the gods made the Messenger, the Traveller, the carrier of offerings, the navel-centre of Immortality.

यस्त्वद्धोता पूर्वो अग्ने यजीयान् द्विता च सत्ता स्वधया च शंभुः ।
तस्यानु धर्म प्र यजा चिकित्वोऽध्या नो घा अध्वरं देववीतौ ॥५॥

5. O Fire, he who was before thee and was the Priest of the call and mighty for sacrifice and was dual entity and by the law of his nature the creator of the Bliss, by his law of action carry on the sacrifice, thou who art awake to knowledge, thou establish our pilgrim-rite in the advent of the gods.

SUKTA 18

भवा नो अग्ने सुमना उपेतौ सखेव सख्ये पितरेव साधुः ।
पुरुद्रुहो हि क्षितयो जनानां प्रति प्रतीचीर्बंहतादरातीः ॥१॥

1. O Fire, in our coming to thee become right-minded accomplishing our aim as a friend to a friend, as father and mother to their child; for these worlds of beings born are full of harm: burn to ashes the hostile forces that come against us.

तपो ष्वग्ने अन्तरां अमित्रान् तपा शंसमररुषः परस्य ।
तपो वसो चिकितानो अचित्तान् वि ते तिष्ठन्तामजरा अयासः ॥२॥

2. Wholly consume our inner foes, consume the self-expression of the enemy who would war against us, O lord of the riches, consume, conscious in knowledge, the powers of ignorance; let them range wide thy ageless marching fires.

इध्मेनाग्न इच्छमानो घृतेन जुहोमि हव्यं तरसे बलाय ।
यावदीशे ब्रह्मणा वन्दमान इमां धियं शतसेयाय देवीम् ॥३॥

3. I desire and offer the oblation, O Fire, with the fuel, with

the pouring of the clarity, for speed, for strength. Until I have the mastery,[1] adoring with the Word I lift to thee for the conquest of the hundreds this thought divine.

उच्छोचिषा सहसस्पुत्र स्तुतो बृहद् वयः शशमानेषु धेहि ।
रेवदग्ने विश्वामित्रेषु शं योर्मंमृंज्मा ते तन्वं भूरि कृत्वः ॥४॥

4. Affirmed by our lauds rise up with thy flame of light, O son of force, found the vast expansion in us who labour at the work, found opulently in the Vishwamitras the peace and the movement, O Fire. We make bright many times over thy body.

कृषि रत्नं सुसनितर्धनानां स घेवग्ने भवसि यत् समिद्धः ।
स्तोतुर्दुरोणे सुभगस्य रेवत् सूप्रा करस्ना वधिषे वपूंषि ॥५॥

5. O conqueror of the riches, create for us the ecstasy, such thou becomest when thou art high kindled. Opulently in the gated house of thy felicitous adorer thou upholdest thy gliding bodies streaming their radiance.

GATHIN KAUSHIKA

Sukta 19

अग्निं होतारं प्र वृणे मियेधे गृत्सं कविं विश्वविदमसूरम् ।
स नो यक्षद् देवताता यजीयान् राये वाजाय वनते मघानि ॥१॥

1. Fire I choose the Priest of the call in the sacrifice, the wise, the seer, the omniscient, free from ignorance: he shall do worship for us strong for sacrifice, in the formation of the godheads; for the wealth, for the plenitude he wins all kinds of amassings.

प्र ते अग्ने हविष्मतीमियर्म्यच्छा सुद्युम्नां रातिनीं घृताचीम् ।
प्रदक्षिणिद् देवतातिमुराणः सं रातिभिर्वसुभिर्यज्ञमश्रेत् ॥२॥

---

[1] Or, as long as I have the power,

2. O Fire, I mission towards thee a power of giving bearing my oblation, luminous, full of lustres. May he come to the sacrifice with his givings, with his treasures turning round it and widening the formation of the godheads.

स तेजीयसा मनसा त्वोत उत शिक्ष स्वपत्यस्य शिक्षोः ।
अग्ने रायो नृतमस्य प्रभूतौ भूयाम ते सुष्टुतयश्च वस्वः ॥३॥

3. So, am I guarded by thee with a mind of shining energy; then do thou teach us of the riches that teach and that give us good children of our works. O Fire, may we become affirmers of thee by our lauds and rich in the power of a wealth most full of the strength of the gods.

भूरीणि हि त्वे दधिरे अनीकाऽग्ने देवस्य यज्यवो जनासः ।
स आ वह देवताति यविष्ठ शर्धो यदद्य विश्यं यजासि ॥४॥

4. For, many flame-forces they have founded in thee, O Fire, men who have the will to sacrifice to the godhead. So, bring to us the formation of the godhead, O youthful god, when thou worshippest with sacrifice the divine host today.

यत् त्वा होतारमनजन् मियेधे निषादयन्तो यजथाय देवाः ।
स त्वं नो अग्नेऽविहेह बोध्यधि श्रवांसि धेहि नस्तनूषु ॥५॥

5. Since the gods seating thee for sacrifice have anointed thee as Priest of the call in the rite, so do thou, O Fire, awake here as our protector and found thy inspirations in our bodies.

SUKTA 20

अग्निमूषससमद्विना दधिक्रां व्युष्टिषु हवते वह्लिरुक्यैः ।
सुज्योतिषो नः शृण्वन्तु देवाः सजोषसो अध्वरं वावशानाः ॥१॥

1. Fire and dawn and the two riders of the horse and Dadhi- kravan the Carrier of the offerings calls by his words in the dawnings. May the gods full of the Light hear us; may they desire and accept with a common pleasure our sacrifice.

अग्ने त्री ते वाजिना त्री षधस्या तिस्रस्ते जिह्वा ऋतजात पूर्वीः ।
तिस्र उ ते तन्वो देववातास्ताभिनंः पाहि गिरो अप्रयुच्छन् ॥२॥

2. O Fire, three are thy steeds, three the worlds of thy session;
   three are thy tongues, O thou born from the Truth, they are
   many: three too are thy bodies desired by the gods, with
   them protect undeviatingly our words.

अग्ने भूरीणि तव जातवेदो देव स्वधावोऽमृतस्य नाम ।
याश्च माया मायिनां विश्वमिन्व त्वे पूर्वीः संदधुः पृष्टबन्धो ॥३॥

3. Many are the names of thee, the Immortal, O Fire, O knower
   of the births, O god who bearest with thee the self-law of
   nature; all the manifold magic of the Lords of magic they
   have combined in thee, O all-ruler, O builder of the levels.

अग्निर्नेता भग इव क्षितीनां देवीनां देव ऋतुपा ऋतावा ।
स वृत्रहा सनयो विश्ववेदाः पर्षद् विश्वाति दुरिता गृणन्तम् ॥४॥

4. The Fire is as the Enjoyer the leader of the divine worlds,
   he is the divine guardian of the fixed time of things, and with
   him is the Truth. He is the slayer of the Coverer, the Eternal,
   the Omniscient; may he carry one who hymns him with the
   word beyond all the difficulty and stumbling.

दधिक्रामग्निमुषसं च देवीं बृहस्पतिं सवितारं च देवम् ।
अश्विना मित्रावरुणा भगं च वसून् रुद्राँ आदित्याँ इह हुवे ॥५॥

5. Dadhikravan, I call here, and the Fire, and the divine dawn,
   Brihaspati and the god Savitri, the two riders of the horse,
   and Mitra and Varuna and Bhaga, the Vasus, the Rudras,
   the Adityas.

SUKTA 21

इमं नो यज्ञममृतेषु धेहीमा हव्या जातवेदो जुषस्व ।
स्तोकानामग्ने मेदसो घृतस्य होतः प्राशान प्रथमो निषद्य ॥१॥

1. Found this our sacrifice in the immortals, accept these
    offerings, O knower of things born. O Priest of the call
    sitting as first and supreme, taste of the drops of understand-
    ing[1] and light.

घृतवन्तः पावक ते स्तोकाः श्चोतन्ति मेदसः ।
स्वधर्मन् देववीतये श्रेष्ठं नो धेहि वार्यम् ॥२॥

2. O purifying Fire, full of light there drip for thee drops of
    understanding; give us the supreme desirable thing in thy
    self-law for the advent of the gods.

तुभ्यं स्तोका घृतश्चुतोऽग्ने विप्राय सन्त्य ।
ऋषिः श्रेष्ठः समिध्यसे यज्ञस्य प्राविता भव ॥३॥

3. To thee, the illumined seer, come these drops dripping light,
    O right and true, O Fire; then thou blazest up as the su-
    preme Rishi. Become the protector of our sacrifice.

तुभ्यं श्चोतन्त्यधिगो शचीवः स्तोकासो अग्ने मेदसो घृतस्य ।
कविशस्तो बृहता भानुनागा हव्या जुषस्व मेधिर ॥४॥

4. On thee they fall, the drops of understanding and light, O
    unseizable[2] Ray! O thou with whom is the puissance!
    Declared by the seers of truth thou hast come with the vast
    light. Accept our offerings, O wise intelligence!

ओजिष्ठं ते मध्यतो मेव उद्भृतं प्र ते वयं वदामहे ।
श्चोतन्ति ते वसो स्तोका अधि त्वचि प्रति तान् देवशो विद्धि ॥५॥

5. Most full of energy is the understanding held up in the
    middle for thee, this is our gift to thee. The drops drip over
    thy skin, O shining one,[3] take them to thee in the way of the
    gods.

---

[1] Or, strength   [2] Or, uncontrollable   [3] Or, Lord of riches,

SUKTA 22

अयं सो अग्निर्यस्मिन् त्सोममिन्द्रः सुतं दधे जठरे वावशानः ।
सहस्रिणं वाजमत्यं न सप्ति ससवान् त्सन् त्स्तूयसे जातवेदः ॥१॥

1. This is that Fire in which Indra, desiring the wine, held it in
   his belly; our laud rises to thee because thou hast won the
   thousandfold plenitude as if a steed of swiftness, O knower
   of all things born!

अग्ने यत् ते दिवि वर्चः पृथिव्यां यदोषधीष्वप्स्वा यजत्र ।
येनान्तरिक्षमुर्वाततन्थ त्वेषः स भानुरर्णवो नृचक्षाः ॥२॥

2. O Fire, that splendour of thine which is in heaven and which
   is in the earth and its growths and its waters, O lord of sacrifice, by which thou hast extended the wide mid-air, it is a
   brilliant ocean of light in which is divine vision.

अग्ने दिवो अर्णमच्छा जिगास्यच्छा देवाँ ऊचिषे धिष्ण्या ये ।
या रोचने परस्तात् सूर्यस्य याश्चावस्ताद्उपतिष्ठन्त आपः ॥३॥

3. O Fire, thou goest towards the ocean of the sky, thou speak-
   est towards the gods who are masters of knowledge,[1] towards
   the waters that abide above in the luminous world of the sun
   and the waters that are below.

पुरीष्यासो अग्नयः प्रावणेभिः सजोषसः ।
जुषन्तां यज्ञमद्रुहोऽनमीवा इषो महीः ॥४॥

4. Let thy Fires that dwell in the waters joining with those that
   descend the slopes accept the sacrifice, mighty impelling
   forces, in which there is no harm nor any distress.

इळामग्ने पुरुदंसं सनिं गोः शश्वत्तमं हवमानाय साध ।
स्यान्नः सूनुस्तनयो विजावाऽग्ने सा ते सुमतिर्भूत्वस्मे ॥५॥

5. O Fire, achieve at my call the Revealing Speech the many-

---

[1] Or, the gods of the planes (seats),

actioned, the lasting conquest of the Light. May there be
for us a Son of our begetting pervading in his birth;[1] O Fire,
may there be created in us that true thinking of thine.

DEVASHRAVAS, DEVAVATA — BHARATAS

Sukta 23

निर्मथितः सुधित आ सधस्थे युवा कविरध्वरस्य प्रणेता ।
जूर्यत्स्वग्निरजरो वनेष्वत्रा दधे अमृतं जातवेदाः ॥१॥

1. Churned out and well-established in the house of his session,
   the Youth, the Seer, the leader of the pilgrim-sacrifice,
   imperishable in the perishing woodlands, the Fire, the
   knower of all things born, has founded here immortality.

अमन्थिष्टां भारता रेवदग्निं देवश्रवा देववातः सुदक्षम् ।
अग्ने वि पश्य बृहताभि रायेषां नो नेता भवतादनु द्यून् ॥२॥

2. The sons of the Bringer, god-inspired and god-beloved,
   have churned out Fire of the perfect discernment. O Fire,
   look widely on us with the vast riches, become the leader
   of our impulsions throughout the days.

दश क्षिपः पूर्व्य सीमजीजनन् त्सुजातं मातृषु प्रियम् ।
अग्निं स्तुहि दैववातं देवश्रवो यो जनानामसद् वशी ॥३॥

3. The ten who throw the Light have brought to birth all
   around the Ancient One well-born in his mothers and well-
   beloved. Affirm with lauds, O god-inspired, the Fire lit by
   the god-beloved, that he may be the controller of men.

नि त्वा दधे वर आ पृथिव्या इळायास्पदे सुदिनत्वे अह्नाम् ।
दृषद्वत्यां मानुष आपयायां सरस्वत्यां रेवदग्ने दिदीहि ॥४॥

4. One has set thee in the supreme seat of the earth, in the seat

---
[1] Or, himself a begetter;

of the Word of Revelation, in the happy brightness of the days: O Fire, opulently shine in the human being, in the river of rocks, in the stream of flowing waters, in the stream of inspiration.[1]

इळामग्ने पुरुदंसं सनि गोः शश्वत्तमं हवमानाय साध ।
स्यान्नः सूनुस्तनयो विजावाऽग्ने सा ते सुमतिर्भूत्वस्मे ॥५॥

5. O Fire, achieve at my call the Revealing Speech the many-actioned, the lasting conquest of the Light. May there be for us a Son of our begetting pervading in his birth;[2] O Fire, may there be created in us that true thinking of thine.

GATHINA VISHWAMITRA

SUKTA 24

अग्ने सहस्व पृतना अभिमातीरपास्य ।
दुष्टरस्तरन्नरातीर्बर्चो धा यज्ञवाहसे ॥१॥

1. O Fire, overpower the hostile armies, hurl them from us; hard to pierce, pierce the enemy-powers, found thy splendour in him who carries through the sacrifice.

अग्न इळा समिध्यसे वीतिहोत्रो अमर्त्यः ।
जुषस्व सू नो अध्वरम् ॥२॥

2. O Fire, thou art kindled by the word of revelation, the immortal who comes to the offering, accept wholly our pilgrim-sacrifice.

अग्ने द्युम्नेन जागृवे सहसः सूनवाहुत ।
एदं बर्हिः सदो मम ॥३॥

3. O Fire, ever-wakeful with thy light, O son of force, invoked sit on my seat of sacrifice.

---

[1] Or, in the river Drishadwati, in Apaya and in Saraswati.   [2] Or, himself a begetter;

अग्ने विश्वेभिरग्निभिर्देवेभिर्महृत्या गिरः ।
यज्ञेषु ये उ चायवः ॥४॥

4.   O Fire, with all thy divine fires greaten in our sacrifices the
word that has sight.

अग्ने दा दाशुषे रयिं वीरवन्तं परीणसम् ।
शिशीहि नः सूनुमतः ॥५॥

5.   O Fire, give to the giver a wealth full of hero-strengths en-
closing us; intensify the force in us having with us the Son.

SUKTA 25

अग्ने दिवः सूनुरसि प्रचेतास्तना पृथिव्या उत विश्ववेदाः ।
ऋधग्देवाँ इह यजा चिकित्वः ॥१॥

1.   O Fire, thou art the son of heaven by the body of the earth,
the conscious knower, even the omniscient. Sacrifice to each
god in turn, O thou who knowest.

अग्निः सनोति वीर्याणि विद्वान् त्सनोति वाजममृताय भूषन् ।
स नो देवाँ एह वह पुरुक्षो ॥२॥

2.   Fire the knower wins the hero-energies, wins the plenitudes
striving towards immortality. So do thou bring to us the
gods, O giver of the manifold plenty.

अग्निर्द्यावापृथिवी विश्वजन्ये आ भाति देवी अमृते अमूरः ।
क्षयन् वाजैः पुरुश्चन्द्रो नमोभिः ॥३॥

3.   The Fire, free from all ignorance, illumines Earth and
Heaven the divine and immortal mothers of all things; possessing all he is manifold in his delights by his plenitudes and
his dispensations.

अग्न इन्द्रश्च दाशुषो दुरोणे सुतावतो यज्ञमिहोप यातम् ।
अमर्धन्ता सोमपेयाय देवा ॥४॥

4. O Fire, and O Indra, here in the gated house of the giver
who offers the wine, come to the sacrifice, gods unforgetting,
for the drinking of the Soma-wine.

अग्ने अपां समिध्यसे दुरोणे नित्यः सूनो सहसो जातवेदः ।
सधस्थानि महयमान ऊती ॥५॥

5. O Fire, thou shinest high, eternal in the house of the waters,
O son of force, O knower of all things born, greatening
under thy guard the worlds of thy session.

SUKTA 26

वैश्वानरं मनसार्गिन निचाय्या हविष्मन्तो अनुषत्यं स्वर्विदम् ।
सुदानुं देवं रथिरं वसूयवो गीर्भी रण्वं कुशिकासो हवामहे ॥१॥

1. We the Kushikas, bringing the offering, desiring the Treasure, call by our words Fire, the universal godhead, discerning him by the mind, as the follower of the truth, who finds
the world of the sun, the great giver, the divine and rapturous charioteer.

तं शुभ्रमग्निमबसे हवामहे वैश्वानरं मातरिश्वानमुक्थ्यम् ।
बृहस्पतिं मनुषो देवतातये विप्रं श्रोतारमतिथिं रघुष्यदम् ॥२॥

2. We call to guard us that brilliant Fire, the universal godhead,
who grows in the mother, the master of the word, the speaker
and the hearer, for the human being's forming of the godhead, the illumined Seer, the Guest, the swift Traveller.

अश्वो न क्रन्दञ्जनिभिः समिध्यते वैश्वानरः कुशिकेभिर्युगेयुगे ।
स नो अग्निः सुवीर्यं स्वश्व्यं दधातु रत्नममृतेषु जागृविः ॥३॥

3. As if the neighing Horse by the mothers, the universal godhead is kindled high by the Kushikas from generation to
generation; may that Fire wakeful in the Immortals give to
us the hero-strength and good power of the Horse and the
ecstasy.

प्र यन्तु वाजास्तविषीभिरग्नयः शुभे संमिश्लाः पृषतीरयुक्षत ।
बृहदुक्षो मरुतो विश्ववेदसः प्र वेपयन्ति पर्वतां अदाभ्याः ॥४॥

4. Let them go forward, the plenitudes with the strengths, thy
Fires; they have yoked the dappled mares mingled together
to reach bliss and make the mountains tremble, before them
the life-gods, omniscient, pouring the Vast, inviolable.

अग्निश्रियो मरुतो विश्वकृष्टय आ त्वेषमुग्रमव ईमहे वयम् ।
ते स्वानिनो रुद्रिया वर्षनिर्णिजः सिंहा न हेषक्रतवः सुदानवः ॥५॥

5. The life-gods with their glory of fire, universal in the
peoples,[1] we desire as our brilliant and forceful guard; great
givers are they, thunderous and terrible, clothed as if in
raiment of rain, they are like roaring lions.

व्रातंव्रातं गणंगणं सुशस्तिभिरग्नेर्भामं मरुतामोज ईमहे ।
पृषदश्वासो अनवभ्रराधसो गन्तारो यज्ञं विदथेषु धीराः ॥६॥

6. Host upon host, troop upon troop with their proclaimings of
the Fire we desire the luminous energy of the life-gods; they
come to the sacrifice driving their dappled horses, their
achievement cannot be taken from them, they are wise thinkers in the discoveries of knowledge.

अग्निरस्मि जन्मना जातवेदा घृतं मे चक्षुरमृतं म आसन् ।
अर्कस्त्रिधातू रजसो विमानोऽजस्रो घर्मो हविरस्मि नाम ॥७॥

7. I am the Fire, I am from my birth the knower of all things
born; light is my eye, in my mouth is immortality; I am the
triple Ray, I am the measurer of the mid-world, I am the
unceasing illumination, I am the offering.

त्रिभिः पवित्रैरपुपोद्ध्यर्कं हृदा मतिं ज्योतिरनु प्रजानन् ।
वर्षिष्ठं रत्नमकृत स्वधाभिरादिद् द्यावापृथिवी पर्यपश्यत् ॥८॥

8. He has purified through the three filters the Ray, following
the thought with the heart he has reached knowledge of the

---

[1] Or, dragging all with them,

light; he has created by the self-laws of his nature the supreme ecstasy and his sight has embraced earth and heaven.

शतधारमुत्समक्षीयमाणं विपश्चितं पितरं वक्त्वानाम् ।
मेळि मदन्तं पित्रोरुपस्थे तं रोदसी पिपृतं सत्यवाचम् ॥९॥

9. He is a fountain with a hundred streams that is never exhausted, with his illumined consciousness he is the father and accorder of all that must be spoken; he takes his rapture in the lap of the Father and Mother and earth and heaven fill him full, the speaker of truth.

SUKTA 27

प्र वो वाजा अभिद्यवो हविष्मन्तो घृताच्या ।
देवाञ्जिगाति सुम्नयुः ॥१॥

1. Forward move the luminous plenitudes bearing the offering with the ladle of light; the seeker of bliss travels to the gods.

ईळे अग्निं विपश्चितं गिरा यज्ञस्य साधनम् ।
श्रुष्टीवानं घितावानम् ॥२॥

2. I pray by the word the Fire with its illumined consciousness, who accomplishes the sacrifice, who has the inspiration, who has the firm holding.

अग्ने शकेम ते वयं यमं देवस्य वाजिनः ।
अति द्वेषांसि तरेम ॥३॥

3. O Fire, may we have the power to rein thee, the divine steed of swiftness, may we cross through the hostile forces.

समिध्यमानो अध्वरेऽग्निः पावक ईड्यः ।
शोचिष्केशस्तमीमहे ॥४॥

4. Fire high-blazing in the rite of the path, Fire whom we must

pray, who purifies, with his tresses of flame — him we desire.

पृथुपाजा अमर्त्यो घृतनिर्णिक् स्वाहुतः ।

अग्निर्यज्ञस्य हव्यवाट् ॥५॥

5. He is the immortal, wide in might, clothed in raiment of light; well-fed with the oblation, Fire is the carrier of the offerings in the sacrifice.

तं सबाधो यतस्रुच इत्था धिया यज्ञवन्तः ।

आ चक्रुरग्निमूतये ॥६॥

6. Assailed by the opponent the doers of sacrifice, setting to work the ladle, keeping the true thought, have made the Fire to guard them.

होता देवो अमर्त्यः पुरस्तादेति माय्या ।

विदथानि प्रचोदयन् ॥७॥

7. The immortal, the godhead, the Priest of the call goes in our front with his mage-wisdom, impelling the discoveries of knowledge.

वाजी वाजेषु धीयतेऽध्वरेषु प्र णीयते ।

विप्रो यज्ञस्य साधनः ॥८॥

8. He is held as the Horse in the plenitudes, he is led along in the rites of the path, he is the illumined Seer who accomplishes the sacrifice.

धिया चक्रे वरेण्यो भूतानां गर्भमा दधे ।

दक्षस्य पितरं तना ॥९॥

9. He was made by the Thought, one Supreme;[1] it held the child of beings, the father of the Understanding in the body.[2]

---

[1] Or, the desirable one;

[2] Or, the daughter of the Understanding set him in us the child born from creatures and their father.

नि त्वा दधे वरेण्यं दक्षस्येळा सहस्कृत ।
अग्ने सुदीतिमुशिजम् ॥१०॥

10. The word of revelation born from the understanding sets thee within, one supreme, O thou forcefully created, O Fire, the perfect thinker and the aspirant.

अग्निं यन्तुरमप्तुरमृतस्य योगे वनुष: ।
विप्रा वाजं: समिन्धते ॥११॥

11. Fire the swift in motion, who crosses through the waters, the illumined seers desiring to conquer in the union with the Truth set ablaze by the plenitudes.

ऊर्जो नपातमध्वरे दीदिवांसमुप द्यवि ।
अग्निमीळे कविक्रतुम् ॥१२॥

12. I pray Fire, the Seer-Will, the Son of Energy flaming out in heaven in the rite of the path.

ईळेन्यो नमस्यस्तिरस्तमांसि दर्शत: ।
समग्निरिध्यते वृषा ॥१३॥

13. One to be prayed, to be worshipped with obeisance, one who sees[1] through the darkness, the Fire is kindled high, the male of the herd.

वृषो अग्नि: समिध्यतेऽश्वो न देववाहन: ।
तं हविष्मन्त ईळते ॥१४॥

14. Mighty and male the Fire is kindled high, he is like a horse that carries the gods, him they pray who bring the offerings.

वृषणं त्वा वयं वृषन् वृषण: समिधीमहि ।
अग्ने दीद्यतं बृहत् ॥१५॥

15. Thee, mighty and male, we male and mighty kindle high, O Bull of the herds, O Fire, and thou illuminest the Vast.

---

[1] Or, is seen

SUKTA 28

अग्ने जुषस्व नो हविः पुरोळाशं जातवेदः ।
प्रातःसावे धियावसो ॥१॥

1. O Fire, accept our offering, the frontal oblation in the dawn
   pressing of the wine, O knower of the births, O rich in
   thought.

पुरोळा अग्ने पचतस्तुभ्यं वा घा परिष्कृतः ।
तं जुषस्व यविष्ठय ॥२॥

2. O Fire, for thee is the frontal offering prepared and dressed,
   that accept, O youthful god.

अग्ने वीहि पुरोळाशमाहुतं तिरोअह्न्यम् ।
सहसः सूनुरस्यध्वरे हितः ॥३॥

3. O Fire, come to[1] the frontal offering that is cast to thee with
   the disappearance of day; O son of force, thou art established in the rite of the path.

माध्यंदिने सवने जातवेदः पुरोळाशमिह कवे जुषस्व ।
अग्ने यह्वस्य तव भागधेयं न प्र मिनन्ति विदथेषु धीराः ॥४॥

4. In the noonday pressing of the wine, O seer, knower of all
   things born, accept the frontal offering. O Fire, the wise
   thinkers in their discoveries of knowledge impair not thy
   portion, who art the mighty one.

अग्ने तृतीये सवने हि कानिषः पुरोळाशं सहसः सूनवाहुतम् ।
अथा देवेष्वध्वरं विपन्यया घा रत्नवन्तममृतेषु जागृविम् ॥५॥

5. O Fire, in the third pressing also thou hast desire of the
   frontal offering cast to thee, O son of force; do thou by the
   illumination establish in the gods the pilgrim-sacrifice full of
   ecstasy and wakeful in the immortals.

---

[1] Or, devour

अग्ने वृधान आहुति पुरोळाशं जातवेदः ।
जुषस्व तिरोअह्न्यम् ॥६॥

6. O Fire, increasing accept the frontal offering, the oblation
cast with the disappearance of the day, O knower of all
things born.

SUKTA 29

अस्तीदमधिमन्थनमस्ति प्रजननं कृतम् ।
एतां विश्पत्नीमा भराग्निं मन्थाम पूर्वथा ॥१॥

1. This is the churning out, this the bringing to birth that is
done; bring the Queen of the peoples, let us churn out the
Fire as of old.

अरण्योर्निहितो जातवेदा गर्भं इव सुधितो गर्भिणीषु ।
दिवेदिव ईड्यो जागृवद्भिर्हविष्मद्भिर्मनुष्येभिरग्निः ॥२॥

2. The knower of all births is set in the two tinders, like an unborn child well-placed in the womb of the mothers, Fire who
is to be prayed from day to day by men wakeful and bearing
their offering.

उत्तानायामव भरा चिकित्वान् त्सद्यः प्रवीता वृषणं जजान ।
अरुषस्तूपो रुशदस्य पाज इळायास्पुत्रो वयुनेऽजनिष्ट ॥३॥

3. Waking to knowledge bring him down in her lying supine; at
once penetrated she has brought to birth the male of the
herd: a ruddy pile of strength his might shines forth, the son
of the Word of revelation is born in the manifestation of
knowledge.

इळायास्त्वा पदे वयं नाभा पृथिव्या अधि ।
जातवेदो नि धीमह्यग्ने हव्याय वोळ्हवे ॥४॥

4. We in the seat of the Word of revelation, on the navel-centre

of the earth, set thee within, O knower of all things born, for the carrying of the oblations.

मन्यता नरः कविमद्ध्वयन्तं प्रचेतसममृतं सुप्रतीकम् ।
यज्ञस्य केतुं प्रथमं पुरस्तादग्निं नरो जनयता सुश्रेवम् ॥५॥

5. Churn out, O men, the seer who creates no duality, the immortal thinker and knower with his fair front; Fire who is the supreme intuition in the sacrifice, the blissful one, bring to birth in your front, O men.

यदी मन्यन्ति बाहुभिर्वि रोचतेऽइवो न वाज्यरुषो वनेष्वा ।
चित्रो न यामश्रिवनोरनिवृतः परि वृणक्त्यश्मनस्तृणा दहन् ॥६॥

6. When they churn him out by the strength of their arms wide he shines, he is like a horse of swiftness, he is luminous in the woodlands; he is like a richly hued chariot in the journeying of the two riders, none can impede him; burning around the rocks he tears the grasses.

जातो अग्नी रोचते चेकितानो वाजी विप्रः कविशस्तः सुवानुः ।
यं देवास ईड्यं विश्वविदं हव्यवाहमदधुरध्वरेषु ॥७॥

7. Agni when he is born shines waking to knowledge, he is the Horse, the illumined who is declared by the seers, the great giver, whom the gods have set in the pilgrim-sacrifices as the carrier of the offerings, the one to be prayed, the omniscient.

सीद होतः स्व उ लोके चिकित्वान् त्सादया यज्ञं सुकृतस्य योनौ ।
देवावीर्देवान् हविषा यजास्यग्ने बृहद् यजमाने वयो धाः ॥८॥

8. Sit, O Priest of the call, in that world which is thy own waking to knowledge, accomplish the sacrifice in the native seat of deeds well done; manifesting the godheads[1] thou sacrificest to the gods with the offering, — O Fire, found in the sacrificer the vast expansion.

---

[1] Or, bringing the gods

कृणोत धूमं वृषणं सखायोऽस्मेधन्त इतन वाजमच्छ ।
अयमग्निः पृतनाषाट् सुवीरो येन देवासो असहन्त दस्यून् ॥९॥

9. O Friends, create his mighty smoke, go with unerring steps towards the plenitude; this is the Fire conqueror in the battle, by whom the gods overcame the destroyers.

अयं ते योनिर्ऋत्विययो यतो जातो अरोचथाः ।
तं जानन्नग्न आ सीदाथा नो वर्धया गिरः ॥१०॥

10. This is thy native seat where is the order of the Truth whence born thou shonest forth, know it and take there thy session, then give increase to our words.

तनूनपादुच्यते गर्भं आसुरो नराशंसो भवति यद् विजायते ।
मातरिश्वा यदमिमीत मातरि वातस्य सर्गो अभवत् सरीमणि ॥११॥

11. A mighty child in the womb he is called the son of the body; when he is born he becomes one who voices the godhead: when as life who grows in the mother he has been fashioned in the mother he becomes a gallop of wind in his movement.

सुनिर्मंथा निर्मथितः सुनिधा निहितः कविः ।
अग्ने स्वध्वरा कृणु देवान् देवयते यज ॥१२॥

12. Churned out with the good churning the seer set within with a perfect placing, — O Fire, make easy the paths of the sacrifice, offer sacrifice to the gods for the seeker of godhead.

अजीजनन्नमृतं मर्त्यासोऽस्मेमाणं तरणि वीळुजम्भम् ।
दश स्वसारो अपुवः समीची: पुमांसं जातमभि सं रभन्ते ॥१३॥

13. Mortals have brought to birth the Immortal, Fire with his strong tusk, the unfailing deliverer.[1] The ten sisters who move as companions passion over the male that is born.

प्र सप्तहोता सनकादरोचत मातुरुपस्थे यदशोचदूधनि ।
न नि मिषति सुरणो दिवेदिवे यदसुरस्य जठरादजायत ॥१४॥

---

[1] Or, one who unfailing crosses through all.

14. He shone out from the eternal with his seven priests of the
call when he blazed on the lap of the mother, in her bosom
of plenty. He is full of joy and closes not his eyes from day
to day, once he has been born from the belly of the Almighty
One.

अमित्रायुधो मरुतामिव प्रयाः प्रथमजा ब्रह्मणो विश्वमिद् विदुः ।
द्युम्नवद् ब्रह्म कुशिकास एरिर एकएको दमे अग्निं समीधिरे ॥१५॥

15. Fighting down the unfriendly powers like the marching
hosts of the life-gods the first-born of the Word come to
know all that is: the Kushikas have sent forth the luminous
word, one by one they have kindled the Fire in the house.

यदद्य त्वा प्रयति यज्ञे अस्मिन् होतश्चिकित्वोऽवृणीमहीह ।
ध्रुवमया ध्रुवमुताशमिष्ठाः प्रजानन् विद्वाँ उप याहि सोमम् ॥१६॥

16. Because here today in the going forward of this sacrifice we
have chosen thee, O Priest of the call, O thou who wakest to
knowledge, thou hast moved to the Permanent, thou hast
achieved by thy toil the Permanent; knowing, come as one
possessed of knowledge to the Soma-wine.

MANDALA FOUR

MANDALA FOUR

VAMADEVA GAUTAMA

Sukta 1

तव्रं ह्यग्ने सदमित् समन्यवो देवासो देवमरतिं न्येरिर इति कृत्वा न्येरिरे ।
अमर्त्यं यजत मर्त्येष्वा देवमादेवं जनत प्रचेतसं विश्वमादेवं जनत प्रचेतसम् ॥१॥

1. Thee, O Fire, ever with one passion the gods have sent inwards, the divine Traveller;[1] with the will they sent thee in; O master of sacrifice, they brought to birth the immortal in mortals, the divine who brings in the divinity, the conscious thinker, they brought to birth the universal who brings in the divinity, the conscious thinker.

स भ्रातरं वरुणमग्न आ ववृत्स्व देवाँ अच्छा सुमती यज्ञवनसं ज्येष्ठं यज्ञवनसम् ।
ऋतावानमादित्यं चर्षणीधृतं राजानं चर्षणीधृतम् ॥२॥

2. Then do thou, O Fire, turn towards the godheads with the right thinking Varuna, thy brother who delights in the sacrifice, the eldest who delights in the sacrifice, — even him who keeps the truth, son of the infinite Mother who upholds seeing-men, the king who upholds seeing-men.

सखे सखायमभ्या ववृत्स्वाशुं न चक्रं रथ्येव रंहास्मभ्यं दस्म रंह्या ।
अग्ने मृळीकं वरुणे सचा विदो मरुत्सु विश्वभानुषु ।
तोकाय तुजे शुशुचान शं कृध्यस्मभ्यं दस्म शं कृधि ॥३॥

3. O Friend, turn towards and to us in his motion the Friend as two rapid chariot-horses turn a swift wheel, for us, O strong worker, like galloping horses; O Fire, mayst thou be with us and find for us bliss in Varuna and in the Life-powers who carry the universal light; for the begetting of the Son, O thou flaming into lustre, create for us peace, for us, O strong worker, create the peace.

---

[1] Or, worker; this root seems to have indicated originally any strong motion, action or work.

तं नो अग्ने वरुणस्य विद्वान् देवस्य हेळोऽव यासिसीष्ठाः ।
यजिष्ठो वह्नितमः शोशुचानो विश्वा द्वेषांसि प्र मुमुग्ध्यस्मत् ॥४॥

4. Do thou, O Fire, for thou knowest, labour away from us the wrath of divine Varuna; flaming into lustre, strongest to sacrifice, mightiest to bear, unloose from us all hostile powers.

स त्वं नो अग्नेऽवमो भवोती नेदिष्ठो अस्या उषसो व्युष्टौ ।
अव यक्ष्व नो वरुणं रराणो वीहि मृळीकं सुहवो न एधि ॥५॥

5. Do thou, O Fire, be most close to us with thy protection, be most near in the dawning of this dawn: rejoicing in us put away from us Varuna[1] by the sacrifice; reach the bliss, be ready to our call.

अस्य श्रेष्ठा सुभगस्य संदृग् देवस्य चित्रतमा मर्त्येषु ।
शुचि घृतं न तप्तमघ्न्यायाः स्पार्हा देवस्य मंहनेव धेनोः ॥६॥

6. Most glorious is the vision of this Godhead, most richly bright in mortals; as if the pure and warm butter of the milch-cow that cannot be slain, her desirable gift is the vision of the Godhead.[2]

त्रिरस्य ता परमा सन्ति सत्या स्पार्हा देवस्य जनिमान्यग्नेः ।
अनन्ते अन्तः परिवीत आगाच्छुचिः शुक्रो अर्यो रोरुचानः ॥७॥

7. Three are they, his supreme truths, the desirable births of the divine Fire; within in the infinite he is spread wide everywhere and has come to us pure and brilliant and noble,

----

[1] i.e. the pressure of the wrath of Varuna against our impurity.

The prayer to put Varuna away sounds strange. But if the inner sense is grasped it becomes cogent and apposite. The sacrificer — the seeker — is praying Agni to be close to him, to protect him. He is aspiring that the Divine Fire should be his protector when the Dawn of the higher light comes to his soul, Varuna being the Lord of wisdom.

[2] Here the connection between Fire and Ray-Cow and Aditi comes out; so also the psychological nature of the clarified butter and its connection with the vision of the Sun.

Who is this cow that "cannot be slain" if not the cow *aditi* — the Infinite Mother — the supreme Divine Consciousness creative of the cosmos, of the gods and the demons, of men and of all that is?

shining in his beauty.[1] One who has spread wide within in the infinite; he in his luminous beauty comes to us.

स दूतो विश्ववेदभि वष्टि सद्या होता हिरण्यरथो रंसुजिह्वः ।
रोहिदश्वो वपुष्यो विभावा सदा रण्वः पितुमतीव संसत् ॥८॥

8. He is a messenger, a Priest of the call, whose yearning is towards all the planes, golden is his chariot, red are his horses, ecstatic his tongue of flame, beautiful his body,[2] wide his lustre, ever is he rapturous like a banquet hall full of the wine.[3]

स चेतयन्मनुषो यज्ञबन्धुः प्र तं मह्या रशनया नयन्ति ।
स क्षेत्यस्य दुर्यासु साधन् देवो मर्तस्य सधनित्वमाप ॥९॥

9. He makes men conscious of the knowledge and is the friend of their sacrifice; they lead him on with a mighty cord; he dwells in the gated house of the being accomplishing his aims; divine, he accepts companionship in the riches of the mortal.

स तू नो अग्निर्नयतु प्रजानन्नच्छा रत्नं देवभक्तं यदस्य ।
धिया यद् विश्वे अमृता अकृण्वन् द्यौष्पिता जनिता सत्यमुक्षन् ॥१०॥

10. Let this Fire taking knowledge of all things lead us towards the ecstasy. That is enjoyed by the Gods, which all the immortals created by the thought, and Father Heaven was its begetter raining the truth.[4]

स जायत प्रथमः पस्त्यासु महो बुध्नें रजसो अस्य योनौ ।
अपादशीर्षा गुहमानो अन्ताऽऽयोयुवानो वृषभस्य नीळे ॥११॥

---

[1] These three births of Fire are not, as usually explained, its three physical forms — which even if accepted (taken) shows the Vedic people far from the mere primitive barbarian — His birth is connected with Truth — His births are "within in the Infinite" — *saccidānanda*. These are the three levels of the earthly evolution on each of which this Divine Fire takes his birth, *parivītaḥ*, on the plane of matter and life and mind.

[2] Or, great is his body, [3] Or, well-stored with food.

[4] This joy — *ratna* — in its origin is created by the immortals with the help of their "thought" — and it was the raining down upon the lower hemisphere of the Truth that gave birth to the joy here.

11. He was born first and supreme in the Rivers,[1] in the founda-
     tion of the vast mid-world, in his native seat; without head,
     without feet, concealing his two ends he joins them in the
     lair of the Bull.[2]

प्र शर्ध आर्तं प्रथमं विपन्यां ऋतस्य योना वृषभस्य नीळे ।
स्पार्हो युवा वपुष्यो विभावा सप्त प्रियासोऽजनयन्त वृष्णे ॥१२॥

12. He came forth with a vibrancy of light, the first and supreme
     force, in the native seat of Truth, in the lair of the Bull,
     desirable and young and beautiful of body[3] and wide in
     lustre; the seven Beloved brought him to birth for the Bull.[4]

अस्माकमत्र पितरो मनुष्या अभि प्र सेदुर्ऋतमाशुषाणाः ।
अश्मव्रजाः सुदुघा वव्रे अन्तरुधा आजन्नुषसो हुवानाः ॥१३॥

13. Here, our human fathers went forward on their way towards
     the Truth desiring to possess it; they drove upwards the
     luminous ones, the good milk-cows in their stone (rocky)
     pen within the hiding cave, calling to the Dawns.[5]

ते ममृजत ददृवांसो अद्रि तदेषामन्ये अभितो वि वोचन् ।
पश्वयन्त्रासो अभि कारमर्वन् विदन्त ज्योतिश्चक्रुपन्त धीभिः ॥१४॥

14. They rent the hill, they made themselves bright and pure,
     others around them proclaimed that work of theirs; drivers
     of the herd,[6] they sang the chant of illumination to the
     Doer of the work; they found the Light, they shone with
     their thoughts.[7]

---

[1] Or, in our habitations,
[2] The same Fire joins his two extremities of the superconscient and the spirit and the
inconscient matter — in the lair of the Bull. This is the Bull which represents the Purusha....
The lair of the Bull is the original status of Him called at other places, *viṣṇoḥ paramaṁ padam,
sadā paśyanti sūrayaḥ.*
    [3] Or, great in body   [4] Or, brought to birth the Bull (but the case is Dative).
    [5] This Rik makes the connection between the hidden cows and the Truth, also the Cows
and the Dawn.
    [6] Literally, having the control over the animal or animals, or, the "instruments of con-
trol",
    [7] Or, they did work by their thoughts. This is Sayana's interpretation.

ते गव्यता मनसा दृढ्रमुब्धं गा येमानं परि षन्तमद्रिम् ।
दृळ्हं नरो वचसा दैव्येन व्रजं गोमन्तमुशिजो बि वव्रुः ॥१५॥

15. By a mind seeking the Rays they rent the firm massed hill
which encircled and repressed the shining herds; men desiring laid open the strong pen full of the Ray-Cows by the
divine word.

ते मन्वत प्रथमं नाम धेनोस्त्रिः सप्त मातुः परमाणि विन्दन् ।
तज्जानतीरभ्यनूषत व्रा आविर्भुवदरुणीर्यंशसा गोः ॥१६॥

16. They meditated[1] on the first name of the Milk-cow, they
discovered the thrice seven supreme planes[2] of the mother;
That knowing the herds lowed towards it, the ruddy Dawn
became manifest by the glory of the Cow of Light.

नेशत् तमो दुधितं रोचत द्यौरुद् देव्या उषसो भानुरर्त ।
आ सूर्यो बृहतस्तिष्ठदज्राँ ऋजु मर्तेषु वृजिना च पश्यन् ॥१७॥

17. The darkness was wounded and vanished, Heaven shone
out, up arose the light of the divine Dawn, the Sun entered
into the fields of the Vast, looking on the straight and
crooked things in mortals.

आदित् पश्चा बुबुधाना व्यख्यन्नादिद् रत्नं धारयन्त द्युभक्तम् ।
विश्वे विश्वासु दुर्यासु देवा मित्र धिये वरुण सत्यमस्तु ॥१८॥

18. Then, indeed, they awoke and saw[3] all behind and wide
around them, then, indeed, they held the ecstasy that is
enjoyed in heaven. In all gated houses were all the gods. O
Mitra, O Varuna, let there be the Truth for the Thought.

अच्छा वोचेय शुशुचानमग्निं होतारं विश्वभरसं यजिष्ठम् ।
शुच्यूधो अतृणन्न गवामन्धो न पूतं परिषिक्तमंशोः ॥१९॥

19. May my speech be towards the upblazing Fire, the Priest
of the call, the bringer of all things, strong to sacrifice. It

---

[1] Or, held in their thought   [2] Or, names
[3] Then, indeed, and after waking they wholly saw

is as if one drank from the pure udder of the cows of light, the purified juice of the Plant of Delight poured on all sides.

विश्वेषामदितिर्यज्ञियानां विश्वेषामतिथिर्मानुषाणाम् ।
अग्निर्देवानामव आवृणानः सुमृळीको भवतु जातवेदाः ॥२०॥

20. The indivisibility of all the gods, the guest of all human beings, may the Fire draw to us the protection of the gods and be blissful to us, the knower of all things born.

SUKTA 2

यो मर्त्येष्वमृत ऋतावा देवो देवेष्वरतिर्निधायि ।
होता यजिष्ठो मह्ना शुचध्यै हव्येरग्निर्मनुष ईरयध्यै ॥१॥

1. He who is immortal in mortals and with him is the Truth, who is the God in the gods, the Traveller,[1] has been set within as the Priest of the call, most strong for sacrifice, to blaze out with the might of his flame, to give men speed on the way by the power of their offerings.

इह त्वं सूनो सहसो नो अद्य जातो जातां उभयां अन्तरग्ने ।
दूत ईयसे युयुजान ऋष्व ऋजुमुष्कान् वृषणः शुक्रांश्च ॥२॥

2. O Son of Force, here today art thou born for us and movest as a messenger between those born of both the Births, yoking, O sublime Flame, thy males straight and massive and bright in lustre.

अत्या वृधस्नू रोहिता घृतस्नू ऋतस्य मन्ये मनसा जविष्ठा ।
अन्तरीयसे अरुषा युजानो युष्मांश्च देवान् विश आ च मर्तान् ॥३॥

3. I hold in thought with my mind thy two red gallopers of the Truth, swiftest, raining increase, raining light; yoking the ruddy-shining pair thou movest between you Gods and the mortal peoples.

---

[1] Or, fighter or worker,

अर्यमणं वरुणं मित्रमेषामिन्द्राविष्णू मरुतो अश्विनोत ।
स्वश्वो अग्ने सुरथः सुराधा एदु वह सुहविषे जनाय ॥४॥

4. Aryaman for them and Mitra and Varuna, Indra, Vishnu
   and the Maruts and the Ashwins do thou well-horsed, well-
   charioted, great in the joy of achievement, bring now, O Fire,
   for the giver of good offerings.

गोमाँ अग्नेऽविमाँ अश्वी यज्ञो नृवत्सखा सदमिदप्रमृष्यः ।
इळावाँ एषो असुर प्रजावान् दीर्घो रयिः पृथुबुध्नः सभावान् ॥५॥

5. O Fire, ever inviolable is this sacrifice and with it is the Cow,
   the Sheep and the Horse, it is like a human friend,[1] and with
   it, O mighty Lord, are the word and the offspring; it is a
   long felicity of riches with a wide foundation, and with it is
   the hall.

यस्त इध्मं जभरत् सिष्विदानो मूर्धानं वा ततपते त्वाया ।
भुवस्तस्य स्वतवाँ पायुरग्ने विश्वस्मात् सीमघायत उरुष्य ॥६॥

6. To him who brings to thee thy fuel with the sweat of his
   labour and heats his head with thee, be a protector in thy
   self-strength, O Fire, and guard him from all around that
   would do him evil.

यस्ते भरादन्नियते चिदन्नं निशिषन्मन्द्रमतिथिमुदीरत् ।
आ देवयुरिनक्षते दुरोणे तस्मिन् रयिर्ध्रुवो अस्तु दास्वान् ॥७॥

7. He who when thou desirest thy food brings thy food to thee,
   who whets thy flame and sends upwards the rapturous guest,
   he who as seeker of the godhead kindles thee in his gated
   house, in him may there be the abiding and bounteous riches.

यस्त्वा दोषा य उषसि प्रशंसात् प्रियं वा त्वा कृणवते हविष्मान् ।
अश्वो न स्वे दम आ हेम्यावान् तमंहसः पीपरो दाश्वांसम् ॥८॥

8. He who in the dusk, he who in the dawn would give expression to thee, or bringing his offering makes thee a beloved

---

[1] Or, it is a comrade with whom are the gods,

friend, as the Horse with golden trappings in his own home mayst thou carry that giver beyond the evil.

यस्तुभ्यमग्ने अमृताय दाशद् दुवस्त्वे कृणवते यतस्रुक् ।
न स राया शशमानो वि योषन्नैनमंहः परि वरदघायोः ॥९॥

9. He who gives to thee, O Fire, to the Immortal, and does in thee the work outstretching the Ladle, may he not in his labour be divorced from the riches, let not the sin of one who would do evil surround him.

यस्य त्वमग्ने अध्वरं जुजोषो देवो मर्तस्य सुधितं रराणः ।
प्रीतेदसद्धोत्रा सा यविष्ठाऽसाम यस्य विधतो वृधासः ॥१०॥

10. He in whose pilgrim-rite thou takest pleasure and, divine, takest delight in the well-founded work of a mortal, may the Power of the Call be pleased with him, O most young Fire, of whom worshipping may we bring about the increase.

चित्तिमचित्ति चिनवद् वि विद्वान् पृष्ठेव वीता वृजिना च मर्तान् ।
राये च नः स्वपत्याय देव दिति च रास्वादितिमुरुष्य ॥११॥

11. Let the knower discriminate the Knowledge and the Ignorance, the straight open levels and the crooked that shut in mortals; O God, for the riches, for the right birth of the Son,[1] lavish on us the finite and guard the Infinite.[2]

कवि शशासुः कवयोऽद्बधा निधारयन्तो दुर्यास्वायोः ।
अतस्त्वं दृश्यां अग्न एतान् पड्भिः पश्येरद्भुतां अर्यं एवैः ॥१२॥

12. Seers unconquered proclaimed the seer, they established him[3] within in the gated house of the human being. Then, O Flame, mayst thou reach with thy journeying feet and, exalted, see those transcendent[4] ones who must come into our vision.[5]

---

[1] Or, for the riches with the fair offspring,
[2] Diti and Aditi, the divided and the undivided Consciousness, the Mother of division and the Indivisible Mother.
[3] Or, commanded the seer, they upheld him   [4] Or, wonderful
[5] Or, made visible; the word means either "visible" or "to be seen".

त्वमग्ने वाघते सुप्रणीतिः सुतसोमाय विघते यविष्ठ ।
रत्नं भर शशमानाय घृष्वे पृथु इचन्द्रमवसे चर्षणिप्राः ॥१३॥

13. O Fire, ever most young, mayst thou giving thy good leading
    to the singer of the word who has pressed the wine and
    performed the sacrifice, bring to him in his labour, lumi-
    nous one, an ecstasy wide in its delight, filling the seeing man
    for his safeguard.

अधा ह यद् वयमग्ने त्वाया पड्भिर्हस्तेभिश्चकृमा तनूभिः ।
रथं न क्रन्तो अपसा भुरिजोर्ऋतं येमुः सुध्य आशुषाणाः ॥१४॥

14. O Fire, as we have done with our hands, with our feet, with
    our bodies in our desire of thee, like men who make a chariot
    with the toil of their two arms, so, the wise thinkers have
    laboured out the Truth and possess it.[1]

अधा मातुरुष्वसः सप्त विप्रा जायेमहि प्रयमा वेधसो नॄन् ।
दिवस्पुत्रा अङ्गिरसो भवेमाऽद्रि रुजेम धनिनं शुचन्तः ॥१५॥

15. Now may we be born as the seven illumined seers of the
    Dawn, the mother, supreme creators creating the Gods with-
    in us; may we become the Angirasas, sons of Heaven and,
    shining with light, break the hill that has within it the riches.

अधा यथा नः पितरः परासः प्रत्नासो अग्न ऋतमाशुषाणाः ।
शुचीदयन् दीधितिमुक्थशासः क्षामा भिन्दन्तो अरुणीरप व्रन् ॥१६॥

16. Now, too, O Fire, even as our supreme and ancient fathers,
    desiring to possess the Truth, speakers of the word, reached
    the very purity, reached the splendour of the Light;[2] as they
    broke through the earth and uncovered the ruddy herds.

सुकर्मणः सुरुचो देवयन्तोऽप्यो न देवा जनिमा धमन्तः ।
शुचन्तो अग्निं ववृधन्त इन्द्रमूर्वं गव्यं परिषदन्तो अग्मन् ॥१७॥

17. Perfect in action, perfect in lustre, desiring the godhead,

---

[1] Or, desiring to possess it.   [2] Or, entered into meditation and reached the very purity;

12

becoming gods, they smelted and forged the Births as one
forges iron, flaming with light they made the Fire to grow,
surrounding Indra they reached the wide mass of the Ray-
Cows.

आ यूथेव क्षुमति पश्वो अख्यद् देवानां यज्जनिमान्त्युग्र ।
मर्तानां चिद्‌उर्वशीरक्कृप्रन् वृषे चिदर्य उपरस्यायोः ॥१८॥

18. There was seen as if herds of the Cows in an opulent place,
     that which, seen near, was the birth of the gods,[1] O Forceful
     Fire; they both illumined[2] the widenesses of mortals and
     were aspirants for the growth[3] of the higher being.

अकर्मं ते स्वपसो अभूम ऋतमवबलमुषसो विभातीः ।
अनूनमग्निं पुरुधा सुश्चन्द्रं देवस्य मर्मृजतश्चार चक्षुः ॥१९॥

19. For thee we worked and became perfect in our works, the
     Dawn shone out and illumined the Truth; we lit the un-
     stinted Fire in the multitude of its kinds, in the fullness of
     his delight, brightening the beautiful eye of the Godhead.

एता ते अग्न उचथानि वेधोऽवोचाम कवये ता जुषस्व ।
उच्छोचस्व कृणुहि वस्यसो नो महो रायः पुरुवार प्र यन्धि ॥२०॥

20. These are the utterances, O creator, O Fire, we have spoken
     to thee the seer, in them take pleasure. Flame upwards,
     make us move full of possessions; O thou of many boons,
     give us the Great Riches.

SUKTA 3

आ वो राजानमध्वरस्य रुद्रं होतारं सत्ययजं रोदस्योः ।
अग्निं पुरा तनयित्नोरचित्ताद्धिरण्यरूपमवसे कृणुध्वम् ॥१॥

---

[1] Or, there was seen like herds of the Cow in an opulent place that which is near to the
birth of the godheads,

[2] Or, achieved the wide illuminations of mortals   [3] Or, warriors for the growth

1. Create for yourselves the King of the pilgrim-rite, the Terrible, the Priest of the invocation who wins by sacrifice the Truth in earth and heaven,[1] create Fire golden in his form for your protection before the outspreading of the Ignorance.[2]

अयं योनिश्चकृमा यं वयं ते जायेव पत्य उशती सुवासाः ।
अर्वाचीनः परिवीतो नि षीदेमा उ ते स्वपाक प्रतीचीः ॥२॥

2. This is thy seat which we have made for thee, even as, desiring, a wife richly robed for her lord; thou art turned towards us and wide-extended around, sit here within: O once far distant Fire, these are fronting thee, O Fire, perfect in wisdom.

आशृण्वते अवृपिताय मन्म नृचक्षसे सुमृळीकाय वेधः ।
देवाय शस्तिममृताय शंस प्रावेव सोता मधुषुद् यमीळे ॥३॥

3. O ordinant of sacrifice, to Fire that hears, inviolate, the strong in vision, the happy, the immortal Godhead speak the Thought, the word expressing him, whom I pray as with the voice of the stone of the pressing when it presses out the honey-wine.

त्वं चिप्रः शम्या अग्ने अस्या ऋतस्य बोध्यृतचित् स्वाधीः ।
कदा त उक्था सधमाद्यानि कदा भवन्ति सख्या गृहे ते ॥४॥

4. Thou, too, O Fire, turn towards our labour, become aware of this word, in perfect answer of thy thought, Truth-Conscious, become aware of the Truth. When shall there be thy utterances that share in our ecstasy, when thy acts of companionship in the house?

कथा ह तद् वरुणाय त्वमग्ने 'कथा दिवे गर्हसे कन्न आगः ।
कथा मित्राय मीळ्हुषे पृथिव्यै ब्रवः कदर्यम्णे कद् भगाय ॥५॥

[1] Or, who worships with sacrifice the Truth for earth and heaven,
[2] Or, before the thunder-crash from the unknown.

5. How dost thou blame it, O Fire, to Varuna, to Heaven, what is that sin we have done? How wouldst thou speak of us to Mitra, the bountiful, how to earth? What wilt thou say to Aryaman, what to Bhaga?

कद् धिष्ण्यासु वृधसानो अग्ने कद् वाताय प्रतवसे शुभंये ।
परिज्मने नासत्याय क्षे ब्रवः कदग्ने रुद्राय नृघ्ने ॥६॥

6. What, O Fire, growing in thy abodes, wouldst thou say for us, what to the wind most forceful, to the seeker of the Good, the all-pervading, to the lord of the journey, to the earth? What, O Fire, to Rudra the slayer of men?

कथा महे पुर्ष्टिभराय पूष्णे कद् रुद्राय सुमखाय हविर्दे ।
कद् विष्णव उरुगायाय रेतो ब्रवः कदग्ने शरवे बृहत्यै ॥७॥

7. How wilt thou speak of us to Pushan, the mighty bringer of increase, what to Rudra great in sacrifice, giver of the offering? What seed of things to wide-striding Vishnu, or what, O Fire, to vast doom?

कथा शर्धाय मरुतामृताय कथा सुरे बृहते पृच्छयमानः ।
प्रति ब्रवोऽदितये तुराय साधा दिवो जातवेदश्चिकित्वान् ॥८॥

8. How when they question thee wouldst thou answer to the host of the Life-Gods in their Truth, or to the Sun in his vastness, to the mother indivisible, to the swift traveller? O knower of all things born, thou knowest the Heaven, for us accomplish.

ऋतेन ऋतं नियतमीळ आ गोरामा सचा मधुमत् पक्वमग्ने ।
कृष्णा सती रुशता धासिनैषा जामर्येण पयसा पीपाय ॥९॥

9. I ask for the truth governed by the Truth, together the unripe things of the Cow of light and that of her which is sweet and ripe, O Fire. Even black of hue, she nourishes with a luminous supporting, with a kindred milk.[1]

_____

[1] The Cow (the Vedic symbol of knowledge) even in the Ignorance where it is black still

ऋतेन हि ष्मा वृषभश्चिदक्तः पुमाँ अग्निः पयसा पृष्ठचेन ।
अस्पन्दमानो अचरद् वयोधा वृषा शुक्रं दुदुहे पृश्निनरूधः ॥१०॥

10. For the Fire the Bull, the Male, is inundated with the Truth,
with milk of the heights: unstirred he ranges abroad establishing the wideness, the dappled Bull has milked out the
bright udder.

ऋतेनाद्रिं व्यसन् भिदन्तः समङ्गिरसो नवन्त गोभिः ।
शुनं नरः परि षदन्नुषासमाविः स्वरभवज्जाते अग्नौ ॥११॥

11. By the Truth the Angiras-seers broke the hill, they parted
it asunder, they moved[1] together with the Ray-Cows; men
sat happily around Dawn, the Sun-world[2] was manifested
when the Fire was born.

ऋतेन देवीरमृता अमृक्ता अर्णोभिरापो मधुमद्भिरग्ने ।
वाजी न सर्गेषु प्रस्तुभानः प्र सदमित् स्रवितवे दधन्युः ॥१२॥

12. By the Truth, divine, immortal and inviolate, the Waters
with their honied floods, Fire, like a steed of swiftness pressing forward[3] in its gallopings, raced ever on to their flow.

मा कस्य यक्षं सदमिद्धुरो गा मा वेशस्य प्रमिनतो मापेः ।
मा भ्रातुरग्ने अनृजोर्ऋणं वेर्मा सख्युर्दक्षं रिपोर्भुजेम ॥१३॥

13. Mayst thou never pass over to the Power[4] of one who is a
thief, or of a neighbour or one intimate who would do us
injury,[5] mayst thou not incur the debt of a brother who is
crooked, may we not suffer by evil thought from[6] friend or
foe.

---

nourishes us with a truth which is still luminous and governed by the Greater Truth which is
hers on higher levels where she is the radiant Cow of Light.

[1] Or, came [2] Or, the Sun [3] Or, urged forward

[4] The word means supernatural or occult Power which captures the force of Agni, the
lord of Tapasya, to use it for harm.

[5] Or, diminishes us,

[6] Or, by the skill of; here, again, it is skill in an occult working, or an occult and hostile
direction of thought that is feared.

रक्षा णो अग्ने तव रक्षणेभी रारक्षाणः सुमख प्रीणानः ।
प्रति ष्फुर वि रुज वीड्वंहो जहि रक्षो महि चिद् वावृधानम् ॥१४॥

14. O Fire, strong in sacrifice, protect us ever guarding us with
thy keepings, taking pleasure in us; burst out in flame, break
the strong evil, slay the (Rakshasa) demon even when he is
increasing into greatness.

एभिर्भव सुमना अग्ने अर्कैरिमान् त्सृष्ट मन्मभिः शूर वाजान् ।
उत ब्रह्माण्यङ्गिरो जुषस्व सं ते शस्तिर्देववाता जरेत ॥१५॥

15. O Fire, become great of mind by these hymns of illumination, by our thinkings touch these plenitudes, O heroic
Flame, so take joy in the words of knowledge, O Angiras,
let our speech expressing thee come close to thee, enjoyed
by the gods.

एता विश्वा विदुषे तुभ्यं वेधो नीथान्यग्ने निण्या वचांसि ।
निवचना कवये काव्यान्यशंसिषं मतिभिर्विप्र उक्थैः ॥१६॥

16. Thus have I, an illumined sage, by my thoughts and utterances spoken to thee, who knowest, O Fire, O creator,
secret words of guidance, seer-wisdoms that speak out their
sense to the seer.[1]

Sukta 4

कृणुष्व पाजः प्रसितिं न पृथ्वीं याहि राजेवामवाँ इभेन ।
तृष्वीमनु प्रसितिं द्रूणानोऽस्तासि विध्य रक्षसस्तपिष्ठैः ॥१॥

1. Make thy mass like a wide marching, go like a king full of
strength with his following, running in the rapid passage of
thy march; thou art the Archer, pierce the demons with thy
most burning shafts.

---

[1] Or, all these in my thoughts and utterances I have spoken to thee, I, an illumined sage,
to thee the knower, O Fire, O creator, words of guidance, secret words, seer-wisdoms that
speak out their meaning to the seer.

तव भ्रमास आशुया पतन्त्यनु स्पृश धृषता शोशुचान: ।
तपूंष्यग्ने जुह्वा पतङ्गगानसंदितो बि सृज विष्वगुल्का: ॥२॥

2. Swiftly rush thy wanderings; blazing up follow and touch
   with thy violence; O Fire, spread by thy tongue thy burning
   heats and thy winged sparks; unleashed, scatter on every
   side thy meteors.

प्रति स्पशो बि सृज तूर्णितमो भव पार्युविशो अस्या अदब्ध: ।
यो नो दूरे अघशंसो यो अन्त्यग्ने माकिष्टे व्यथिरा दधर्षीत् ॥३॥

3. Swiftest to act, spread abroad thy scouts to their places,
   and become the indomitable protector of this being: he
   who would bring evil by speech against us from afar or one
   from near, let not any such bringer of anguish do violence to
   thee, O Fire!

उदग्ने तिष्ठ प्रत्या तनुष्व न्यमित्रां ओषतात् तिग्महेते ।
यो नो अराति समिधान चक्रे नीचा तं धक्ष्यतसं न शुष्कम् ॥४॥

4. Arise, O Fire, spread out towards us, consume utterly the
   unfriendly, O sharp-missiled Flame; O high-kindled! who-
   ever has done enmity against us burn him down like a dry
   log.

ऊर्ध्वो भव प्रति विध्याध्यस्मदाविष्कृणुष्व दैव्यान्यग्ने ।
अव स्थिरा तनुहि यातुजूनां जामिमजामिं प्र मृणीहि शत्रून् ॥५॥

5. High-uplifted be, piercing through reveal in us the things
   divine, O Fire; lay low what the demon forces[1] have established: companion or single, crush the foe.

स ते जानाति सुमतिं यविष्ठ य ईवते ब्रह्मणे गातुमेरत् ।
विश्वान्यस्मै सुविनानि रायो द्युम्नान्यर्यो रायो बि दुरो अभि द्यौत् ॥६॥

6. He knows thy right-mindedness, O youngest of the Gods,
   who hastens the journey[2] for the Word in its march. For him

---

[1] Or, demon impulsions [2] Or, who drives the path

the high doer of works has made to shine about his doors
all brightness of the day, all treasures and splendours of the
light.

सेदग्ने अस्तु सुभगः सुदानुर्यस्त्वा नित्येन हविषा य उक्थैः ।
पिप्रीषति स्व आयुषि दुरोणे विश्ववेदस्मै सुदिना सासदिष्टिः ॥७॥

7. May he, O Fire, be fortunate and munificent who with the
eternal offering, who with his utterances, seeks to satisfy thee
in his own life, in his gated house; may there be for him all
brightnesses of the day, may such be his sacrificing.[1]

अर्चामि ते सुमतिं घोष्यर्वाक् सं ते वावाता जरतामियं गीः ।
स्वश्वास्त्वा सुरथा मर्जयेमास्मे क्षत्राणि धारयेरनु द्यून् ॥८॥

8. I make to shine thy right thought in me, may this word
diffused in its peal approach close to thee. Rich in horses
and chariots may we make all bright and pure for thee,
mayst thou hold up thy mights in us from day to day.

इह त्वा भूर्या चरेदुप त्मन् दोषावस्तर्दीदिवांसमनु द्यून् ।
क्रीळन्तस्त्वा सुमनसः सपेमाऽभि द्युम्ना तस्थिवांसो जनानाम् ॥९॥

9. Here in this world should one largely act from one's self in
the presence of thee as day by day thou shinest out in morn
and in dusk: right-minded may we touch thee as we play,
taking our stand on the luminous inspirations[2] of men.

यस्त्वा स्वश्वः सुहिरण्यो अग्न उपयाति वसुमता रथेन ।
तस्य त्राता भवसि तस्य सखा यस्त आतिथ्यमानुषग् जुजोषत् ॥१०॥

10. He who comes to thee, O Fire, with strong horses, with
fine gold, with his chariot full of riches, thou becomest his
deliverer, his friend and comrade, — he who takes joy in
thy uninterrupted guesthood.

---

[1] Or, may all that sacrifice of his be bright in its days.
[2] Or, luminous energies

महो रुजामि बन्धुता वचोभिस्तन्मा पितुर्गोतमादन्वियाय ।
त्वं नो अस्य वचसश्चिकिद्धि होतर्यविष्ठ सुक्रतो दमूनाः ॥११॥

11. I break great ones by my words, by my friendship with thee;
that came down to me from Gotama, my father: domiciled
in the house do thou become conscious of this word of ours,
O youngest God! O Priest of the call! O strong Will!

अस्वप्नजस्तरणयः सुशेवा अतन्द्रासोऽवृका अश्रमिष्ठाः ।
ते पायवः सध्रयञ्चो निषद्याग्ने तव नः पान्त्वमूर ॥१२॥

12. Undreaming, ever in movement, blissful, undrowsing,
untorn, untired may thy guardian powers sitting linked
together guard us, O thou untouched by ignorance, O Fire!

ये पायवो मामतेयं ते अग्ने पश्यन्तो अन्धं दुरितादरक्षन् ।
ररक्ष तान् सुक्रतो विश्ववेदा दिप्सन्त इद् रिपवो नाह देभुः ॥१३॥

13. Thy guardian powers, O Fire, which protected the son of
Mamata from evil, for they saw and he was blind, omniscient
guarded them in their good work; the foe who would have
hurt them could not hurt.

त्वया वयं सधन्यस्त्वोतास्तव प्रणीत्यश्याम वाजान् ।
उभा शंसा सूदय सत्यतातेऽनुष्ठुया कृणुह्यह्रयाण ॥१४॥

14. By thee as thy companions, guarded by thee, by thy leading, may we win the plenitudes; impel to their way both
annnuciations, O builder of Truth: straightaway, confident,
create.

अया ते अग्ने समिधा विधेम प्रति स्तोमं शस्यमानं गृभाय ।
दहाशसो रक्षसः पाह्यस्मान् द्रुहो निदो मित्रमहो अवद्यात् ॥१५॥

15. With the fuel may we do thee worship, O Fire, accept the
hymn which we utter, burn the demons who speak not the
word of blessing, guard us from the doer of harm, from the
censurer and his blame, O friendly Light!

SUKTA 5

वैश्वानराय मीळ्हुषे सजोषाः कथा दाशेमाग्नये बृहद् भाः ।
अनूनेन बृहता वक्षयेनोप स्तभायदुपमिन्न रोधः ॥१॥

1. How should we give, one in our joy in him, vast in light,[1] to
   the bounteous Universal Fire? With his vast and ample
   upbearing he props up the firmament like a pillar.

मा निन्दत य इमां मह्यं रातिं देवो दधौ मर्त्याय स्वधावान् ।
पाकाय गृत्सो अमृतो विचेता वैश्वानरो नृतमो यह्वो अग्निः ॥२॥

2. Blame not him who in his self-law has given this gift, divine
   to me the mortal, the wise to the ignorant, the immortal,
   the wide in consciousness, the most strong and mighty
   Universal Fire.

साम द्विबर्हा महि तिग्मभृष्टिः सहस्ररेता वृषभस्तुविष्मान् ।
पदं न गोरपगूळ्हं विविद्वानग्निर्मह्यां प्रेदु वोचन्मनीषाम् ॥३॥

3. In his twofold mass[2] may the puissant Bull with his thousandfold seed, with his keen blaze discovering the great
   Possession, the deeply hidden seat of the Cow, declare to
   me that Mind of wisdom.

प्र तां अग्निर्बभसत् तिग्मजम्भस्तपिष्ठेन शोचिषा यः सुराधाः ।
प्र ये मिनन्ति वरुणस्य धाम प्रिया मित्रस्य चेततो ध्रुवाणि ॥४॥

4. May the Fire sharp-tusked with his most burning flame of
   light, he who is full of felicity,[3] consume them, they who
   impair the domain of Varuna and the beloved and abiding
   things of Mitra the conscious knower.

अभ्रातरो न योषणो व्यन्तः पतिरिपो न जनयो दुरेवाः ।
पापासः सन्तो अनृता असत्या इदं पदमजनता गभीरम् ॥५॥

---

[1] Or, shining with the light of the vast,   [2] Or, force
[3] Or, he who is ever happy in achievement.

5. Going they go on their way like women who have no brothers, like wives[1] with evil movements who do hurt[2] to their lord, sinful, and untrue and full of falsehood they have brought into being this profound plane.

इदं मे अग्ने कियते पावकाऽमिनते गुरुं भारं न मन्म ।
बृहद् दधाथ धृषता गभीरं यह्वं पृष्ठं प्रयसा सप्तधातु ॥६॥

6. For me who howso small, impair not the heavy burden of this thought, O purifying Fire, uphold with the violence of thy delight this vast and profound and mighty sevenfold plane.[3]

तस्मिन्नेव समना समानमभि ऋत्वा पुनती धीतिरश्याः ।
ससस्य चर्मन्नधि चारु पृश्नेरग्रे रुप आरुपितं जबारु ॥७॥

7. Him, now may the purifying Thought reach and possess by the will, like attaining to its like; in the movement[4] of the peace, over the form of the dappled Mother figured out on the summit in its might and its beauty.

प्रवाच्यं वचसः किं मे अस्य गुहा हितमुप निणिग् वदन्ति ।
यदुस्रियाणामप वारिव व्रन् पाति प्रियं रुपो अग्रं पदं वेः ॥८॥

8. What of this word do they say to me, what that has to be declared and is mysterious and hidden in the secrecy?[5] What was as if a covering defence of the rays[6] they have uncovered, — he guards the beloved form, the summit plane of the being.[7]

इदमु त्यन्महि महामनीकं यदुस्रिया सचत पूर्व्यं गौः ।
ऋतस्य पदे अधि दीद्यानं गुहा रघुष्यद् रघुयद् विवेद ॥९॥

9. This which is that great front of the Great Ones to which as its supreme place adheres the shining Cow, he came to know flaming in the plane of the Truth, hastening in its speed in the secrecy.[8]

---

[1] Or, mothers [2] Or, deceive [3] Or, plane with its seven layers. [4] Or, the action [5] Or, cave? [6] Or, the shining Cows [7] Or, the Bird. [8] Or, cave.

अध द्युतानः पित्रोः सचासाऽमनुत गुह्यां चारु पृश्नेः ।
मातुष्पदे परमे अन्ति षद् गोर्वृष्णः शोचिषः प्रयतस्य जिह्वा ॥१०॥

10. Now shining in union with the two Parents, close to him,
he perceived the beautiful and secret abode of the dappled
Cow. There was the tongue of the Bull of flame intent on
its action, it was near the Cow of Light, in the supreme plane
of the Mother.

ऋतं वोचे नमसा पृच्छद्यमानस्तवाशसा जातवेदो यदीदम् ।
त्वमस्य क्षयसि यद्ध विश्वं दिवि यद् द्रविणं यत् पृथिव्याम् ॥११॥

11. Asked with obeisance I voice the Truth, this which I have
won by thy declaring of it,[1] O knower of all things born;
thou possessest all this that is, the treasure which is in
heaven and that which is on the earth.

किं नो अस्य द्रविणं कद्ध रत्नं वि नो वोचो जातवेदश्चिकित्वान् ।
गुहाध्वनः परमं यन्नो अस्य रेकु पदं न निदाना अगन्म ॥१२॥

12. What is the treasure of this Truth, what the delight of it,
wholly declare to us, O knower of the births, for thou art
aware. That supreme plane in the secrecy which is the highest goal of our path, which is over and above all, that we
have reached, free from bondage.

का मर्यादा वयुना कद्ध वाममच्छा गमेम रघवो न वाजम् ।
कदा नो देवीरमृतस्य पत्नीः सूरो वर्णेन ततनन्नुषासः ॥१३॥

13. What is its boundary, its manifestation of knowledge, what
the joy of it towards which we must move like gallopers
towards the plenitude? When have the divine Dawns, wives
of the immortal, woven it into shape by the hue of light of
the sun?

अनिरेण वचसा फल्ग्वेन प्रतीत्येन कृधुनातृपासः ।
अधा ते अग्ने किमिहा वदन्त्यनायुधास आसता सचन्ताम् ॥१४॥

---

[1] Or, by thy wish,

14. Those who live undelighted with the word that is languid and scanty, narrow and dependent on their belief, what now and here can they say to thee, O Fire? Uninstrumented let them remain united with the unreal.

अस्य श्रिये समिधानस्य वृष्णो वसोरनीकं दम आ रुरोच ।
रुशद् वसानः सुदृशीकरूपः क्षितिर्न रायाः पुरुवारो अद्यौत् ॥१५॥

15. For the glory and beauty of the Bull in his high burning the flame-force of the master of riches glowed in its splendour; clothing himself with brilliance in his form of perfect vision, he has shone out full of many boons like a dwelling with its treasure.

SUKTA 6

ऊर्ध्व ऊ षु णो अध्वरस्य होतरग्ने तिष्ठ देवताता यजीयान् ।
त्वं हि विश्वमभ्यसि मन्म प्र वेधसश्चित् तिरसि मनीषाम् ॥१॥

1. O Fire, summoner Priest of the pilgrim-rite, stand up very high for us, strong for sacrifice in the forming of the gods: thou art the ruler over every Thought and thou carriest forward the mind of thy worshipper.

अमूरो होता न्यसादि विश्वग्निर्मन्द्रो विदयेषु प्रचेताः ।
ऊर्ध्वं भानुं सवितेवाश्रेन्मेतेव धूमं स्तभायदुप द्याम् ॥२॥

2. Free from ignorance, Fire, the rapturous Priest of the Call has taken his seat in creatures, the conscious thinker in their findings of knowledge. He enters into a high lustre like a creator Sun, like a pillar he makes his smoke a prop to heaven.

यता सुजूर्णी रातिनी घृताची प्रदक्षिणिद् देवतातिमुराणः ।
उदु स्वरुर्नवजा नाक्रः पश्वो अनक्ति सुधितः सुमेकः ॥३॥

3. A luminous force of giving, swift and put forth into action,

he widens the formation of the gods as he turns round it;
new-born he stands up high[1] like an arrow-shaft well-planted
and firm and shows by his light the herds.[2]

स्तीर्णे बर्हिषि समिधाने अग्ना ऊर्ध्वो अध्वर्युर्जुजुषाणो अस्थात् ।
पर्यग्निः पशुपा न होता त्रिविष्टघेति प्रदिव उराणः ॥४॥

4. When the sacred grass is strewn and kindled burns the
flame, the leader of the pilgrim-rite stands up to high rejoicing in his work; Fire, the Priest of the call, like a
guardian of the herds thrice moves round them, the Ancient
of days, ever widening his circle.

परि त्मना मितद्रुरेति होताऽग्निर्मन्द्रो मधुवचा ऋतावा ।
द्रवत्यस्य वाजिनो न शोका भयन्ते विश्वा भुवना यदभ्राट् ॥५॥

5. He goes round in his self-motion with measured run, Fire,
the rapturous Priest of the call, sweet of word, possessing the
Truth; his flames gallop like horses, all the worlds are in
fear when he blazes.

भद्रा ते अग्ने स्वनीक संदृग् घोरस्य सतो विषुणस्य चारुः ।
न यत् ते शोचिस्तमसा वरन्त न ध्वस्मानस्तन्वी रेप आ धुः ॥६॥

6. O Fire of the fair front! happy is thy vision; even when
thou art terrible and adverse great is thy beauty: for they
hem not in thy flame with the darkness, for the destroyers
cannot set evil in thy body.

न यस्य सातुर्जनितोरवारि न मातरापितरा नू चिदिष्टौ ।
अधा मित्रो न सुधितः पावकोऽग्निर्दीदाय मानुषीषु विक्षु ॥७॥

7. He is the begetter of things and his conquest cannot be held
back, not even the father and the mother can stay him any
longer in his impulsion. Now like a friend well-established,
the purifying Fire has shone out in the human peoples.

---

[1] Greek: *akra*.

[2] Or, a sun-beam fixed and constant. Or, it may possibly mean, a pole, banner well-
planted and firm he shows (the place of) the herds.

द्वियं पञ्च जीजनन् त्संवसानाः स्वसारो अग्नि मानुषीषु विक्षु ।
उषर्बुधमथर्यो न दन्तं शुक्रं स्वासं परशुं न तिग्मम् ॥८॥

8. The twice five sisters who dwell together have given birth to
the Fire in the human peoples, the waker in the dawn, like
a tusk of flame, brilliant and fair of face, like a sharp axe.

तव त्ये अग्ने हरितो घृतस्ना रोहितास ऋज्वञ्चः स्वञ्चः ।
अरुषासो वृषण ऋजुमुष्का आ देवतातिमह्वन्त दस्माः ॥९॥

9. Bay-coloured are those horses of thine, dripping light, or
they are red, straight is their motion, swift is their going,
males, ruddy-shining, straight and massive, great in their
deeds they are called to our forming of the Gods.

ये ह त्ये ते सहमाना अयासस्त्वेषासो अग्ने अर्चयश्चरन्ति ।
श्येनासो न दुवसनासो अर्थं तुविष्वणसो मारुतं न शर्धः ॥१०॥

10. These are thy rays, O Fire, that put forth overwhelming
force, moving, impetuous in their blaze, they move towards
the goal like hawks in their action, with many voices of storm
like an army of the life-god.

अकारि ब्रह्म समिधान तुभ्यं श्ंसात्युक्थं यजते व्यू धाः ।
होतारमग्निं मनुषो नि षेदुर्नमस्यन्त उशिजः श्ंसमायोः ॥११॥

11. O high-kindled Fire, the Word has been formed for thee,
one voices the utterance, one sacrifices, — now ordain:
men set the Fire within as the Priest of the call, making
to him their prostration of surrender, aspirants to the self-
expression of the human being.

SUKTA 7

अयमिह प्रथमो धायि धातृभिर्होता यजिष्ठो अध्वरेष्वीड्यः ।
यमप्नवानो भृगवो विरुरुचुर्वनेषु चित्रं विभ्वं विशेविशे ॥१॥

1. This is he who was established as chief and first by the
    Founders of things, the Priest of the call, most strong for
    sacrifice, to be prayed in the pilgrim-rites, — he whom the
    doer of works and the flame-seers[1] set shining wide in the
    forests, rich in light, all-pervading, for man and man.

अग्ने कदा त आनुषग् भुवद् देवस्य चेतनम् ।
अधा हि त्वा जगृभ्रिरे मर्तासो विश्ववीडिडघम् ॥२॥

2. O Fire, when shall the conscious waking of thy godhead be-
    come uninterrupted? For, now mortals have laid hold on
    thee as one desirable in human creatures.

ऋतावानं विचेतसं पश्यन्तो द्यामिव स्तृभिः ।
विश्वेषामध्वराणां हस्कर्तारं दमेदमे ॥३॥

3. For they see thee, possessor of the Truth and wide in know-
    ledge like waking heaven with its stars, the smile of light of
    all these pilgrim-sacrifices in house and house, —

आशुं दूतं विवस्वतो विश्वा यश्चर्षणीरभि ।
आ जभ्रुः केतुमायवो भृगवाणं विशेविशे ॥४॥

4. The swift messenger of the illumining Sun who comes to
    all the seeing people; men hold him as the ray of intuition
    and he shines as the Bhrigu-flame-seer for each being.

तमीं होतारमानुषक् चिकित्वांसं नि षेदिरे ।
रण्वं पावकशोचिषं यजिष्ठं सप्त धामभिः ॥५॥

5. This is the Priest of the call whom they set within, who un-
    interruptedly wakes to knowledge, rapturous with his puri-
    fying flame, most strong to sacrifice by his seven seats.[2]

तं शश्वतीषु मातृषु वन आ वीतमश्रितम् ।
चित्रं सन्तं गुहा हितं सुवेदं कूचिद्दर्थिनम् ॥६॥

---

[1] Apnavan and the Bhrigus   [2] Or, with his seven lights.

6. Him in the many mothers linked together, wide-spread and unapproached in the forest, abiding in the secret Cave and rich with many lights, full of knowledge or moving to some unknown goal.

ससस्य यद् वियुता सस्मिन्भूधमृतस्य धामन् रणयन्त देवा: ।
महाँ अग्निनमसा रातहव्यो वेरध्वराय सदमिदृतावा ॥७॥

7. When in the separation from sleep the Gods have joy in that udder of the Cow, in the plane of the Truth, great becomes the Fire by the offering given with prostration and journeys for the pilgrim-sacrifice and the Truth is ever with him.

वेरध्वरस्य दूत्यानि विद्वानुभे अन्ता रोदसी संचिकित्वान् ।
दूत ईयसे प्रदिव उराणो विदुष्टरो दिव आरोधनानि ॥८॥

8. He journeys knowing the embassies of the pilgrim-sacrifice between both the firmaments, utterly awakened to knowledge. A messenger, the Ancient of days, ever widening, ever greater in knowledge, thou travellest the mounting slopes of heaven.[1]

कृष्णं त एम रुशत: पुरो भाश्चरिष्ण्वर्चिर्वपुषामिदेकम् ।
यदप्रवीता दधते ह गर्भं सद्यश्चिज्जातो भवसीदु दूत: ॥९॥

9. Black is the path of thy shining, thy light goes in front, a journeying ray, the one supreme of all thy bodies; when one unimpregnated bears thee as the child of her womb, in the sudden moment of thy birth thou art already the messenger.

सद्यो जातस्य ददृशानमोजो यदस्य वातो अनुवाति शोचि: ।
वृणक्ति तिग्मामतसेषु जिह्वां स्थिरा चिदन्ना दयते वि जम्भै: ॥१०॥

10. The moment he is born his might becomes visible when the wind blows behind his flame; he turns his sharp tongue round the trunks and tears his firm food with his jaws of flame.

---

[1] Or, thou travellest to the inmost places of heaven.

13

तृषु यदन्ना तृषुणा ववक्ष तृषुं दूतं कृणुते यह्वो अग्निः ।
वातस्य मेळिं सचते निजूर्वन्नाशुं न वाजयते हिन्वे अर्वा ॥११॥

11. When quickly he carries his foods on his rapid tongue, this
mighty Fire fashions himself into a swift messenger; consuming all he clings to the mad course[1] of the wind, as a driver a swift horse he sets it to gallop for the seeker of the
plenitude.

SUKTA 8

दूतं वो विश्ववेदसं हव्यवाहममर्त्यम् ।
यजिष्ठमृञ्जसे गिरा ॥१॥

1. Array with your word the messenger, the carrier of your
offerings, most strong to sacrifice, the omniscient, the Immortal.

स हि वेदा वसुधिति महाँ आरोषणं दिवः ।
स देवाँ एह वक्षति ॥२॥

2. For, he knows the place of the possession of the riches, he
knows the ascending slope of heaven, he shall bring here the
gods.

स वेद देव आनमं देवाँ ऋतायते दमे ।
वाति प्रियाणि चिद् वसु ॥३॥

3. A God, he knows for the seeker of the Truth his way of submission to the gods in the house of Truth, and he gives the
beloved treasures.

स होता सेदु दूत्यं चिकित्वाँ अन्तरीयते ।
विद्वाँ आरोषणं दिवः ॥४॥

4. He is the Priest of the call, it is he who travels between,
aware of his embassy, knowing the ascending slope of
heaven.

---

[1] Or, to the roar

ते स्याम ये अग्नये ददाशुर्हव्यदातिभिः ।
य ईं पुष्यन्त इन्धते ॥५॥

5. May we be of those who have given to the Fire with the gift of their offerings, who kindle him and increase.

ते राया ते सुवीर्यैः ससवांसो वि शृण्विरे ।
ये अग्ना दधिरे दुवः ॥६॥

6. They by the treasure, by the hero-strengths have conquered and have heard who have upheld their work in the Fire.

अस्मे रायो दिवेदिवे सं चरन्तु पुरुस्पृहः ।
अस्मे वाजास ईरताम् ॥७॥

7. In us may the riches move from day to day bringing the multitude of our desires, may we receive the impulsion of the plenitudes.

स विप्रश्चर्षणीनां शवसा मानुषाणाम् ।
अति क्षिप्रेव विध्यति ॥८॥

8. An illumined seer, by the might of seeing human beings he pierces beyond like a swift arrow.

SUKTA 9

अग्ने मृळ महाँ असि य ईमा देवयुं जनम् ।
इयेथ बर्हिरासदम् ॥१॥

1. O Flame, be gracious, for great art thou who comest to the seeker of the godheads to sit on his seat of sacrifice.

स मानुषीषु दूळभो विक्षु प्रावीरमर्त्यः ।
दूतो विश्वेषां भुवत् ॥२॥

2. He becomes manifest in human beings,[1] invincible,[2] im-

---

[1] Or, he becomes in human beings a protector, [2] Or, indestructible,

mortal, the messenger of all.

स सद्म परि णीयते होता मन्द्रो दिविष्टिषु ।
उत पोता नि षीदति ॥३॥

3. He is borne round the house, a rapturous Priest of the call in
   our heavenward urges; he takes his seat as the Priest of the
   purification.

उत ग्ना अग्निरध्वर उतो गृहपतिर्दमे ।
उत ब्रह्मा नि षीदति ॥४॥

4. The Fire is the Goddess-powers in the pilgrim-rite and he is
   the master of the house in his home, he sits too as the Priest
   of the word.

वेषि ह्यध्वरीयतामुपवक्ता जनानाम् ।
हव्या च मानुषाणाम् ॥५॥

5. Thou comest to the offerings as the speaker of the sanction
   for human beings when they would perform the pilgrim-
   sacrifice.

वेषीद्वस्य दूत्यं यस्य जुजोषो अध्वरम् ।
हव्यं मर्तस्य वोळ्हवे ॥६॥

6. Thou comest to be his envoy to him in whose sacrifice thou
   takest pleasure to carry the offerings of the mortal.

अस्माकं जोष्यध्वरमस्माकं यज्ञमङ्गिरः ।
अस्माकं शृणुधी हवम् ॥७॥

7. Take pleasure in our pilgrim-rite, in our sacrifice, O Angiras,
   hear our call.

परि ते दूळभो रथोऽस्मां अश्नोतु विश्वतः ।
येन रक्षसि दाशुषः ॥८॥

8. Let thy invincible car reach us and move round us on every side by which thou guardest the givers of the offering.

SUKTA 10

अग्ने तमद्याऽश्वं न स्तोमैः क्रतुं न भद्रं हृदिस्पृशम् ।
ऋध्यामा त ओहैः ॥१॥

1. O Fire, let us today make thee affluent with our lauds as thy vehicles to bear thee, — even that of thee which is as if the Horse, as if a happy will touching the heart.

अधा ह्यग्ने क्रतोर्भद्रस्य दक्षस्य साधोः ।
रथीर्ऋंतस्य बृहतो बभूथ ॥२॥

2. For now, O Fire, thou hast become the charioteer of a happy Will, of an all-accomplishing Discernment, of the Vast Truth.

एभिर्नो अर्कैर्भवा नो अर्वाङ् स्वर्ण ज्योतिः ।
अग्ने विश्वेभिः सुमना अनीकैः ॥३॥

3. Become close to us, O Fire, by these hymns of illumination, right-minded with all thy flame-powers, thy light like the sun-world.

आभिष्टे अद्य गीर्भिर्गृणन्तोऽग्ने दाशेम ।
प्र ते दिवो न स्तनयन्ति शुष्माः ॥४॥

4. Today uttering thee with these utterances may we give to thee, O Fire; thy strengths thunder forth like the heavens.[1]

तव स्वादिष्ठाग्ने संदृष्टिरिदा चिदह्न इदा चिदक्तोः ।
श्रिये रुक्मो न रोचत उपाके ॥५॥

5. Most sweet is thy vision, now in the day, now in the night; it

---
[1] Or, like the strength of heaven.

shines out close to us like gold for its beauty and splendour.

घृतं न पूतं तनूररेपाः शुचि हिरण्यम् ।
तत् ते रुक्मो न रोचत स्वधावः ॥६॥

6. Free from evil is thy body; it is like pure clarified butter, it
is pure gold; that in thee is golden in its shining, for such is
thy self-law.

कृतं चिद्धि ष्मा सनेमि द्वेषोऽग्न इनोषि मर्तात् ।
इत्था यजमानादृतावः ॥७॥

7. Even the lasting hostility done, O thou who possessest the
Truth, thou drivest away perfectly from the mortal sacrificer.[1]

शिवा नः सख्या सन्तु भ्रात्राग्ने देवेषु युष्मे ।
सा नो नाभिः सवने सस्मिन्भूवन् ॥८॥

8. O Fire, auspicious may be all our friendship and brother-
hood with you Gods. That is our centre, where is our home,
where is that udder of the Cow of Light.

SUKTA 11

भद्रं ते अग्ने सहसिन्ननीकमुपाक आ रोचते सूर्यस्य ।
रुशद् वृशे ववृशे नक्तया चिदरुक्षितं वृश आ रूपे अन्नम् ॥१॥

1. Happy is that flame-power of thine, O forceful Fire; it
shines close to the Sun, glowing to vision it is seen even in
the night, it is as if in its beauty[2] there were an unarid feast
for the eye.

वि षाह्यग्ने गृणते मनीषां खं वेपसा तुविजात स्तवानः ।
विश्वेभिर्यद् वावनः शुक्र देवैस्तन्नो रास्व सुमहो भूरि मन्म ॥२॥

---

[1] Or, away from the mortal who is exact in his sacrifice.   [2] Or, in its form

2. O Fire, O thou with thy many births, even as we hymn thee
force open the heavens[1] with thy quivering lustre[2] for him
who utters the mind of wisdom; O Brilliant, O glorious
Flame, what thou with all the gods hast won, that give to us,
that mighty thought.

त्वदग्ने काव्या त्वन्मनीषास्त्वदुक्था जायन्ते राध्यानि ।
त्वदेति द्रविणं वीरपेशा इत्याधिये दाशुषे मर्त्याय ॥३॥

3. O Fire, from thee are born the seer-wisdoms, from thee the
mind of knowledge, from thee the utterances that achieve;
from thee come the riches that take the hero's form to the
mortal giver who has the true thought.

त्वद् वाजी वाजंभरो विहाया अभिष्टिकृज्जायते सत्यशुष्मः ।
त्वद् रयिर्देवजूतो मयोभुस्त्वदाशुर्जूजुवाँ अग्ने अर्वा ॥४॥

4. From thee is born the steed of swiftness that carries the
plenitude, that has the force of Truth, that makes the great
approach, that has the vastness; from thee is the treasure
sent by the gods that creates the bliss, from thee the rapid
speeding war-horse, O Fire.

त्वामग्ने प्रथमं देवयन्तो देवं मर्ता अमृत मन्द्रजिह्वम् ।
द्वेषोयुतमा विवासन्ति धीभिर्वंसूनसं गृहपतिममूरम् ॥५॥

5. Thee, O Fire, O immortal, first and chief of the godheads,
mortals who are seekers of the godheads illumine by their
thoughts, Fire with the rapturous tongue who pushest away
the hostiles, the one domiciled within, the master of our
house untouched by ignorance.

आरे अस्मदमतिमारे अंह आरे विश्वां दुर्मतिं यन्निपासि ।
दोषा शिवः सहसः सूनो अग्ने यं देव आ चित् सचसे स्वस्ति ॥६॥

6. Far from us all unconsciousness, sin and evil mind when
thou art on guard, a benignant Power in the night, O Fire,

---

[1] Or, the door or entrance [2] Or, with thy lustre of knowledge

O son of force, over him to whom thou cleavest for his weal.

SUKTA 12

यस्त्वामग्न इनधते यतस्रुक् त्रिस्ते अन्नं कृणवत् सस्मिन्नहन् ।
स सु द्युम्नैरभ्यस्तु प्रसक्षत् तव क्रत्वा जातवेदश्चिकित्वान् ॥१॥

1. He who kindles thee, O Fire, and with his ladle in action
   creates food for thee thrice in the day may he, awakened to
   knowledge, be ever with thy illuminations and wholly put
   forth his force and overcome by thy will, O knower of all
   things born.

इध्मं यस्ते जभरच्छश्रमाणो महो अग्ने अनीकमा सपर्यन् ।
स इधानः प्रति दोषामुषासं पुष्यन् रयिं सचते घ्नन्नमित्रान् ॥२॥

2. He who labours and brings to thee thy fuel serving the
   flame-force of thy greatness, O Fire, he kindling thee every
   day and night ever grows and cleaves to the Treasure slaying
   the unfriendly Powers.

अग्निरीशे बृहतः क्षत्रियस्याऽग्निर्वाजस्य परमस्य रायः ।
दधाति रत्नं विधते यविष्ठो व्यानुषङ् मर्त्याय स्वधावान् ॥३॥

3. The Fire is the master of the vast might, the Fire is master
   of the supreme plenitude and riches; ever young, faithful to
   his self-law, he founds wholly uninterruptedly the ecstasy
   for the mortal who worships him.

यच्चिद्धि ते पुरुषत्रा यविष्ठाऽचित्तिभिश्चकृमा कच्चिदागः ।
कृधी ह्वस्मां अदितेरनागान् व्येनांसि शिश्रथो विश्वगग्ने ॥४॥

4. If at all in our humanity by our movements of ignorance we
   have done any evil against thee, O Fire, make us wholly
   sinless before the mother indivisible; O Fire, mayst thou
   loosen from us the bonds of our sins to every side.

महश्चिदग्न एनसो अभीक ऊर्वाद् देवानामृत मर्त्यानाम् ।
मा ते सखाय: सदमिद् रिषाम यच्छा तोकाय तनयाय शं यो: ॥५॥

5. Even though our sin be great before gods and men, even
though it be wide, O Fire, may we not come ever to harm
from it who are thy friends and comrades; give to our Son,
our begotten, the peace and the well-doing.

यथा ह त्यद् वसवो गौर्यं चित् पदि षिताममुञ्चता यजत्रा: ।
एवो ब्वस्मन्मुञ्चता व्यंहु: प्र तार्यग्ने प्रतरं न आयु: ॥६॥

6. Even as that was done when the Masters of Riches, the
Lords of sacrifice released the bright cow tethered by her
foot, so release us utterly from evil; mayst thou carry forward our life so that it crosses beyond, O Fire.

SUKTA 13

प्रत्यग्निरुषसामग्रमख्यद् विभातीनां सुमना रत्नधेयम् ।
यातमश्विना सुकृतो दुरोणमुत् सूर्यो ज्योतिषा देव एति ॥१॥

1. The Fire facing the front of the dawns as they shine out has
revealed the founding of ecstasy; the two Riders of the
horse are coming to the gated house of the doer of good
works; the divine Sun is rising up with its light.

ऊर्ध्वं भानुं सविता देवो अश्रेद् द्रप्सं दविध्वद् गविषो न सत्वा ।
अनु व्रतं वरुणो यन्ति मित्रो यत् सूर्यं दिव्यारोहयन्ति ॥२॥

2. The divine creator Sun has reached his high shining, he is
like a warrior seeker of the Light brandishing his flag. There
is Varuna, there is Mitra, all follow the working of the Law
when they make the Sun to rise up in heaven.

यं सीमकृण्वन् तमसे विपृचे ध्रुवक्षेमा अनवस्यन्तो अर्यम् ।
तं सूर्यं हरित: सप्त यह्वी: स्पशं विश्वस्य जगतो वहन्ति ॥३॥

3. Him whom, firm in their foundation, never ceasing from

their aim they have made for the removing of the darkness, this Sun seven mighty brilliant mares bear as the scouts of the whole world.

वहिष्ठेभिर्विहरन्त्यासि तन्तुमवव्ययप्रसितं देव वस्म ।
रविध्वतो रश्मयः सूर्यस्य चर्मेवावाधुस्तमो अप्स्वन्तः ॥४॥

4. O God, thou goest with steeds most strong to bear separating the weft woven, unweaving the black garment; the streaming rays of the Sun cast the darkness like a covering skin down within the waters.

अनायतो अनिबद्धः कथायं न्यङ्ङुत्तानोऽव पद्यते न ।
कया याति स्वधया को ददर्श दिवः स्कम्भः समृतः पाति नाकम् ॥५॥

5. Unextended, unbound, facing downwards, facing upwards, how does he not sink? By what self-law does he go on his journey? Who has seen when he joins heaven and is its pillar and guards the firmament?

SUKTA 14

प्रत्यग्निरुषसो जातवेदो अस्थाद् देवो रोचमाना महोभिः ।
आ नासत्योरुगाया रथेनेमं यज्ञमुप नो यातमच्छ ॥१॥

1. Fire, the godhead has been revealed, the knower of all things born, fronting the dawns as they gleam with the greatness of their lustres; wide-moving, lords of the journey, come moving in their chariot towards this our sacrifice.

ऊर्ध्वं केतुं सविता देवो अश्रेज्ज्योतिर्विश्वस्मै भुवनाय कृण्वन् ।
आप्रा द्यावापृथिवी अन्तरिक्षं वि सूर्यो रश्मिभिश्चेकितानः ॥२॥

2. The creator Sun is lodged in his high Ray of intuition fashioning the light for the whole world; the Sun in his universal knowledge has filled earth and heaven and the midworld with his rays.

आवहन्त्यरुणीज्योतिषागान्मही चित्रा रश्मिभिश्चेकिताना ।
प्रबोधयन्ती सुविताय देव्युषा ईयते सुयुजा रथेन ॥३॥

3. The Dawn bearing him has come with the Light, Dawn vast
   and rich in her lustres, knowing all by her rays; the divine
   Dawn awakening to the happy path is journeying in her
   well-yoked chariot.

आ वां वहिष्ठा इह ते वहन्तु रथा अश्वास उषसो व्युष्टौ ।
इमे हि वां मधुपेयाय सोमा अस्मिन् यज्ञे वृषणा मादयेथाम् ॥४॥

4. May these horses and chariots, strong to bear, bring you
   both in the shining out of the dawn: for, here for you are the
   juices of the Wine for the drinking of the sweetness; O strong
   Ones, may you take rapture of them in this sacrifice.

अनायतो अनिबद्धः कथायं न्यङ्ङुत्तानोऽव पद्यते न ।
कया याति स्वधया को ददर्श दिवः स्कम्भः समृतः पाति नाकम् ॥५॥

5. Unextended, unbound, facing downwards, facing upwards
   how does he not sink? By what self-law does he go on his
   journey? Who has seen when he joins heaven and is its
   pillar and guards the firmament?

SUKTA 15

अग्निर्होता नो अध्वरे वाजी सन् परि णीयते ।
देवो देवेषु यज्ञियः ॥१॥

1. The Fire is our Priest of the call in the pilgrim-sacrifice; he is
   led around as the horse, he is the godhead in the gods who is
   lord of the sacrifice.

परि त्रिविष्टिपध्वरं यात्यग्नी रथीरिव ।
आ देवेषु प्रयो दधत् ॥२॥

2. The Fire goes thrice around the pilgrim-sacrifice and is like
   one driving a chariot, he founds our delight in the gods.

परि वाजपतिः कविरग्निर्हव्यान्यक्रमीत् ।
दधद् रत्नानि दाशुषे ॥३॥

3. The Fire moves around the offerings, a seer, a master of the plenitudes and founds for the giver the ecstasies.

अयं यः सृञ्जये पुरो देववाते समिध्यते ।
द्युमां अमित्रदम्भनः ॥४॥

4. This is he who is kindled in the front in Srinjaya, son of Devavata, he is luminous and a destroyer of foes.

अस्य घा वीर ईवतोऽग्नेरीशीत मर्त्यः ।
तिग्मजम्भस्य मीळ्हुषः ॥५॥

5. The mortal who is a hero can have mastery over the Fire in its march, the sharp-tusked bountiful Fire.

तमर्वन्तं न सानसिमरुषं न दिवः शिशुम् ।
मर्मृज्यन्ते दिवेदिवे ॥६॥

6. They make him bright from day to day like a conquering war-horse, like a shining babe of heaven.

बोधद्यन्मा हरिभ्यां कुमारः साहदेव्यः ।
अच्छा न हूत उदरम् ॥७॥

7. When the prince, the son of Sahadeva, woke me with his two bay horses, though called towards him I was not ready to rise.

उत त्या यजता हरी कुमारात् साहदेव्यात् ।
प्रयता सद्य आ ददे ॥८॥

8. Even so, I took at once from the prince, the son of Sahadeva, those two sacred horses he gave.

एष वां देवावश्विना कुमारः साहदेव्यः ।
दीर्घायुरस्तु सोमकः ॥९॥

9. O divine Riders, here before you is the prince Somaka, son
of Sahadeva; long-lived may he be!

तं युवं देवावश्विना कुमारं साहदेव्यम् ।
दीर्घायुषं कृणोतन ॥१०॥

10. Even him the prince, the son of Sahadeva, O divine Riders,
make long of life.

SUKTA 40

दधिक्राव्ण इदु नु चर्किराम विश्वा इन्मामुषसः सूदयन्तु ।
अपामग्नेरुषसः सूर्यस्य बृहस्पतेराङ्गिरसस्य जिष्णोः ॥१॥

1. Dadhikravan is he of whom now we must do the work; may
all the Dawns speed me on the path! For the Waters and for
the Dawn and the Sun and Brihaspati, he of the puissance,
the Victor.

सत्वा भरिषो गविषो दुवन्यसच्छवस्यादिष उषसस्तुरण्यसत् ।
सत्यो द्रवो द्रवरः पतङ्गरो दधिक्रावेषमूर्जं स्वर्जनत् ॥२॥

2. May this Power of being who seeks the full-bringing and
seeks the Light and who abides in all activity turn into inspiration the impulsions of the Dawn, may he abide in their
speed that carries us beyond. Dadhikravan who is the
truth in his running, — yea, he gallops and he flies, — brings
into being the impulsion, the abundant force, the heavenly
light.

उत स्मास्य द्रवतस्तुरण्यतः पर्णं न वेरनु वाति प्रगर्धिनः ।
श्येनस्येव ध्रजतो अङ्कसं परि दधिक्राव्णः सहोर्जा तरित्रतः ॥३॥

3. When he runs, when he speeds in his passage, as the wing
of the Bird is a wind that blows about him in his greed of
the gallop; as the wing that beats about the breast of the
rushing Eagle, so about the breast of Dadhikravan when

with the Force he carries us beyond.

उत स्य वाजी क्षिपर्णि तुरण्यति ग्रीवायां बद्धो अपिकक्ष आसनि ।
क्रतुं दधिक्रा अनु संतवीत्वत् पथामङ्कान्स्यन्वापनीफणत् ॥४॥

4. For the abundance of his strength he carries his impeller
    beyond, a rein binds his neck and a rein holds him about the
    chest and a rein is in his mouth. Dadhikravan puts forth his
    energy according to the will in the mind and gallops along
    the turning of the path.

हंसः शुचिषद्वसुरन्तरिक्षसद्धोता वेदिषदतिथिर्दुरोणसत् ।
नृषद्वरसदृतसद् व्योमसदब्जा गोजा ऋतजा अद्रिजा ऋतम् ॥५॥

5. This is the swan that dwells in the purity, the lord of subs-
    tance in the middle world, the Priest of the offering whose
    seat is upon the altar, the guest in the gated house. He
    dwells in the Man, he dwells in the Truth, he dwells in
    the wide Ether; he is born of the Waters, he is born of the
    Light, he is born of the Law, he is born of the Hill of Subs-
    tance, he is the Law of the Truth.

MANDALA FIVE

THE ATRIS

BUDHA AND GAVISHTHIRA

SUKTA 1

अबोध्यग्निः समिधा जनानां प्रति धेनुमिवायतीमुषासम् ।
यह्वा इव प्र वयामुज्जिहानाः प्र भानवः सिस्रते नाकमच्छ ॥१॥

1. Fire is awake by the kindling of the peoples, he fronts the dawn that comes to him like a fostering milch-cow; like the mighty ones casting upward their branching his lustres spread towards heaven.

अबोधि होता यजथाय देवानूर्ध्वो अग्निः सुमनाः प्रातरस्थात् ।
समिद्धस्य रुशददर्शि पाजो महान् देवस्तमसो निरमोचि ॥२॥

2. The Priest of the call is awake for sacrifice to the gods, Fire with his right thinking has stood up high ablaze. The red-glowing mass of him is seen: a great god has been delivered out of the darkness.

यदीं गणस्य रशनामजीगः शुचिरङ्क्ते शुचिभिर्गोभिरग्निः ।
आद् दक्षिणा युज्यते वाजयन्त्युत्तानामूर्ध्वो अधयज्जुहूभिः ॥३॥

3. When he put out the long cord of his troop, Fire in his purity reveals all by the pure herds of his rays; the goddess of understanding is yoked to her works, she supine he standing high, he has drunk from her breasts with his tongues of flame.

अग्निमच्छा देवयतां मनांसि चक्षूंषीव सूर्ये सं चरन्ति ।
यदीं सुवाते उषसा विरूपे श्वेतो वाजी जायते अग्रे अह्नाम् ॥४॥

4. The minds of men who seek the godhead converge towards the flame even as their seeings converge in the sun; when two dawns of different forms give birth to this Fire the white Horse is born in front of the days.

जनिष्ट हि जेन्यो अग्रे अह्नां हितो हितेष्वरुषो वनेषु ।
दमेदमे सप्त रत्ना दधानोऽग्निर्होता नि षसादा यजीयान् ॥५॥

5. He was born victorious in front of the days, established in
established things, ruddy-bright in the woodlands of our
pleasure; in house and house founding the seven ecstasies
the Fire took up his session as a Priest of the call strong for
sacrifice.

अग्निर्होता न्यसीदद् यजीयानुपस्थे मातुः सुरभा उ लोके ।
युवा कविः पुरुनिःष्ठ ऋतावा कृष्टीनामुत मध्य इद्धः ॥६॥

6. Strength has taken his seat as the Priest of the offering
mighty for sacrifice in the lap of the Mother, in that rapturous other world, the youth, the seer, manifold in his
fixed knowledge, possessed of the Truth, the upholder of the
peoples; in between too, is he kindled.

प्र नु त्यं विप्रमध्वरेषु साधुमग्निं होतारमीळते नमोभिः ।
आ यस्ततान रोदसी ऋतेन नित्यं मृजन्ति वाजिनं घृतेन ॥७॥

7. Men pray with their prostrations of surrender that illumined
seer, who achieves perfection in the pilgrim-sacrifices, Fire,
the Priest of the call, for he has extended earth and heaven
by the Truth, they rub bright with the Light the eternal
Horse of power.

मार्जाल्यो मृज्यते स्वे दमूनाः कविप्रशस्तो अतिथिः शिवो नः ।
सहस्रशृङ्गो वृषभस्तदोजा विश्वाँ अग्ने सहसा प्रास्यन्यान् ॥८॥

8. The purifier he is rubbed bright and pure, he who is proclaimed by the seers, one who is the dweller in his own house,
and is our benignant guest; the bull of the thousand horns
because thou hast the strength of That, O Fire, thou pre-
cedest in puissance all others.

प्र सद्यो अग्ने अत्येष्वन्यानाविर्यस्मै चारुतमो बभूथ ।
ईळेन्यो वपुष्यो विभावा प्रियो विशामतिथिर्मानुषीणाम् ॥९॥

9. At once thou goest forward, O Fire, and overpassest all others in whomsoever thou hast become manifest in all the glory of thy beauty; adorable, great of body, wide of light thou art the beloved guest of human beings.

तुभ्यं भरन्ति क्षितयो यविष्ठ बलिमग्ने अन्तित ओत दूरात् ।
आ भन्दिष्ठस्य सुमतिं चिकिद्धि बृहत् ते अग्ने महि शर्म भद्रम् ॥१०॥

10. To thee, O ever youthful Fire, all the worlds and their peoples bring the offering from near and from far; awake to that right-mindedness of man's happiest state: vast and great and happy is that peace of thee,[1] O Fire.

आद्य रथं भानुमो भानुमन्तमग्ने तिष्ठ यजतेभिः समन्तम् ।
विद्वान् पथीनामुर्वन्तरिक्षमेह देवान् हविरद्याय वक्षि ॥११॥

11. Today, O luminous one, mount the luminous wholeness of thy car with the lords of sacrifice, thou knowest the wide mid-world with all its paths, bring here the gods to partake of our sacrifice.

अवोचाम कवये मेध्याय वचो वन्दारु वृषभाय वृष्णे ।
गविष्ठिरो नमसा स्तोममग्नौ दिवीव रुक्ममुरुव्यञ्चमश्रेत् ॥१२॥

12. To the seer, the understanding one, we have uttered the word of our adoration, to the Bull, the male; the Steadfast in Light has taken refuge in his laud as in a far-reaching mass of gold.

KUMAR ATREYA OR VRISHA JANA

SUKTA 2

कुमारं माता युवतिः समुब्धं गुहा बिभर्ति न ददाति पित्रे ।
अनीकमस्य न मिनज्जनासः पुरः पश्यन्ति निहितमरतौ ॥१॥

---

[1] Or, is thy house of refuge,

1. The young Mother carries the boy suppressed in the secret cavern and she gives him not to the father; his force is undiminished, men see him in front established inwardly in the movement.

कमेतं त्वं युवते कुमारं पेषी बिभर्षि महिषी जजान ।
पूर्वीर्हि गर्भ: शरदो ववर्धाऽपश्यं जातं यदसूत माता ॥२॥

2. Who is this boy, O young mother, whom thou carriest in thyself when thou art compressed into form, but when thou art vast thou hast given him birth? Through many years grew the child in the womb, I saw him born when the mother brought him forth.

हिरण्यदन्तं शुचिवर्णमारात् क्षेत्रादपश्यमायुधा मिमानम् ।
ददानो अस्मा अमृतं विपृक्वत् किं मामनिन्द्राः कृणवन्ननुक्थाः ॥३॥

3. I saw him in a distant field, one golden-tusked and purebright of hue shaping his weapons: to him I am giving immortality in my several parts and what shall they do to me who possess not Indra and have not the word?

क्षेत्रादपश्यं सनुतश्चरन्तं सुमद् यूथं न पुरु शोभमानम् ।
न ता अगृभ्रन्नजनिष्ट हि षः पलिक्नीरिद् युवतयो भवन्ति ॥४॥

4. In that field I saw ranging apart what seemed a happy herd in its many forms of beauty; none could seize on them, for he was born, even those of them who were grey with age became young again.

के मे मर्यकं वि यवन्त गोभिर्न येषां गोपा अरणिश्चिदास ।
य ईं जगृभुरव ते सृजन्त्वाजाति पश्व उप नश्चिकित्वान् ॥५॥

5. Who were they that divorced my strength from the herds of light? Against them there was no protector nor any fighter in this war. Let those who seized them release them back to me, he has become aware and is driving back to me my herds of vision.

वसां राजानं वसतिं जनानामरातयो नि दधुर्मत्येषु ।
ब्रह्माण्यत्रेरव तं सृजन्तु निन्दितारो निन्द्यासो भवन्तु ॥६॥

6. The hostile powers have hidden within in mortals the king of those who dwell in creatures in whom all creatures dwell; let the wisdom-words of Atri release him, let the binders themselves become the bound.

शुनश्चिच्छेपं निदितं सहस्राद् यूपादमुञ्चो अशमिष्ट हि षः ।
एवास्मदग्ने वि मुमुग्धि पाशान् होतश्चिकित्व इह तू निषद्य ॥७॥

7. Shunahshepa too was bound to the thousandfold post of sacrifice, him didst thou release and he attained to calm;[1] so do thou take thy seat here in us, O conscious knower, O Priest of the call, and loose from us the cords of our bondage.

हृणीयमानो अप हि मद्भयेः प्र मे देवानां व्रतपा उवाच ।
इन्द्रो विद्वाँ अनु हि त्वा चचक्ष तेनाहमग्ने अनुशिष्ट आगाम् ॥८॥

8. Mayst thou not grow wroth and depart from me: he who guards the law of working of the gods declared it to me; Indra knew and sought after and saw thee, and taught by him, O Fire, I have come to thee.

वि ज्योतिषा बृहता भात्यग्निराविर्विश्वानि कृणुते महित्वा ।
प्रादेवीर्मायाः सहते दुरेवाः शिशीते शृङ्गे रक्षसे विनिक्षे ॥९॥

9. This Fire shines with the Vast Light and makes all things manifest by his greatness. He overpowers the workings of knowledge that are undivine and evil in their impulse, he sharpens his horns to gore the Rakshasa.

उत स्वानासो दिवि षन्त्वग्नेस्तिग्मायुधा रक्षसे हन्तवा उ ।
मदे चिदस्य प्र रुजन्ति भामा न वरन्ते परिबाधो अदेवीः ॥१०॥

10. May the voices of the Fire be sharp weapons to slay the Rakshasa. In his ecstasy his angers break down, all the

---

[1] Or, he achieved the work;

undivine obstructions that besiege us cannot hem him in.

एतं ते स्तोमं तुविजात विप्रो रथं न धीरः स्वपा अतक्षम् ।
यदीदग्ने प्रति त्वं देव हर्याः स्वर्वतीरप एना जयेम ॥११॥

11. O thou of the many births, I the sage, the thinker, the man of perfect works have fashioned for thee this laud like a chariot. If, indeed, O god, thou shouldst take an answering joy in it, by this we could conquer the waters that carry the light of the sun-world.

तुविग्रीवो वृषभो वावृधानोऽश्वर्यः समजाति वेदः ।
इतीममग्निममृता अवोचन् बर्हिष्मते मनवे शर्म यंस-
द्धविष्मते मनवे शर्म यंसत् ॥१२॥

12. The bull with the neck of might, whom no enemy can oppose, grows and comes driving from the foe the riches of knowledge. So have the immortals spoken to this Fire that he may work out peace for man when he prepares the sacred seat, work out peace for man when he brings the offering.

VASUSHRUTA

SUKTA 3

त्वमग्ने वरुणो जायसे यत् त्वं मित्रो भवसि यत् समिद्धः ।
त्वे विश्वे सहसस्पुत्र देवास्त्वमिन्द्रो दाशुषे मर्त्याय ॥१॥

1. Thou art Varuna, O Fire, when thou art born, thou becomest Mitra when thou blazest high; in thee are all the gods, O son of Force, thou art Indra for the mortal giver.

त्वमर्यमा भवसि यत् कनीनां नाम स्वधावन् गुह्यं बिभर्षि ।
अञ्जन्ति मित्रं सुधितं न गोभिर्यद् दंपती समनसा कृणोषि ॥२॥

2. O holder of the self-law, thou becomest Aryaman when thou bearest the secret name of the Virgins; they reveal thee

with the Rays as Mitra firmly founded when thou makest
of one mind the Lord of the house and the Spouse.

तव श्रिये मरुतो मर्जयन्त रुद्र यत् ते जनिम चारु चित्रम् ।
पदं यद् विष्णोरुपमं निधायि तेन पासि गुह्यं नाम गोनाम् ॥३॥

3. For the glory of thee, O Rudra, the life-powers make bright
thy birth into a richly manifold beauty. When that highest
step[1] of Vishnu is founded within, thou guardest by it the
secret name of the Ray-cows.

तव श्रिया सुवृशो देव देवाः पुरू दधाना अमृतं सपन्त ।
होतारमग्निं मनुषो नि षेदुर्दशस्यन्त उशिजः शंसमायोः ॥४॥

4. By the glory of thee who hast the true seeing, the gods hold
a multiple completeness and taste[2] immortality; men take
up their session with Fire, the Priest of the call, aspiring,
making a gift of the self-expression of the human being.

न त्वद्धोता पूर्वो अग्ने यजीयान् न काव्यः परो अस्ति स्वधावः ।
विशश्च यस्या अतिथिर्भवासि स यज्ञेन वनवद् देव मर्तान् ॥५॥

5. There is none who precedes thee as priest of the call, O Fire,
none mightier for sacrifice, there is none supreme over thee
in the seer-wisdoms, O master of the self-law, and of whatsoever man thou becomest the guest, he conquers by sacrifice, O godhead, those who are mortals.

वयमग्ने वनुयाम त्वोता वसूयवो हविषा बुध्यमानाः ।
वयं समर्ये विदथेष्वह्नां वयं राया सहस्पुत्र मर्तान् ॥६॥

6. May we who seek the Riches win them by the offering, we
guarded by thee and awakened, O Fire, — we in the clash
of the battle, in our discoveries of knowledge through days,
we by the Treasure overcome mortal men, O son of Force.

---

[1] The supreme plane of the three. [2] Or, touch

यो न आगो अभ्येनो भरत्यधीदघमघशंसे दधात ।
जही चिकित्वो अभिशस्तिमेतामग्ने यो नो मर्चयति द्वयेन ॥७॥

7. He who brings sin and transgression upon us, on him who
    gives expression to evil, on himself may there be put that evil;
    O thou who art conscious, slay this hostile assault, O Fire,
    even him who oppresses us with the duality.[1]

त्वामस्या व्युषि देव पूर्वे दूतं कृण्वाना अयजन्त हव्यैः ।
संस्थे यदग्न ईयसे रयीणां देवो मर्तैर्वसुभिरिध्यमानः ॥८॥

8. Thee in the dawning of this night, O godhead, the ancients
    made their messenger and gave sacrifice with their oblations;
    for thou art the godhead kindled by mortals who have the
    light[2] and thou travellest to the House of the Treasures.

अव स्पृधि पितरं योधि विद्वान् पुत्रो यस्ते सहसः सून ऊहे ।
कदा चिकित्वो अभि चक्षसे नोऽग्ने कदा ऋतचिद् यातयासे ॥९॥

9. Rescue thy father, in thy knowledge keep him safe, thy
    father who becomes thy son and bears thee, O son of Force.
    O conscious knower, when wilt thou look upon us? When
    with thy Truth-Consciousness wilt thou set us to our jour-
    ney?

भूरि नाम वन्दमानो दधाति पिता वसो यदि तज्जोषयासे ।
कुविद् देवस्य सहसा चकानः सुम्नमग्निर्निर्वन्ते वावृधानः ॥१०॥

10. The father adores and establishes the mighty name because
    thou, O shining one, bringest him to accept and take pleasure
    in it; once and again, the Fire increases and desiring the bliss
    of the godhead he conquers it by force.

त्वमग्न जरितारं यविष्ठ विश्वान्यग्ने दुरिताति पर्षि ।
स्तेना अदृश्रन् रिपवो जनासोऽज्ञातकेता वृजिना अभूवन् ॥११॥

11. O youthful god, thou, indeed, carriest safe thy adorer beyond

---

[1] The division or the twofoldness of the nature divided between good and evil.
[2] Or, the riches

all stumblings, O Fire; for the hostile beings are seen, the thieves, even they who know not the light of intuitive knowledge and turn to crookedness.

इमे यामासस्त्वद्रिगभूवन् वसवे वा तदिदागो अवाचि ।
नाहायमग्निरभिशस्तये नो न रीषते वावृधानः परा दात् ॥१२॥

12. These journeys have turned towards thee, that evil in us has been declared to the Shining One, O this Fire as he grows will not deliver us to the assailant and the hurter.

SUKTA 4

त्वामग्ने वसुपतिं वसूनामभि प्र मन्दे अध्वरेषु राजन् ।
त्वया वाजं वाजयन्तो जयेमाऽभि ध्याम पृत्सुतीर्मर्त्यानाम् ॥१॥

1. O Fire, O king, towards thee the Wealth-master of the riches I turn and delight in thee in the pilgrim-sacrifice; replenishing thee may we conquer the plenitude, may we overcome the battle-hosts of mortals.

हव्यावाळग्निरजरः पिता नो विभुर्विभावा सुदृशीको अस्मे ।
सुगार्हपत्याः समिधो दिदीह्यास्मद्रयक् सं मिमीहि श्रवांसि ॥२॥

2. The ageless Fire that carries the offering is the father of us, he in us is pervasive in his being, extended in light, perfect in vision. Accomplished in the works of the master of the house blaze out thy forces, form and turn towards us thy inspirations.

विशां कविं विश्पतिं मानुषीणां शुचिं पावकं घृतपृष्ठमग्निम् ।
नि होतारं विश्वविदं दधिध्वे स देवेषु वनते वार्याणि ॥३॥

3. The seer, the master of men, lord of the human peoples, Fire, pure and purifying with its back of light set within you as the omniscient priest of the call; he shall win our desirable things in the godheads.

जुषस्वाग्न इळया सजोषा यतमानो रश्मिभिः सूर्यस्य ।
जुषस्व नः समिधं जातवेद आ च देवान् हविरद्याय वक्षि ॥४॥

4. Of one mind with the goddess of revelation take pleasure in us, O Fire, labouring with the rays of the sun; accept with pleasure our fuel, O knower of all things born, and bring the gods to us to partake of our sacrifice.

जुष्टो दमूना अतिथिर्दुरोण इमं नो यज्ञमुप याहि विद्वान् ।
विश्वा अग्ने अभियुजो विहृत्या शत्रूयतामा भरा भोजनानि ॥५॥

5. A cherished guest domiciled in our gated house come to this sacrifice of ours as the knower; O Fire, slaying all who assail us bring to us the enjoyments of those who make themselves the enemy.

वधेन दस्युं प्र हि चातयस्व वयः कृण्वानस्तन्वे स्वायै ।
पिपर्षि यत् सहसस्पुत्र देवान् त्सो अग्ने पाहि नृतम वाजे अस्मान् ॥६॥

6. Drive away from us the Destroyer with thy stroke making free space for thy own body; when thou carriest the gods over safe, O son of Force, us, O Fire, strongest godhead, guard in the plenitude.

वयं ते अग्न उक्थैर्विधेम वयं हव्यैः पावक भद्रशोचे ।
अस्मे रयिं विश्ववारं समिन्वास्मे विश्वानि द्रविणानि धेहि ॥७॥

7. O Fire, may we worship thee with our words, thee with our offerings, O purifier, O happy light; into us bring the treasure in which are all desirable things, in us establish substance of every kind of riches.

अस्माकमग्ने अध्वरं जुषस्व सहसः सूनो त्रिषधस्थ हव्यम् ।
वयं देवेषु सुकृतः स्याम शर्मणा नस्त्रिवरूथेन पाहि ॥८॥

8. Accept our pilgrim-sacrifice, O Fire, accept, O son of Force, O holder of the triple world of thy session, our offering. May we be doers of good deeds before the godheads, protect us with a triple armour of peace.

विश्वानि नो दुर्गहा जातवेदः सिन्धुं न नावा दुरितातिं पर्षि ।
अग्ने अत्रिवन्नमसा गृणानोऽस्माकं बोध्यविता तनूनाम् ॥९॥

9. O knower of all things born, carry us through all difficult passages, through all calamities as a ship over the ocean. O Fire, voiced by us with our obeisance even as did Atri, awake and be the guardian of our bodies.

यस्त्वा हृदा कीरिणा मन्यमानोऽमर्त्यं मर्त्यो जोहवीमि ।
जातवेदो यशो अस्मासु धेहि प्रजाभिरग्ने अमृतत्वमश्याम् ॥१०॥

10. I think of thee with a heart that is thy bard and mortal I call to thee immortal; O knower of all things born, establish the glory in us, by the children of my works, O Fire, may I win immortality.

यस्मै त्वं सुकृते जातवेद उ लोकमग्ने कृणवः स्योनम् ।
अश्विनं स पुत्रिणं वीरवन्तं गोमन्तं रयिं नशते स्वस्ति ॥११॥

11. The doer of great deeds for whom thou shalt make that happy other world, O knower of all things born, reaches in peace a wealth in which are the Horses of swiftness, the Ray-Cows, the Son, the Heroes.

Sukta 5

सुसमिद्धाय शोचिषे घृतं तीव्रं जुहोतन ।
अग्नये जातवेदसे ॥१॥

1. On the high-kindled flame pour as offering a poignant clarity, to Fire, the knower of all things born.

नराशंसः सुषूदतीमं यज्ञमदाभ्यः ।
कविर्हि मधुहस्त्यः ॥२॥

2. The spokesman of the godhead, the inviolable hastens the sacrifice on its way, for this is the seer who comes with the wine of sweetness in his hands.

ईळितो अग्न आ वहेन्द्रं चित्रमिह प्रियम् ।
सुखै रथेभिरूतये ॥३॥

3. O Fire, we have sought thee with our adoration, bring
    hither Indra the rich in light, the beloved with his happy
    chariots to protect us.

ऊर्णम्रदा वि प्रथस्वाभ्यर्का अनूषत ।
भवा नः शुभ्र सातये ॥४॥

4. Spread wide, O seat, soft as wool the songs of illuminations
    sound high; O bright one, be with us for the conquest.

देवीद्वारो वि श्रयध्वं सुप्रायणा न ऊतये ।
प्रप्र यज्ञं पृणीतन ॥५॥

5. Swing wide, O divine doors; be easy of approach that you
    may be our guard: lead further further and fill full our
    sacrifice.

सुप्रतीके वयोवृधा यह्वी ऋतस्य मातरा ।
दोषामुषासमीमहे ॥६॥

6. Dawn and night we seek with desire the two mighty Mothers
    of the Truth with their fair front to us who increase our
    being's space.

वातस्य पत्मन्नीळिता दैव्या होतारा मनुषः ।
इमं नो यज्ञमा गतम् ॥७॥

7. O worshipped twain, O divine priests of man's call, arrive
    on the path of the wind to this our sacrifice.

इळा सरस्वती मही तिस्रो देवीर्मयोभुवः ।
बर्हिः सीदन्त्वस्रिधः ॥८॥

8. May Ila, Saraswati, and Mahi,[1] the three goddesses who
    create the bliss sit on the sacred seat, they who never err.

---

[1] Ila, goddess of revelation; Saraswati, goddess of inspiration; Mahi, goddess of the
Vast Truth, Mahas or *ṛtaṁ bṛhat*.

शिवस्त्वष्टरिहा गहि विभुः पोष उत त्मना ।
यज्ञेयज्ञे न उदव ॥९॥

9. O maker of forms, hither benignant arrive all-pervading in thy fostering to us and in thyself; in sacrifice on sacrifice us upward guard.

यत्र वेत्थ वनस्पते देवानां गुह्या नामानि ।
तत्र हव्यानि गामय ॥१०॥

10. O Tree,[1] there where thou knowest the secret names of the gods make rich our offerings.

स्वाहाग्नये वरुणाय स्वाहेन्द्राय मरुद्भ्यः ।
स्वाहा देवेभ्यो हविः ॥११॥

11. Swaha to the Fire and to Varuna, Swaha to Indra and the Life-powers, Swaha to the gods be our offering.

SUKTA 6

अग्नि तं मन्ये यो वसुरस्तं यं यन्ति धेनवः ।
अस्तमर्वन्त आशवोऽस्तं नित्यासो वाजिन इषं स्तोतृभ्य आ भर ॥१॥

1. I meditate on the Fire who is the dweller in things,[2] to whom the milch-cows go as to their home, to their home the swift war-horses, to their home the eternal steeds of swiftness.[3] Bring to those who laud thee the force of thy impulse.

सो अग्निर्यो वसुगृणे सं यमायन्ति धेनवः ।
समर्वन्तो रघुद्रुवः सं सुजातासः सूरय इषं स्तोतृभ्य आ भर ॥२॥

2. This is the Fire who is the dweller in things voiced by me, in whom meet the milch-cows, and in him the swift galloping war-horses and in him the illuminates who have come to the perfect birth. Bring to those who laud thee the force of thy impulse.

---

[1] Or, O master of delight,   [2] Or, who is the Shining One,   [3] Or, steeds of the plenitude.

अग्निर्हि वाजिनं विशे ददाति विश्वचर्षणिः ।
अग्नी राये स्वाभुवं स प्रीतो याति वार्यमिषं स्तोतृभ्य आ भर ॥३॥

3. The all-seeing Fire gives the steed of the plenitude to man,
Fire the horse that comes swiftly to him for the riches;
when he is pleased he journeys to the desirable good. Bring
to those who laud thee the force of thy impulse.

आ ते अग्न इधीमहि द्युमन्तं देवाजरम् ।
यद्ध स्या ते पनीयसी समिद् दीदयति द्यवीषं स्तोतृभ्य आ भर ॥४॥

4. O Fire, we kindle thy luminous and ageless flame; when the
fuel of thee becomes more effective in its labour, it blazes
up in heaven. Bring to those who laud thee the force of thy
impulse.

आ ते अग्न ऋचा हविः शुक्रस्य शोचिषस्पते ।
सुश्चन्द्र दस्म विश्पते हव्यवाद् तुभ्यं हूयत इषं स्तोतृभ्य आ भर ॥५॥

5. O Fire, O Master of the brilliant Light, the offering is cast
to thee with the word of illumination, O bearer of the
offering, O master of the creature, achiever of works, O
delightful Flame. Bring to those who laud thee the force of
thy impulse.

प्रो त्ये अग्नयोऽग्निषु विश्वं पुष्यन्ति वार्यम् ।
ते हिन्विरे त इन्विरे त इषण्यन्त्यानुषगिषं स्तोतृभ्य आ भर ॥६॥

6. In thy fires those greater fires of thee nurse every desirable
good; they, they race, they run, they drive on in their impulse without a break. Bring to those who laud thee the force
of thy impulse.

तव त्ये अग्ने अर्चयो महि व्राधन्त वाजिनः ।
ये पत्वभिः शफानां व्रजा भुरन्त गोनामिषं स्तोतृभ्य आ भर ॥७॥

7. O Fire, those rays of thine, thy steeds of plenitude greaten
the Vast; they gallop with tramplings of their hooves to

the pens of the ray-cows. Bring to those who laud thee the
force of thy impulse.

नवा नौ अग्न आ भर स्तोतृभ्यः सुक्षितीरिषः।
ते स्याम य आनृचुस्त्वादूतासो दमेदम इषं स्तोतृभ्य आ भर॥८॥

8. Bring to us who laud thee, O Fire, new impelling forces that
    lead to happy worlds; may we be of those who with thee
    for their messenger sing the hymn of illumination in home and
    home. Bring to those who laud thee the force of thy impulse.

उभे सुश्चन्द्र सर्पिषो दर्वी श्रीणीष आसनि।
उतो न उत् पुपूर्या उक्थेषु शवसस्पत इषं स्तोतृभ्य आ भर॥९॥

9. O delightful Flame, thou turnest both the ladles of the
    streaming clarity towards thy mouth; then mayst thou carry
    us high beyond in the utterances, O Master of might. Bring
    to those who laud thee the force of thy impulse.

एवाँ अग्निमजुर्यमुर्गीभिर्यज्ञेभिरानुषक्।
दधदस्मे सुवीर्यमुत त्यदाश्वश्व्यमिषं स्तोतृभ्य आ भर॥१०॥

10. Thus have they driven and controlled the Fire without a
    break by their words and their sacrifices; may he found in
    us the perfect hero-might and the perfect power of the
    Horse. Bring to those who laud thee the force of thy
    impulse.

ISHA

SUKTA 7

सखायः सं वः सम्यञ्चमिषं स्तोमं चाग्नये।
वर्षिष्ठाय क्षितीनामूर्जो नप्त्रे सहस्वते॥१॥

1. O comrades, in you an integral force and complete laud
    to Fire the most powerful among the peoples, to the

mighty child of energy.

कुत्रा चिद् यस्य समृतौ रण्वा नरो नृषदने ।
अहं न्तश्चिद् यमिन्धते संजनयन्ति जन्तवः ॥२॥

2. Whom wheresoever they come into contact with, him men
    who have the power rapturously set alight in this house of
    man and all beings born strive to bring to birth.

सं यदिषो वनामहे सं हव्या मानुषाणाम् ।
उत द्युम्नस्य शवस ऋतस्य रश्मिमा ददे ॥३॥

3. Whenso we win completely the impulsions of force,
    completely the offerings human beings must give, then he
    gathers to himself the Ray of the light and the might and
    the Truth.

सः स्मा कृणोति केतुमा नक्तं चिद् दूर आ सते ।
पावको यद् वनस्पतीन् प्र स्मा मिनात्यजरः ॥४॥

4. Yea, he creates the light of intuition even for one who is
    far off in the night, the purifying and imperishable Fire
    ravages the trees of the forest.

अव स्म यस्य वेषणे स्वेदं पथिषु जुह्वति ।
अभीमह स्वजेन्यं भूमा पृष्ठेव रुरुहुः ॥५॥

5. When in his service men cast down their sweat on the paths,
    they ascend to a self-born ground as if to wide levels.

यं मर्त्यः पुरुस्पृहं विदद् विश्वस्य धायसे ।
प्र स्वादनं पितूनामस्ततार्ति चिदायवे ॥६॥

6. Him mortal man must come to know as one who holds the
    multitude of his desires so that he may establish in him all;
    he moves towards the sweet taste of the draughts of the wine
    and to the building of the house for man.

स हि ष्मा धन्वाक्षितं वाता न वात्या पशुः ।
हिरिइमश्रुः शुचिदञ्भुरनिभृष्टतविषिः ॥७॥

7. Pure and bright, verily, is he and he tears our desert dwelling place,[1] like a beast who tears, a beast with golden beard and tusks of bright purity, he is like a smith whose force is unafflicted by the heat of the Fire.

शुचिः ष्म यस्मा अत्रिवत् प्र स्वधितीव रीयते ।
सुषूरसूत माता क्राणा यदानशे भगम् ॥८॥

8. Yes, he is pure and bright and he is as one whose axe is like an eater and ever enters deeper; with a happy delivery his mother bore him, for he is an achiever of the work and wins enjoyment of the bliss.

आः यस्ते सर्पिरासुतेऽग्ने शमस्ति धायसे ।
ऐषु द्युम्नमुत श्रव आ चित्तं मर्त्येषु धाः ॥९॥

9. O Fire, to whom is poured the running stream of the offering of light, the man who is a happy ground for establishing thee, — in such mortals found the light, and the inspiration and the knowledge.

इति चिन्मन्युमधिजस्त्वादातमा पशुं ददे ।
आदग्ने अपृणतोऽत्रिः सासह्याद् दस्यूनिषः सासह्यान्नृन् ॥१०॥

10. Even so, irresistible born, I receive the force of mind, the cow of vision given by thee. O Fire, then may Atri overcome the destroyers who satisfy thee not, may he overcome forces and men.

SUKTA 8

त्वामग्न ऋतायवः समीधिरे प्रत्नं प्रत्नास ऊतये सहस्कृत ।
पुरुश्चन्द्रं यजतं विश्वधायसं दमूनसं गृहपतिं वरेण्यम् ॥१॥

---

[1] Or, the solid ground on which we dwell,

1. O Fire, created by our force, thee the Ancient One, the ancient seekers of Truth set blazing for their guard the master of sacrifice with his many delights who establishes all, Fire who dwells in the house, master of the house, the supremely desirable.

त्वामग्ने अतिथिं पूर्व्यं विशः शोचिष्केशं गृहपतिं नि षेदिरे ।
बृहत्केतुं पुरुरूपं धनस्पृतं सुशर्माणं स्ववसं जरद्विषम् ॥२॥

2. Thee, O Fire, men seated within as the ancient guest, the master of the house with his tresses of light, — vast is his intuition, many are his forms, he brings out the riches, he is a giver of perfect peace and protection and a destroyer of the foe.

त्वामग्ने मानुषीरीळते विशो होत्राविदं विविचि रत्नधातमम् ।
गुहा सन्तं सुभग विश्ववदर्शतं तुविष्वणसं सुयजं घृतश्रियम् ॥३॥

3. Thee the human people pray, O Fire, who knowest the word of invocation, who hast the just discernment, who art strongest to found the ecstasy, — thee who dwellest in the secret cave, O happy Flame, and hast the vision of all things, the perfect sacrificer with the multitude of thy voices and the glory and beauty of thy light.

त्वामग्ने धर्णसि विश्ववधा वयं गीर्भिर्गृणन्तो नमसोप सेदिम ।
स नो जुषस्व समिधानो अङ्गिरो देवो मर्तस्य यशसा सुवीतिभिः ॥४॥

4. Thee, O Fire, who upholdest all things in every way we voicing thee with our words have approached with obeisance; so do thou accept us, O Angiras, a godhead kindled by the glory of a mortal and by his high illuminings.

त्वमग्ने पुरुरूपो विशेविशे वयो दधासि प्रत्नथा पुरुष्टुत ।
पुरूण्यन्ना सहसा वि राजसि त्विषिः सा ते तित्विषाणस्य नाधृषे ॥५॥

5. O Fire, thou takest many forms for man and man and thou foundest for him his growth as of old, O thou lauded by

many voices; many are the things on which thou feedest and thou illuminest them all with thy force, and none can do violence to the fury of thy blaze when thou blazest up in thy might.

त्वामग्ने समिधानं यविष्ठ्य देवा दूतं चक्रिरे हव्यवाहनम् ।
उरुज्रयसं घृतयोनिमाहुतं त्वेषं चक्षुर्दधिरे चोदयन्मति ॥६॥

6. Thee, O youthful Fire, in thy high kindling the gods have made a messenger and a carrier of the offerings; thee of whom light is the native seat and wide are the spaces through which thou movest, they have set when thou hast received the offerings as a keen burning eye that urges the thought.

त्वामग्ने प्रदिव आहुतं घृतैः सुम्नायवः सुषमिधा समीधिरे ।
स वावृधान ओषधीभिरुक्षितोऽभि ज्रयांसि पार्थिवा वि तिष्ठसे ॥७॥

7. Thee, O Fire, fed with offerings of light from the higher heaven the seekers of bliss[1] kindled with an entire kindling, so now growing on the herbs to thy full might thou spreadest over wide earth-spaces.

GAYA

SUKTA 9

त्वामग्ने हविष्मन्तो देवं मर्तास ईळते ।
मन्ये त्वा जातवेदसं स हव्या वक्ष्यानुषक् ॥१॥

1. Thee, O Fire, men bringing offerings pray, mortals the godhead; I meditate on thee as the knower of all things born and as such thou carriest our offerings without a break.

अग्निर्होता वास्वतः क्षयस्य वृक्तबर्हिषः ।
सं यज्ञासश्चरन्ति यं सं वाजासः श्रवस्यवः ॥२॥

---

[1] Or, from of old; or, the ancient seekers of bliss

2. Fire is the priest of the call in the house of the giver who has plucked the grass for the seat of sacrifice and in him our sacrifices meet and our plenitudes of inspired knowledge.

उत स्म यं शिशुं यथा नवं जनिष्टारणी ।
धर्तारं मानुषीणां विशामग्निं स्वध्वरम् ॥३॥

3. Verily, the two tinders have brought to birth as if a new-born infant Fire who does aright the pilgrim-sacrifice, to be the upholder of the human beings.

उत स्म दुर्गृभीयसे पुत्रो न ह्वार्याणाम् ।
पुरू यो दधासि वनाऽग्ने पशुर्न यवसे ॥४॥

4. Verily, thou art hard to seize like a son of crookednesses; many are the trees of the forest thou consumest, O Fire, like a beast in his pasture.

अध स्म यस्यार्चयः सम्यक् संयन्ति धूमिनः ।
यदीमह त्रितो दिव्युप धमातेव धमति शिशीते धमातरी यथा ॥५॥

5. Now, verily, his rays with their smoke meet perfectly together when Trita, the triple one, blows upon him in heaven like a smelter, it is as if in the smelter that he whets his flame.

तवाहमग्न ऊतिभिर्मित्रस्य च प्रशस्तिभिः ।
द्वेषोयुतो न दुरिता तुर्याम मर्त्यानाम् ॥६॥

6. I by thy guardings, O Fire, and by thy utterances as the friend — like men beset by hostile powers so may we pass beyond the stumbling-places of mortals.

तं नो अग्ने अभी नरो रयिं सहस्व आ भर ।
स क्षेपयत् स पोषयद् भुवद् वाजस्य सातय उतैधि पृत्सु नो वृषे ॥७॥

7. O forceful Fire, bring to us, to men, the treasure; may he cast his shafts, may he foster us, may he be with us for the conquest of the plenitude. Be with us in our battles that we may grow.

SUKTA 10

अग्न ओजिष्ठमा भर द्युम्नमस्मभ्यमध्रिगो ।
प्र नो राया परीणसा रत्सि वाजाय पन्थाम् ॥१॥

1. O Fire, bring to us a light full of energy, O unseizable Ray;
   for us by thy opulence pervading on every side cut out in our
   front a path to the plenitude.

त्वं नो अग्ने अद्भुत क्रत्वा दक्षस्य मंहना ।
त्वे असुर्यमारुहत् क्राणा मित्रो न यज्ञियः ॥२॥

2. O Fire, O Wonderful, come to us with thy will and the
   growth of the judgment; in thee the sacrificial Friend,
   achiever of the work can climb to almightiness.

त्वं नो अग्न एषां गयं पुष्टिं च वर्धय ।
ये स्तोमेभिः प्र सूरयो नरो मघान्यानशुः ॥३॥

3. Increase for us, O Fire, the acquisition and the growth of
   these who are men that are illuminates and by their laudings
   of thee have attained to the plenitudes of the riches, —

ये अग्ने चन्द्र ते गिरः शुम्भन्त्यश्वराधसः ।
शुष्मेभिः शुष्मिणो नरो दिवश्चिद् येषां बृहत् सुकीर्तिर्बोधति त्मना ॥४॥

4. who, O delightful Fire, have achieved the power of the horse
   and make beautiful their words of thee, strong men with
   their strength whose is the Vast that is greater even than
   heaven, for in them that glory by itself awakes.

तव त्ये अग्ने अर्चयो भाजन्तो यन्ति धृष्णुया ।
परिज्मानो न विद्युतः स्वानो रथो न वाजयुः ॥५॥

5. These are those flaming rays of thine, O Fire, and they go
   blazing and violent, like lightnings that run over all quar-

ters, like the voice of a chariot seeking the plenitude.

नू नो अग्न ऊतये सबाधसश्च रातये ।
अस्माकासश्च सूरयो विश्वा आशास्तरीषणि ॥६॥

6. Soon, O Fire, may alike those of us who are opposed and
obstructed attain to protection and the giving of the riches
and our illuminates break through all directions and beyond.

त्वं नो अग्ने अङ्गिरः स्तुतः स्तवान आ भर ।
होतर्विभ्वासहं रयिं स्तोतृभ्यः स्तवसे च न उतैधि पृत्सु नो वृषे ॥७॥

7. Thou, O Fire, O Angiras, after and during the laud bring
to us riches of a far-reaching force, O Priest of the call, for
those who laud thee and for our further laud. Be with us in
our battles that we may grow.

SUTAMBHARA

SUKTA 11

जनस्य गोपा अजनिष्ट जागृविरग्निः सुदक्षः सुविताय नव्यसे ।
घृतप्रतीको बृहता दिविस्पृशा द्युमद् वि भाति भरतेभ्यः शुचिः ॥१॥

1. Fire the guardian of men has been born, wakeful and discerning for a new happy journey; luminous is his front and
with his heaven-touching vast he shines out full of light and
brilliant in his purity for the Bringers.

यज्ञस्य केतुं प्रथमं पुरोहितमग्निं नरस्त्रिषधस्थे समीधिरे ।
इन्द्रेण देवैः सरथं स बर्हिषि सीदन्नि होता यजथाय सुक्रतुः ॥२॥

2. Fire the supreme intuition of the sacrifice, the representative
priest, men have kindled high in the triple world of his
session; let him come in one chariot with Indra and the gods
and take his seat on the sacred grass, the Priest of the call,
strong in will to sacrifice.

असंमृष्टो जायसे मात्रोः शुचिर्मन्द्रः कविरुदतिष्ठो विवस्वतः ।
घृतेन त्वावर्धयन्नग्न आहुत धूमस्ते केतुरभवद् दिवि श्रितः ॥३॥

3. Unoppressed thou art born brilliant-pure from the mothers
   twain, a rapturous Priest of the call thou hast risen up from
   the sun; they have increased thee with the offering of light,
   O Fire, fed with the oblation and thy smoke has become a
   ray of intuition lodged in heaven.

अग्निर्नो यज्ञमुप वेतु साधुयाऽग्निं नरो वि भरन्ते गृहेगृहे ।
अग्निर्दूतो अभवद्ध्यवाहनोऽग्निं वृणाना वृणते कविक्रतुम् ॥४॥

4. May the Fire come to our sacrifice with power to accomplish, men carry the Fire severally in house and house; the
   Fire has become the messenger and carrier of our offering;
   when men accept the Fire it is the seer-will that they accept.

तुभ्येदमग्ने मधुमत्तमं वचस्तुभ्यं मनीषा इयमस्तु शं हृदे ।
त्वां गिरः सिन्धुमिवावनीर्महीरा पृणन्ति शवसा वर्धयन्ति च ॥५॥

5. For thee, O Fire, this word most full of the honey-sweetness,
   for thee this Thinking, let it be a happiness to thy heart;
   thee our words fill with force as the great rivers fill the sea
   and make thee grow.

त्वामग्ने अङ्गिरसो गुहा हितमन्वविन्दञ्छिश्रियाणं वनेवने ।
स जायसे मथ्यमानः सहो महत् त्वामाहुः सहसस्पुत्रमङ्गिरः ॥६॥

6. Thee, O Fire, the Angiras sought and found hidden in the
   secrecy lodging in tree and tree; by our pressure on thee
   thou art born a mighty force, the Son of Force they call thee,
   O Angiras!

SUKTA 12

प्राग्नये बृहते यज्ञियाय ऋतस्य वृष्णे असुराय मन्म ।
घृतं न यज्ञ आस्ये सुपूतं गिरं भरे वृषभाय प्रतीचीम् ॥१॥

1. To Fire, the vast sacrificial Flame, to the Bull of the Truth,
    to the mighty lord I bring my thought as if the offering of
    light in the sacrifice, purified in the mouth I bring the word
    turned to meet him for the master of the herds.

ऋतं चिकित्व ऋतमिच्चिकिद्धृतस्य धारा अनु तृन्धि पूर्वीः ।
नाहं यातुं सहसा न द्वयेन ऋतं सपाम्यरुषस्य वृष्णः ॥२॥

2. O thou conscious of the Truth, of the Truth alone be con-
    scious, cut out in succession many streams of the Truth; I
    know not how to travel by force or by division to the Truth
    of the shining lord.

कया नो अग्न ऋतयन्नृतेन भुवो नवेदा उचथस्य नव्यः ।
वेदा मे देव ऋतुपा ऋतूनां नाहं पतिं सनितुरस्य रायः ॥३॥

3. By what thought of ours seeking the Truth by the Truth shalt
    thou become for us, O Fire, a new discoverer of the word?
    The god who is guardian of the order and laws of the Truth
    knows me but I know him not, the master of the conquering
    riches.

के ते अग्ने रिपवे बन्धनासः के पायवः सनिषन्त द्युमन्तः ।
के धासिमग्ने अनृतस्य पान्ति क आसतो वचसः सन्ति गोपाः ॥४॥

4. O Fire, who are these that are binders of the Adversary,
    who are the guardians, the luminous ones that shall possess
    and conquer? who keep the foundation of the Falsehood,
    O Fire? who are the guardians of the untrue Word?

सखायस्ते विषुणा अग्न एते शिवासः सन्तो अशिवा अभूवन् ।
अधूर्षत स्वयमेते वचोभिऋंजूयते वृजिनानि ब्रुवन्तः ॥५॥

5. These were thy comrades, O Fire, who have turned away
    from thee, they were benignant and have become malign;
    they have done violence to themselves by their words speak-
    ing crooked things to the seeker after straightness.

यस्ते अग्ने नमसा यज्ञमीट्टू ऋतं स पात्यरुषस्य वृष्ण: ।
तस्य क्षय: पृथुरा साधुरेतु प्रसर्साणस्य नहुषस्य शेष: ॥६॥

6. But he, O Fire, who desires with obeisance the sacrifice,
   guards the Truth of the luminous lord; let there come to
   him his wide and perfect habitation, the last state of man as
   he advances on his journey.

SUKTA 13

अर्चन्तस्त्वा हवामहेऽर्चन्त: समिधीमहि ।
अग्ने अर्चन्त ऊतये ॥१॥

1. Singing the word of illumination we call to thee, singing the
   word of illumination we kindle, singing the word of illumination, O Fire, that thou mayst be our guard.

अग्ने: स्तोमं मनामहे सिध्रमद्य दिविस्पृश: ।
देवस्य द्रविणस्यव: ॥२॥

2. Seekers of the riches we meditate today the all-achieving
   laud of the divine, heaven-touching Fire.

अग्निर्जुषत नो गिरो होता यो मानुषेष्वा ।
स यक्षद् दैव्यं जनम् ॥३॥

3. May Fire accept our words, he who is the priest of the call
   in men; may he sacrifice to the divine kind.

त्वमग्ने सप्रथा असि जुष्टो होता वरेण्य: ।
त्वया यज्ञं वि तन्वते ॥४॥

4. Great is thy wideness, O Fire, our priest of the call, beloved
   and supremely desirable; by thee men carry out the sacrifice.

त्वामग्ने वाजसातमं विप्रा वर्धन्ति सुष्टुतम् ।
स नो रास्व सुवीर्यम् ॥५॥

5.   Thee high-lauded, O Fire, the strong conqueror of the pleni-
     tudes, the illumined wise increase; so do thou give us the
     gift of a complete hero-might.

अग्ने नेमिररॉं इव देवॉस्त्वं परिभूरसि ।
आ राधश्चित्रमृञ्जसे ॥६॥

6.   As the rim of a wheel the spokes, so dost thou encompass
     the gods; thou shalt arrange for us our rich achievement.

SUKTA 14

अग्निं स्तोमेन बोधय समिधानो अमर्त्यम् ।
हव्या देवेषु नो दघत् ॥१॥

1.   Awake by the laud the Fire, let the immortal be kindled
     and let him set our offerings in the godheads.

तमध्वरेष्वीळते देवं मर्तो अमर्त्यम् ।
यजिष्ठं मानुषे जने ॥२॥

2.   Him they pray in the pilgrim-sacrifices, mortals the divine
     and immortal who is strong for sacrifice in human kind.

तं हि शश्वन्त ईळते स्रुचा देवं घृतश्चुता ।
अग्निं हव्याय वोळ्हवे ॥३॥

3.   Him, the divine Fire, the perpetual generations pray with
     the ladle dripping the clarity for the carrying of their of-
     ferings.

अग्निर्जातो अरोचत घ्नन् दस्यूञ्ज्योतिषा तमः ।
अविन्दद् गा अपः स्वः ॥४॥

4.   Fire at his birth has shone out slaying the destroyers, dark-
     ness by the light, he found the Ray-Cows, the Waters, the
     Sun-World.

अग्निमीळेन्यं कविं घृतपृष्ठं सपर्यंत ।
वेतु मे शृणवढ्ढवम् ॥५॥

5. Serve Fire the supremely desirable, the seer with his back
of Light; may he come, may he hear my call.

अग्निं घृतेन वावृधुः स्तोमेभिर्विश्वचर्षणिम् ।
स्वाधीभिर्वंचस्युभिः ॥६॥

6. The Fire they have made to grow by the light, the all-seeing
by their lauds that place rightly the thought, that seek for
the word.

DHARUNA ANGIRASA

SUKTA 15

प्र वेधसे कवये वेद्याय गिरं भरे यशसे पूर्व्याय ।
घृतप्रसत्तो असुरः सुश्रेवो रायो धर्ता धरुणो वस्वो अग्निः ॥१॥

1. I bring my word to the creator and seer, him whom we must
know, the glorious, the ancient one; Fire the Mighty One
seated in the light, full of bliss, the holder of the Treasure,
the continent of the Riches.

ऋतेन ऋतं धरुणं धारयन्त यज्ञस्य शाके परमे व्योमन् ।
दिवो धर्मन् धरुणे सेदुषो नॄञ्जातैरजातां अभि ये ननक्षुः ॥२॥

2. By the Truth they held the Truth that holds all, in the might
of the sacrifice, in the supreme ether, they who reached the
gods seated in the law that is the upholder of heaven, reached
by the godheads born the unborn.

अंहोयुवस्तन्वस्तन्वते वि वयो महद् दुष्टरं पूर्व्याय ।
स संवतो नवजातस्तुतुर्यात् सिंहं न क्रुद्धमभितः परि ष्ठुः ॥३॥

3. They weave bodies that reject evil, they weave a vast expansion hard to cross for the ancient one; he new-born can

cross through the regions[1] though they stand around him as
around an angry lion.

मातेव यद् भरसे पप्रथानो जनंजनं धायसे चक्षसे च ।
वयोवयो जरसे यद् दधानः परि त्मना विषुरूपो जिगासि ॥४॥

4. When growing wide thou bearest like a mother birth after
   birth for firm foundation, for vision, when thou holdest and
   wearest out manifestation after manifestation, taking many
   forms thou encompassest all things with thyself.

वाजो नु ते शवसस्पात्वन्तमुरं बोघं धरणं देव रायः ।
पदं न. तायुर्गूंहा दधानो महो राये चितयन्नत्रिमस्पः ॥५॥

5. May thy plenitude guard the last limit of thy force, the wide
   continent of the riches that milks out its abundance, O
   godhead: like a thief thou holdest in the secrecy that plane,
   awakening him to the consciousness of the great riches thou
   hast rescued Atri.

PURU

SUKTA 16

बृहद् वयो हि भानवेऽर्चा देवायाग्नये ।
यं मित्रं न प्रशस्तिभिर्मर्तासो दधिरे पुरः ॥१॥

1. Create by the illumining word a wide expansion for the
   Light, for the divine Fire, whom mortals by their proclaimings of him set in their front as Mitra the friend.

स हि द्युभिर्जनानां होता दक्षस्य बाह्वोः ।
वि हव्यमग्निरानुषग्भगो न वारमृण्वति ॥२॥

2. He is men's priest of the call who by his illuminations
   carries in his two arms of the Understanding the offerings
   wholly in a continuous order; as Bhaga, the enjoyer, he

---

[1] Or, breaks through his converging hunters

reaches our desirable good.

अस्य स्तोमे मधोनः सख्ये वृद्धशोचिषः ।
विश्वा यस्मिन् तुविष्वणि समर्ये शुष्ममादधुः ॥३॥

3. In the lauding of this master of plenty, in his friendship as his light grows, for all things are in this Fire of the many voices, men have founded their strength in him, the Noble One.

अधा ह्यग्न एषां सुवीर्यस्य मंहना ।
तमिद् यह्वं न रोदसी परि श्रवो बभूवतुः ॥४॥

4. Now, indeed, O Fire, these have reached a plenitude of heroic strength, around him as around one mighty, earth and heaven have become an inspired knowledge.

नू न एहि वार्यमग्ने गृणान आ भर ।
ये वयं ये च सूरयः स्वस्ति धामहे सचोतैधि पृत्सु नो वृधे ॥५॥

5. Now, voiced by our word, come to us and bring to us our desirable good; we here and the illumined seers, let us together found our blissful state. And do thou be with us in our battles that we may grow.

SUKTA 17

आ यज्ञैर्देव मर्त्य इत्था तव्यांसमूतये ।
अग्निं कृते स्वध्वरे पूरुरीळीतावसे ॥१॥

1. Mortal man should pray thee, O God, by the sacrifices because thou hast the right strength for his guard; when well-done is the pilgrim-sacrifice man must pray the Fire that he may protect him.

अस्य हि स्वयशस्तर आसा विधर्मन् मन्यसे ।
तं नाकं चित्रशोचिषं मन्द्रं परो मनीषया ॥२॥

2. By his mouth, in his complete law, thou becomest greater
    in the self-glory and holdest in mind that rapturous heaven
    manifoldly brilliant in its light beyond the thinking mind.

अस्य वासा उ अर्चिषा य आयुक्त तुजा गिरा ।
दिवो न यस्य रेतसा बृहच्छोचन्त्यर्चयः ॥३॥

3. This, indeed, is he who by the ray of this Fire has become
    possessed of the force and the word and whose rays by the
    seed of heaven blaze into a vast light.

अस्य क्रत्वा विचेतसो दस्मस्य वसु रथ आ ।
अधा विश्वासु हव्योऽग्निर्विक्षु प्र शस्यते ॥४॥

4. By the will of this completely conscious achiever of works the
    riches are there in his car; so now is the Fire the one to be
    called and he is proclaimed in all the peoples.

नू न इद्धि वार्यमासा सचन्त सूरयः ।
ऊर्जो नपादभिष्टये पाहि शग्धि स्वस्तय उतैधि पृत्सु नो वृषे ॥५॥

5. Now, indeed, by the mouth of the Fire, can the luminous
    seers cleave to that desirable good; O son of energy, protect
    us that we may enter in, have power for the happy state.
    And do thou be with us in our battles that we may conquer.

DWITA MRIKTAWAHAS

SUKTA 18

प्रातरग्निः पुरुप्रियो विशः स्तवेतातिथिः ।
विश्वानि यो अमर्त्यो हव्या मर्तेषु रण्यति ॥१॥

1. Let the Fire with his multitude of delightful things, the
    guest of man, receive the laud at dawn, he who is immortal
    in mortals and takes joy in all their offerings.

द्विताय मृक्तवाहसे स्वस्य दक्षस्य मंहना ।
इन्दुं स धत्त आनुषक् स्तोता चित् ते अमर्त्य ॥२॥

2. The plenitude of his own understanding for the twofold
power that carries the purified offering; he holds uninterruptedly the moon-wine and he too who lauds thee, holds
it, O immortal.

तं वो दीर्घायुशोचिषं गिरा हुवे मघोनाम् ।
अरिष्टो येषां रथो व्यश्वदावन्त्रीयते ॥३॥

3. I call him by the word who is the light of long-extended life
for you the lords of plenty, you whose chariot goes abroad
without hurt, O giver of the Horse, —

चित्रा वा येषु दीधितिरासन्नुक्था पान्ति ये ।
स्तीर्णं बर्हिः स्वर्णरे श्रवांसि दधिरे परि ॥४॥

4. in whom is the richly brilliant light of thought and they
guard the utterances in their mouths; spread is the sacred
seat and they found the inspirations all around it in the
Godhead of the sun-world.

ये मे पञ्चाशतं ददुरश्वानां सधस्तुति ।
द्युमदग्ने महि श्रवो बृहत् कृधि मघोनां नृवदमृत नृणाम् ॥५॥

5. They who have given me in the moment of the laud the fifty
steeds of swiftness create for those lords of plenty a great
and luminous inspired knowledge, create for those gods the
Vast, with its gods, O Immortal, O Fire.

VAVRI

SUKTA 19

अभ्यवस्थाः प्र जायन्ते प्र वव्रेर्वव्रिश्चिकेत ।
उपस्थे मातुर्वि चष्टे ॥१॥

1. State upon state is born, covering upon covering has be-

come conscious and aware, in the lap of the mother he sees.

जुहुरे वि चितयन्तोऽनिमिषं नृम्णं पान्ति ।
आ वृल्हां पुरं विविशुः ॥२॥

2. Awaking to an entire knowledge they have called and guard
a sleepless strength, they have entered the strong fortified
city.

आ श्वेत्रेयस्य जन्तवो द्युमद् वर्धन्त कृष्टयः ।
निष्कग्रीवो बृहदुक्थ एना मध्वा न वाजयुः ॥३॥

3. Creatures born, men who people the earth have increased
the luminosity of the son of the white mother; his neck wears
the golden necklace, he has the utterance of the Vast, and
with his honey-wine he is the seeker of the plenitude.

प्रियं दुग्धं न काम्यमजामि जाम्योः सचा ।
घर्मो न वाजजठरोऽदब्धः शश्वतो दभः ॥४॥

4. He is as if the delightful and desirable milk of the mother, he
is that which is uncompanioned abiding with the two companions; he is the blaze of the light, and the belly of the
plenitude, he is the eternal invincible and the all-conqueror.

क्रीळन् नो रश्म आ भुवः सं भस्मना वायुना वेविदानः ।
ता अस्य सन् धृषजो न तिग्माः सुसंशिता वक्ष्यो वक्षणेस्थाः ॥५॥

5. O Ray, mayst thou be with us and play with us, unifying
thy knowledge with the shining of the breath of life; may
those flames of him be for us violent and intense and keenly
whetted, strong to carry and settled in the breast.

PRAYASWATS

SUKTA 20

यमग्ने वाजसातम त्वं चिन् मन्यसे रयिम् ।
तं नो गीर्भिः श्रवाय्यं देवत्रा पनया युजम् ॥१॥

1. O Fire, O thou who art most strong to conquer the plenitudes, the wealth which thou holdest in mind that make full
of inspiration by the words and set it to work in the gods as
our ally.

ये अग्ने नेरयन्ति ते वृद्धा उग्रस्य शवसः ।
अप द्वेषो अप ह्वरोऽन्यव्रतस्य सश्चिरे ॥२॥

2. They have grown on thy forceful strength, O Fire, yet impel
us not on the way, they fall away and cleave to the hostility,
cleave to the crookedness of one who has a law alien to
thine.

होतारं त्वा वृणीमहेऽग्ने दक्षस्य साधनम् ।
यज्ञेषु पूर्व्यं गिरा प्रयस्वन्तो हवामहे ॥३॥

3. Thee, O Fire, the ancient one, we choose in our sacrifices as
the Priest of the call, one who accomplishes a discerning
knowledge, and bringing the pleasant offering we call thee
by the word.

इत्था यथा त ऊतये सहसावन् दिवेदिवे ।
राय ऋताय सुक्रतो गोभिः ष्याम सधमादो वीरैः स्याम सधमादः ॥४॥

4. So rightly make it that we may live in thy protection and
that we may grow towards the Truth day by day, O forceful
Fire, O strong in will, together rejoicing in the light of the
Ray-Cow, together rejoicing in the strength of the Heroes.

SASA

SUKTA 21

मनुष्वत् त्वा नि धीमहि मनुष्वत् समिधीमहि ।
अग्ने मनुष्वदङ्गिरो देवान् देवयते यज ॥१॥

1 As the human we set thee within us, as the human we kindle

thee; O Fire, O Angiras, as the human offer sacrifice to the gods for the seeker of the godheads.

त्वं हि मानुषे जनेऽग्ने सुप्रीत इध्यसे ।
स्रुचस्त्वा यन्त्यानुषक् सुजात सर्पिरासुते ॥२॥

2.   O Fire, thou art kindled in the human being and well-satisfied; unceasing ladles go to thee, O perfect in thy birth, O thou who receivest as oblation the stream of his clarities!

त्वां विश्वे सजोषसो देवासो दूतमक्रत ।
सपर्यन्तस्त्वा कवे यज्ञेषु देवमीळते ॥३॥

3.   Thee all the gods with one mind of acceptance made their envoy; men serving thee pray thee as the godhead in their sacrifices, O seer.

देवं वो देवयज्ययाऽग्निमीळीत मर्त्यः ।
समिद्धः शुक्र दीदिहि ऋतस्य योनिमासदः ससस्य योनिमासदः ॥४॥

4.   Let mortal man with will to the divine sacrifice to you, pray to the divine Fire; O brilliant Flame, high-kindled shine; mayst thou take thy seat in the native home of the Truth, take thy seat in the native home of the peace.

VISHWASAMAN

SUKTA 22

प्र विश्वसामन्नत्रिवदर्चा पावकशोचिषे ।
यो अध्वरेष्वीडघो होता मन्द्रतमो विशि ॥१॥

1.   O thou of the universal peace, as the Atri sing the word of illumination to Fire of the purifying light who is to be prayed in the pilgrim-sacrifices, the Priest of the call, most rapturous in man.

न्याग्निं जातवेदसं दधाता देवमृत्विजम् ।
प्र यज्ञ एत्वानुषगद्या देवव्यचस्तमः ॥२॥

2. Set within you Fire, the knower of all things born, as the
divine ordinant of the rite; let your sacrifice march forward
today most strong to bring the epiphany of the gods.

चिकित्विन्मनसं त्वा देवं मर्तास ऊतये ।
वरेण्यस्य तेज्वस इयानासो अमन्महि ॥३॥

3. Mortals we fix our minds on thee the godhead who hast the
mind of conscious knowledge for the protection as we
journey, for the guardian supremely desirable.

अग्ने चिकिद्धघस्य न इदं वचः सहस्य ।
तं त्वा सुशिप्र वंपते स्तोमैर्वर्धन्त्यत्रयो गीर्भिः शुम्भन्त्यत्रयः ॥४॥

4. O Fire, become conscious of this in us, this is our word,
O forceful Flame: O strong-jawed master of the house this
is thou whom the Atris magnify with their lauds, whom the
Atris glorify with their words.

DYUMNA VISHWACHARSHANI

SUKTA 23

अग्ने सहन्तमा भर द्युम्नस्य प्रासहा रयिम् ।
विश्वा यश्चर्षणीरभ्यासा वाजेषु सासहत् ॥१॥

1. O Fire, bring by the force of the light a forceful wealth which
shall overcome by thy mouth in the plenitudes all the
peoples.

तमग्ने पृतनाषहं रयिं सहस्व आ भर ।
त्वं हि सत्यो अद्भुतो दाता वाजस्य गोमतः ॥२॥

2. O forceful Fire, bring that wealth which overcomes armies,

for thou art the true, the wonderful, the giver of the plenitude
of the Ray-Cows.

विश्वे हि त्वा सजोषसो जनासो वृक्तबर्हिषः ।
होतारं सद्मसु प्रियं व्यन्ति वार्या पुरु ॥३॥

3. All men who have plucked the sacred grass with one mind of
    acceptance approach thee, the beloved Priest of the call in
    their houses and reach in thee the multitude of desirable
    things.

स हि क्ष्मा विश्वचर्षणिरभिमाति सहो दधे ।
अग्न एषु क्षयेष्वा रेवन्नः शुक्र दीदिहि द्युमत् पावक दीदिहि ॥४॥

4. This is the labourer in all man's works and he holds in him-
    self an all-besieging force. O pure brilliant Flame, shine out
    full of joy and opulence in these our habitations, shine out
    full of light, O our purifier.

GAUPAYANAS OR LAUPAYANAS

SUKTA 24

अग्ने त्वं नो अन्तम उत त्राता शिवो भवा वरूथ्यः ।
वसुरग्निर्वसुश्रवा अच्छा नक्षि द्युमत्तमं रयिं दाः ॥१॥२॥

1-2. O Will, become our inmost inmate, become auspicious to us,
      become our deliverer and our armour of protection. Thou
      who art the lord of substance and who of that substance hast
      the divine knowledge, come towards us, give us its most
      luminous opulence.

स नो बोधि श्रुधी हवमुरुष्या णो अघायतः समस्मात् ।
तं त्वा शोचिष्ठ दीदिवः सुम्नाय नूनमीमहे सखिभ्यः ॥३॥४॥

3-4. Awake! hear our call! keep us far from all that seeks to
      turn us to evil. O shining One, O Flame of purest Light,

thee for our comrades we desire that even now they may have
the bliss and peace.

VASUYUS

SUKTA 25

अच्छा वो अग्निमवसे देवं गासि स नो वसुः ।
रासत् पुत्र ऋषूणामृतावा पर्षति द्विषः ॥१॥

1. Raise thy song towards the Will, towards the divine for thy
   increasing, for he is our lord of substance and he lavishes;
   he is the son of the seekers of knowledge; he is the keeper
   of the Truth who ferries us beyond the surge of our destroyers.

स हि सत्यो यं पूर्वे चिद् देवासश्चिदद् यमीधिरे ।
होतारं मन्द्रजिह्वमित् सुदीतिभिर्विभावसुम् ॥२॥

2. This is the true in his being whom the seers of old kindled,
   yea, the gods too kindled him with perfect outshinings into
   his wide substance of the light, the Priest of the oblation with
   his tongue of ecstasy.

स नो धीती वरिष्ठया श्रेष्ठया च सुमत्या ।
अग्ने रायो दिदीहि नः सुवृक्तिभिर्वरेण्य ॥३॥

3. O Flame supremely desirable, so by our supreme thinking,
   by our brightest perfected mentality, by its utter cleaving
   away of all evil, let thy light give unto us the bliss.

अग्निर्देवेषु राजत्यग्निर्मर्तेष्वाविशन् ।
अग्निर्नो हव्यवाहनोऽग्नि धीभिः सपर्यत ॥४॥

4. The Will is that which shines out in the gods, the Will is that
   which enters with its light into mortals, the Will is the carrier
   of our oblation; the Will seek and serve in all your thoughts.

अग्निस्तुविश्रवस्तमं तुविब्रह्माणमुत्तमम् ।
अतूतं श्रावयत्पति पुत्रं ददाति दाशुषे ॥५॥

5. The Will gives to the giver of sacrifice the Son[1] born of his
    works who teems with the many inspirations and many
    voices of the soul, the highest, the unassailable, the Master
    of things who opens our ears to the knowledge.

अग्निर्ददाति सत्पति सासाह यो युधा नृभिः ।
अग्निरत्यं रघुष्यदं जेतारमपराजितम् ॥६॥

6. Yea, 'tis the Will that gives to us the Lord of existences who
    conquers in the battle by souls of power; Will gives to us
    our swift-galloping steed of battle ever conquering, never
    conquered.

यद् वाहिष्ठं तदग्नये बृहदर्चं विभावसो ।
महिषीव त्वद् रयिस्त्वद् वाजा उवीरते ॥७॥

7. That which is strongest in us to upbear, we give it to the Will.
    Sing out the Vast, O thou whose wide substance is its light.
    Thy opulence is as if the largeness of the Goddess[2] herself;
    upward is the rush of thy plenitudes.

तव द्युमन्तो अर्चयो ग्रावेबोच्यते बृहत् ।
उतो ते तन्यतुर्यथा स्वानो अर्तं त्मना दिवः ॥८॥

8. Luminous are thy flaming radiances; there rises from thee
    a vast utterance like the voice of the pressing-stone of de-
    light; yea, thy cry of itself rises up like a thunder-chant
    from the heavens.

एवां अग्नि वसूयवः सहसानं ववन्दिम ।
स नो विश्वा अति द्विषः पर्षन्नावेव सुक्रतुः ॥९॥

---

[1] The Son of the sacrifice is a constant image in the Veda. Here it is the godhead himself,
Agni who gives himself as a son to man, a Son who delivers his father. Agni is also the War-
Horse and the steed of the journey, the White Horse, the mystic galloping Dadhikravan who
carries us through the battle to the goal of our voyaging.

[2] Aditi, the vast Mother.

9. Thus, desiring substance, we adore the Will who is forceful to conquer. May he who has the perfect power of his workings, carry us beyond all the forces that seek to destroy us, like a ship over the waters.

SUKTA 26

अग्ने पावक रोचिषा मन्द्रया देव जिह्वया ।
आ देवान् वक्षि यक्षि च ॥१॥

1. O Flame, O purifier, bring to us by thy tongue of rapture, O god, the gods and offer to them sacrifice.

तं त्वा घृतस्नवीमहे चित्रभानो स्वर्दृशम् ।
देवाँ आ वीतये वह ॥२॥

2. Thou who drippest the clarity, thou of the rich and varied luminousness, we desire thee because thou hast the vision of our world of the Truth. Bring to us the gods for their manifesting.[1]

वीतिहोत्रं त्वा कवे द्युमन्तं समिधीमहि ।
अग्ने बृहन्तमध्वरे ॥३॥

3. O Seer, we kindle thee in thy light and thy vastness in the march of our sacrifice who carriest the offerings on their journey.

अग्ने विश्वेभिरा गहि देवेभिर्हव्यदातये ।
होतारं त्वा वृणीमहे ॥४॥

4. Come, O Will, with all the godheads for the giving of the oblation; thee we accept as the Priest of the offering.

---

[1] Or, "for the journeying" to the luminous world of the Truth, or "for the eating" of the oblations.

यजमानाय सुन्वत आग्ने सुवीर्यं वह ।
देवैरा सत्सि बर्हिषि ॥५॥

5. For the sacrificer who presses the wine of his delight, bring,
    O Flame, a perfect energy. Sit with the gods on the seat of
    the soul's fullness.

समिधानः सहस्रजिदग्ने धर्माणि पुष्यसि ।
देवानां दूत उक्थ्यः ॥६॥

6. O Flame, thou burnest high and increasest the divine laws
    and art the conqueror of a thousandfold riches; thou art
    the messenger of the gods who hast the word.

न्यर्ग्निं जातवेदसं होत्रवाहं यविष्ठगम् ।
दधाता देवमृत्विजम् ॥७॥

7. Set within you the Flame who knows the births, bearer of
    the offering, youngest vigour, divine sacrificer in the seasons
    of the Truth.

प्र यज्ञ एत्वानुषगद्या देवव्यचस्तमः ।
स्तृणीत बर्हिरासदे ॥८॥

8. Today let thy sacrifice march forward unceasingly, thy sacri-
    fice that shall bring the whole epiphany of the godheads.
    Strew the seat of thy soul that there they may sit.

एवं मरुतो अश्विना मित्रः सीदन्तु वरुणः ।
देवासः सर्वया विशा ॥९॥

9. There let the Life-powers[1] take their seat and the Riders of
    the Horse[2] and the Lord of Love[3] and the Lord of Wideness,[4]
    even the gods with all their nation.

---

[1] The Maruts.   [2] The twin Ashwins.   [3] Mitra.   [4] Varuna.

TRYARUNA TRAIVRISHNA, TRASADASYU PAURUKUTSA, ASHWAMEDHA BHARATA

SUKTA 27

अनस्वन्ता सत्पतिर्मामहे मे गावा चेतिष्ठो असुरो मघोन: ।
त्रैवृष्णो अग्ने दशभि: सहस्त्रंवैश्वानर ञ्यरुणश्चिकेत ॥१॥

1. O Will, O Universal Power,[1] the mighty One supreme in vision, master of his being, lord of his plenitudes has given me his two cows of the Light that draw his wain. He of the triple dawn, son of the triple Bull,[2] has awakened to knowledge with the ten thousands[3] of his plenitude.

यो मे शता च विंशतिं च गोनां हरी च युक्ता सुधुरा ददाति ।
वैश्वानर सुष्टुतो वावृधानोऽग्ने यच्छ ञ्यरुणाय शर्म ॥२॥

2. He gives to me the hundred and twenty[4] of the cows of dawn; his two shining[5] horses he gives, yoked to the car, that bear aright the yoke. O Will, O Universal Power, do thou rightly affirmed and increasing extend peace and bliss to the lord of the triple dawn.

एवा ते अग्ने सुमतिं चकानो नविष्ठाय नवमं त्रसदस्यु: ।
यो मे गिरस्तुविजातस्य पूर्वीर्युक्तेनाभि ञ्यरुणो गृणाति ॥३॥

---

[1] Or, Godhead,

[2] The Triple Bull is Indra, lord of the three luminous realms of Swar, the Divine Mind; Tryaruna Trasadasyu is the half-god, man turned into the Indra type; therefore he is described by all the usual epithets of Indra, "Asura", "Satpati", "Maghavan". The triple dawn is the dawn of these three realms on the human mentaity.

[3] Thousand symbolises absolute completeness. But there are ten subtle powers of the illumined mind each of which has to have its entire plenitude.

[4] The symbolic figure of the illuminations of divine knowledge as the series of dawns (cows) of the twelve months of the year and twelve periods of the sacrifice. There are again ten times twelve to correspond to the ten subtle sisters, powers of the illumined mentality.

[5] The two shining horses of Indra identical probably with the two cows of light of the first verse; they are the two vision-powers of the supramental Truth-Consciousness, right-hand and left-hand, probably direct truth-discernment and intuition. As cows symbolising light of knowledge they yoke themselves to the material mind, the wain; as horses symbolising power of knowledge to the chariot of Indra, the liberated pure mind.

3. For thus has he done desiring thy grace of mind, new-given
for him, new-manifested, — he, the disperser of the destroyers,[1] the lord of the triple dawn who with attentive mind
gives response to the many words of my many births.[2]

यो म इति प्रवोचत्यश्वमेधाय सुरये ।
वददृचा सनि यते वदन्मेधामृतायते ॥४॥

4. May he who answers to me with assent give to the illumined
giver of the Horse-sacrifice,[3] by the word of illumination,
possession of the goal of his journey; may he give power of
intelligence to the seeker of the Truth.

यस्य मा परुषाः शतमुद्धर्षयन्त्युक्षणः ।
अश्वमेधस्य दानाः सोमा इव त्र्याशिरः ॥५॥

5. A hundred strong bulls of the diffusion[4] raise me up to joy;
the gifts of the sacrificer of the steed are as outpourings of
the wine of delight with their triple infusions.[5]

इन्द्राग्नी शतदाभ्यश्वमेधे सुवीर्यम् ।
क्षत्रं धारयतं बृहद् दिवि सूर्यमिवाजरम् ॥६॥

---

[1] Trasadasyu; in all things he reproduces the characteristics of Indra.

[2] The seer by this self-fulfilment on the higher plane is born, as it were, into many realms
of consciousness and from each of these there go up its words that express the impulses in it
which seek a divine fulfilment. The Mind-Soul answers to these and gives assent, it supplies to
the word of expression the answering word of illumination and to the Life that seeks the Truth
it gives the power of intelligence that finds and holds the Truth.

[3] The Horse-sacrifice is the offering of the Life-power with all its impulses, desires, enjoyments to the divine existence. The Life-soul (Dwita) is itself the giver of this sacrifice which it
performs when by the power of Agni it attends to vision on its own vital plane, when it becomes,
in the figure of the hymn, the illumined seer, *aśvamedha*.

[4] The complete hundred powers of the Life by whom all the abundance of the vital plane
is showered upon the growing man. The vital forces being the instrument of desire and enjoyment, this diffusion is like the outpouring of the wine of delight that raises the soul to new and
intoxicating joys.

[5] The delight extracted from existence is typefied by the honey-wine of the Soma; it is
mixed with the milk, the curds and the grain, the milk being that of the luminous cows, the
curds the fixation of their yield in the intellectual mind and the grain the formulation of
the light in the force of the physical mind. These symbolic senses are indicated by the double
meaning of the words used, *go, ḍadhi, yava*.

6. May the God-Mind and the God-Will uphold in the sacrificer of the Horse and giver of his hundred a perfect energy and a vast force of battle even as in heaven the Sun of Light indestructible.[1]

VISHWAWARA

SUKTA 28

समिद्धो अग्निर्दिवि शोचिरश्रेत् प्रत्यङ्ङुषसमुर्विया वि भाति ।
एति प्राची विश्ववारा नमोभिर्देवाँ ईळाना हविषा घृताची ॥१॥

1. The Flame of Will burning high rises to his pure light in the heaven of mind; wide he extends his illumination and fronts the Dawn. She comes, moving upward, laden with all desirable things, seeking the gods with the oblation, luminous with the clarity.

समिध्यमानो अमृतस्य राजसि हविष्कृण्वन्तं सचसे स्वस्तये ।
विश्वं स धत्ते द्रविणं यमिन्वस्यातिथ्यमग्ने नि च धत्त इत् पुरः ॥२॥

2. When thou burnest high thou art king of immortality and thou cleavest to the doer of sacrifice to give him that blissful state; he to whom thou comest to be his guest, holds in himself all substance and he sets thee within in his front.

अग्ने शर्धं महते सौभगाय तव द्युम्नान्युत्तमानि सन्तु ।
सं जास्पत्यं सुयममा कृणुष्व शत्रूयतामभि तिष्ठा महांसि ॥३॥

3. O Flame, put forth thy battling might for a vast enjoyment[2] of bliss, may there be thy highest illumination; create a well-governed union of the Lord and his Spouse, set thy foot

---

[1] Perfect and vast energy in the vital being corresponding to the infinite and immortal light of the Truth in the mental being.

[2] The Vedic immortality is a vast beatitude, a large enjoyment of the divine and infinite existence reposing on a perfect union between the Soul and Nature; the soul becomes King of itself and its environment, conscious on all its planes, master of them, with Nature for its bride delivered from divisions and discords into an infinite and luminous harmony.

on the greatness of hostile powers.

समिद्धस्य प्रमहसोऽग्ने वन्दे तव श्रियम् ।
वृषभो द्युम्नवाँ असि समध्वरेष्विध्यसे ॥४॥

4. I adore, O Flame, the glory of thy high-blazing mightiness.
Thou art the Bull with the illuminations; thou burnest up
in the march of our sacrifices.

समिद्धो अग्न आहुत देवान् यक्षि स्वध्वर ।
त्वं हि हव्यवाळसि ॥५॥

5. O Flame that receivest our offerings, perfect guide of the
sacrifice, high-kindled offer our oblation to the godheads;
for thou art the bearer of our offerings.

आ जुहोता दुवस्यताऽग्निं प्रयत्यध्वरे ।
वृणीध्वं हव्यवाहनम् ॥६॥

6. Cast the offering, serve the Will with your works[1] while your
sacrifice moves forward to its goal, accept the carrier of our
oblation.

---

[1] Or, set the Will to its workings

MANDALA SIX

BHARADWAJA BARHASPATYA

SUKTA 1

त्वं ह्यग्ने प्रथमो मनोताऽस्या धियो अभवो दस्म होता ।
त्वं सीं वृषन्कृणोर्दुष्टरीतु सहो विश्वस्मै सहसे सहध्यै ॥१॥

1. O potent Fire, thou wert the first thinker of this thought and
the Priest of the call. O Male, thou hast created everywhere
around thee a force invulnerable to overpower every force.

अधा होता न्यसीदो यजीयानिळस्पद इषयन्नीडघः सन् ।
तं त्वा नरः प्रथमं देवयन्तो महो राये चितयन्तो अनु ग्मन् ॥२॥

2. And now strong for sacrifice, thou hast taken thy session
in the seat of aspiration, one aspired to, a flamen of the
call, an imparter of the impulse. Men, building the godheads,
have grown conscious of thee, the chief and first, and followed to a mighty treasure.

वृतेव यन्तं बहुभिर्वसव्यैस्त्वे रयिं जागृवांसो अनु ग्मन् ।
रुशन्तमग्निं दर्शतं बृहन्तं वपावन्तं विश्वहा दीदिवांसम् ॥३॥

3. In thee awake, they followed after the Treasure as in the wake
of one who walks on a path with many possessions, in the
wake of the vast glowing-visioned embodied Fire that casts
its light always and for ever.

पदं देवस्य नमसा व्यन्तः श्रवस्यवः श्रव आपन्नमृक्तम् ।
नामानि चिद् दधिरे यज्ञियानि भद्रायां ते रणयन्त संदृष्टौ ॥४॥

4. Travellers with surrender to the plane of the godhead,
seekers of inspired knowledge, they won an inviolate inspiration, they held the sacrificial Names and had delight in thy
happy vision.

त्वां वर्धन्ति क्षितयः पृथिव्यां त्वां राय उभयासो जनानाम् ।
त्वं त्राता तरणे चेत्यो भूः पिता माता सदमिन्मानुषाणाम् ॥५॥

5. The peoples increase thee on the earth; both kinds of riches
of men increase thee. O Fire, our pilot through the battle,
thou art the deliverer of whom we must know, ever a father
and mother to human beings.

सपर्येण्यः स प्रियो विक्ष्वग्निर्होता मन्द्रो नि षसादा यजीयान् ।
तं त्वा वयं दम आ दीदिवांसमुप ज्ञुबाधो नमसा सदेम ॥६॥

6. Dear and servable is this Fire in men; a rapturous Priest of
the call has taken up his session, strong for sacrifice. Pressing the knee may we come to thee with obeisance of surrender when thou flamest alight in the house.

तं त्वा वयं सुध्यो नव्यमग्ने सुम्नायव ईमहे देवयन्तः ।
त्वं विश्वो अनयो दीद्यानो दिवो अग्ने बृहता रोचनेन ॥७॥

7. O Fire, we desire thee, the god to whom must rise our cry,
we the right thinkers, the seekers of bliss, the builders of the
godheads. O Fire, shining with light thou leadest men
through the vast luminous world of heaven.

विशां कविं विश्पतिं शश्वतीनां नितोशनं वृषभं चर्षणीनाम् ।
प्रतीषणिमिषयन्तं पावकं राजन्तमग्निं यजतं रयीणाम् ॥८॥

8. To the seer, the Master of creatures who rules over the
eternal generations of peoples, the Smiter, the Bull of those
that see, the mover to the journey beyond who drives us, the
purifying Flame, the Power in the sacrifice, Fire the Regent
of the Treasures!

सो अग्न ईजे शशमे च मर्तो यस्त आनट् समिधा हव्यदातिम् ।
य आहुतिं परि वेदा नमोभिर्विश्वेत् स वामा दधते त्वोतः ॥९॥

9. O Fire, the mortal has done his sacrifice and achieved his
labour who has worked out the gift of the oblation with the

fuel of thy flame and wholly learned the way of the offering by his prostrations of surrender; he lives in thy guard and holds in himself all desirable things.

अस्मा उ ते महि महे विधेम नमोभिरग्ने समिधोत हव्यैः ।
वेदी सूनो सहसो गीर्भिरुक्थैरा ते भद्रायां सुमतौ यतेम ॥१०॥

10. O Fire, O son of Force, may we offer to thy greatness that which is great, worshipping thee with the obeisance and the fuel and the offering, the altar and the word and the utterance. For we would work and strive in thy happy right thinking, O Fire.

आ यस्ततन्थ रोदसी वि भासा श्रवोभिश्च श्रवस्यस्तरुत्रः ।
बृहद्भिर्वाजैः स्थविरेभिरस्मे रेवद्भिरग्ने वितरं वि भाहि ॥११॥

11. O thou who art filled with inspiration and a passer of barriers, O thou who has extended earth and heaven by the wideness of thy light and thy inspired discoveries of knowledge, shine wider yet in us with thy large and solid and opulent amassings, O Fire.

नृवद्वसो सदमिद्धेह्यस्मे भूरि तोकाय तनयाय पश्वः ।
पूर्वीरिषो बृहतीरारेअघा अस्मे भद्रा सौश्रवसानि सन्तु ॥१२॥

12. O Prince of Riches, fix always in us that in which are the Gods, settle here many herds for the begotten son. In us may there be the happy things of true inspiration and the multitude of the large impulsions from which evil is far.

पुरूण्यग्ने पुरुधा त्वाया वसूनि राजन्वसुता ते अश्याम् ।
पुरूणि हि त्वे पुरुवार सन्त्यग्ने वसु विधते राजनि त्वे ॥१३॥

13. O King, O Fire, let me enjoy by thee and thy princehood of the riches many riches in many ways; for, O Fire of many blessings, there are many treasures for thy worshipper in thee, the King.

SUKTA 2

त्वं हि क्षैतवद्यशोऽग्ने मित्रो न पत्यसे ।
त्वं विचर्षणे श्रवो वसो पुर्ष्टि न पुष्यसि ॥१॥

1. O Fire, thou travellest like a friend to the glory where is our home. O wide-seeing Prince of the Treasure, thou nurturest our inspiration and our growth.

त्वां हि ष्मा चर्षणयो यज्ञेभिर्गीर्भिरीळते ।
त्वां वाजी यात्यवृको रजस्तूर्विश्वचर्षणिः ॥२॥

2. Men who see aspire to thee with the word and the sacrifice. To thee comes the all-seeing Horse that crosses the mid-world, the Horse that no wolf tears.

सजोषस्त्वा दिवो नरो यज्ञस्य केतुमिन्धते ।
यद्ध स्य मानुषी जनः सुम्नायुर्जुह्वे अध्वरे ॥३॥

3. The Men of Heaven with a single joy set thee alight to be the eye of intuition of the sacrifice when this human being, this seeker of bliss, casts his offering in the pilgrim-rite.

ऋषद्यस्ते सुदानवे धिया मर्तः शशमते ।
ऊती ष बृहतो दिवो द्विषो अंहो न तरति ॥४॥

4. The mortal should grow in riches who achieves the work by the Thought for thee, the great giver; he is in the keeping of the Vast Heaven and crosses beyond the hostile powers and their evil.

समिधा यस्त आहुति निशिति मर्त्यो नशत् ।
वयावन्तं स पुष्यति क्षयमग्ने शतायुषम् ॥५॥

5. O Fire, when mortal man arrives by the fuel of thy flame to the way of the oblation and the sharpening of thy intensities, he increases his branching house, his house of the hundred of life.

त्वेषस्ते धूम ऋण्वति दिवि षञ्छुक्र आततः ।
सूरो न हि द्युता त्वं कृपा पावक रोचसे ॥६॥

6. The smoke from thy blaze journeys and in heaven is out-stretched brilliant-white. O purifying Fire, thou shinest with a flame like the light of the sun.

अधा हि विश्ववीड्योऽसि प्रियो नो अतिथिः ।
रण्वः पुरीव जूर्यः सूनृतं त्रययाय्यः ॥७॥

7. Now art thou here in men, one to be aspired to and a beloved guest; for thou art like one delightful and adorable in the city and as if our son and a traveller of the triple world.

कृत्वा हि द्रोणे अज्यसेऽग्ने वाजी न कृत्व्यः ।
परिज्मेव स्वधा गयोऽत्यो न ह्वार्यः शिशुः ॥८॥

8. O Fire, thou art driven by the will in our gated house like a horse apt for our work; thou art by thy nature like a far-spreading mansion and like a galloper of winding ways and a little child.

त्वं त्या चिदच्युताऽग्ने पशूर्न यवसे ।
धामा ह यत्ते अजर वना वृश्चन्ति शिक्वसः ॥९॥

9. O Fire, thou art like a beast in thy pasture and devourest even the unfallen things; the lustres of thy blaze tear to pieces the woodlands, O ageless Flame.

वेषि ह्यध्वरीयतामग्ने होता दमे विशाम् ।
समृधो विश्पते कृणु जुषस्व हव्यमङ्गिरः ॥१०॥

10. O Fire, thou comest a Priest of the call into the house of men that do the Rite of the Path. Make us complete in the treasure, O Master of men! O Angiras flame-seer, rejoice in our oblation.

अच्छा नो मित्रमहो देव देवानग्ने वोचः सुमतिं रोदस्योः ।
वीहि स्वस्ति सुक्षितिं दिवो नॄन्दिषो अंहांसि दुरिता तरेम ता
तरेम तवावसा तरेम ॥११॥

11. O Fire, O friendly Light, O Godhead, turn to the Godheads, mayst thou speak for us the true thought of Earth and Heaven; move to the peace and the happy abode and the men of Heaven. Let us pass beyond the foe and the sin and the stumbling; let us pass beyond these things, pass in thy keeping through them safe.

SUKTA 3

अग्ने स क्षेषवृतपा ऋतेजा उरु ज्योतिर्नंशते देवयुष्टे ।
यं त्वं मित्रेण वरुणः सजोषा देव पासि त्यजसा मर्तमंहः ॥१॥

1. The mortal who longs for the Godhead shall take up his home with thee, O Fire, he is born into the Truth and a guardian of the Truth and comes to thy wide Light, — he in whom thou being Varuna takest with Mitra a common delight and thou guardest that mortal, O God, by thy casting away from him of evil.

ईजे यज्ञेभिः शशमे शमीभिर्ऋधद्वारायाग्नये ददाश ।
एवा चन तं यशसामजुष्टिनाँहो मर्तं नशते न प्रवृत्तिः ॥२॥

2. He has sacrificed with sacrifices, he has achieved his labour by his works, he has given to the Fire whose boons grew ever in opulence. And so there befalls him not the turning away of the Glorious Ones; evil comes not to him nor the insolence of the adversary.

सूरो न यस्य दृशतिररेपा भीमा यदेति शुचतस्त आ धीः ।
हेषस्वतः शुरुधो नायमक्तोः कुत्रा चिद्रण्वो वसतिर्वनेजाः ॥३॥

3. Faultless is thy seeing like the sun's; terrible marches thy thought when blazing with light thou neighest aloud like a

force of battle. This Fire was born in the pleasant woodland and is a rapturous dweller somewhere in the night.

तिग्मं चिदेम महि वर्षो अस्य भसदश्वो न यमसान आसा ।
विजेहमानः परशुनं जिह्वां द्रविनं द्रावयति दारु धक्षत् ॥४॥

4. Fiery-sharp is his march and great his body, — he is like a horse that eats and champs with his mouth: he casts his tongue like an axe to every side, like a smelter he melts the log that he burns.

स इदस्तेव प्रति धावसिष्य्ञ्छिशीत तेजोऽप्यसो न धाराम् ।
चित्रध्रजतिररतिर्यो अक्तोर्वेनं द्रुषद्वा रघुपत्मजंहाः ॥५॥

5. He sets like an archer his shaft for the shooting, he sharpens his powers of light like an edge of steel. He is the traveller of the night with rich rapid movements; he has thighs of swift motion and is like a bird that settles on a tree.

स ईं रेभो न प्रति वस्त उस्राः शोचिषा रारपीति मित्रमहाः ।
नक्तं य ईमरुषो यो दिवा नुनमर्त्यो अरुषो यो दिवा नुन् ॥६॥

6. This friendly Light is like a singer of the word and clothes himself with the Rays, he rhapsodises with his flame. This is the shining One who journeys by night and by day to the Gods, the shining Immortal who journeys through the day to the Gods.

दिवो न यस्य विधतो नवीनोद् वृषा रुक्ष ओषधीषु नूनोत् ।
घृणा ना यो ध्रजसा पत्मना यन्ना रोदसी वसुना दं सुपत्नी ॥७॥

7. The cry of him is like the voice of ordaining Heaven;[1] he is the shining Bull that bellows aloud in the growths of the forest. He goes with his light and his race and his running and fills Earth and Heaven with his riches; they are like wives happy in their spouse.

---

[1] Or, the cry of him in his worship of sacrifice is like the voice of Heaven;

धायोभिर्वा यो युज्येभिरर्कैर्विद्युन्न दविद्योत्स्वेभिः शुष्मैः ।
शर्धो वा यो मरुतां ततक्ष ऋभुनं त्वेषो रभसानो अद्यौत् ॥८॥

8.   He flashes like the lightning with his own proper strength,
      his own founding and helpful illuminations. As if heaven's
      craftsman he has fashioned the army of the Life-Gods and
      lightens ablaze in his exultant speed.

SUKTA 4

यथा होतर्मनुषो देवताता यज्ञेभिः सूनो सहसो यजासि ।
एवा नो अद्य समना समानानुशत्रग्न उशतो यक्षि देवान् ॥१॥

1.   O Son of Force, O Priest of the call, even as always in man's
      forming of the godhead thou sacrificest with his sacrifices,
      sacrifice so for us to the Gods today, O Fire, an equal power
      to equal powers, one who desires to the Gods who desire.

स नो विभावा चक्षणिर्न वस्तोरग्निर्निर्वन्दार वेद्यश्चनो धात् ।
विश्वायुर्यो अमृतो मर्त्येष्वषूषुर्भुद् भूवतिथिर्जातवेदाः ॥२॥

2.   He is wide in his light like a seer of the Day; he is the one we
      must know and founds an adorable joy. In him is universal
      life, he is the Immortal in mortals; he is the Waker in the
      Dawn, our Guest, the Godhead who knows all births that
      are.

द्यावो न यस्य पनयन्त्यभ्वं भासांसि वस्ते सूर्यो न शुक्रः ।
वि य इनोत्यजरः पावकोऽद्नस्य चिच्छिश्नथत्पूर्व्याणि ॥३॥

3.   The heavens seem to praise his giant might; he is robed in
      lustre and brilliant like the Sun. Ageless the purifying Fire
      moves abroad and cuts down even the ancient things of the
      Devourer.[1]

---

[1] Or, the enjoyer.

वग्रा हि सूनो अस्यदघसद्धा चक्रे अग्निर्जनुषाज्मान्नम् ।
स त्वं न ऊर्जसन ऊर्जं धा राजेव जेरवृके क्षेष्यन्तः ॥४॥

4. O Son, thou art the speaker, thy food is thy seat; Fire from
his very birth has made his food the field of his race. O
Strength-getter, found strength in us! Thou conquerest like
a king and thy dwelling is within, there where there comes
not any render.

नितिक्ति यो वारणमन्नमत्ति वायुनं राष्ट्रचत्येत्यक्तून् ।
तुर्याम यस्त आविशामरातीरत्यो न ह्रृतः पततः परिहृत् ॥५॥

5. He eats his food and sharpens his sword of defence; he is
like the Life-God a master of kingdoms and passes beyond
the nights. O Fire, may we pierce through the foe, O thou
who breakest like a galloping steed all that battle against thy
appointings, hurting around thee our hurters as they fall
upon us.

आ सूर्यो न भानुमद्भिरर्कैरग्ने ततन्थ रोदसी वि भासा ।
चित्रो नयत्परि तमांस्यक्तः शोचिषा पत्मन्नौशिजो न दीयन् ॥६॥

6. O Fire, thou art like the Sun with thy splendid illuminations
and hast wide extended Earth and Heaven with thy light.
Smeared with lustre,[1] rich in brilliance he shepherds away the
darkness and like a son of the desire of the Gods rushes
onward in his march.

त्वां हि मन्द्रतममर्कंशोकैर्ववृमहे महि नः श्रोष्यग्ने ।
इन्द्रं न त्वा शवसा देवता वायुं पृणन्ति राधसा नृतमाः ॥७॥

7. We have chosen thee most rapturous with the flaming lights
of thy illuminations; O Fire, hear for us that which is great.
O Godhead of Fire, the most strong Gods fill thee like
Indra with might and like the Life-God with riches.

---

[1] Or, anointed with light,

नू नो अग्नेऽवृकेभिः स्वस्ति वेषि रायः पथिभिः पर्ष्यंहः ।
ता सूरिभ्यो गृणते रासि सुम्नं मदेम शतहिमाः सुवीराः ॥८॥

8. O Fire, thou journeyest happily to the treasures by paths
   where the wolf rends not, and carriest us beyond all evils.
   These high things thou givest to the luminous wise; thou
   lavishest the bliss on him who voices thee with the word.
   May we revel in rapture, strong with the strength of the
   Heroes, living a hundred winters.

SUKTA 5

हुवे वः सूनुं सहसो युवानमद्रोघवाचं मतिभिर्यविष्ठम् ।
य इन्वति द्रविणानि प्रचेता विश्ववाराणि पुरुवारो अध्रुक् ॥१॥

1. I call to you by my thoughts, Fire, the youngest of the gods
   in whose words is no bale, the Youth, the Son of Force. He
   is a mind of the knowledge free from all that hurts; his gifts
   are many and he journeys to the riches where all boons are.

त्वे वसूनि पुर्वणीक होतर्दोषा वस्तोरेरिरे यज्ञियासः ।
क्षामेव विश्वा भुवनानि यस्मिन्त्सं सौभगानि दधिरे पावके ॥२॥

2. O Priest of the call, Priest with thy many flame-forces,[1] in
   the night and in the light the Lords of sacrifice cast on thee
   their treasures. As in earth are founded all the worlds, they
   founded all happinesses in the purifying Fire.

त्वं विक्षु प्रदिवः सीद आसु क्रत्वा रथीरभवो वार्याणाम् ।
अत इनोषि विघते चिकित्वो व्यानुषग्जातवेदो वसूनि ॥३॥

3. Thou art the Ancient of Days and hast taken thy seat in these
   peoples and becomest by the will their charioteer of desirable things. O Conscient, O thou who knowest all births
   that are, thou walkest wide for thy worshipper in unbroken order to the Treasures.

---

[1] Or, forms of flame,

यो नः सनुत्यो अभिदासदग्ने यो अन्तरो मित्रमहो वनुष्यात् ।
तमजरेभिर्वृषभिस्तव स्वेस्तपा तपिष्ठ तपसा तपस्वान् ॥४॥

4. O Fire, O friendly Light, O most burning Power, the enemy
who is hidden and would destroy us, the enemy who is within
us and would conquer, leap fiery-forceful with thy affliction
of flame and consume him with thy male and ageless fires.

यस्ते यज्ञेन समिधा य उक्थैरर्कैभिः सूनो सहसो ददाशत् ।
स मर्त्येष्वमृत प्रचेता राया द्युम्नेन श्रवसा वि भाति ॥५॥

5. When man gives to thee with the sacrifice and the fuel and
with his spoken words and his chants of illumination, he becomes, O Immortal, O Son of Force, a mind of knowledge
among mortals and shines with the riches and inspiration
and light.

स तत्कृधीषितस्तूयमग्ने स्पृधो बाधस्व सहसा सहस्वान् ।
यच्छस्यसे द्युभिरक्तो वचोभिस्तज्जुषस्व जरितुर्घोषि मन्म ॥६॥

6. Missioned create that swiftly, O Fire. Force is thine, resist
with thy force our confronters. When revealed by thy lights,
thou art formulated by our words, rejoice in the far-sounding
thought of thy adorer.

अश्याम तं काममग्ने तवोती अश्याम रयिं रयिवः सुवीरम् ।
अश्याम वाजमभि वाजयन्तोऽश्याम द्युम्नमजराजरं ते ॥७॥

7. O Fire, may we possess in thy guard that high desire, — possess, O Lord of the treasures, that Treasure and its heroes,
possess replenishing thee thy plenitude, possess, O ageless
Fire, thy ageless light.

SUKTA 6

प्र नव्यसा सहसः सूनुमच्छा यज्ञेन गातुमव इच्छमानः ।
वृश्चद्वनं कृष्णयामं रुशन्तं वीती होतारं दिव्यं जिगाति ॥१॥

1. Man turns with a new sacrifice to the Son of Force when he
    desires the Way and the guard. He arrives in his journeyings
    to the heavenly Priest of the call, the Priest shining with
    light, but black is his march through the forests he tears.

स शिवतानस्तन्यतू रोचनस्था अजरेभिर्नानदर्द्रूर्यविष्ठः ।
यः पावकः पुरुतमः पुरूणि पृथून्यग्निरनुयाति भर्वन् ॥२॥

2. He grows white and thunderous, he stands in a luminous
    world; he is most young with his imperishable clamouring
    fires. This is he that makes pure and is full of his multitudes
    and, even as he devours, goes after the things that are many,
    the things that are wide.

वि ते विष्वग्वातजूतासो अग्ने भामासः शुचे शुचयश्चरन्ति ।
तुविम्रक्षासो दिव्या नवग्वा वना वनन्ति धृषता रुजन्तः ॥३॥

3. O Fire, thy lights range wind-impelled on every side, pure as
    thou art pure. Many things they violate and break in their
    rashness and enjoy the forests of their pleasure, heavenly
    lights, seers of the ninefold-ray.

ये ते शुक्रासः शुचयः शुचिष्मः क्षां वपन्ति विषितासो अश्वाः ।
अध भ्रमस्त उर्विया वि भाति यातयमानो अधि सानु पृष्ने ॥४॥

4. O Fire of the burning purities, pure and flaming-bright are
    these thy horses that loosed to the gallop raze the earth.
    Then wide is thy wandering and its light shines far as it drives
    them up to the dappled Mother's heights.

अध जिह्वा पापतीति प्र वृष्णो गोषुयुधो नाशनिः सृजाना ।
शूरस्येव प्रसितिः क्षातिरग्नेर्दुर्बर्तुर्भीमो दयते वनानि ॥५॥

5. Then the tongue of the Bull leaps constantly like the thunder-
    bolt loosed of the God who fights for the herds of the Light.
    The destruction of Fire is like the charge of a hero; he is
    terrible and irresistible, he hews the forests asunder.

आ भानुना पार्थिवानि ज्रयांसि महस्तोदस्य धृषता ततन्थ ।
स बाधस्वाप भया सहोभिः स्पृधो वनुष्यन्वनुषो नि जूर्व ॥६॥

6. Thou hast spread out the earthly speed-ranges by thy light
   and the violence of thy mighty scourge. Repel by thy forceful powers all dangerous things; turn to conquer those who
   would conquer us, shatter our confronters.

स चित्र चित्रं चितयन्तमस्मे चित्रक्षत्र चित्रतमं वयोधाम् ।
चन्द्रं रयिं पुरुवीरं बृहन्तं चन्द्र चन्द्राभिर्गृणते युवस्व ॥७॥

7. O rich in thy brilliances, Fire with thy manifold luminous
   mights, rivet to us the rich and various treasure, most richly
   diverse, that awakens us to knowledge and founds our
   expanding growth. O delightful God, to him who voices
   thee with delightful words the vast delightful wealth and its
   many hero-keepers!

SUKTA 7

मूर्धानं दिवो अरतिं पृथिव्या वैश्वानरमृत आ जातमग्निम् ।
कविं सम्राजमतिथिं जनानामासन्ना पात्रं जनयन्त देवाः ॥१॥

1. Head of heaven and traveller of the earth a universal Power
   was born to us in the Truth, a Guest of men, a seer and absolute King; the Gods brought to birth universal Fire and
   made him in the mouth a vessel of the oblation.

नाभिं यज्ञानां सदनं रयीणां महामाहावमभि सं नवन्त ।
वैश्वानरं रथ्यमध्वराणां यज्ञस्य केतुं जनयन्त देवाः ॥२॥

2. All they together came to him, a navel knot of sacrifice, a
   house of riches, a mighty point of call in the battle. Charioteer of the Works of the way, eye of intuition of the sacrifice, the Gods brought to birth the universal Godhead.

त्वद्विप्रो जायते वाज्यग्ने त्वद्वीरासो अभिमातिषाहः ।
वैश्वानर त्वमस्मासु धेहि वसूनि राजन्त्स्पृहयाय्याणि ॥३॥

3. O Fire, from thee is born the Seer, the Horse and of thee
are the Heroes whose might overcomes the adversary. O
King, O universal Power, found in us the desirable treasures.

त्वां विश्वे अमृत जायमानं शिशुं न देवा अभि सं नवन्ते ।
तव क्रतुभिरमृतत्वमायन्वैश्वानर यत्पित्रोरदीदेः ॥४॥

4. O Immortal, all the Gods come together to thee in thy
birth as to a new-born child. O universal Power, they
travelled to immortality by the works of thy will when thou
leapedst alight from the Father and Mother.

वैश्वानर तव तानि व्रतानि महान्यग्ने नकिरा दधर्ष ।
यज्जायमानः पित्रोरुपस्थेऽविन्दः केतुं वयुनेष्वह्नाम् ॥५॥

5. O Fire, universal Godhead, none could do violence to the
laws of thy mighty workings because even in thy birth in
the lap of the Father and the Mother thou hast discovered
the light of intuition of the Days in manifested things.[1]

वैश्वानरस्य विमितानि चक्षसा सानूनि दिवो अमृतस्य केतुना ।
तस्येदु विश्वा भुवनाधि मूर्धनि वया इव रुरुहुः सप्त विस्रुहः ॥६॥

6. The heights of heaven were measured into form by the eye
of this universal Force, they were shaped by the intuition of
the Immortal. All the worlds are upon his head; the seven
far-flowing rivers climbed from him like branches.

वि यो रजांस्यमिमीत सुक्रतुर्वैश्वानरो वि दिवो रोचना कविः ।
परि यो विश्वा भुवनानि पप्रथेऽदब्धो गोपा अमृतस्य रक्षिता ॥७॥

7. The Universal mighty of will measured into form the kingdom of middle space; a Seer, he shaped the luminous planes
of Heaven. He has spread around us all these worlds; he is
the guardian of immortality and its indomitable defender.

---

[1] Or, in all sorts of knowledge.

SUKTA 8

पृक्षस्य वृष्णो अरुषस्य नू सहः प्र नु वोचं विदथा जातवेदसः ।
वैश्वानराय मतिर्नव्यसी शुचिः सोम इव पवते चारुरग्नये ॥१॥

1. Now have I spoken aloud the force of the brilliant Male
who fills the world, the discoveries of knowledge of the god
who knows all things that are. A new and pure and beautiful
thought is streaming like sacramental wine to Fire, the universal Godhead.

स जायमानः परमे व्योमनि व्रतान्यग्निर्व्रतपा अरक्षत ।
व्यन्तरिक्षममिमीत सुक्रतुर्वैश्वानरो महिना नाकमस्पृशत् ॥२॥

2. Fire is the guardian of the laws of all workings and he kept
safe the laws of his action and motion even in the moment
of his birth in the supreme ether. The Universal mighty of
will measured into shape the middle world and touched
heaven with his greatness.

व्यस्तभ्नाद्रोदसी मित्रो अद्भुतोऽन्तर्वावदक्रुणोज्ज्योतिषा तमः ।
वि चर्मणीव धिषणे अवर्तयद्वैश्वानरो विश्वमधत्त वृष्ण्यम् ॥३॥

3. The Wonderful, the Friend propped up earth and heaven
and made the darkness a disappearing thing by the Light.
He rolled out the two minds like skins; the Universal
assumed every masculine might.

अपामुपस्थे महिषा अगृभ्णत विशो राजानमुप तस्युर्ऋग्मियम् ।
आ दूतो अग्निमभरद्विवस्वतो वैश्वानरं मातरिश्वा परावतः ॥४॥

4. The Great Ones seized him in the lap of the waters and the
Peoples came to the King with whom is the illumining Word.
Messenger of the luminous Sun, Life that expands in the
Mother brought Fire the universal Godhead from the
supreme Beyond.

युगेयुगे विदथ्यं गृणडुचोऽग्ने रयिं यशसं धेहि नव्यसीम् ।
गव्येव राजन्नघशंसमजर नीचा नि वृश्च वनिनं न तेजसा ॥५॥

5. Found for those who from age to age speak the word that is
    new, the word that is a discovery of knowledge, O Fire, their
    glorious treasure; but cut him in twain who is a voice of
    evil, cast him low by thy force of light like a tree with the
    thunderbolt, imperishable[1] king.

अस्माकमग्ने मघवत्सु धारयाऽनामि क्षत्रमजरं सुवीर्यम् ।
वयं जयेम शतिनं सहस्रिणं वैश्वानर वाजमग्ने तवोतिभिः ॥६॥

6. O Fire, uphold in our masters of the treasure their indestruc-
    tible[2] hero-force and unbending might of battle. O universal
    Fire, may we by thy safe keepings conquer the plenitude
    of the hundreds and the plenitude of the thousands.

अदब्धेभिस्तव गोपाभिरिष्टेऽस्माकं पाहि त्रिषधस्थ सूरीन् ।
रक्षा च नो ददुषां शर्धो अग्ने वैश्वानर प्र च तारीः स्तवानः ॥७॥

7. O our impeller,[3] holder of the triple session, shield our lumi-
    nous seers with thy indomitable guardian fires. Keep safe, O
    Fire, the army of those who have given, O Universal, hearing
    our hymn to thee deliver to its forward march.

SUKTA 9

अहश्च कृष्णमहरर्जुनं च वि वर्तेते रजसी वेद्याभिः ।
वैश्वानरो जायमानो न राजावातिरज्ज्योतिषाग्निस्तमांसि ॥१॥

1. A day that is black and a day that is argent bright, two
    worlds revolve in their different paths by forces that we must
    know. Fire, the universal Godhead, like a king that comes to
    birth has thrust the Darknesses down by the Light.

---

[1] Or, ageless   [2] Or, unaging   [3] Or, O doer of sacrifice,

नाहं तन्तुं न वि जानाम्योतुं न यं वयन्ति समरेऽतमानाः ।
कस्य स्विंत् पुत्र इह वक्त्वानि परो वदात्यवरेण पित्रा ॥२॥

2. I know not the woof, I know not the warp, nor what is this
   web that they weave moving to and fro in the field of their
   motion and labour. There are secrets that must be told and
   of someone the son speaks them here, one highest beyond
   through his father lower than he.

स इत्तन्तुं स वि जानात्योतुं स वक्त्वान्यृतुथा वदाति ।
य ईं चिकेतदमृतस्य गोपा अवश्चरन्परो अन्येन पश्यन् ॥३॥

3. He knows the warp, he knows the woof, he tells in their time
   the things that must be spoken. This is the guardian of immortality who wakes to the knowledge of these things;
   walking here below he is one highest beyond who sees
   through another.

अयं होता प्रथमः पश्यतेममिदं ज्योतिरमृतं मर्त्येषु ।
अयं स जज्ञे ध्रुव आ निषत्तोऽमर्त्यस्तन्वा वर्धमानः ॥४॥

4. This is the pristine Priest of the call, behold him! this is the
   immortal Light in mortals. This is he that is born and grows
   with a body and is the Immortal seated and steadfast for
   ever.

ध्रुवं ज्योतिर्निहितं दृशये कं मनो जविष्ठं पतयत्स्वन्तः ।
विश्वे देवाः समनसः सकेता एकं क्रतुमभि वि यन्ति साधु ॥५॥

5. An immortal Light set inward for seeing, a swiftest mind
   within in men that walk on the way. All the Gods with a
   single mind, a common intuition, move aright in their divergent paths towards the one Will.

वि मे कर्णा पतयतो वि चक्षुर्वीदं ज्योतिर्हृदय आहितं यत् ।
वि मे मनश्चरति दूरआधीः किं स्विद्वक्ष्यामि किमु नू मनिष्ये ॥६॥

6. My ears range wide to hear and wide my eyes to see, wide
   this Light that is set in the heart; wide walks my mind and I

set my thought afar; something there is that I shall speak;
something that now I shall think.

विश्वे देवा अनमस्यन्निभयानास्त्वामग्ने तमसि तस्थिवांसम् ।
वैश्वानरोऽवतूतये नोऽमत्योऽवतूतये नः ॥७॥

7. All the gods were in awe of thee when thou stoodest in the
darkness and bowed down before thee, O Fire. May the
Universal Godhead keep us that we may be safe, may the
Immortal keep us that we may be safe.

SUKTA 10

पुरो वो मन्द्रं दिव्यं सुवृक्ति प्रयति यज्ञे अग्निमध्वरे दधिध्वम् ।
पुर उक्येभिः स हि नो विभावा स्वध्वरा करति जातवेदाः ॥१॥

1. When the pilgrim-rite moves on its way, set in your front
the divine ecstatic Fire, place him in front by your words,
the Flame of the good riddance:[1] he is the Knower of all
things born; his light shines wide and he shall make easy
for us the progressions of the sacrifice.

तमु द्युमः पुर्वणीक होतरग्ने अग्निभिर्मनुष इधानः ।
स्तोमं यमस्मे ममतेव शूषं घृतं न शुचि मतयः पवन्ते ॥२॥

2. O Fire, kindled by man's fires, Priest of the call who comest
with thy light, Priest of the many flame-armies, hearken to
the anthem our thoughts strain out pure to the godhead like
pure clarified butter,[2] even as Mamata chanted to him her
paeon.

पीपाय स श्रवसा मत्येषु यो अग्नये ददाश विप्र उक्यैः ।
चित्राभिस्तमूतिभिश्चित्रशोचिर्व्रंजस्य साता गोमतो दधाति ॥३॥

---

[1] The word *suvṛkti* corresponds to the *katharsis* of the Greek mystics — the clearance,
riddance or rejection of all perilous and impure stuff from the consciousness. It is Agni Pavaka,
the purifying Fire who brings to us this riddance or purification, "suvrikti".

[2] Here we have the clue to the symbol of the "clarified butter" in the sacrifice; like the

3. He among mortals is fed on inspiration, the illumined who
gives with his word to the Fire, the seer whom the Fire of
the brilliant illuminations settles by his luminous safeguardings in the conquest of the Pen where are the herds of the
Light.

आ यः पत्रौ जायमान उर्वीं दूरेदृशा भासा कृष्णाध्वा ।
अध बहु चित्तम ऊर्म्याद्यास्तिरः शोचिषा ददृशे पावकः ॥४॥

4. Fire of the blackened trail in his very birth has filled wide
earth and heaven with his far-seeing light. Now has Fire
that makes pure been seen by his bright flame even through
much darkness of the billowing Night.

नू नश्चित्रं पुरुवाजाभिरूती अग्ने रयिं मघवद्भ्यश्च धेहि ।
ये राधसा श्रवसा चात्यन्यान्त्सुवीर्येभिश्चाभि सन्ति जनान् ॥५॥

5. Found, O Fire, for us and the masters of plenty by thy safeguardings packed with the plenitudes a treasure of richly
brilliant kinds; for these are they who surpass all others in
their opulence and inspiration and hero-mights.

इमं यज्ञं चनो धा अग्न उशन् यं त आसनो जुह्वते हविष्मान् ।
भरद्वाजेषु दधिषे सुवृक्तिमवीर्वाजस्य गध्यस्य सातौ ॥६॥

6. O Fire, yearn to the sacrifice that the bringer of the offering
casts to thee; found the rapture. Hold firm in the Bhara-
dwajas the perfect purification; guard them in their seizing
of the riches of the quest.

वि द्वेषांसीनुहि वर्धयेळां मदेम शतहिमाः सुवीराः ॥७॥

7. Scatter all hostile things, increase the revealing Word. May
we revel in the rapture, strong with strength of the Heroes,
living a hundred winters.

---

others it is used in its double meaning, "clarified butter" or, as we may say, "the light-offering".

18

SUKTA 11

यजस्व होतरिषितो यजीयानग्ने बाधो मरुतां न प्रयुक्ति ।
आ नो मित्रावरुणा नासत्या द्यावा होत्राय पृथिवी ववृत्याः ॥१॥

1. Missioned and strong to sacrifice, offer the sacrifice, Priest
   of the call; O Fire, put away from us as if by the applied
   force of the Life-gods all that opposes. Turn in their paths
   towards our offering Mitra and Varuna and the twin Lords
   of the journey and Earth and Heaven.

त्वं होता मन्द्रतमो नो अध्रुगन्तर्देवो विदथा मर्त्येषु ।
पावकया जुह्वा वह्निरासाग्ने यजस्व तन्वं तव स्वाम् ॥२॥

2. To us thou art our priest of the invocation, harmless and
   perfect in ecstasy; thou art the god within in mortals that
   makes the discoveries of knowledge; thou art the carrier
   with the burning mouth, with the purifying flame of oblation. O Fire, worship with sacrifice thy own body.

धन्या चिद्धि त्वे धिषणा वष्टि प्र देवाञ्जन्म गृणते यजध्यै ।
वेपिष्ठो अङ्गिरसां यद्ध विप्रो मधु छन्दो भनति रेभ इष्टौ ॥३॥

3. In thee the understanding is full of riches and it desires the
   gods, the divine births, that the word may be spoken and
   the sacrifice done, when the singer, the sage, wisest of the
   Angirasas chants his honey-rhythm in the rite.

अविद्युतत्स्वपाको विभावाग्ने यजस्व रोदसी उरूची ।
आयुं न यं नमसा रातहव्या अञ्जन्ति सुप्रयसं पञ्च जनाः ॥४॥

4. He has leaped into radiance and is wise of heart and wide
   of light; O Fire, sacrifice to the largeness of Earth and
   Heaven. All the five peoples lavish the oblation with obeisance of surrender and anoint as the living being Fire the

bringer of their satisfactions.

वृञ्जे ह यन्नमसा बर्हिरग्नावयामि सुग्धृतवती सुवृक्तिः ।
अम्यक्षि सद्य सदने पृथिव्या अश्रायि यज्ञः सूर्ये न चक्षुः ॥५॥

5. When the sacred grass has been plucked with prostration of surrender to the Fire, when the ladle of the purification full of the light-offering has been set to its labour, when the home has been reached in the house of Earth and the sacrifice lodged like an eye in the sun, —

दशस्या नः पुर्वणीक होतर्देवेभिरग्ने अग्निभिरिधानः ।
रायः सूनो सहसो वावसाना अति ह्रसेम वृजनं नांहः ॥६॥

6. O Son of Force, O Fire, kindling with the gods thy fires, Priest of the call, Priest with thy many flame-armies, dispense to us the Treasures; shining with light let us charge beyond the sin and the struggle.

SUKTA 12

मध्ये होता दुरोणे बर्हिषो राळग्निस्तोदस्य रोदसी यजध्यै ।
अयं स सूनुः सहस ऋतावा दूरात्सूर्यो न शोचिषा ततान ॥१॥

1. In the midmost of the gated house Fire, the Priest of the call, the King of the sacred seat and the whip of swiftness, to sacrifice to Earth and Heaven! This is the Son of Force in whom is the Truth; he stretches out from afar with his light like the sun.

आ यस्मिन् त्वे स्वपाके यजत्र यक्षद्राजन्त्सर्वतातेव नु द्यौः ।
त्रिषधस्थस्ततरुषो न जंहो हव्या मघानि मानुषा यजध्यै ॥२॥

2. When a man sacrifices in thee, O King, O Lord of sacrifice, when he does well his works in the wise and understanding Fire like Heaven in its all-forming labour, triple thy session;

thy speed is as if of a deliverer, when thou comest to give the sacrifice whose offerings are man's human fullnesses.

तेजिष्ठा यस्यारतिर्वनेराट् तोदो अध्वन्न वृधसानो अद्यौत् ।
अद्रोघो न द्रविता चेतति त्मन्नमर्त्योऽवर्त्रं ओषधीषु ॥३॥

3. A splendour in the forest, most brilliant-forceful is the speed of his journeying; he is like a whip on the path and ever he grows and blazes. He is like a smelter who does hurt to none; he is the Immortal who wakes of himself to know-ledge: he cannot be turned from his way mid the growths of the earth.

सास्माकेभिरेतरी न शूषैरग्निः ष्टवे दम आ जातवेदाः ।
द्रुग्धो वन्वन् कृत्वा नार्वोल्तः पितेव जारयायि यज्ञैः ॥४॥

4. Fire, the knower of all things born, is hymned by our paeans in the house as if in one that walks on the way. He feeds on the Tree and conquers by our will like a war-horse; this shining Bull is adored by us with sacrifice like a father.

अध स्मास्य पनयन्ति भासो वृथा यत्तक्षदनुयाति पृथ्वीम् ।
सद्यो यः स्पन्द्रो विषितो धवीयानृणो न तायुरति धन्वा राट् ॥५॥

5. And now his splendours chant aloud and he hews with ease and walks along the wideness of the earth. He is rapid in his race and in a moment is loosed speeding to the gallop: he is like a thief that runs; his light is seen beyond the desert places.

स त्वं नो अर्वन्निदाया विश्वेभिरग्ने अग्निभिरिधानः ।
वेषि रायो वि यासि दुच्छुना मदेम शतहिमाः सुवीराः ॥६॥

6. O War-Horse, us from the bondage deliver, kindling, O Fire, with all thy fires; for thou travellest to the Riches and scatterest the forces of affliction and sorrow. May we revel in the rapture, strong with the strength of the Heroes, living a hundred winters.

Sukta 13

त्वद्विश्वा सुभग सौभगान्यग्ने वि यन्ति वानिनो न वया: ।
श्रुष्टी रयिर्वाजो वृत्रतूर्यं दिवो वृष्टिरीड्यो रीतिरपाम् ॥१॥

1. O felicitous Fire, of thee are all felicities and they grow wide
   from thee like branches from a tree. For quickly come, in
   the piercing of the Python adversary, the Riches and the
   desirable plenty and the Rain of Heaven and the flowing of
   the Waters.

त्वं भगो न आ हि रत्नमिवे परिज्मेव क्षयसि दस्मवर्चा: ।
अग्ने मित्रो न बृहत् ऋतस्याऽसि क्षत्ता वामस्य देव भूरे: ॥२॥

2. Thou art Bhaga of the felicities and thou pourest on us the
   ecstasy and takest up thy house in us, a pervading presence
   and a potent splendour. O divine Fire, like Mitra thou art
   a feeder on the vast Truth and the much joy and beauty.

स सत्पति: शवसा हन्ति वृत्रमग्ने विप्रो वि पणेर्भर्ति वाजम् ।
यं त्वं प्रचेत ऋतजात राया सजोषा नप्त्रापां हिनोषि ॥३॥

3. O Fire born of the Truth, O thinker and knower, when con-
   senting with the Child of the Waters thou takest pleasure in
   a man and speedest him with the Treasure, he becomes a
   master over beings and in his might slays the Python
   adversary and becomes a seer and carries out with him the
   riches of the Dweller in the Cave.

यस्ते सूनो सहसो गीर्भिरुक्थैर्यज्ञेमर्तो निशिंति वेद्यानट् ।
विश्वं स देव प्रति वारमग्ने धत्ते धान्यं पत्यते वसव्यै: ॥४॥

4. O Son of Force, the mortal who has reached to the intensity
   of thee by the word and the utterance and the altar and the
   sacrifice, draws to him sufficiency of every kind of wealth,
   O divine Fire, and walks on the way with his riches.

ता नृभ्य आ सौश्रवसा सुवीराऽग्ने सूनो सहसः पुष्यसे धाः ।
कृणोषि यच्छवसा भूरि पश्वो वयो वृकायारये जसुरये ॥५॥

5. O Fire, O Son of Force, found for men that they may grow,
    happy riches of inspiration with strength of its hero-keepers,
    — many herds, thy creation in thy might, but now a food
    for the wolf and the foe and the destroyer.

वया सूनो सहसो नो विहाया अग्ने तोकं तनयं वाजि नो दाः ।
विश्वाभिर्गीर्भिरभि पूर्तिमश्यां मदेम शतहिमाः सुवीराः ॥६॥

6. O Son of Force, become the vast speaker within us; give us
    the Son of our begetting, give us all that is packed with the
    plenitudes; let me enjoy by my every word satisfaction of
    fullness. May we revel in the rapture, strong with the
    strength of the Heroes, living a hundred winters.

SUKTA 14

अग्ना यो मर्त्यो दुवो धियं जुजोष धीतिभिः ।
भसन्नु ष प्र पूर्व्यं इषं वुरीतावसे ॥१॥

1. When mortal man by his musings comes to take pleasure of
    work and thought in the Fire, he shines with light and is one
    supreme; he receives the impulsion that leads him to safety.

अग्निरिद्धि प्रचेता अग्निर्वेधस्तम ऋषिः ।
अग्निं होतारमीळते यज्ञेषु मनुषो विशः ॥२॥

2. The Fire is the thinker and knower, the Fire is a mightiest
    disposer of works and a seer. To Fire the Priest of the in-
    vocation the peoples of men aspire in their sacrifices.

नाना ह्याग्नेऽवसे स्पर्धन्ते रायो अर्यः ।
तूर्वन्तो दस्युमायवो व्रतैः सीक्षन्तो अवतम् ॥३॥

Of many kinds are they who seek thy safeguard and strive
with the Fire for his riches; men breaking through the

Destroyer seek to overcome his lawless strength by the order
of their works.

अग्निरप्सामृतीषहं वीरं बदाति सत्पतिम् ।
यस्य त्रसन्ति शवसः संचक्षि शत्रवो भिया ॥४॥

4. The Fire gives to man a Master of beings, a Warrior who
overbears the charge of the foe and wins the Waters; the
enemies are afraid at his very sight and scatter in panic from
his puissance.

अग्निर्हि विघना निदो देवो मर्तमुरुष्यति ।
सहावा यस्यावृतो रयिर्वाजेष्ववृतः ॥५॥

5. The Fire is the godhead who rescues mortal man by knowledge from the Binder. A forceful thing is the treasure of
his riches, unencircled by the adversary, unbesieged in its
plenitudes.

अच्छा नो मित्रमहो देव देवानग्ने वोचः सुमतिं रोदस्योः ।
वीहि स्वास्ति सुक्षितिं दिवो नॄन् द्विषो अंहांसि दुरिता तरेम
ता तरेम तवावसा तरेम ॥६॥

6. O Fire, O friendly Light, O Godhead turn to the Godheads,
mayest thou speak for us the true thought of Earth and
Heaven; march in peace to the happy abode and the Men of
Heaven. Let us pass safe beyond the foe and the sin and the
stumbling.
Let us pass beyond these things, pass in thy keeping through
them safe.

BHARADWAJA BARHASPATYA OR
VITAHAVYA ANGIRASA

SUKTA 15

इममू षु वो अतिथिमुषर्बुधं विश्वासां विशां पतिमृञ्जसे गिरा ।
वेतोर्दिवो जनुषा कच्चिदा शुचिज्योक् चिदत्ति गर्भो यदच्युतम् ॥१॥

1. Thou must crown with the word the guest who wakes from
    sleep with the dawn, Master of all these peoples. He is pure
    from his very birth and surely he comes to us from heaven in
    his time; long too, a child from the womb, he feeds on all
    that is unfallen.

मित्रं न यं सुधितं भृगवो दधुर्वनस्पतावीडघमूर्ध्वंशोचिषम् ।
स त्वं सुप्रीतो वीतहव्ये अद्भुत प्रशस्तिभिर्मंहयसे दिवेदिवे ॥२॥

2. The Bhrigus set in the Tree the godhead of our aspiration
    with his high flame of light like a friend well-confirmed in
    his place. And now, O Wonderful, well-pleased in him who
    has cast to thee the offering, thou art magnified by wordings
    of thy power from day to day.

स त्वं दक्षस्यावृको वृधो भूर्यः परस्यान्तरस्य तरुषः ।
रायः सूनो सहसो मर्त्येष्वा छर्दिर्यच्छ वीतहव्याय सप्रथो
भरद्वाजाय सप्रथः ॥३॥

3. Be in us the one whom the wolf cannot rend, the god who
    makes grow the discernment, makes grow the supreme inner
    Warrior who delivers.[1] O Son of Force, extend in mortals
    the Riches, the wide-spreading House, for the caster of the
    offering, for Bharadwaja the wide-spreading House.

द्युतानं वो अतिथिं स्वर्णरमग्निं होतारं मनुषः स्वध्वरम् ।
विप्रं न द्युक्षवचसं सुवृक्तिभिर्हव्यवाहमरति देवमृञ्जसे ॥४॥

4. Crown must thou the guest shining with light, the Male of
    the Sun-world, the Priest of man's invocation who makes
    perfect the Rite of the Path. Crown with your acts of puri-
    fication the Seer whose speech has its home in the Light,[2]
    the Carrier of offerings, the Traveller, the Godhead of Fire.

पावकया यश्चितयन्त्या कृपा क्षामन् रुरुच उषसो न भानुना ।
तूर्वन्न यामन्नेतशस्य नू रण आ यो घृणे न ततृषाणो अजरः ॥५॥

---

[1] Or, be our deliverer from the enemy beyond and within us.
[2] Or, has its home in the Heaven, or, houses the Light,

5. He shines with the light that makes pure, the light that awakens to knowledge, shines in beauty on the earth as if with a splendour of Dawn. He is as if one hewing his way in the march and battle of the shining Horse; he is like one athirst and luminously blazing, the ageless Fire.

अग्निमग्निं वः समिधा डुवस्यत प्रियंप्रियं वो अतिथिं गृणीषणि ।
उप वो गीर्भिरमृतं विवासत देवो देवेषु वनते हि वार्यं
देवो देवेषु वनते हि नो डुवः ॥६॥

6. Fire and again Fire set to work with your fuel, chant with your speech the dear, the beloved Guest. Approach and set the Immortal alight with your words; a god he enjoys in the gods our desirable things, — a god, he enjoys our works in the gods.

समिद्धमग्निं समिधा गिरा गृणे शुचिं पावकं पुरो अध्वरे ध्रुवम् ।
विप्रं होतारं पुरुवारमद्रुहं कविं सुम्नैरीमहे जातवेदसम् ॥७॥

7. I chant the Fire that is kindled with the word for fuel, the Fire that is pure and makes pure; Fire that is steadfast for ever and marches in front in the Rite of the Path. We desire with his felicities the Illumined, the Priest of the call, the harmless, rich with many blessings, the Seer who knows all births that are.

त्वां दूतमग्ने अमृतं युगेयुगे हव्यवाहं दधिरे पायुमीड्यम् ।
देवासश्च मर्तासश्च जागृवि विभुं विश्पतिं नमसा नि षेदिरे ॥८॥

8. O Fire, they have set thee here the Messenger, the Immortal in generation after generation, the Carrier of offerings, protector of man and the Godhead of his prayer. Gods alike and mortals sit with obeisance before the all-pervading Master of the peoples, the ever-wakeful Fire.

विभूषन्नग्न उभयाँ अनु व्रता दूतो देवानां रजसी समीयसे ।
यत्ते धीति सुमतिमावृणीमहेऽध स्मा नस्त्रिवरूथः शिवो भव ॥९॥

9. O Fire, according to the laws of thy works thou pervadest either race; thou art the messenger of the Gods and rangest both the worlds. Since we have accepted thy thinking and the right understanding that is thine, be to us our triple armour of defence and benignant helper.

तं सुप्रतीकं सुदृशं स्वञ्चमविद्वांसो विदुष्टरं सपेम ।
स यक्षद्विश्वा वयुनानि विद्वान् प्र हव्यमग्निरमृतेषु वोचत् ॥१०॥

10. May we who know not come into touch with this great knower with his true front and just walk and perfect vision. May he who knows all manifested things[1] do sacrifice for us, may Fire voice our offering in the world of the Immortals.

तमग्ने पास्युत तं पिपर्षि यस्त आनट् कवये शूर धीतिम् ।
यज्ञस्य वा निशितिं वोदिदिति वा तमित्पृणक्षि शवसोत राया ॥११॥

11. O heroic Fire, thou guardest and bringest safe to the other side the man who has reached to the Thought for thee the Seer and achieved the intensity of the sacrifice or its ascending movement; thou fillest him with might and riches.

त्वमग्ने वनुष्यतो नि पाहि त्वमु नः सहसावन्नवद्यात् ।
सं त्वा ध्वस्मन्वदभ्येतु पाथः सं रयिः स्पृह्याय्यः सहस्री ॥१२॥

12. O Fire that hast the Force, guard us from fault, guard from one who would subject us. May there come to thee along the path full of destructions the thousandfold delectable treasure.

अग्निहोंता गृहपतिः स राजा विश्वा वेद जनिमा जातवेदाः ।
देवानामुत यो मर्त्यानां यजिष्ठः स प्र यजतामृतावा ॥१३॥

13. Fire, the Priest of the invocation, is a king and the Master in our house; all the births he knows, he is of all things born the Knower. He is strong to sacrifice and the Truth is in him; let him do sacrifice for gods and mortals.

---

[1] Or, all kinds of knowledge

अग्ने यदद्य विशो अध्वरस्य होतः पावकशोचे वेष्ट्वं हि यज्वा ।
ऋता यजासि महिना वि यद् भूर्हव्या वह यविष्ठ या ते अद्य ॥१४॥

14. O Fire, O Light that makest pure, O summoning Priest of
man's sacrifice, today when thou comest as a doer of worship, today when thou growest all-pervading in thy greatness and offerest the things of the Truth for sacrifice, today
carry with thee our offerings, O ever-youthful Fire, even the
truths that are thine.

अभि प्रयांसि सुधितानि हि ख्यो नि त्वा दधीत रोदसी यजध्यै ।
अवा नो मघवन्वाजसातावग्ने विश्वानि दुरिता तरेम
ता तरेम तवावसा तरेम ॥१५॥

15. Open thy manifesting eye on our firm-based pleasant things;
let a man set thee within him to sacrifice to Earth and
Heaven. Protect us, O King of Riches, in our conquest of
the plenitudes; O Fire, may we pass safe through all the
stumbling-places.
Let us pass beyond these things, pass in thy keeping through
them safe.

अग्ने विश्वेभिः स्वनीक देवैरूर्णावन्तं प्रथमः सीद योनिम् ।
कुलायिनं घृतवन्तं सवित्रे यज्ञं नय यजमानाय साधु ॥१६॥

16. O Fire with thy strong armies of flame, sit with the gods,
first of them all, in the wool-flecked lair where the Nest is
ready and the light-offering; lead for the doer of the rite,
for the presser of the wine rightly on its paths the sacrifice.

इममु त्यमथर्ववदग्निं मन्थन्ति वेधसः ।
यमङ्कूयन्तमानयन्नमूरं श्याव्याभ्यः ॥१७॥

17. This is that Fire whom the ordainers of works churn out
like Atharvan of old; a Power unbewildered, they led him
in his zigzag walk from the dusky Nights.

जनिष्वा देववीतये सर्वताता स्वस्तये ।
आ देवान्वक्ष्यमृतां ऋतावृधो यज्ञं देवेषु पिस्पृशः ॥१८॥

18.   Be born to us in our all-forming labour for the coming of
      the Gods, for our peace. Bring the gods to us, the Immor-
      tals, the builders of the growing Truth; give to our sacrifice
      touch on the gods.

वयमु त्वा गृहपते जनानामग्ने अकर्म समिधा बृहन्तम् ।
अस्थूरि नो गार्हपत्यानि सन्तु तिग्मेन नस्तेजसा सं शिशाधि ॥१९॥

19.   O Fire, O man's master of the house, we have fed thee with
      our fuel and made thee a vastness; let the works of the house-
      master be unhalting, make us utterly keen with thy intense
      force of light.

BHARADWAJA BARHASPATYA

SUKTA 16

त्वमग्ने यज्ञानां होता विश्वेषां हितः ।
देवेभिर्मानुषे जने ॥१॥

1.   O Fire, thou art set here in all as the Priest of the call in the
      sacrifice, set by the gods in the human being.

स नो मन्द्राभिरध्वरे जिह्वाभिर्यज मह: ।
आ देवान्वक्षि यक्षि च ॥२॥

2.   Offer worship with thy rapturous tongues in the Rite of the
      Path to the Great Ones. Bring the gods to us, do them
      sacrifice.

वेत्था हि वेधो अध्वनः पथश्च देवाञ्जसा ।
अग्ने यज्ञेषु सुक्रतो ॥३॥

3.   O ordainer of works, mighty of will, by thy revealing light[1]
      in the sacrifice thou knowest the tracks of the gods and their
      highways.

_____
[1] Or, with thy straight going

त्वामीळे अध द्विता भरतो वाजिभिः शुनम् ।
ईजे यज्ञेषु यज्ञियम् ॥४॥

4. Now has the Bringer of the Treasure with his horses of swiftness aspired to thee for a twofold bliss; he has sacrificed in the sacrifices to the king of sacrifice.

त्वमिमा वार्या पुरु दिवोदासाय सुन्वते ।
भरद्वाजाय दाशुषे ॥५॥

5. O Fire, for the Servant of Heaven[1] who presses the wine, for Bharadwaja the giver of the offering, the multitude of these desirable things!

त्वं दूतो अमर्त्य आ वहा दैव्यं जनम् ।
शृण्वन्विप्रस्य सुष्टुतिम् ॥६॥

6. Thou art the Immortal messenger; lend ear to the laud of the seer and bring the Divine People.

त्वामग्ने स्वाध्यो मर्तासो देववीतये ।
यज्ञेषु देवमीळते ॥७॥

7. Men deeply meditating aspire to thee that the godheads may come to them; mortals they aspire to the God in the sacrifice.

तव प्र यक्षि संदृशमुत क्रतुं सुदानवः ।
विश्वे जुषन्त कामिनः ॥८॥

8. Bring into sacrifice thy perfect sight and thy will; rich are thy gifts and in thee is the joy of all who desire.

त्वं होता मनुर्हितो वह्निरासा विदुष्टरः ।
अग्ने यक्षि दिवो विशः ॥९॥

9. Thou art the Priest of the call set here in thinking man, his carrier with mouth of flame wiser in knowledge than he. O Fire, sacrifice to the people of heaven.

---

[1] Divodasa

अग्न आ याहि वीतये गृणानो हव्यदातये ।
नि होता सत्सि बर्हिषि ॥१०॥

10.   Come, O Fire, for the advent; voiced by the word, come for
the gift of the oblation: sit, the Priest of our invocation, on
the grass of the altar.

तं त्वा समिद्भिरङ्गिरो घृतेन वर्धयामसि ।
बृहच्छोचा यविष्ठय ॥११॥

11.   O Angiras, we make thee to grow by our fuel and our offering of the clarity; flame into a vast light, O ever-youthful
Fire.

स नः पृथु श्रवाय्यमच्छा देव विवाससि ।
बृहदग्ने सुवीर्यम् ॥१२॥

12.   O God, O Fire, thou illuminest towards us a wide light of
inspired knowledge and the vastness of a perfect force.

त्वामग्ने पुष्करादध्यथर्वा निरमन्थत ।
मूर्ध्नो विश्वस्य वाघतः ॥१३॥

13.   O Fire, Atharvan churned thee out from the Lotus, from
the head of every chanting sage.[1]

तमु त्वा दध्यङङृषिः पुत्र ईधे अथर्वणः ।
वृत्रहणं पुरंदरम् ॥१४॥

14.   And Dadhyang too, the Seer, Atharvan's son, kindled thee
a slayer of the Python adversary and shatterer of his cities.

तमु त्वा पाथ्यो वृषा समीधे दस्युहन्तमम् ।
धनंजयं रणेरणे ॥१५॥

15.   Thee the Bull of the paths set full alight, most mighty to slay
the Destroyers, a conqueror of riches in battle upon battle.

---

[1] Or, on Pushkara; or, the Lotus of the head of every chanting sage.

एहचू षु ब्रवाणि तेऽग्न इत्येतरा गिरः ।
एभिर्वर्धास इन्दुभिः ॥१६॥

16. Come to me and let me voice to thee, O Fire, true other
words; for thou growest by these moon-powers of the Wine.

यत्र क्व च ते मनो दक्षं दधस उत्तरम् ।
तत्रा सदः कृणवसे ॥१७॥

17. Wheresoever is thy mind and thou plantest that higher discernment, there thou makest thy house.

नहि ते पूर्तमक्षिपद् भुवन्नेमानां वसो ।
अया दुबो वनवसे ॥१८॥

18. O Prince of Riches, the fullness of thy treasures meets not
the eye and it is for the few;[1] take then joy in our work.

आग्निरगामि भारतो वृत्रहा पुरुचेतनः ।
विवोवासस्य सत्पतिः ॥१९॥

19. Fire of the Bringers is approached by us, the slayer of the
Python adversary conscious with a multiple knowledge, the
Servant of Heaven's Fire, master of beings.

स हि विश्वाति पार्थिवा रयिं दाशन्महित्वना ।
वन्वन्नवातो अस्तृतः ॥२०॥

20. This is he that unconquered, unoverthrown shall by his
greatness win and give to us a treasure beyond all earthly
things.

स प्रत्नवन्नवीयसाऽग्ने द्युम्नेन संयता ।
बृहत्ततन्य भानुना ॥२१॥

21. O Fire, by a new illumination like the old and joining it, thou
hast stretched out the Vast with thy light.[2]

---

[1] Or, let not the fullness of thy treasures meet the eye only of the few;
[2] Or, built the Vast with thy light.

प्र वः सखायो अग्नये स्तोमं यज्ञं च धृष्णुया ।
अर्च गाय च वेधसे ॥२२॥

22. O friends, offer to the impetuous violence of Fire the hymn
and the sacrifice; sing the illumining verse, chant to the
Ordainer of works.

स हि यो मानुषा युगा सीदद्धोता कविक्रतुः ।
दूतश्च हव्यवाहनः ॥२३॥

23. This is he that must sit through the human generations,
man's Priest of the call with the seer-will, the Messenger,
the Carrier of the oblation.

ता राजाना शुचिव्रताऽऽदित्यान्मारुतं गणम् ।
वसो यक्षीह रोदसी ॥२४॥

24. O Prince of the Treasure, do worship here with sacrifice to
the Two Kings who are ever pure in their works, to the sons
of the Indivisible Mother, to the company of the Life-Gods,
to Earth and Heaven.

वस्वी ते अग्ने संदृष्टिरिषयते मर्त्याय ।
ऊर्जो नपादमृतस्य ॥२५॥

25. O Fire, O Child of Energy, full of riches is thy vision for the
mortal, the vision of the immortal, and it imparts to him its
impulse.

क्रत्वा दा अस्तु श्रेष्ठोऽद्य त्वा वन्वन्त्सुरेक्णाः ।
मर्तं आनाश सुवृक्तिम् ॥२६॥

26. Let the giver be the best by work of the will; today winning
thee let him become one overflowing with affluence: a mortal, he shall taste the perfect purification.

ते ते अग्ने त्वोता इषयन्तो विश्वमायुः ।
तरन्तो अर्यो अरातीर्वन्वन्तो अर्यो अरातीः ॥२७॥

27. These are thy men whom thou guardest, O Fire, and they find the speed of thy impulse and move to universal Life, fighters piercing through the armies of the enemy, fighters conquering the armies of the enemy.[1]

अग्निस्तिग्मेन शोचिषा यासद्विश्वं न्यत्रिणम् ।
अग्निर्नो वनते रयिम् ॥२८॥

28. Let the Fire with his keen energy of light overwhelm every devourer; Fire conquers for us the riches.

सुवीरं रयिमा भर जातवेदो विचर्षणे ।
जहि रक्षांसि सुक्रतो ॥२९॥

29. O wide-seeing Fire, God who knowest all births that are, bring to us the treasure with its strength of the Heroes; O mighty of will, slay the demon-keepers.

त्वं नः पाह्यंहसो जातवेदो अघायतः ।
रक्षा णो ब्रह्मणस्कवे ॥३०॥

30. O God who knowest all births that are, guard us from sin and from him that worketh calamity; O Seer of the Word, protect us.

यो नो अग्ने दुरेव आ मर्तो वधाय दाशति ।
तस्मान्नः पाह्यंहसः ॥३१॥

31. The mortal of evil movements who gives us over to the stroke, guard us, O Fire, from him and his evil.

तं तं देव जिह्वया परि बाधस्व दुष्कृतम् ।
मर्तो यो नो जिघांसति ॥३२॥

32. O God, repulse on every side with thy tongue of flame that doer of wickedness; oppose the mortal who would slay us.

---

[1] Or, piercing through the enemies who war against them, (bis).

19

भरद्वाजाय सप्रथः शर्म यच्छ सहन्त्य ।
अग्ने वरेण्यं वसु ॥३३॥

33.   O forceful Fire, extend to Bharadwaja the peace[1] with its
       wideness; extend to him the desirable riches.

अग्निर्वृत्राणि जङ्घनद् द्रविणस्युर्विपन्यया ।
समिद्धः शुक्र आहुतः ॥३४॥

34.   Let Fire the seeker of the treasure kindled and brilliant and
       fed with our offerings slay with his flame of illumination the
       encircling Adversaries.

गर्भे मातुः पितुष्पिता विदिद्युतानो अक्षरे ।
सीदन्नृतस्य योनिमा ॥३५॥

35.   Let him become the father of the Father in the womb of the
       Mother; let him break out into lightnings in the Imperi-
       shable, let him take his seat in the native home of the Truth.

ब्रह्म प्रजावदा भर जातवेदो विचर्षणे ।
अग्ने यद्दीदयद्दिवि ॥३६॥

36.   O wide-seeing Fire, God who knowest all births that are,
       bring us the Word with its issue, the Word whose light shines
       in Heaven.

उप त्वा रण्वसंदृशं प्रयस्वन्तः सहस्कृत ।
अग्ने ससृज्महे गिरः ॥३७॥

37.   O thou who art made by our force, we come to thee of the
       rapturous vision bringing our offerings for thy pleasure and
       let forth towards thee, O Fire, our words.

उप च्छायामिव घृणेरगन्म शर्म ते वयम् ।
अग्ने हिरण्यसंदृशः ॥३८॥

38.   Like men that take refuge in the shade, we have arrived to

---

[1] Or, the wide-spreading house of refuge

the refuge of thy peace, there where thou blazest with light
and art a vision of gold, O Fire.

य उग्र इव शर्यंहा तिग्मशृङ्गो न वंसगः ।
अग्ने पुरो ररोजिथ ॥३९॥

39. Thou art like a fierce fighter shooting arrows and like a
sharp-horned Bull; O Fire, thou breakest the cities.

आ यं हस्ते न खादिनं शिशुं जातं न बिभ्रति ।
विशामग्निं स्वध्वरम् ॥४०॥

40. They bring him like a beast of prey, like a new-born child
they bear him in their hands, Fire that effects the Rite of the
Path for the peoples.

प्र देवं देवबीतये भरता वसुवित्तमम् ।
आ स्वे योनौ नि षीदतु ॥४१॥

41. Bring to us this great discoverer of riches, bring the god for
the coming of the gods; let him take his seat in his own
native home.

आ जातं जातवेदसि प्रियं शिशीतातिथिम् ।
स्योन आ गृहपतिम् ॥४२॥

42. In the felicitous Fire that knows all things born the Master
of your House is born to you; sharpen to his intensity the
beloved guest.

अग्ने युक्ष्वा हि ये तवाऽश्वासो देव साधवः ।
अरं वहन्ति मन्यवे ॥४३॥

43. O God, O Fire, yoke those horses of thine that do well the
work and can bear thee sufficient for our passion.

अच्छा नो याह्या वहाऽभि प्रयांसि वीतये ।
आ देवान्त्सोमपीतये ॥४४॥

44.   Come to us, bear towards us the Gods that they may eat of [1]
our pleasant offerings and drink our Soma-wine.

उदग्ने भारत द्युमदजस्रेण दविद्युतत् ।
शोचा वि भाह्यजर ॥४५॥

45.   O Fire of the Bringers luminously lightening with thy in-
cessant flame upward burn; spread wide thy light, O ageless [2]
power.

वीती यो देवं मर्तो दुवस्येदग्निमीळीताध्वरे हविष्मान् ।
होतारं सत्ययजं रोदस्योरुत्तानहस्तो नमसा विवासेत् ॥४६॥

46.   Let the mortal who would serve with his works the God in
the advent, aspire bringing his offering to the Fire in the
Rite of the Path; let him with uplifted [3] hands and with
obeisance of surrender make shine the summoning Priest
of Earth and Heaven, the fire of true sacrifice. [4]

आ ते अग्न ऋचा हविर्हृदा तष्टं भरामसि ।
ते ते भवन्तूक्षण ऋषभासो वशा उत ॥४७॥

47.   We bring to thee, O Fire, by the illumining word an offering
that is shaped by the heart. Let there be born from it thy
impregnating bulls and thy heifers.

अग्नि देवासो अग्रियमिन्धते वृत्रहन्तमम् ।
येना वसून्याभृता तृळ्हा रक्षांसि वाजिना ॥४८॥

48.   The Gods kindle, most strong to slay the Python adversary,
the supreme Fire, the Horse of swiftness by whom the
Riches are brought and pierced the demon-keepers.

---

[1] Or, come to   [2] Or, imperishable   [3] Or, outstretched
[4] Or, who worships the Truth with sacrifice.

MANDALA SEVEN

VASISHTHA MAITRAVARUNI

SUKTA 1

अग्निं नरो दीधितिभिररण्योर्हस्तच्युती जनयन्त प्रशस्तम् ।
दूरेदृशं गृहपतिमथर्युम् ॥१॥

1. Men have brought to birth from the two tinders by the
    hands' fall the Fire voiced by the light of their meditations;[1]
    Fire that sees afar the flaming master of the house.

तमग्निमस्ते वसवो न्यृण्वन् त्सुप्रतिचक्षमवसे कुतश्चित् ।
दक्षाय्यो यो दम आस नित्यः ॥२॥

2. The Shining Ones[2] have set within in our dwelling-house
    closely regarding all to guard us from whatever side — that
    Fire which in his home sits eternal and all-discerning.

प्रेद्धो अग्ने दीदिहि पुरो नोऽजस्रया सूर्म्या यविष्ठ ।
त्वां शश्वन्त उप यन्ति वाजाः ॥३॥

3. Verily shine out in front of us, O Fire, with thy perpetual
    radiance; to thee continuous come plenitudes.

प्र ते अग्नयोऽग्निभ्यो वरं निः सुवीरासः शोशुचन्त द्युमन्तः ।
यत्रा नरः समासते सुजाताः ॥४॥

4. Fires come blazing out supremely from thy Fires, lumi-
    nous, full of hero-might, there where are assembled men
    born to the perfect birth.

दा नो अग्ने धिया रयिं सुवीरं स्वपत्यं सहस्य प्रशस्तम् ।
न यं यावा तरति यातुमावान् ॥५॥

5. Give us, O Fire, O Forceful One, by the thought the wealth

---

[1] Or, by the scintillations of their thought the Fire voiced by them;

[2] Or, the lords of the riches

full of hero-power, full of progeny high-proclaimed which
the Assailant with his demon magic cannot pierce.

उप यमेति युवतिः सुदक्षं दोषा वस्तोहंर्विष्मती घृताची ।
उप स्वैनमरमतिर्वसूयुः ॥६॥

6. He to whom there comes in the light and in the dusk the
    young Damsel, luminous bearing the offering — it is his own
    dynamic thought that comes to him desiring the Riches.

विश्वा अग्नेऽप्र दहारातीर्येभिस्तपोभिरदहो जरूथम् ।
प्र निस्वरं चातयस्वामीवाम् ॥७॥

7. O Fire, burn away from us all hostile powers with the con-
    suming flames with which thou didst burn the afflicting
    demon, destroy Pain so that no voice of her is left.

आ यस्ते अग्न इधते अनीकं वसिष्ठ शुक्र दीदिवः पावक ।
उतो न एभिः स्तवथैरिह स्याः ॥८॥

8. O bright and most opulent, O Fire, who shinest and puri-
    fiest, as with whosoever kindles thy flame-forces, so with us
    too, by those lauds abide.

वि ये ते अग्ने भेजिरे अनीकं मर्ता नरः पित्र्यासः पुरत्रा ।
उतो न एभिः सुमना इह स्याः ॥९॥

9. As with those who have turned to thy flame-force, mortal
    men, our forefathers in many lands, with us too by these
    lauds in thy right-mindedness abide.

इमे नरो वृत्रहत्येषु शूरा विश्वा अदेवीरभि सन्तु मायाः ।
ये मे धियं पनयन्त प्रशस्ताम् ॥१०॥

10. May these men, heroes in the slayings of the Coverer, who
    work out the thought I have voiced, overcome all undivine
    mage-knowledge.

मा शूने अग्ने नि षदाम नृणां मानेषसोऽवीरता परि त्वा ।
प्रजावतीषु दुर्यासु दुर्य ॥११॥

11. O Fire, may we not dwell in the emptiness, nor in houses of
men where there is no son[1] and the hero is not, but around
thee may we dwell in homes where there is good progeny,
O dweller in the home.

यमश्वी नित्यमुपयाति यज्ञं प्रजावन्तं स्वपत्यं क्षयं नः ।
स्वजन्मना शेषसा वावृधानम् ॥१२॥

12. This is the eternal sacrifice to which there comes the Rider
of the Horse, to our house full of progeny and good offspring, our house increasing with the self-born Son.

पाहि नो अग्ने रक्षसो अजुष्टात् पाहि धूर्तेररुषो अघायोः ।
त्वा युजा पृतनायूँरभि ष्याम् ॥१३॥

13. Protect us, O Fire, from the abhorred Rakshasa, protect
from the harm of one who would war against us and do us
evil; with thee as ally may we overcome those who would
battle against us.

सेदग्निररत्येरत्यस्त्वन्यान् यत्र वाजी तनयो वीळुपाणिः ।
सहस्रपाथा अक्षरा समेति ॥१४॥

14. May that Fire go beyond all other fires where is the Horse
and the Son with the strong hand; traveller of the thousand
paths reaches the imperishable things.

सेदग्निर्यो वनुष्यतो निपाति समेद्धारमंहस उरुष्यात् ।
सुजातासः परि चरन्ति वीराः ॥१५॥

15. This is that Fire who guards those who would conquer, he
protects from evil the man who sets him ablaze; the heroes
of the perfect birth move around him.

---

[1] Or, where no remainder is left

अयं सो अग्निराहुतः पुरुत्रा यमीशानः समिदिन्धे हविष्मान् ।
परि यमेत्यध्वरेषु होता ॥१६॥

16. This is that Fire who is called[1] in many lands, whom the
giver of the offering sets ablaze and has lordship, round
whom moves the Priest of the call in the rites of the path.

त्वे अग्न आहवनानि भूरीशानास आ जुहुयाम नित्या ।
उभा कृण्वन्तो वहतू मियेधे ॥१७॥

17. In thee, O Fire, we cast many offerings gaining lordship,
creating in the sacrifice both the eternal Travellers.

इमो अग्ने वीततमानि हव्याऽजस्रो वक्षि देवतातिमच्छ ।
प्रति न ईं सुरभीणि व्यन्तु ॥१८॥

18. O Fire, these offerings most desired, incessantly bring to
our formation of the godhead; to us may there come all
delightful Powers.

मा नो अग्नेऽवीरते परा दा दुर्वाससेऽमतये मा नो अस्यै ।
मा नः क्षुधे मा रक्षस ऋतावो मा नो दमे मा वन आ जुहूर्थाः ॥१९॥

19. Deliver us not, O Fire, to strengthlessness, nor to the ill-clad
mindlessness, nor to hunger, nor to the Rakshasa, O thou
with whom is the Truth, lead us not astray in the house or
in the forest.

नू मे ब्रह्माण्यग्न उच्छशाधि त्वं देव मघवद्भ्यः सुषूदः ।
रातौ स्यामोभयास आ ते यूयं पात स्वस्तिभिः सदा नः ॥२०॥

20. Now, O Fire, teach to us the Words, do thou, O God,
speed them to the lords of plenty, may both we and they
abide in thy grace, do you protect us ever with all kinds of
weal.

[1] Or, given offering

त्वमग्ने मुहवो रण्वसंदृक् सुदीती सूनो सहसो दिदीहि ।

मा त्वे सचा तनये नित्य आ धङ्मा वीरो अस्मन्नर्यो वि दासीत् ॥२१॥

21. Thou, O Fire, art swift to our call and rapturous is thy
vision; O son of force, shine with a bright light. Burn us not
since in thee and with thee is the eternal Son, let not the
strength of the hero in us break us to pieces.

मा नो अग्ने दुर्भृतये सचैषु देवेद्धेष्वग्निषु प्र वोच: ।

मा ते अस्मान् दुर्मतयो भूमाच्चिद् देवस्य सूनो सहसो नशन्त ॥२२॥

22. Mayst thou not, who art with us in these god-kindled fires,
denounce us for difficulty to bear thee; may not wrong
thinkings from thee, O son of force, even by error come to
us.

स मर्तो अग्ने स्वनीक रेवानमर्त्ये य आजुहोति हव्यम् ।

स देवता वसुवर्नि दधाति यं सूरिरर्थीं पृच्छमान एति ॥२३॥

23. O Fire, O thou with thy flame-force, rich with Treasure, become the mortal who casts his offerings in the immortal;
that godhead founds in him the conquest of the riches to
whom comes questioning the illumined seer, the seeker.

महो नो अग्ने सुवितस्य विद्वान् रयिं सूरिभ्य आ वहा बृहन्तम् ।

येन वयं सहसावन् मदेमाऽविक्षितास आयुषा सुवीरा: ॥२४॥

24. O Fire, thou art the knower of the great and happy path,
bring to the illumined seers the vast Treasure by which,
O forceful one, with a life unwasting, heroic in strength we
may take rapture.

नू मे ब्रह्माण्यग्न उच्छशाधि त्वं देव मघवद्भ्य: सुषूद: ।

रातौ स्यामोभयास आ ते यूयं पात स्वस्तिभि: सदा न: ॥२५॥

25. Now, O Fire, teach to us the Words, do thou, O God, speed
them to the lords of plenty, may both we and they abide in
thy grace, do you protect us ever with all kinds of weal.

SUKTA 2

जुषस्व नः समिधमग्ने अद्य शोचा बृहद् यजतं धूममृण्वन् ।
उप स्पृश दिव्यं सानु स्तूपैः सं रश्मिभिस्ततनः सूर्यस्य ॥१॥

1. Cleave to our fuel, O Fire, today, illumine the vast[1] pouring
   thy smoke of sacrifice, touch the peak celestial with thy up-
   piled masses, then stretch them out to unite with the rays of
   the Sun.

नराशंसस्य महिमानमेषामुप स्तोषाम यजतस्य यज्ञैः ।
ये सुक्रतवः शुचयो धियंधाः स्वदन्ति देवा उभयानि हव्या ॥२॥

2. Let us invoke, by the sacrifices of the lord of sacrifice who
   voices the godheads, the greatness of these who are pure,
   who are perfect in will, who are founders of the Thought-
   gods, they take the taste of both kinds of offerings.

ईळेन्यं वो असुरं सुदक्षमन्तर्दूतं रोदसी सत्यवाचम् ।
मनुष्वदग्निं मनुना समिद्धं समध्वराय सदमिन्महेम ॥३॥

3. Fire who is to be prayed by you the mighty, the wise of
   understanding, the messenger between earth and heaven,
   whose speech is truth kindled as the human by the thinking
   man, let us greaten ever for the pilgrim-sacrifice.

सपर्यवो भरमाणा अभिज्ञु प्र वृञ्जते नमसा बर्हिरग्नौ ।
आजुह्वाना घृतपृष्ठं पृषद्वद्ध्यर्वयवो हविषा मर्जयध्वम् ॥४॥

4. Desiring to serve, bringing the offering, kneeling with prostration they pluck the sacred grass; O priests of the pilgrim-
   sacrifice, casting it into the Fire speckled, with luminous
   back, brighten him with the offering.

स्वाध्यो वि दुरो देवयन्तोऽशिश्रयू रथ्युर्देवताता ।
पूर्वी शिशुं न मातरा रिहाणे समग्रुवो न समनेष्वञ्जन् ॥५॥

---

[1] Or, blaze out vastly

5. The seekers of the godhead perfected in their thinking have
   come with yoked chariots and flung wide open the doors in
   their formation of the godheads, they have anointed him as
   if the two ancient Mothers caressing their child, as if rivers
   moving through level spaces.

उत योषणे दिव्ये मही न उषासानक्ता सुदुघेव धेनुः ।
बर्हिषदा पुरुहूते मघोनी आ यज्ञिये सुविताय श्रयेताम् ॥६॥

6. May too dawn and night, matrons great and divine, like
   good milch-cows, queens of sacrifice, queens of plenty called
   by many seekers, sit on the sacred grass and lodge with us
   for our happiness.[1]

विप्रा यज्ञेषु मानुषेषु कारू मन्ये वां जातवेदसा यजध्यै ।
ऊर्ध्वं नो अध्वरं कृतं हवेषु ता देवेषु वनथो वार्याणि ॥७॥

7. I meditate on you, O ye two illumined Seers, doers of the
   work in our human sacrifices, knowers of all things born,
   for sacrifice; make high our pilgrim-sacrifice when we call:
   you win our desirable things in the gods.

आ भारती भारतीभिः सजोषा इळा देवैर्मनुष्येभिरग्निः ।
सरस्वती सारस्वतेभिरर्वाक् तिस्रो देवीर्बर्हिरेदं सदन्तु ॥८॥

8. In unison may Bharati with her Muses of invocation, Ila
   with gods and men, and Fire, Saraswati with her powers of
   inspiration come down to us, the three goddesses sit upon
   this seat of sacrifice.

तन्नस्तुरीपमध पोषयित्नु देव त्वष्टर्वि रराणः स्यस्व ।
यतो वीरः कर्मण्यः सुदक्षो युक्तग्रावा जायते देवकामः ॥९॥

9. O divine maker of forms who hast the utter rapture, cast
   upon us that supreme transcendence, cause of our growth,
   from which is born in us the hero ever active with wise

---

[1] Or, be with us for our happy journey.

discernment, the seeker of the gods who sets to work the stone of the wine-pressing.

वनस्पतेऽव सृजोप देवानग्निर्हविः शमिता सूदयाति ।
सेदु होता सत्यतरो यजाति यथा देवानां जनिमानि वेद ॥१०॥

10. O tree, release thy yield to the gods; Fire the achiever of the work speeds the offering on its way. It is he who does worship as the Priest of the call, the more true in his act because he knows the birth of the gods.

आ याह्याग्ने समिधानो अर्वाङिन्द्रेण देवैः सरथं तुरेभिः ।
बर्हिनं आस्तामदितिः सुपुत्रा स्वाहा देवा अमृता मादयन्ताम् ॥११॥

11. Come down to us, O Fire, high-kindled, in one chariot with Indra and swiftly journeying gods; let Aditi, mother of mighty sons, sit on the sacred grass, let the gods, the immortals, take rapture in Swaha.

SUKTA 3

अग्नि वो देवमग्निभिः सजोषा यजिष्ठं दूतमध्वरे कृणुध्वम् ।
यो मर्त्येषु निध्रुविर्ऋंतावा तपुर्मूर्धा घृतान्नः पावकः ॥१॥

1. Create for yourselves in the sacrifice with a common joy in him the divine Fire along with all the fires, the strong for sacrifice, the messenger who is in mortals the possessor of Truth, inwardly permanent, whose food is Light, with his head of burning flame, the purifying Fire.

प्रोथदश्वो न यवसेऽविष्यन् यदा महः संवरणाद् व्यस्थात् ।
आदस्य वातो अनु वाति शोचिरध स्म ते व्रजनं कृष्णमस्ति ॥२॥

2. He neighs in his desire like a horse in his pasture, when he breaks out from a mighty encirclement the wind blows in the wake of his flame; now black is thy marching.

उद् यस्य ते नवजातस्य वृष्णोऽग्ने चरन्त्यजरा इधानाः ।
अच्छा द्यामरुषो धूम एति सं दूतो अग्न ईयसे हि देवान् ॥३॥

3. O Fire, when are kindled the imperishable flames of thee, the new-born Bull, and they journey upwards, thy smoke mounts ruddy to heaven, for thou travellest, O Fire, as a messenger to the gods.

वि यस्य ते पृथिव्यां पाजो अश्रेद् तृषु यदन्ना समवृक्त जम्भैः ।
सेनेव सृष्टा प्रसितिष्ट एति यवं न दस्म जुह्वा विवेक्षि ॥४॥

4. The might of thee moves wide over earth, when swiftly thou tearest thy food with thy jaws, the movement of thy march is like a charging army; O strong doer, with thy tongue of flame thou art like one sifting-grain of barley.

तमिद् दोषा तमुषसि यविष्ठमग्निमत्यं न मर्जयन्त नरः ।
निशिशाना अतिथिमस्य योनौ दीदाय शोचिराहुतस्य वृष्णः ॥५॥

5. Him in the dusk, him in the dawn, the ever youthful Fire men groom like a horse whetting the strength of the guest in his native seat; when the offerings are cast to him there shines out the light of the Bull.

सुसंदृक् ते स्वनीक प्रतीकं वि यद् रुक्मो न रोचस उपाके ।
दिवो न ते तन्यतुरेति शुष्मश्चित्रो न सूरः प्रति चक्षि भानुम् ॥६॥

6. O thou of the bright flame-force, fair to vision is thy front when nearest thou shinest out like gold, thy strength moves like the thunder of heaven, rich in thy brilliance thou showest thy light like a Sun.[1]

यथा वः स्वाहाग्नये दाशेम परीळाभिर्घृतवद्भिरश्च हव्यैः ।
तेभिर्नो अग्ने अमितैर्महोभिः शतं पूर्भिरायसीभिर्नि पाहि ॥७॥

7. So that we may give for you with Swaha, to the Fire, we

---

[1] Or, like the light of the Sun.

stand around him with the words of revelation and luminous
offerings; do thou, O Fire, guard us with those measureless
greatnesses, with thy hundred iron cities.

या वा ते सन्ति दाशुषे अधृष्टा गिरो वा याभिर्नृवतीररुष्याः ।
ताभिर्नः सूनो सहसो नि पाहि स्मत् सुरीञ्जरितृञ्जातवेदः ॥८॥

8. The inviolate powers which are there for the giver, the
Words with which thou guardest the powers that are human,
with these protect us, at once illumined seers and thy adorers, O son of force, O knower of all things born!

नियन्तं पूतेव स्वधितिः शुचिर्गात् स्वया कृपा तन्वा रोचमानः ।
आ यो मात्रोरुशेन्यो जनिष्ट देवयज्याय सुक्रतुः पावकः ॥९॥

9. When he goes out pure like a bright axe shining with his own
light for his body, he who was born from two mothers for
sacrifice to the gods, strong of will, the desirable purifying
Fire.

एता नो अग्ने सौभगा दिदीह्यपि क्रतुं सुचेतसं वतेम ।
विश्वा स्तोतृभ्यो गृणते च सन्तु यूयं पात स्वस्तिभिः सदा नः ॥१०॥

10. O Fire, light up for us these happinesses; let us wake to an
understanding of thy perfectly conscious will; let all be there
for those who laud thee, for him who utters thee; may you
protect us always with all kinds of weal.

SUKTA 4

प्र वः शुक्राय भानवे भरध्वं हव्यं मतिं चाग्नये सुपूतम् ।
यो दैव्यानि मानुषा जनूंष्यन्तर्विश्वानि विद्मना जिगाति ॥१॥

1. Bring forward for the Fire, for the brilliant Light, thy mind
and thy purified offering, the Fire who travels with knowledge between all the divine and human births.

स गृत्सो अग्निस्तरुणश्चिदस्तु यतो यविष्ठो अजनिष्ट मातुः ।
सं यो वना युवते शुचिदन् भूरि चिदन्ना समिदत्ति सद्यः ॥२॥

2. May Fire be the wise one and the deliverer when he is born
the youngest from the mother, he who pure-bright of tooth
clings to the forests, many foods he devours in a moment.

अस्य देवस्य संसद्यनीके यं मर्तासः श्येतं जगृभ्रे ।
नि यो गृभं पौरुषेयीमुवोच दुरोकमग्निरायवे शुशोच ॥३॥

3. In the rendezvous of this god in his flame-force, one whom
mortals have seized, a white flame, and he has proclaimed
that strong human grasp, Fire has illumined that which is
ill-lit to the human being.

अयं कविरकविषु प्रचेता मर्तेष्वग्निरमृतो नि धायि ।
स मा नो अत्र जुहुरः सहस्वः सदा त्वे सुमनसः स्याम ॥४॥

4. This is the seer, the conscious thinker in those who are not
seers, Fire has been set as the Immortal in mortals; then
lead us not here astray, O forceful Fire, may we be ever
right-minded in thee.

आ यो योनिं देवकृतं ससाद क्रत्वा ह्यग्निरमृताँ अतारीत् ।
तमोषधीश्च वनिनश्च गर्भं भूमिश्च विश्वधायसं बिभर्ति ॥५॥

5. He who has come to his native seat made by the gods, Fire
delivered the gods by his will; the plants and the trees and
the earth bear him who is the foundation of all.

ईशे ह्यग्निरमृतस्य भूरेरीशे रायः सुवीर्यस्य वातोः ।
मा त्वा वयं सहसावन्नवीरा माप्सवः परि षदाम मादुवः ॥६॥

6. Fire has power for a large Immortality, he is master of a
wealth bounteous and full of hero-strength; O thou who
hast strength with thee, let us not sit around thee shapeless,
actionless, without hero-force.

परिषद्यं ह्वारणस्य रेक्णो नित्यस्य रायः पतयः स्याम ।
न शेषो अग्ने अन्यजातमस्त्यचेतानस्य मा पथो वि दुक्षः ॥७॥

7. To be rejected is the abundance of the riches that bring no
    delight, let us be the masters of a wealth that is eternal; that
    which is born from another is not the Son; O Fire, turn not
    to wrong the paths of one who knows not.

नहि प्रभायारणः सुशेवोऽन्योदर्यो मनसा मन्तवा उ ।
अधा चिदोकः पुनरित् स एत्या नो वाज्यभीषाळेतु नव्यः ॥८॥

8. Not to be accepted even though blissful is the son of an-
    other womb, not to be thought of even by the mind, for he
    brings with him no delight, soon even he returns to his home,
    let rather the new Horse come to us, the all-conquering.

त्वमग्ने वनुष्यतो नि पाहि त्वमु नः सहसावन्नवद्यात् ।
सं त्वा ध्वस्मन्वदभ्येतु पायः सं रयिः स्पृह्याय्यः सहस्री ॥९॥

9. Do thou, O Fire, protect us from one who would conquer
    us, protect us thou, too, O forceful Fire, from blame; may
    there come to thee on a path full of destruction, come utterly
    a wealth thousandfold and desirable.

एता नो अग्ने सौभगा दिदीह्यपि ऋतुं सुचेतसं वतेम ।
विश्वा स्तोतृभ्यो गृणते च सन्तु यूयं पात स्वस्तिभिः सदा नः ॥१०॥

10. O Fire, light up for us these happinesses; let us wake to an
    understanding of thy perfectly conscious will; let all be there
    for those who laud thee, for him who utters thee; may you
    protect us always with all kinds of weal.

SUKTA 5

प्राग्नये तवसे भरध्वं गिरं दिवो अरतये पृथिव्याः ।
यो विश्वेषाममृतानामुपस्थे वैश्वानरो वावृधे जागृवद्भिः ॥१॥

1. Bring to the Fire in his strength a Word for the traveller of earth and heaven who, in the lap of all the Immortals, the universal godhead, grows by those who are ever wakeful.

पृष्टो दिवि धाय्यग्निः पृथिव्यां नेता सिन्धूनां वृषभः स्तियानाम् ।
स मानुषीरभि विशो वि भाति वैश्वानरो वावृधानो वरेण ॥२॥

2. Fire, sought for, was set in heaven and in earth, the leader of the rivers, the Bull of things that are stable; he shines upon the human peoples, the universal godhead growing by that which is supreme.

त्वद्भिया विश आयन्नसिक्नीरसमना जहतीर्भोजनानि ।
वैश्वानर पूर्वे शोशुचानः पुरो यदग्ने दरयन्नदीदेः ॥३॥

3. In fear of thee the black Tribe, creatures unharmonious, came away casting behind them their enjoyments, when O Fire, O universal godhead, thy light shone upon man when thou torest them and flamedst forth in his front.

तव त्रिधातु पृथिवी उत द्यौर्वैश्वानर व्रतमग्ने सचन्त ।
त्वं भासा रोदसी आ ततन्थाज्जस्त्रेण शोचिषा शोशुचानः ॥४॥

4. O Fire, O universal godhead, earth and heaven and the mid-realm clove to the triple law of thy workings; shining with thy uninterrupted flame thou hast spread out the two firmaments by thy light.

त्वामग्ने हरितो वावशाना गिरः सचन्ते धुनयो घृताचीः ।
पतिं कृष्टीनां रथ्यं रयीणां वैश्वानरमुषसां केतुमह्राम् ॥५॥

5. To thee, O Fire, the Words, thy shining horses, impetuous and luminous cleave in their desire, to the universal godhead, lord of the peoples, charioteer of the Riches, ray of intuition of the dawns and the days.

त्वे असुर्यं वसवो न्यृण्वन् क्रतुं हि ते मित्रमहो जुषन्त ।
त्वं दस्यूँरोकसो अग्न आज उरु ज्योतिर्जनयन्नार्याय ॥६॥

6. Into thee, the Shining Ones[1] cast the Mightiness, for they clove to thy will, O friendly Light; O Fire, thou threwest the Destroyers out from the house bringing to birth a wide Light for the Aryan.

स जायमानः परमे व्योमन् वायुर्न पायः परि पासि सद्यः ।
त्वं भुवना जनयन्नभि क्षत्रपत्याय जातवेदो दशस्यन् ॥७॥

7. As thou camest to birth in the supreme ether at once as Vayu thou didst guard the path, thou criest aloud bringing to birth the worlds, according them as a gift to the Son, O knower of all things born!

तामग्ने अस्मे इषमेरयस्व वैश्वानर द्युमतीं जातवेदः ।
यया राधः पिन्वसि विश्ववार पृथु श्रवो दाशुषे मर्त्याय ॥८॥

8. O Fire, O universal godhead, O knower of all things born, send into us that luminous impulsion by which, O thou in whom are all desirable things, thou nourishest the achievement of a wide inspired knowledge for the mortal giver.

तं नो अग्ने मघवद्भ्यः पुरुक्षुं रयिं नि वाजं श्रुत्यं युवस्व ।
वैश्वानर महि नः शर्म यच्छ रुद्रेभिरग्ने वसुभिः सजोषाः ॥९॥

9. O Fire, join to us within, to us made masters of the riches a plenitude of the knowledge inspired wide in its store; O universal godhead, do thou in union with the Rudras and the Vasus extend to us a vast peace.[2]

SUKTA 6

प्र सम्राजो असुरस्य प्रशस्तिं पुंसः कृष्टीनामनुमाद्यस्य ।
इन्द्रस्येव प्र तवसस्कृतानि वन्दे दारुं वन्दमानो विवक्मि ॥१॥

1. I adore the Render, adoring I proclaim by my speech the

---

[1] Or, the Lords of the riches　　[2] Or, a vast refuge.

deeds of the all-ruler, the almighty, the male, as Indra strong
and to be rejoiced in by the peoples.

कवि केतुं धासि भानुमद्रेहिन्वन्ति शं राज्यं रोदस्योः ।
पुरंदरस्य गीर्भिरा विवासेऽग्नेवंतानि पूर्व्या महानि ॥२॥

2. Him they send the seer, the ray of intuition, the foundation,
   the light on the hill, the kingdom of peace in earth and
   heaven; I illumine with my words the great and ancient laws
   of working of Fire who rends the cities.

न्यक्रतून् ग्रथिनो मृध्रवाचः पणीँरश्रद्धाँ अवृधाँ अयज्ञान् ।
प्रप्र तान् दस्यूँरग्निर्निर्विवाय पूर्वश्चकारापराँ अयज्यून् ॥३॥

3. The traffickers who have not the will for the work, the
   binders in knots, who have the speech that destroys, who
   have neither faith nor growth in the being, nor sacrifice,
   these the Destroyers Fire has scattered before him; supreme
   he has made nether in their realm those who will not to do
   sacrifice.

यो अपाचीने तमसि मदन्तीः प्राचीश्चकार नृतमः शचीभिः ।
तमीशानं वस्वो अग्निं गृणीषेऽनानतं दमयन्तं पृतन्यून् ॥४॥

4. The powers that rejoice in the darkness behind, he most
   mighty in his godhead has made by his energies powers in
   front; that Fire I proclaim, lord of the Treasure, who is
   never bowed, who tames those that make battle against
   him.

यो देह्यो अनमयद् वधस्नैर्यो अर्यपत्नीरुषसश्चकार ।
स निरुध्या नहुषो यह्वो अग्निर्विशश्चक्रे बलिहृतः सहोभिः ॥५॥

5. He bent down the walls by his showering blows, he who
   has made the dawns wives of the Noble Ones; he the
   mighty Fire has put his restraint upon men and made the
   peoples bringers to him of his taxes by his forceful mights.

यस्य शर्मन्नुप विश्वे जनास एवैस्तस्थुः सुर्मतिं भिक्षमाणाः ।
वैश्वानरो वरमा रोदस्योराग्निः ससाद पित्रोरुपस्थम् ॥६॥

6. He to whose peace all beings come by their movements
    praying for a right mind, the universal godhead came to
    that which is supreme above earth and heaven, Fire to the
    lap of the father and mother.

आ देवो ददे बुध्न्या वसूनि वैश्वानर उदिता सूर्यस्य ।
आ समुद्रादवरादा परस्मादाग्निर्ददे दिव आ पृथिव्याः ॥७॥

7. The god took to him the riches of the Foundation, the uni-
    versal godhead in the rising of the Sun gathered wealth from
    the nether and the upper ocean, Fire took to him the riches
    of earth and heaven.

SUKTA 7

प्र वो देवं चित् सहसानमग्निमश्वं न वाजिनं हिषे नमोभिः ।
भवा नो दूतो अध्वरस्य विद्वान् त्मना देवेषु विविदे मितद्रुः ॥१॥

1. Even though a god putting forth his force, I drive him for-
    ward as my steed of swiftness by my prostrations of surren-
    der; become the messenger of our pilgrim-sacrifice, one who
    has knowledge; of himself in the gods he becomes known in
    his measured race.

आ याह्यग्ने पथ्या अनु स्वा मन्द्रो देवानां सख्यं जुषाणः ।
आ सानु शुष्मैर्नदयन् पृथिव्या जम्भेभिर्विश्वमुशधग्वनानि ॥२॥

2. O Fire, come to us along thy own paths, rapturous, taking
    pleasure in the comradeship of the gods; making the high
    plateaus of earth to roar with his rushing strengths, with his
    tusks of flame he burns the woodlands, all he burns in his
    desire.

प्राचीनो यज्ञः सुधितं हि बर्हिः प्रीणीते अग्निरीळितो न होता ।
आ मातरा विश्ववारे हुवानो यतो यविष्ठ जज्ञिषे सुशेवः ॥३॥

3. In front is the sacrifice, well-placed is the sacred grass, pleased is the Fire; one prayed, thou art like a Priest of the call, calling to the two mothers in whom are all desirable things, whence thou art born most young and blissful.

सद्यो अध्वरे रथिरं जनन्त मानुषासो विचेतसो य एषाम् ।
विशामधायि विश्पतिर्दुरोणेऽग्निर्मन्द्रो मधुवचा ऋतावा ॥४॥

4. Men accomplished in conscious knowledge have brought at once into birth the charioteer who has been set as master of the peoples in their house, Fire the rapturous, the sweet of speech, one who has with him the Truth.

असादि वृतो वह्निराजगन्वानग्निर्ब्रह्मा नृषदने विधर्ता ।
द्यौश्च यं पृथिवी वावृधाते आ यं होता यजति विश्ववारम् ॥५॥

5. He has come and taken his seat in the house of Man, the chosen bearer of the offering, Fire, the Priest of the Word, he who upholds all things, he whom earth and heaven increase, to whom the Priest of the call sacrifices for in him are all desirable things.

एते द्युम्नेभिर्विश्वमातिरन्त मन्त्रं ये वारं नर्या अतक्षन् ।
प्र ये विशस्तिरन्त श्रोषमाणा आ ये मे अस्य दीधयन्नृतस्य ॥६॥

6. These have crossed beyond all by their lights, the men of strength who have fashioned excellently the Word, human beings who have gone forward eager to hear and have illumined for me something of this Truth.

नू त्वामग्न ईमहे वसिष्ठा ईशानं सूनो सहसो वसूनाम् ।
इषं स्तोतृभ्यो मघवद्भ्य आनड् यूयं पात स्वस्तिभिः सदा नः ॥७॥

7. Now we desire thee, O Fire, O son of force, as the master of the Riches, we the Vasishthas; thou hast obtained the impulsion for those who laud thee, those who have the plenty. Do you always guard us with all kinds of weal.

SUKTA 8

इन्धे राजा समर्यो नमोभिर्यस्य प्रतीकमाहुतं घृतेन ।
नरो हृव्येभिरीळते सबाध आग्निरग्र उषसामशोचि ॥१॥

1. The King, the Noble One is kindled high with prostrations
    of surrender, he whose front receives the oblation of the
    Light; men oppressed and opposed pray with offerings and
    the Fire is born in front of the dawns.

अयमु ष्य सुमहाँ अवेदि होता मन्द्रो मनुषो यह्वो अग्निः ।
वि भा अकः ससृजानः पृथिव्यां कृष्णपविरोषधीभिर्ववक्षे ॥२॥

2. He verily is that great one whom one knew, the rapturous
    Priest of man, the mighty one, the Fire; he has found wide
    his lustres when he is let loose on the wide earth, black is
    the rim of his wheel when he is declared by her growths.

कया नो अग्ने वि वसः सुवृक्तिं कामु स्वधामृणवः शस्यमानः ।
कदा भवेम पतयः सुदत्र रायो वन्तारो दुष्टरस्य साधोः ॥३॥

3. By what law of thee, O Fire, dost thou illumine our puri-
    fication? To what self-law of thee dost thou move when
    thou art proclaimed aloud? O great giver, when may we
    become the lords and conquerors of a wealth that is all-
    accomplishing[1] and unassailable?

प्रप्रायमग्निर्भरतस्य शृण्वे वि यत् सूर्यो न रोचते बृहद् भाः ।
अभि यः पूरं पृतनासु तस्थौ द्युतानो दैव्यो अतिथिः शुशोच ॥४॥

4. The voice of the Fire of the bringer is heard more and more
    when he shines like a sun, a vast light; Fire who stands over
    man in his battles has broken flaming into a blaze, the divine
    guest.

असन्नित् ते त्वे आहवनानि भूरि भुवो विश्वेभिः सुमना अनीकैः ।
स्तुतश्चिदग्ने शृण्विषे गृणानः स्वयं वर्धस्व तन्वं सुजात ॥५॥

---

[1] Or, perfect

5. In thee were our many callings and thou becamest right-
thoughted with all thy flame-forces. When thou art proclaimed by the word, thou hearest, O Fire; perfect in thy
birth, thyself increase thy body.

इदं वचः शतसाः संसहस्रमुदग्नये जनिषीष्ट द्विबर्हाः ।
शं यत् स्तोतृभ्य आपये भवाति द्युमदमीवचातनं रक्षोहा ॥६॥

6. This is the word that rose into birth for the Fire it is a
conqueror of the hundreds and with it are the thousands, it
is twofold in its greatness when it creates the bliss for those
who laud him for the friend; it is luminous, a driver away
of evil, a slayer of the Rakshasa.

नू त्वामग्न ईमहे वसिष्ठा ईशानं सूनो सहसो वसूनाम् ।
इषं स्तोतृभ्यो मघवद्भ्य आनड् यूयं पात स्वस्तिभिः सदा नः ॥७॥

7. Now we desire thee, O Fire, O son of force, as the master
of the Riches, we the Vasishthas; thou hast obtained the
impulsion for those who laud thee, those who have the
plenty. Do you always guard us with all kinds of weal.

SUKTA 9

अबोधि जार उषसामुपस्थाद्धोता मन्द्रः कवितमः पावकः ।
दधाति केतुमुभयस्य जन्तोर्हव्या देवेषु द्रविणं सुकृत्सु ॥१॥

1. He awoke from the lap of the dawns, their lover, the rapturous Priest of the call, the great seer, the purifying Fire;
he founds the ray of intuition for both kinds of being born,
the offerings in the gods, the riches in the doers of good.

स सुक्रतुर्यो वि दुरः पणीनां पुनानो अर्कं पुरुभोजसं नः ।
होता मन्द्रो विशां दमूनास्तिरस्तमो ददृशे राम्याणाम् ॥२॥

2. Strong in will this is he who has flung wide the doors of the
Traffickers purifying for us the illumining ray which gives

the many enjoyments; the rapturous Priest of the call, who dwells in the house of men, is seen through the darkness of the nights.

अमूर: कविरदितिर्विवस्वान् त्लुसंसन्मित्रो अतिथि: शिवो न: ।
चित्रभानुरुषसां भात्यग्रेऽपां गर्भ: प्रस्व आ विवेश ॥३॥

3. The seer free from ignorance, the boundless, the luminous, a friend happily met,[1] our benignant guest, rich in his lustres he shines in front of the dawns, a child of the waters he enters into his mothers.

ईळेन्यो वो मनुषो युगेषु समनगा अशुचज्जातवेदा: ।
सुसंदृशा भानुना यो विभाति प्रति गाव: समिधानं बुधन्त ॥४॥

4. One to be prayed by you in the generations of man, equal in his rays shone out the knower of all things born, Fire who dawns with his light of perfect vision, the rays woke into his high blazing.

अग्ने याहि दूत्यं मा रिषण्यो देवाँ अच्छा ब्रह्मकृता गणेन ।
सरस्वतीं मरुतो अश्विनापो यक्षि देवान् रत्नधेयाय विश्वान् ॥५॥

5. O Fire, go on thy embassy and fail not towards the gods with the company of those who fashion the Word: sacrifice to Saraswati and the life-powers, and two riders of the horse and the waters and to all the gods for the giving of the ecstasy.

त्वामग्ने समिधानो वसिष्ठो जरूथं हन् यक्षि राये पुरंधिम् ।
पुरुणीथा जातवेदो जरस्व यूयं पात स्वस्तिभि: सदा न: ॥६॥

6. Vasishtha kindles thee, O Fire, slaying the destroying demon, sacrifice for the Wealth to the many-thoughted goddess:[2] many are the roads of thy approach, O knower of all things born. Do you always guard us with all kinds of weal.

---

[1] Or, happy in thy sessions, our friend,   [2] Or, to her who is the tenant of the city:

SUKTA 10

उषो न जारः पृथु पाजो अश्रेदृविद्युतहद्यच्छोशुचानः ।
वृषा हरिः शुचिरा भाति भासा धियो हिन्वान उशतीरजीगः ॥१॥

1. As the lover of dawn he has reached to a wide strength
   shining, flaming out with his play of lightnings; the Bull
   pure and resplendent he shines on us, illumining with his
   light our thoughts he wakes our dawnings.

स्वर्ण वस्तोरुषसामरोचि यज्ञं तन्वाना उशिजो न मन्म ।
अग्निर्जन्मानि देव आ वि विद्वान् द्रवद् दूतो देवयावा वनिष्ठः ॥२॥

2. It is as if the sun-world shone out from the day and the
   dawns; they are forming the sacrifice as aspirants the
   Thought: Fire the godhead knowing the births runs wide to
   his goal, the Messenger, the Traveller to the godheads,
   strong to conquer.

अच्छा गिरो मतयो देवयन्तीरग्निं यन्ति द्रविणं भिक्षमाणाः ।
सुसंदृशं सुप्रतीकं स्वञ्चं हव्यवाहमरति मानुषाणाम् ॥३॥

3. Our words are thoughts seeking for godhead. Come to the
   Fire asking for the Treasure, Fire the carrier of offerings,
   fair of front, perfect in vision, true in movement, the traveller of the ways for men.

इन्द्रं नो अग्ने वसुभिः सजोषा रुद्रं रुद्रेभिरा वहा बृहन्तम् ।
आदित्येभिरदिति विश्वजन्यां बृहस्पतिमृक्वभिर्विश्ववारम् ॥४॥

4. O Fire, companioning the shining ones bring to us Indra,
   companioning the Rudras bring vast Rudra, with the
   Adityas bring the boundless and universal Mother, with
   those who have the illumined word bring the master of the
   word in whom are all desirable things.

मन्द्रं होतारमुशिजो यविष्ठमग्निं विश ईळते अध्वरेषु ।
स हि क्षपावाँ अभवद् रयीणामतन्द्रो दूतो यजथाय देवान् ॥५॥

5.   Men who are aspirants pray in the pilgrim-rites to Fire the
      youthful and rapturous Priest of the call; for he has become
      the ruler of the earth and the Riches, a sleepless messenger
      for sacrifice to the gods.

SUKTA 11

महाँ अस्यध्वरस्य प्रकेतो न ऋते त्वदमृता मादयन्ते ।
आ विश्वेभिः सरथं याहि देवैर्न्यग्ने होता प्रथमः सदेह ॥१॥

1.   Thou art the great conscious perception of the pilgrim-
      sacrifice, without thee the immortals have no rapture; come
      in one chariot with all the gods, take thy seat within, O Fire,
      as the supreme Priest of the call.

त्वामीळते अजिरं दूत्याय हविष्मन्तः सदमिन्मानुषासः ।
यस्य देवैरासदो बर्हिरग्नेऽहान्यस्मै सुदिना भवन्ति ॥२॥

2.   Men who bring the offering ever pray for thee, the swift in
      movement, for their envoy: when thou sitst with the gods
      on a man's seat of sacrifice, happy for him become the days.

त्रिश्चिदक्तोः प्र चिकितुर्वसूनि त्वे अन्तर्दाशुषे मर्त्याय ।
मनुष्वदग्न इह यक्षि देवान् भवा नो दूतो अभिशस्तिपावा ॥३॥

3.   Even thrice in the night within thee they woke to the know-
      ledge of the Riches for the mortal giver; as the human here
      sacrifice to the gods, become our messenger and protector
      from the assailant.

अग्निरीशे बृहतो अध्वरस्याग्निर्विश्वस्य हविषः कृतस्य ।
ऋतुं ह्यस्य वसवो जुषन्ताथा देवा दधिरे हव्यवाहम् ॥४॥

4.   The Fire has power for a vast pilgrim-sacrifice, Fire is a
      master of every offering made, for to his will cleave
      the Shining Ones, so the gods established him as the

carrier of the offerings.

आग्ने वह हविरद्याय देवानिन्द्रज्येष्ठास इह मादयन्ताम् ।
इमं यज्ञं दिवि देवेषु घेहि यूयं पात स्वस्तिभिः सदा नः ॥५॥

5. O Fire, bring the gods to eat of the offerings, may they with
   Indra as their eldest take here their rapture, establish this
   sacrifice in heaven in the gods. Do you always guard us
   with all kinds of weal.

SUKTA 12

अगन्म महा नमसा यविष्ठं यो दीदाय समिद्धः स्वे दुरोणे ।
चित्रभानुं रोदसी अन्तरुर्वी स्वाहुतं विश्वतः प्रत्यञ्चम् ॥१॥

1. We have come with a great prostration of surrender to the
   ever-young Fire who has shone out blazing in his own home
   rich of lustre between the wide firmaments and filled with
   the offerings cast in him he moves facing every side.

स मह्ना विश्वा दुरितानि साह्वानग्निः ष्टवे दम आ जातवेदाः ।
स नो रक्षिषद् दुरितादवद्यादस्मान् गृणत उत नो मघोनः ॥२॥

2. He overcomes all evils by his mights: the Fire is affirmed
   by the lauds in the home, the knower of all things born; may
   he guard us from stumbling and from blame, us when we
   speak the words and us when we are lords of the plenty.

त्वं वरुण उत मित्रो अग्ने त्वां वर्धन्ति मतिभिर्वसिष्ठाः ।
त्वे वसु सुषणनानि सन्तु यूयं पात स्वस्तिभिः सदा नः ॥३॥

3. Thou art Varuna and thou art Mitra, O Fire, thee the
   Vasishthas make to grow by their thoughts, in thee may the
   riches be easily won. Do you always guard us with all kinds
   of weal.

SUKTA 13

प्राग्नये विश्वशुचे धियंधेऽसुरघ्ने मन्म धीति भरध्वम् ।
भरे हविर्न बर्हिषि प्रीणानो वैश्वानराय यतये मतीनाम् ॥१॥

1. To Fire all-illumining, founder of the thought, slayer of the
   Asuras, bring your thinking and the thought formed; glad
   I bring to our sacrificial seat the offering for the universal
   godhead who has mastery over minds.

त्वमग्ने शोचिषा शोशुचान आ रोदसी अपृणा जायमानः ।
त्वं देवाँ अभिशस्तेरमुञ्चो वैश्वानर जातवेदो महित्वा ॥२॥

2. Thou, O Fire, illumining with thy light fillest earth and
   heaven even in thy birth: thou hast released the gods from
   the Assailant by thy might, thou the universal godhead, the
   knower of all things born.

जातो यदग्ने भुवना व्यख्यः पशून् न गोपा इर्यः परिज्मा ।
वैश्वानर ब्रह्मणे विन्द गातुं यूयं पात स्वस्तिभिः सदा नः ॥३॥

3. When born, O Fire, thou lookest on the world as a herds-
   man on his cattle, one to be missioned, pervading everywhere, as the universal godhead thou foundest the Path for
   the Lord. Do you always guard us with all kinds of weal.

SUKTA 14

समिधा जातवेदसे देवाय देवहूतिभिः ।
हविर्भिः शुक्रशोचिषे नमस्विनो वयं दाशेमाग्नये ॥१॥

1. To the godhead knower of all things born, by our fuel, by
   our invocations of the god, by our offerings may we give
   making prostration, to the Fire of the brilliant light.

वयं ते अग्ने समिधा विधेम वयं दाशेम सुष्टुती यजत्र ।
वयं घृतेनाध्वरस्य होतर्वयं देव हविषा भद्रशोचे ॥२॥

2. May we worship thee, O Fire, with the fuel, may we give to thee with the laud, O master of sacrifice, we with the oblation, O Priest of the call of the pilgrim-sacrifice, we with the offerings, O god of the happy flame.

आ नो देवेभिरुप देवहूतिमग्ने याहि वषट्कृतिं जुषाणः ।
तुभ्यं देवाय दाशतः स्याम यूयं पात स्वस्तिभिः सदा नः ॥३॥

3. Come, O Fire, with the gods to our invocation of the gods taking pleasure in the cry "Vashat", to thee, O god, may we be givers of the offerings. Do you guard us always with all kinds of weal.

SUKTA 15

उपसद्याय मीळ्हुष आस्ये जुहुता हविः ।
यो नो नेदिष्ठमाप्यम् ॥१॥

1. To the bounteous, one to be approached with worship, cast in the mouth the offering, who brings to us closest alliance.

यः पञ्च चर्षणीरभि निषसाद दमेदमे ।
कविर्गृहपतिर्युवा ॥२॥

2. He who comes to the five peoples of seeing men and takes his seat within in house and house, the seer, the master of the house, the youth.

स नो वेदो अमात्यमग्नी रक्षतु विश्वतः ।
उतास्मान् पात्वंहसः ॥३॥

3. May that Fire guard the knowledge that is our inmate from every side, may he protect us from evil.

नवं नु स्तोममग्नये दिवः श्येनाय जीजनम् ।
वस्वः कुविद् वनाति नः ॥४॥

4.   Now have I brought forth a new laud to Fire, the Hawk of
      Heaven; he wins for us repeatedly the Riches.

स्पार्हा यस्य श्रियो दृशे रयिर्वीरवतो यथा ।
अग्ने यज्ञस्य शोचतः ॥५॥

5.   He whose glories are desirable for vision and are like the
      Riches with their hero-powers, for he flames in front of the
      sacrifice.

सेमां वेतु वषट्कृतिमग्निर्जुषत नो गिरः ।
यजिष्ठो हव्यवाहनः ॥६॥

6.   May he take knowledge of this cry of "Vashat", may the Fire
      cleave to[1] our words who is the carrier of the offerings and
      most strong for sacrifice.

नि त्वा नक्ष्य विश्पते द्युमन्तं देव धीमहि ।
सुवीरमग्न आहुत ॥७॥

7.   O Lord of the peoples to whom we must reach, to whom
      the offerings are cast, we have set thee within luminous in
      thy hero-force, O godhead, O Fire.

क्षप उस्रश्च दीदिहि स्वग्नयस्त्वया वयम् ।
सुवीरस्त्वमस्मयुः ॥८॥

8.   Shine through the nights and the days, by thee may we be
      well-armed with fire; a hero-force art thou and thy desire is
      towards us.

उप त्वा सातये नरो विप्रासो यन्ति धीतिभिः ।
उपाक्षरा सहस्रिणी ॥९॥

9.   To thee men illumined come with their thinkings for the
      conquest, to thee the imperishable One with her thousands.

_____
[1] Or, take pleasure in

अग्नी रक्षांसि सेधति शुक्रशोचिरमर्त्यः ।
शुचिः पावक ईड्यः ॥१०॥

10. The Fire repels the Rakshasas, the immortal with its brilliant light, one to be prayed, the pure and purifying flame.

स नो राधांस्या भरेशानः सहसो यहो ।
भगश्च दातु वार्यम् ॥११॥

11. Bring us our effectuations for thou hast the mastery, O son of force, and may the lord of enjoyment give us the object of our desire.

त्वमग्ने वीरवद् यशो देवश्च सविता भगः ।
दितिश्च दाति वार्यम् ॥१२॥

12. Thou, O Fire, givest us heroic glory and the divine Creator-Sun and Lord of enjoyment and the Mother of the finite gives us the object of our desire.

अग्ने रक्षा णो अंहसः प्रति ष्म देव रीषतः ।
तपिष्ठैरजरो दह ॥१३॥

13. O Fire, guard us from evil, against the doer of harm protect us, O god; imperishable, burn him with thy most afflicting fires.

अधा मही न आयस्यनाधृष्टो नृपीतये ।
पूर्भवा शतभुजिः ॥१४॥

14. Now unviolated become to us a mighty iron city hundred fortressed for the protection of men.

त्वं नः पाह्यंहसो दोषावस्तरघायतः ।
दिवा नक्तमदाभ्य ॥१५॥

15. Do thou guard us from evil in dusk and in dawn from the bringer of calamity — thou art by day and night inviolable.

SUKTA 16

एना वो अग्नि नमसोर्जो नपातमा हुवे ।
प्रियं चेतिष्ठमरतिं स्वध्वरं विश्वस्य दूतममृतम् ॥१॥

1. With this prostration I invoke for you Fire the son of
   Energy, the beloved, the traveller most awake to knowledge
   who carries out well the pilgrim-sacrifice, the immortal
   messenger of every man.

स योजते अरुषा विश्वभोजसा स दुद्रवत् स्वाहुतः ।
सुब्रह्मा यज्ञः सुशमी वसूनां देवं राधो जनानाम् ॥२॥

2. He yokes the two shining steeds that bring all enjoyments,
   well-fed with the offerings swiftly may he run; to be worshipped with sacrifice he of the perfect Word, accomplisher
   of the riches, the divine achievement of men.

उदस्य शोचिरस्थादाजुह्वानस्य मीळ्हुषः ।
उद् धूमासो अरुषासो दिविस्पृशः समग्निमिन्धते नरः ॥३॥

3. Up stands the flame of light of this bounteous One when to
   him are cast the offerings, his ruddy smoke goes up and
   touches heaven; men kindle high the Fire.

तं त्वा दूतं कृण्महे यशस्तमं देवाँ आ वीतये वह ।
विश्वा सूनो सहसो मर्तभोजना रास्व तद् यत् त्वेमहे ॥४॥

4. Thou art that most glorious messenger whom we create,
   bring to us the advent of the gods, O son of force, give us all
   mortal enjoyments, give us that which from thee we desire.

त्वमग्ने गृहपतिस्त्वं होता नो अध्वरे ।
त्वं पोता विश्ववार प्रचेता यक्षि वेषि च वार्यम् ॥५॥

5. Thou, O Fire, art the master of the house, thou art the Priest
   of the call in our pilgrim-sacrifice, thou art the purifying
   Priest, he in whom are all desirable things, the conscious

thinker; sacrifice and reach the object of our desire.

कृधि रत्नं यजमानाय सुकृतो त्वं हि रत्नधा असि ।
आ न ऋते शिशीहि विश्वमृत्विजं सुशंसो यश्च दक्षते ॥६॥

6. O strong in will, create the ecstasy for the doer of the sacrifice for thou art the founder of ecstasy: sharpen in the Truth for us every doer of the rite and whosoever is perfect in expression and skilful in thought.

त्वे अग्ने स्वाहुत प्रियासः सन्तु सूरयः ।
यन्तारो ये मघवानो जनानामूर्वान् दयन्त गोनाम् ॥७॥

7. O Fire fed with the offerings, let them abide in thee, the beloved, the illumined wise and those lords of plenty among men who are they that travel to and allot to us the widenesses of the Rays.

येषामिळा घृतहस्ता दुरोण आँ अपि प्राता निषीदति ।
तांस्त्रायस्व सहस्य द्रुहो निदो यच्छा नः शर्म दीर्घश्रुत् ॥८॥

8. Those within whose gated house the goddess of Revelation with her hands of light sits filled with her fullnesses, them deliver from the doer of harm and the Censurer,[1] O forceful Fire; give to us the peace that hears the Truth from afar.

स मन्द्रया च जिह्वया वह्निरासा विदुष्टरः ।
अग्ने रयिं मघवद्भ्यो न आ वह हव्यदातिं च सूदय ॥९॥

9. Do thou then with thy rapturous tongue, for thou art the bearer of the oblation with thy mouth and great is thy knowledge, bring to our lords of the plenty the riches and hasten on its way our gift of the offering.

ये राधांसि ददत्यश्व्या मघा कामेन श्रवसो महः ।
ताँ अंहसः पिपृहि पर्तृभिष्ट्वं शतं पूर्भिर्यविष्ठ्य ॥१०॥

---
[1] Or from betrayal and from bondage,

10. They who give to us the achieving plenitudes of the power
     of the Horse because of our desire of the great inspired
     knowledge, them, O most young godhead, bring safe out of
     all evil by thy hundred fortresses of rescue.

देवो वो द्रविणोदाः पूर्णां विवष्ट्याऽसिचम् ।
उद् वा सिञ्चध्वमुप वा पृणध्वमादिद् वो देव ओहते ॥११॥

11. The divine giver of your Treasure desires from you the full
     pouring of the oblations; pour out and fill: then the god-
     head carries you on your way.[1]

तं होतारमध्वरस्य प्रचेतसं वह्निं देवा अकृण्वत ।
दधाति रत्नं विधते सुवीर्यमग्निर्जनाय दाशुषे ॥१२॥

12. The gods have made him the Priest of the call of the pilgrim-
     sacrifice, the conscious thinker, the carrier of flame; Fire
     founds the ecstasy and the heroic strength for the man who
     performs the sacrifice for the giver.

SUKTA 17

अग्ने भव सुषमिधा समिद्ध उत बर्हिरूर्विया वि स्तृणीताम् ॥१॥

1. O Fire, become high kindled with the plenty of thy fuel,
    let the sacred grass be spread wide.

उत द्वार उशतीरिव श्रयन्तामुत देवाँ उशत आ वहेह ॥२॥

2. Let the doors of aspiration swing open; bring here the aspi-
    rant gods.

अग्ने वीहि हविषा यक्षि देवान् त्वध्वरा कृणुहि जातवेदः ॥३॥

3. Go, O Fire, sacrifice to the gods with the offering; make
    good the ways of the pilgrim-sacrifice, O knower of all things
    born.

---

[1] Or, brings to you the Riches.

स्वध्वरा करति जातवेदा यक्षद् देवां अमृतान् पिप्रयच्च ॥४॥

4. He makes good the ways of the pilgrim-sacrifice, the knower of all things born; he sacrifices and gladdens the immortal gods.

वंस्व विश्वा वार्याणि प्रचेतः सत्या भवन्त्वाशिषो नो अद्य ॥५॥

5. Conquer all desirable things, O conscious thinker, may our yearning today become the Truth.

त्वामु ते दधिरे हव्यवाहं देवासो अग्न ऊर्जं आ नपातम् ॥६॥

6. Thee they have established as the carrier of offerings, O Fire, the gods have founded thee, the Son of Energy.

ते ते देवाय दाशतः स्याम महो नो रत्ना वि दध इयानः ॥७॥

7. Those may we be who give to thee, the godhead, go vast upon thy way and found for us the ecstasies.

MANDALA EIGHT

VATSA KANWA

SUKTA 11

त्वमग्ने व्रतपा असि देव आ मर्त्येष्वा ।
त्वं यज्ञेष्वीड्यः ॥१॥

1. O Fire, thou art the guardian of the law of all workings,
thou art the divine in mortals; thou art one to be prayed in
the sacrifices.

त्वमसि प्रशस्यो विदथेषु सहन्त्य ।
अग्ने रथीरध्वराणाम् ॥२॥

2. O forceful one, it is thou who art to be expressed in the
findings of knowledge; O Fire, thou art the charioteer of
the pilgrim-sacrifices.

स त्वमस्मदप द्विषो युयोधि जातवेदः ।
अदेवीरग्ने अरातीः ॥३॥

3. So do thou remove away from us the enemies, O knower
of all things born, even the undivine and hostile forces,
O Fire.

अन्ति चित् सन्तमह यज्ञं मर्तस्य रिपोः ।
नोप वेषि जातवेदः ॥४॥

4. Even when it is near, O surely thou comest not to the sacrifice of our mortal foe, O knower of all things born.

मर्ता अमर्त्यस्य ते भूरि नाम मनामहे ।
विप्रासो जातवेदसः ॥५॥

5. Mortals illumined we meditate on the many names of thee

the immortal, the knower of all things born.

विप्रं विप्रासोऽवसे देवं मर्तास ऊतये ।
अग्निं गीर्भिर्हवामहे ॥६॥

6. We call the Fire with our words, illumined we call the illumined for our guard, mortals we call the god for our protection.

आ ते वत्सो मनो यमत् परमाच्चित् सधस्थात् ।
अग्ने त्वांकामया गिरा ॥७॥

7. Vatsa compels thy mind even from the supreme world of thy
session, O Fire, by his Word that longs for thee

पुरुत्रा हि सदृङङसि विशो विश्वा अनु प्रभुः ।
समत्सु त्वा हवामहे ॥८॥

8. Thou art the equal lord of all peoples in many lands; we
call to thee in the battles.

समत्स्वग्निमवसे वाजयन्तो हवामहे ।
वाजेषु चित्रराधसम् ॥९॥

9. We call to the Fire to guard us in our battles, we who
seek the plenitudes; in the plenitudes richly manifold is his
achievement.

प्रत्नो हि कमीडघो अध्वरेषु सनाच्च होता नव्यश्च सत्सि ।
स्वां चाग्ने तन्वं पिप्रयस्वास्मभ्यं च सौभगमा यजस्व ॥१०॥

10. For thou art of old one to be prayed in the pilgrim-sacrifices,
and from time eternal thou sittest as the ever-new Priest of
the call; O Fire, gladden thy own body and bring happiness
to us by the sacrifice.

SOBHARI KANWA

SUKTA 19

तं गूर्धया स्वर्णरं देवासो देवमरतिं दधन्विरे ।
देवत्रा हव्यमोहिरे ॥१॥

1. Affirm that godhead of the sun-world, the gods set the
divine traveller to his race, they brought the offering to the
world of the gods.

विभूतरातिं विप्र चित्रशोचिषमग्निमीळिष्व यन्तुरम् ।
अस्य मेधस्य सोम्यस्य सोभरे प्रेमध्वाराय पूर्व्यम् ॥२॥

2. O illumined seer, pray the Fire opulent in his gifts, rich in
his lustres; the guide of this Soma-sacrifice pray, O Sobhari,
for the rite of the path, the Ancient One.

यजिष्ठं त्वा ववृमहे देवं देवत्रा होतारममर्त्यम् ।
अस्य यज्ञस्य सुक्रतुम् ॥३॥

3. We have chosen thee the mightiest for sacrifice, the divine
in the divine, the immortal as the Priest of call of this sacrifice, the strong of will, —

ऊर्जो नपातं सुभगं सुदीदितिमग्निं श्रेष्ठशोचिषम् ।
स नो मित्रस्य वरुणस्य सो अपामा सुम्नं यक्षते दिवि ॥४॥

4. the Son of Energy, the Fire, happy and radiant and most
glorious in his light; may he win for us by sacrifice the bliss
in heaven of Mitra and Varuna and the bliss of the waters.

यः समिधा य आहुती यो वेदेन ददाश मर्तो अग्नये ।
यो नमसा स्वध्वरः ॥५॥

5. The mortal who with the fuel and the oblation, with knowledge and with surrender has given to the Fire, who is perfect in the pilgrim-rite, —

तस्येदर्वन्तो रंहयन्त आशवस्तस्य द्युम्नितमं यशः ।
न तमंहो देवकृतं कुतश्चन न मर्त्यकृतं नशत् ॥६॥

6. swift gallop his war-horses, most luminous is his glory,
neither calamity wrought by the gods nor evil wrought of
men can come to him from any part.

स्वग्नयो वो अग्निभिः स्याम सूनो सहस ऊर्जां पते ।
सुवीरस्त्वमस्मयुः ॥७॥

7. High of fire may we be with your fires, O son of force, O
lord of Energies! for thou hast the hero-strength and thy
desire is towards us.

प्रशंसमानो अतिथिनं मित्रियोऽग्नी रथो न वेद्यः ।
त्वे क्षेमासो अपि सन्ति साधवस्त्वं राजा रयीणाम् ॥८॥

8. As our friendly guest finding our expression for us, Fire must
be known, and as our chariot; in thee are all-accomplishing
foundations of ease, thou art the king of the Treasures.

सो अद्धा दाश्वध्वरोऽग्ने मर्तं सुभग स प्रशंस्यः ।
स धीभिरस्तु सनिता ॥९॥

9. That mortal is sure in the giving of his pilgrim-sacrifice, O
happy Fire, he is one to be proclaimed, may he be a conqueror by his thoughts, —

यस्य त्वमूर्ध्वो अध्वराय तिष्ठसि क्षयद्वीरः स साधते ।
सो अर्वद्भिः सनिता स विपन्युभिः स शूरैः सनिता कृतम् ॥१०॥

10. one for whom thou standest high exalted over his pilgrim-
sacrifice, he is a master and hero and accomplishes, — he
conquers by the war-horses, by the luminous seers, by the
heroes, wins his work achieved.

यस्याग्निर्वपुर्गृहे स्तोमं चनो दधीत विश्ववार्यः ।
हव्या वा वेविषद् विषः ॥११॥

11. He in whose house Fire, in whom are all desirable things, maintains his body and his affirming laud and his delight and the offerings, he occupies the field of his occupancy.

विप्रस्य वा स्तुवतः सहसो यहो मक्षूतमस्य रातिषु ।
अवोदेवमुपरिमर्त्यं कृधि वसो विविद्षो वचः ॥१२॥

12. O son of force, for the illumined seer who lauds thee and is most swift in his givings, create for that seeker of knowledge, O Shining One,[1] the word in which the mortal is above the godhead below.

यो अग्नि हव्यदातिभिर्नमोभिर्वा सुदक्षमाविवासति ।
गिरा वाजिरशोचिषम् ॥१३॥

13. He who by his gifts of the oblations or by prostrations of surrender, or by his word illumines the Fire, who brings his right judgment, and the swift action of his light, —

समिधा यो निशिती दाशदर्वित धामभिरस्य मर्त्यः ।
विश्वेत् स धीभिः सुभगो जनाँ अति द्युम्नैरुद्न इव तारिषत् ॥१४॥

14. he who with his stimulation by the fuel serves with the seats of the session of the Fire, the Boundless, that happy mortal exceeding men by his thoughts and by his lights passes beyond all things as one who crosses over waters.

तदग्ने द्युम्नमा भर यत् सासहत् सदने कं चिदत्रिणम् ।
मन्युं जनस्य दूढचः ॥१५॥

15. Bring, O Fire, that light which overcomes in the house whatever devourer or wrath of any being with evil thoughts.

येन चष्टे वरुणो मित्रो अर्यमा येन नासत्या भगः ।
वयं तत् ते शवसा गातुवित्तमा इन्द्रत्वोता विधेमहि ॥१६॥

16. The light by which Mitra sees and Varuna and Aryaman, by

[1] Or, O lord of the Riches,

which lords of the journey and Bhaga, that light may we
worship, we made by thy force perfect knowers of the path
guarded by the lordship of the Puissant.

ते घेदग्ने स्वाध्यो ये त्वा विप्र निदधिरे नृचक्षसम् ।
विप्रासो देव सुक्रतुम् ॥१७॥

17. O Fire, those are perfect in their thought who, themselves
    illumined, have set thee within them, O illumined seer, thee,
    O godhead, divine in vision and strong in will.

त इद् वेदि सुभग त आहुति ते सोतुं चक्रिरे दिवि ।
त इद् वाजेभिर्जिग्युर्महद् धनं ये त्वे कामं न्येरिरे ॥१८॥

18. They have made their altar and their offering, O happy Fire,
    and their libation of the wine in heaven, they have con-
    quered by their plenitudes a mighty wealth who have cast
    into thee their desire.

भद्रो नो अग्निराहुतो भद्रा रातिः सुभग भद्रो अध्वरः ।
भद्रा उत प्रशस्तयः ॥१९॥

19. O felicitous god, happy to us art thou fed with the offerings,
    happy thy giving, happy the pilgrim-sacrifice, happy our
    utterances.

भद्रं मनः कृणुष्व वृत्रतूर्ये येना समत्सु सासहः ।
अव स्थिरा तनुहि भूरि शर्धतां वनेमा ते अभिष्टिभिः ॥२०॥

20. Create for us a happy mind in the piercing of the Coverers
    by which thou mayst overcome in the battles; lay prostrate
    many firm positions of those who challenge us, may we
    conquer them by thy attacks.

ईळे गिरा मनुर्हितं यं देवा दूतमरतिं न्येरिरे ।
यजिष्ठं हव्यवाहनम् ॥२१॥

21. I pray with the word the Fire set in man whom the god sent

in as the messenger and traveller, the carrier of offerings,
strong to sacrifice.

तिग्मजम्भाय तरुणाय राजते प्रयो गायस्यग्नये ।
यः पिंशते सूनृताभिः सुवीर्यमग्निर्घृतेभिराहुतः ॥२२॥

22. To the ever-young Fire shining with his sharp tusks of flame,
thou singest delight, Fire who fed with the offerings of light
forms by true words a great strength.

यदी घृतेभिराहुतो वाशीमग्निर्भरत उच्चाव च ।
असुर इव निर्णिजम् ॥२३॥

23. When he is fed with the offerings of light the Fire like one full
of might, works his blade upwards and downwards and
carves for himself a shape.

यो हव्यान्यैरयता मनुर्हितो देव आसा सुगन्धिना ।
विवासते वार्याणि स्वध्वरो होता देवो अमर्त्यः ॥२४॥

24. The godhead set in man who speeds the offerings in its
fragrant mouth, perfect in the pilgrim-sacrifice illumines all
desirable things, the divine and immortal Priest of the call.

यदग्ने मर्त्यस्त्वं स्यामहं मित्रमहो अमर्त्यः ।
सहसः सूनवाहुत ॥२५॥

25. O Fire, fed with the offerings, O son of force, O friendly
light, if thou wert the mortal and I the immortal, —

न त्वा रासीयाभिशस्तये वसो न पापत्वाय सन्त्य ।
न मे स्तोतामतीवा न दुर्हितः स्यादग्ने न पापया ॥२६॥

26. I would not give thee over to the Assailant or to sinfulness,
O benignant, O shining one; he who lauded me would not
be one without understanding or miserable nor one plagued
by guilt, O Fire.

पितुर्न पुत्रः सुभृतो दुरोण आ देवाँ एतु प्र णो हविः ॥२७॥

27. He is like a son well nourished in the house of his father;
may our offerings reach the gods.

तवाहमग्न ऊतिभिर्नेदिष्ठाभिः सचेय जोषमा वसो ।
सदा देवस्य मर्त्यः ॥२८॥

28. O Fire, O shining one, by thy closest guardings may I, the
mortal, be ever companioned by the favour of the god.

तव क्रत्वा सनेयं तव रातिभिरग्ने तव प्रशस्तिभिः ।
त्वामिदाहुः प्रमति वसो ममाग्ने हर्षस्व दातवे ॥२९॥

29. By thy will may I conquer, O Fire, by thy gifts, by thy revealing utterances; for of thee they speak as the guiding
Thought in me. O Fire, have joy for the giving.

प्र सो अग्ने तवोतिभिः सुवीराभिस्तिरते वाजभर्मभिः ।
यस्य त्वं सख्यमावरः ॥३०॥

30. By thy guardings in which is the strength of the heroes and
the bringing of the plenitudes, he drives forward on his way
with whom thou hast chosen friendship, O shining one.

तव द्रप्सो नीलवान् वाश ऋत्विय इन्धानः सिष्णवा ददे ।
त्वं महीनामुषसामसि प्रियः क्षपो वस्तुषु राजसि ॥३१॥

31. ....[1] the blue stream of thee with its cry is faithful to the
law of its Truth, even as it is kindled it takes what is cast in
it; thou art beloved of the great Dawns and thou shinest in
the dwelling places of the night.

तमागन्म सोभरयः सहस्रमुष्कं स्वभिष्टिमवसे ।
सम्राजं त्रासदस्यवम् ॥३२॥

32. We the sons of Sobhari have come to the Fire with its thousandfold mass of flame, strong in its approach for protec-

---

[1] *Siṣṇo* not translated.

tion, imperial, the Fire of the Terror of the Destroyer.[1]

यस्य ते अग्ने अन्ये अग्नय उपक्षितो वया इव ।
विपो न द्युम्ना नि युवे जनानां तव क्षत्राणि वर्धयन् ॥३३॥

33. O Fire, other fires dwell dependent on thee as on a tree its branches; I annex to me the illuminations of men and their lights, increasing so thy warrior forces.

यमादित्यासो अद्रुहः पारं नयथ मर्त्यम् ।
मघोनां विश्वेषां सुदानवः ॥३४॥

34. O sons of the boundless mother, you who betray not, great givers, the mortal whom out of all possessors of riches you lead to the other shore, —

यूयं राजानः कं चिच्चर्षणीसहः क्षयन्तं मानुषाँ अनु ।
वयं ते वो वरुण मित्रार्यमन् त्यामेदृतस्य रथ्यः ॥३५॥

35. for you, the kings, who have power over seeing men, choose one or another to have mastery in the human ways, — such may we be, O Varuna, O Mitra, O Aryaman, charioteers, indeed, of the Truth.

अदान्मे पौरुकुत्स्यः पञ्चाशतं त्रसदस्युर्वधूनाम् ।
मंहिष्ठो अर्यः सत्पतिः ॥३६॥

36. The Terror of the Destroyers, son of the master of wide vision, has given me the brides five hundred, he is a bounteous giver, the noble, a lord of beings.

उत मे प्रयियोर्वयियोः सुवास्त्वा अधि तुग्वनि ।
तिसृणां सप्ततीनां श्यावः प्रणेता भुवद् वसुर्दियानां पतिः ॥३७॥

37. And so, for me at the ford of the wide-flowing and forward streaming river of the happy dwelling places,[2] came the bay horse, leader of the three seventies. May he become an opulent master of the things that are to be given.

---

[1] Or, Fire of Trasadasyu. [2] Or, the river Suvastu,

VISHWAMANAS VAIYASHWA

SUKTA 23

ईळिष्वा हि प्रतीव्यं यजस्व जातवेदसम् ।
चरिष्णुधूममगृभीतशोचिषम् ॥१॥

1. Pray the Fire as he fronts you, worship with sacrifice the knower of all things born, Fire with his driving smoke and his unseizable light, —

दामानं विश्वचर्षणेऽग्निं विश्वमनो गिरा ।
उत स्तुषे विष्पर्धसो रथानाम् ॥२॥

2. fire who is like the string of speeding chariots to a competitor in the race; O all-seeing universal mind, laud him with the word.

येषामाबाध ऋग्मिय इषः पृक्षश्च निग्रभे ।
उपविदा वह्निर्विन्दते वसु ॥३॥

3. Those on whom he presses, possessor of the word of illumination and seizes on their impulsions and their satisfactions, by their approach to knowledge the Fire finds the Treasure.

उदस्य शोचिरस्थाद् दीदियुषो व्यजरम् ।
तपुर्जम्भस्य सुद्युतो गणश्रियः ॥४॥

4. Up stands his ageless light as he flames out with his burning tusks, in his beautiful splendour, in the glory of his companies.

उदु तिष्ठ स्वध्वर स्तवानो देव्या कृपा ।
अभिख्या भासा बृहता शुशुक्वनिः ॥५॥

5. Even so, stand up as they laud thee, O doer of the pilgrim-rite, shining out with thy divine light, with thy vast all-regarding lustre.

अग्ने याहि सुशस्तिभिर्हव्या जुह्वान आनुषक् ।
यथा दूतो बभूथ हव्यवाहनः ॥६॥

6. Go, O Fire, with perfect utterances of the word offering uninterruptedly the oblations, since thou hast become the
messenger and the carrier of the offerings.

अग्ने वः पूर्व्यं हुवे होतारं चर्षणीनाम् ।
तमया वाचा गृणे तमु वः स्तुषे ॥७॥

7. I call for you the ancient Fire, the Priest of the call of seeing
men; him with this word I declare, him for you I laud.

यज्ञेभिरद्भुतक्रतुं यं कृपा सूदयन्त इत् ।
मित्रं न जने सुधितमृतावनि ॥८॥

8. Fire whom with the sacrifices, with the light verily they speed
like a friend firmly established in the man who possesses the
Truth.

ऋतावानमृतायवो यज्ञस्य साधनं गिरा ।
उपो एनं जुजुषुर्नमसस्पदे ॥९॥

9. To Fire the possessor of the Truth, the accomplisher of the
sacrifice, the seekers of the Truth have come with the word
and cleave to him in the seat of the adoration.

अच्छा नो अङ्गिरस्तमं यज्ञासो यन्तु संयतः ।
होता यो अस्ति विक्ष्वा यशस्तमः ॥१०॥

10. Let our sacrifices go towards him united in their effort, to
him most fiery-wise of the Angirasas who is the Priest of the
call in men and most glorious.

अग्ने तव त्ये अजरेन्धानासो बृहद् भाः ।
अश्वा इव वृषणस्तविषीयवः ॥११॥

11. O ageless Fire, those lights of thine kindling the Vast are
like male and mighty horses;

स त्वं न ऊर्जां पते रयिं रास्व सुवीर्यम् ।
प्राव नस्तोके तनये समत्स्वा ॥१२॥

12. So do thou, O Lord of Energies, give us the wealth, hero-
     might; protect us in our battles, in the Son of our begetting.

यद् वा उ विश्पतिः शितः सुप्रीतो मनुषो विशि ।
विश्वेदग्निः प्रति रक्षांसि सेधति ॥१३॥

13. Since, indeed, the lord of the peoples, keen and glad in the
     house of man, wards off all demon-powers, —

श्रुष्टयग्ने नवस्य मे स्तोमस्य वीर विश्पते ।
नि मायिनस्तपुषा रक्षसो दह ॥१४॥

14. O Fire, with thy hearing of my new laud, with thy burning
     flame, consume utterly the demon magicians, O hero, O lord
     of the peoples.

न तस्य मायया चन रिपुरीशीत मर्त्यः ।
यो अग्नये ददाश हव्यदातिभिः ॥१५॥

15. Not even by magic can the mortal foe master the man who
     offers worship to the Fire with his gifts of the oblation.

व्यश्वस्त्वा वसुविदमुक्षण्युरप्रीणादृषिः ।
महो राये तमु त्वा समिधीमहि ॥१६॥

16.*

उशना काव्यस्त्वा नि होतारमसादयत् ।
आयाजि त्वा मनवे जातवेदसम् ॥१७॥

17. Thee Ushana of the inspired wisdom set within for men as
     the Priest of the call, the doer of sacrifice, the knower of all
     things born.

---

* Translation not found in MSS.

विश्वे हि त्वा सजोषसो देवासो दूतमक्रत ।
श्रुष्टी देव प्रथमो यज्ञियो भुवः ॥१८॥

18. For all the gods with one mind made thee the messenger;
O godhead, thou becamest by inspired knowledge supreme
and a lord of sacrifice.

इमं घा वीरो अमृतं दूतं कृण्वीत मर्त्यः ।
पावकं कृष्णवर्तनिं विहायसम् ॥१९॥

19. Him immortal let the mortal hero make his envoy, the
purifying Fire with his black path, vast in his wideness.

तं हुवेम यतस्रुचः सुभासं शुक्रशोचिषम् ।
विशामग्निमजरं प्रत्नमीडयम् ॥२०॥

20. Him let us call putting forth the ladle, the luminous, the
brilliant in light, one to be prayed by men, the ancient and
unaging Fire.

यो अस्मै हव्यदातिभिराहुतिं मर्तोऽविधत् ।
भूरि पोषं स धत्ते वीरवद् यशः ॥२१॥

21. For the mortal who performs sacrifice to him by his gifts of
the offering he founds much increase and a glory of his hero-
strengths.

प्रथमं जातवेदसमग्निं यज्ञेषु पूर्व्यम् ।
प्रति स्नुगेति नमसा हविष्मती ॥२२॥

22. To the Fire, the ancient, the first and supreme, the knower
of all things born in the sacrifices with the obeisance comes
the ladle full of the oblation.

आभिर्विधेमाग्नये ज्येष्ठाभिर्व्यश्ववत् ।
मंहिष्ठाभिर्मतिभिः शुक्रशोचिषे ॥२३॥

23. May we offer sacrifice as did Vyashwa with these greatest
and richest thinkings to Fire, the brilliant in light.

नूतमचं विहायसे स्तोमेभिः स्यूरयूपवत् ।
ऋषे वैयश्व दम्यायाग्नये ॥२४॥

24. O Rishi, son of Vyashwa, now sing the word of illumination
     as did Sthurayupa, to the Fire, vast in his wideness, the
     dweller in the house.

अतिथ्य मानुषाणां सूनुं वनस्पतीनाम् ।
विप्रा अग्निमबसे प्रत्नमीळते ॥२५॥

25. The guest of men, the son of the Trees, the illumined seers
     praise for his protection, the ancient Fire.

महो विश्वाँ अभि षतोऽभि हव्यानि मानुषा ।
अग्ने नि षत्सि नमसाधि बर्हिषि ॥२६॥

26. Turned towards all the great beings, turned towards our
     human offerings, by our obeisance, O Fire, thou takest thy
     seat on the sacred grass.

वंस्वा नो वार्या पुरु वंस्व रायः पुरुस्पृहः ।
सुवीर्यस्य प्रजावतो यशस्वतः ॥२७॥

27. Conquer for us many desirable things, take possession of
     the wealth that brings us our many longings and hero-energy
     and the offspring and the glory.

त्वं वरो सुषाम्णेऽग्ने जनाय चोदय ।
सदा वसो रातिं यविष्ठ शश्वते ॥२८॥

28.*

त्वं हि सुप्रतूरसि त्वं नो गोमतीरिषः ।
महो रायः सातिमग्ने अपा वृधि ॥२९॥

29. Thou art he who breaks through,[1] thou openest to us the
     luminous impulsions; open to us the conquest of the great
     Riches, O Fire.

---

* Translation not found in MSS.   [1] Or, he who overcomes,

अग्ने त्वं यशा अस्या मित्रावरुणा वह ।
ऋतावाना सम्राजा पूतदक्षसा ॥३०॥

30. O Fire, thou art the glorious one; bring to us Varuṇa and
Mitra, the all-rulers who possess the Truth and have the
purified judgment.

SHYAVASHWA ATREYA

SUKTA 38

यज्ञस्य हि स्थ ऋत्विजा सस्नी वाजेषु कर्मसु ।
इन्द्राग्नी तस्य बोधतम् ॥१॥

1. You (two) are the ritual-priests of the sacrifice, conquerors
in our plenitudes and our works; to this awake, O Indra,
O Fire.

तोशासा रययावाना वृत्रहणापराजिता ।
इन्द्राग्नी तस्य बोधतम् ॥२॥

2. O smiters who journey in the chariot, slayers of the coverer,
ever unconquered — to this awake, O Indra, O Fire.

इदं वां मदिरं मध्वधुक्षन्नद्रिभिर्नरः ।
इन्द्राग्नी तस्य बोधतम् ॥३॥

3. Men have pressed out for you by the stones this rapturous
honey-wine — to this awake, O Indra, O Fire.

जुषेथां यज्ञमिष्टये सुतं सोमं सधस्तुती ।
इन्द्राग्नी आ गतं नरा ॥४॥

4. Take pleasure in the sacrifice, for the sacrifice come to the
Soma-wine pressed out, gods to whom rises the common
laud, O Indra, O Fire.

इमा जुषेथां सवना येभिर्हव्यान्यूहथुः ।
इन्द्राग्नी आ गतं नरा ॥५॥

5. May you take pleasure in these Soma-pressings by them who
    have the offering, — O gods come to us, O Indra, O Fire.

इमां गायत्रवर्तनि जुषेथां सुष्टुतिं मम ।
इन्द्राग्नी आ गतं नरा ॥६॥

6. May you take pleasure in this laud of mine, this path of song,
    O gods, come to us, O Indra, O Fire.

प्रातर्यावभिरा गतं देवेभिर्जेन्यावसू ।
इन्द्राग्नी सोमपीतये ॥७॥

7. Come for the drink of the Soma-wine with the gods who
    arrive at dawn, you who have the victor-riches,[1] O Indra,
    O Fire.

श्यावाश्वस्य सुन्वतोऽत्रीणां शृणुतं हवम् ।
इन्द्राग्नी सोमपीतये ॥८॥

8. Hear the call of the Atris, of Shyavashwa[2] pressing the wine,
    come for the drinking of the Soma, O Indra, O Fire.

एवा वामह्व ऊतये यथाहुवन्त मेधिराः ।
इन्द्राग्नी सोमपीतये ॥९॥

9. Thus have I called you for protection as the wise have ever
    called you, for the drinking of the Soma (wine), O Indra, O
    Fire.

आहं सरस्वतीवतोरिन्द्राग्न्योरवो वृणे ।
याभ्यां गायत्रमृच्यते ॥१०॥

10. I choose the protection of Indra and the Fire with Saraswati
    at their side, for whom the sacred song breaks into light.[3]

---

[1] Or, you who have the riches which are for the victor, or the true riches,
[2] He who has the bay-horse.   [3] Or, is chanted.

SUKTA 39

अग्निमस्तोष्यृग्मियमग्निमीळा यजध्यै ।
अग्निर्देवाँ अनक्तु न उभे हि विदथे कविरन्तश्चरति दूत्यं नभन्तामन्यके समे ॥१॥

1. To Fire I give laud, the possessor of the illumined word, to
   worship the Fire with the speech of revelation; let the Fire
   reveal the gods to us, for he is the seer who goes on his
   embassy between the two worlds in the knowledge, — let
   all that are hostile be rent asunder.

न्यग्ने नव्यसा वचस्तनूषु शंसमेषाम् ।
न्यराती ररावणां विश्वा अर्यो अरातीरितो युच्छन्त्वामुरो नभन्तामन्यके समे ॥२॥

2. O Fire, destroy with a new word the expression of these
   within in the bodies, destroy within us the beings hostile to
   those who give thee, let all the enemy forces, the hostile
   spirits depart from here who would do hurt to us, — let all
   that are hostile be rent asunder.

अग्ने मन्मानि तुभ्यं कं घृतं न जुह्व आसनि ।
स देवेषु प्र चिकिद्धि त्वं ह्यसि पूर्व्यः शिवो दूतो विवस्वतो नभन्तामन्यके समे ॥३॥

3. O Fire, to thee I offer my thoughts as if an offering of light[1]
   cast into thy mouth; so do thou awake to knowledge in the
   gods, for thou art the ancient and benign messenger of the
   Sun, — let all that are alien be rent asunder.

तत्तदग्निनर्वयो दधे यथायथा कृपण्यति ।
ऊर्जाहुतिर्वसूनां शं च योश्च मयो दधे विश्वस्यै देवहूत्यै नभन्तामन्यके समे ॥४॥

4. He founds growth upon growth of the being even as one[2]
   desires; offered the oblation of offered energy for every call
   to the gods he founds both the peace and the movement
   of the Shining Ones, he founds the bliss, — let all that are

---

[1] *Ghṛtam*, clarified butter or light. [2] Or, he

alien be rent asunder.

स चिकेत सहीयसाऽग्निश्चित्रेण कर्मणा ।
स होता शश्वतीनां दक्षिणाभिरभीवृत इनोति च प्रतीव्यं नभन्तामन्यके समे ॥५॥

5. He awakes to knowledge by his forceful and many-sided
   works; he is the Priest of the call of many powers sur-
   rounded by lights of discernment and he takes possession
   of all that faces him, — let all that are alien be rent asunder.

अग्निर्जाता देवानामग्निर्वेद मर्तानामपीच्यम् ।
अग्निः स द्रविणोदा अग्निर्द्वारा व्यूर्णुते स्वाहुतो नवीयसा नभन्तामन्यके समे ॥६॥

6. The Fire knows the births of the gods and the secret thing
   of mortals; this is the Fire that gives the treasures, the Fire
   when there is cast into him as offering that is new uncovers
   the hidden doors, — let all that are alien be rent asunder.

अग्निर्देवेषु संवसुः स विक्षु यज्ञियास्वा ।
स मुदा काव्या पुरु विश्वं भूमेव पुष्यति देवो देवेषु यज्ञियो नभन्तामन्यके समे ॥७॥

7. Fire is the companion dwelling in the gods, dwelling in the
   beings who are masters of sacrifice; he increases by his rapture many seer-wisdoms, even as all that is large, he is a god
   in the gods and a lord of sacrifice, — let all that are alien be
   rent asunder.

यो अग्निः सप्तमानुषः श्रितो विश्वेषु सिन्धुषु ।
तमागन्म त्रिपस्त्यं मन्धातुर्दस्युहन्तममग्निं यज्ञेषु पूर्व्यं नभन्तामन्यके समे ॥८॥

8. Fire is the sevenfold human, he is lodged in all the rivers;
   to him we have come, the dweller in the triple abode, the Fire
   of the thinker, slayer of the Destroyers, ancient and supreme
   in the sacrifices, — let all that are alien be rent asunder.

अग्निस्त्रीणि त्रिधातून्या क्षेति विदथा कविः ।
स त्री रेकादशां इह यक्षच्च पिप्रयच्च नो
विप्रो दूतः परिष्कृतो नभन्तामन्यके समे ॥९॥

9. Fire is the seer who takes up his dwelling in his three abodes
   of knowledge of three kinds; may he sacrifice to the Three
   and Thirty and satisfy us, perfected, the illumined thinker
   and messenger, — let all that are alien be rent asunder.

त्वं नो अग्न आयुषु त्वं देवेषु पूर्व्य वस्व एक इरज्यसि ।
त्वामाप: परिस्रुत: परि यन्ति स्वसेतवो नभन्तामन्यके समे ॥१०॥

10. O ancient and supreme Fire, thou art in us who are mortals,
    thou in the gods, one and sole thou rulest over the Treasures;
    around thee the wide-flowing waters go each with its own
    bridge, — let all that are alien be rent asunder.

SUKTA 40

इन्द्राग्नी युवं सु न: सहन्ता दासथो रयिम् ।
येन दृळ्हा समत्स्वा वीळु चित् साहिषीमह्याग्निर्वनेव वात इन्नभन्तामन्यके समे ॥१॥

1. O Indra, O Fire, forceful you give to us the treasure by
   which we shall overcome in our battles even all that is firm
   and strong, as Fire the trees in a wind, — let all that are alien
   be rent asunder.

नहि वां वव्रयामहेऽध्येन्द्रमिद् यजामहे शविष्ठं नृणां नरम् ।
स न: कदा चिदर्वता गमदा वाजसातये गमदा मेधसातये नभन्तामन्यके समे ॥२॥

2. May we not shut you away from us, then may we truly worship Indra with sacrifice, the god most potent of the gods;
   may he sometime come to us with the war-horse, may he
   come to us for the winning of the plenitudes, for the winning
   of the purity,[1] — let all that are alien be rent asunder.

ता हि मध्यं भराणामिन्द्राग्नी अधिक्षित: ।
ता उ कवित्वना कवी पृच्छ्यमाना सखीयते
सं धीतमश्नुतं नरा नभन्तामन्यके समे ॥३॥

---

[1] Or, for the getting of sacrifices,

3.   For they, Indra and Fire, dwell in the midst of mellays;
      gods, seers, questioned, they by their seerhood gain for
      one who seeks their friendship the knowledge won by the
      thought, — let all that are alien be rent asunder.

अभ्यर्चं नभाकवदिन्द्राग्नी यजसा गिरा ।
ययोर्विश्वमिदं जगदियं द्यौः पृथ्वी महृयुपस्थे बिभृतो वसु नभन्तामन्यके समे ॥४॥

4.   To Indra and the Fire sing the illumined chant even as
      Nabhaka, doing them homage with sacrifice and speech,
      whose is all this world and this heaven and great earth bear
      for them in their lap the treasures, — let all that are alien be
      rent asunder.

प्र ब्रह्माणि नभाकवदिन्द्राग्निभ्यामिरज्यत ।
या सप्तबुध्नमर्णवं जिह्वाबारमपोर्णुत इन्द्र ईशान ओजसा नभन्तामन्यके समे ॥५॥

5.   Even as Nabhaka direct towards Indra and Fire the Words
      who uncovered the sea of the seven foundations with its dim[1]
      doors, — even Indra ruling all by his might, — let all that
      are alien be rent asunder.

अपि वृश्च पुराणवद् व्रततेरिव गुष्पितमोजो दासस्य दम्भय ।
वयं तदस्य संभृतं वस्विन्द्रेण वि भजेमहि नभन्तामन्यके समे ॥६॥

6.   Even as of old cleave like clustering mass of a creeper,
      crush the might of the demon; that wealth amassed by him
      may we by Indra share, — let all that are alien be rent
      asunder.

यदिन्द्राग्नी जना इमे विह्वयन्ते तना गिरा ।
अस्माकेभिर्नृभिर्वयं सासह्याम पृतन्यतो वनुयाम वनुष्यतो नभन्तामन्यके समे ॥७॥

7.   When, O Indra, O Fire, these who are here call you with
      speech and act, may we overcome by our men those who
      battle against us, may we conquer those who would conquer
      us, — let all that are alien be rent asunder.

---

[1] Or, oblique

या नु श्वेताववो दिव उच्चरात उप द्युभिः ।
इन्द्राग्न्योरनु व्रतमुहाना यन्ति सिन्धवो
यान् त्सीं बन्धादमुञ्चतां नभन्तामन्यके समे ॥८॥

8. White gods are they who from below ascend to the heavens
by their lights; according to the law of the working of Indra
and Fire, flowing move the Rivers whom they loosed from
bondage to every side, — let all that are alien be rent
asunder.

पूर्वीष्ट इन्द्रोपमातयः पूर्वीरुत प्रशस्तयः सूनो हिन्वस्य हरिवः ।
वस्वो वीरस्यापृचो या नु साधन्त नो धियो नभन्तामन्यके समे ॥९॥

9. O Indra, O thou of the bright horses, O begetter of the shining hero, the shooter who strikes into his mark, many are
thy measurings of things, many thy expressions of the truth
which accomplish[1] our thoughts, — let all that are alien be
rent asunder.

तं शिशीता सुवृक्तिभिस्त्वेषं सत्वानमृग्मियम् ।
उतो न चिद् य ओजसा शुष्णस्याण्डानि भेदति
जेषत् स्वर्वतीरपो नभन्तामन्यके समे ॥१०॥

10. Intensify him by your purifications, the brilliant warrior
with the illumined word, even him who with might breaks
the serpent-eggs of Shushna, may he conquer the waters
that bear the light of the Sun-world, — let all that are alien
be rent asunder.

तं शिशीता स्वध्वरं सत्यं सत्वानमृत्वियम् ।
उतो नु चिद् य ओहत आण्डा शुष्णस्य भेद-
त्यजैः स्वर्वतीरपो नभन्तामन्यके समे ॥११॥

11. Intensify him who is perfect in the rite of the path, the true
warrior who follows the law of the Truth; it is he who
observes, who breaks the serpent-eggs of Shushna, conquers
the waters that bear the light of the Sun-world, — let all that
are alien be rent asunder.

---

[1] Or bring to perfection

एवेन्द्राग्निभ्यां पितृवन्नवीयो मन्धातृवदङ्गिरस्वदवाचि ।
त्रिधातुना शर्मणा पातमस्मान् वयं स्याम पतयो रयीणाम् ॥१२॥

12. So has the new word been spoken to Indra and to Fire, even
as by my father, by Mandhata, by the Angiras; protect us
with triple peace, may we be masters of the riches.

VIRUPA ANGIRASA

SUKTA 43

इमे विप्रस्य वेधसोऽग्नेरस्तृतयज्वनः ।
गिरः स्तोमास ईरते ॥१॥

1. Him pray our words, even these lauds of Fire, the illumined
seer, the creator, invincible in his sacrifice.

अस्मे ते प्रतिहर्यंते जातबेदो विचर्षणे ।
अग्ने जनामि सुष्टुतिम् ॥२॥

2. Such art thou for whom I bring to birth perfect laud and glad
is thy response, O seeing Fire, O knower of all things born!

आरोका इव घेदह तिग्मा अग्ने तव त्विषः ।
वड्डूर्वनानि बप्सति ॥३॥

3. Oh, like jets of light thy keen energies of flame devour with
their teeth the woods.

हर्यो धूमकेतवो वातजूता उप द्यवि ।
यतन्ते वृथगग्नयः ॥४॥

4. Bright, with smoke for their flag against heaven, urged by
the winds, labour separate thy fires.

एते त्ये वृथगग्नय इद्धासः समदृक्षत ।
उषसामिव केतवः ॥५॥

5. These are those separate fires of thine that kindled are seen like rays of the Dawns.

कृष्णा रजांसि पत्सुतः प्रयाणे जातवेदसः ।
अग्निर्यद् रोधति क्षमि ॥६॥

6. Black is the dust under his feet in the march of the knower of all things born when Fire sprouts upon the earth.

धासि कृष्वान ओषधीर्बप्सदग्निनं वायति ।
पुनर्यन् तरुणीरपि ॥७॥

7. Making his foundation, consuming the herbs Fire wearies not but goes even to the young shoots.

जिह्वाभिरह नन्नमर्दचिषा जञ्जणाभवन् ।
अग्निर्वनेषु रोचते ॥८॥

8. Oh, laying all low with his tongues of flame, flashing out with his ray Fire shines in the woodlands.

अप्स्वग्ने सधिष्टव सौषधीरनु रुध्यसे ।
गर्भे सञ्जायसे पुनः ॥९॥

9. In the waters, O Fire, is thy seat,[1] thou besiegest the plants; thou becomest a child in the womb and art born again.

उदग्ने तव तद् घृतादर्ची रोचत आहुतम् ।
निसानं जुह्वो मुखे ॥१०॥

10. O Fire, that ray of thine fed with the oblation rises up shining from the offering of light,[2] licking the mouth of the ladle.

उक्षान्नाय वशान्नाय सोमपृष्ठाय वेधसे ।
स्तोर्मविधेमाग्नये ॥११॥

---

[1] Or, goal,   [2] Or, clarified butter,

11.   May we ordain sacrifice with the lauds to Fire, the ordainer
       of things, Fire who makes the ox and the cow his food and
       he bears on his back the Soma-wine.

उत त्वा नमसा वयं होतर्वरेण्यक्रतो ।
अग्ने समिद्धिरीमहे ॥१२॥

12.   O Fire, we come to thee with prostration and with the fuel,
       O Priest of the call, O supreme will!

उत त्वा भृगुवच्छुचे मनुष्वदग्न आहुत ।
अङ्गिरस्वद्धवामहे ॥१३॥

13.   O pure Flame, fed with offerings we call thee as did Bhrigu,
       as did Manu, as did Angiras.

त्वं ह्यग्ने अग्निना विप्रो विप्रेण सन् त्सता ।
सखा सख्या समिध्यसे ॥१४॥

14.   For thou art kindled, O Fire, by the fire, thou who art the
       illumined seer art kindled by one who is illumined, as a
       comrade thou art kindled by thy comrade.

स त्वं विप्राय दाशुषे रयिं देहि सहस्रिणम् ।
अग्ने वीरवतीमिषम् ॥१५॥

15.   So do thou to the illumined who gives to thee give the thou-
       sandfold wealth and the hero-force.

अग्ने भ्रातः सहस्कृत रोहिदश्व शुचिव्रत ।
इमं स्तोमं जुषस्व मे ॥१६॥

16.   O Fire, my brother, created by my force, drawn by thy red
       horses, pure in the law of thy workings, take pleasure in this
       laud of mine.

उत त्वाग्ने मम स्तुतो वाश्राय प्रतिहर्यते ।
गोष्ठं गाव इवाशत ॥१७॥

17. My lauds reach thee, O Fire, as to the calf lowing in glad response the cows reach their stall.

तुभ्यं ता अङ्गिरस्तम विश्वाः सुक्षितयः पृथक् ।
अग्ने कामाय येमिरे ॥१८॥

18. For thee, O most luminous Angiras, all those worlds of happy dwelling, each in its separate power, labour for thy desire, O Flame.

अग्निं धीभिर्मनीषिणो मेधिरासो विपश्चितः ।
अध्वसद्याय हिन्विरे ॥१९॥

19. In thinkers the wise, the illumined seers urged by their thoughts the Fire to dwell in their house.

तं त्वामज्मेषु वाजिनं तन्वाना अग्ने अध्वरम् ।
वह्निं होतारमीळते ॥२०॥

20. So thee as the horse in its gallopings performing the pilgrim-sacrifice, O Fire, they desire as the carrier of the offering and the Priest of the call.

पुरुत्रा हि सदृङ्ङसि विशो विश्वा अनु प्रभुः ।
समत्सु त्वा हवामहे ॥२१॥

21. Thou art the lord who looks with equal eyes on all the peoples in many lands; we call to thee in our battles.

तमीळिष्व य आहुतोऽग्निर्विभ्राजते घृतैः ।
इमं नः शृणवद्धवम् ॥२२॥

22. Pray the Fire who fed with the pouring of the clarities blazed wide; may he hear this our call.

तं त्वा वयं हवामहे शृण्वन्तं जातवेदसम् ।
अग्ने घ्नन्तमप द्विषः ॥२३॥

23. Such art thou whom we call, Fire, the knower of all things born who hears our cry and smites away from us the foe.

विशां राजानमद्भुतमध्यक्षं धर्मणामिमम् ।
अग्निमीळे स उ श्रवत् ॥२४॥

24. I pray this Fire, the marvellous king of the peoples who presides over the laws of their action, may he hear.

अग्निं विश्वायुवेपसं मर्यं न वाजिनं हितम् ।
सप्तिं न वाजयामसि ॥२५॥

25. Fire who illumines the universal life like a male horse urged to its gallop, we speed like a racer to the goal.

घ्नन् मृध्राण्यप द्विषो दहन् रक्षांसि विश्वहा ।
अग्ने तिग्मेन दीदिहि ॥२६॥

26. Smiting away the foes and things that hurt, burning the Rakshasas, on every side, O Fire, shine out with thy keen flame.

यं त्वा जनास इन्धते मनुष्वदङ्गिरस्तम ।
अग्ने स बोधि मे वचः ॥२७॥

27. Thou whom men kindle as the human thinker,[1] O most luminous Angiras, O Fire, become aware of my word.

यदग्ने दिविजा अस्यप्सुजा वा सहस्कृत ।
तं त्वा गीर्भिर्हवामहे ॥२८॥

28. Because, O Fire, created by our force thou art the flame born in heaven, or the flame born in the waters, as such we call thee with our words.

तुभ्यं छेत् ते जना इमे विश्वाः सुक्षितयः पृथक् ।
धासिं हिन्वन्त्यत्तवे ॥२९॥

---

[1] Or, like Manu,

29. To thee, verily, these beings born and these worlds of a happy dwelling each separately in its place, lay a foundation where thou canst devour thy food.[1]

ते घेदग्ने स्वाध्योऽग्रा विश्वा नुचक्षसः ।
तरन्तः स्याम दुर्गहा ॥३०॥

30. O Fire, may we be those who have the right thought and the divine vision, and through all the days, pass safe beyond the danger.

अग्निं मन्द्रं पुरप्रियं शीरं पावकशोचिषम् ।
हृद्भिर्मन्द्रेभिरीमहे ॥३१॥

31. We seek with rapturous hearts Fire, the rapturous, in whom are many things that are dear to us, — Fire with his intense and purifying light.

स त्वमग्ने विभावसुः सृजन् सूर्यो न रश्मिभिः ।
शर्धन् तमांसि जिघ्नसे ॥३२॥

32. O Fire, shining with thy light, loosing forth thy lustre like the sun with its rays, thou puttest forth thy force and slayest the darknesses.

तत् ते सहस्व ईमहे दात्रं यन्नोपदस्यति ।
त्वदग्ने वार्यं वसु ॥३३॥

33. We seek from thee, O forceful Fire, that gift of thine, — the desirable wealth which never fails.

SUKTA 44

समिधाग्निं दुवस्यत घृतैर्बोधयतातिथिम् ।
आस्मिन् हव्या जुहोतन ॥१॥

---

[1] Or, cast nourishment for thy eating.

1. Set to his action by the fuel, awaken the guest by the offer-
    ings of the clarities; cast in him the offerings.

अग्ने स्तोमं जुषस्व मे वर्धस्वानेन मन्मना ।
प्रति सूक्तानि हर्य नः ॥२॥

2. O Fire, take pleasure in my laud, grow by this thought; let
    thy joy respond to our utterances.

अग्निं दूतं पुरो दधे हव्यवाहमुप ब्रुवे ।
देवाँ आ सादयादिह ॥३॥

3. I set in front Fire, the messenger, and speak to the carrier of
    the offerings; may he bring to their session here the gods.

उत् ते बृहन्तो अर्चयः समिधानस्य दीदिवः ।
अग्ने शुक्रास ईरते ॥४॥

4. O luminous Fire, vast and bright thy rays upwards ascend
    as thou art kindled high.

उप त्वा जुह्वो मम घृताचीर्यन्तु हर्यत ।
अग्ने हव्या जुषस्व नः ॥५॥

5. O joyful Flame, to thee may my ladles go bright with the
    clarities; O Fire, take pleasure in our offerings.

मन्द्रं होतारमृत्विजं चित्रभानुं विभावसुम् ।
अग्निमीळे स उ श्रवत् ॥६॥

6. I pray the Fire, the rapturous Priest of the call, the sacri-
    ficant, shining with his light, rich in his lustres, may he hear.

प्रत्नं होतारमीडयं जुष्टमग्निं कविक्रतुम् ।
अध्वराणामभिश्रियम् ॥७॥

7. The ancient Priest of the call, desirable and accepted, Fire
    the seer-will, joiner of the pilgrim-rites.

जुषाणो अङ्गिरस्तमेमा हव्यान्यानुषक् ।
अग्ने यज्ञं नय ऋतुथा ॥८॥

8. O most luminous Angiras, taking pleasure in these offerings lead the sacrifice uninterruptedly in the way of the Truth,[1] O Fire.

समिधान उ सन्त्य शुक्रशोच इहा वह ।
चिकित्वान् दैव्यं जनम् ॥९॥

9. High-kindled, O Right and True, O brilliant light, awakened to knowledge bring here the divine people.

विप्रं होतारमद्रुहं धूमकेतुं विभावसुम् ।
यज्ञानां केतुमीमहे ॥१०॥

10. The illumined seer and Priest of the call, free from harms, shining with light, carrying his banner of smoke, him we seek, the ray of intuition of the sacrifices.

अग्ने नि पाहि नस्त्वं प्रति ष्म देव रीषतः ।
भिन्धि द्वेषः सहस्कृत ॥११॥

11. O Fire, made by our force, protect us against the doers of harm, pierce the hostile power.

अग्निः प्रत्नेन मन्मना शुम्भानस्तन्वं स्वाम् ।
कविर्विप्रेण वावृधे ॥१२॥

12. Fire by the ancient thought making beautiful his own body, a seer, grows by each illumined sage.

ऊर्जो नपातमा हुवेऽग्निं पावकशोचिषम् ।
अस्मिन् यज्ञे स्वध्वरे ॥१३॥

13. I call to me the Child of Energy, Fire of the purifying light in this sacrifice which is perfect rite of the path.

---

[1] Or, according to the rule of the rites,

स नो मित्रमहस्त्वमग्ने शुक्रेण शोचिषा ।
देवैरा सत्सि बर्हिषि ॥१४॥

14. So do thou, O Fire, O friendly light, with thy brilliant flame
     sit with the gods on the sacred grass.

यो अग्निं तन्वो दमे देवं मर्तः सपर्यति ।
तस्मा इद् दीदयद् वसु ॥१५॥

15. The mortal who serves the divine Fire in the house of the
     body, to him he gives the Riches.

अग्निर्मूर्धा दिवः ककुत् पतिः पृथिव्या अयम् ।
अपां रेतांसि जिन्वति ॥१६॥

16. Fire is the head and peak of heaven and lord of earth and
     he sets moving the waters.

उदग्ने शुचयस्तव शुक्रा भ्राजन्त ईरते ।
तव ज्योतींष्यर्चयः ॥१७॥

17. O Fire, upward dart blazing thy pure and brilliant tongues;
     make to shine out thy lights.

ईशिषे वार्यस्य हि दात्रस्याग्ने स्वर्पतिः ।
स्तोता स्यां तव शर्मणि ॥१८॥

18. Thou art the lord of the Sun-world, O Fire, and hast power
     for the gifts desirable; may I who laud thee abide in thy
     peace.

त्वामग्ने मनीषिणस्त्वां हिन्वन्ति चित्तिभिः ।
त्वां वर्धन्तु नो गिरः ॥१९॥

19. Thee, O Fire, the thinkers urge on thy road, thee by their
     perceivings of knowledge; may our words increase thee.

अवध्यस्य स्वधावतो द्यूतस्य रेभतः सदा ।
अग्नेः सख्यं वृणीमहे ॥२०॥

20. We choose the comradeship of the Fire inviolate in the law of his nature, the ever-chanting messenger.

अग्निः शुचिव्रततमः शुचिर्विप्रः शुचिः कविः ।
शुची रोचत आहुतः ॥२१॥

21. Most pure in his workings is the Fire, he is the pure illumined sage, the pure seer of Truth; pure he shines out fed by our offerings.

उत त्वा धीतयो मम गिरो वर्धन्तु विश्वहा ।
अग्ने सख्यस्य बोधि नः ॥२२॥

22. So thee may my thinkings and my words increase always; O Fire, awake to the comradeship between us.

यदग्ने स्यामहं त्वं त्वं वा घा स्या अहम् ।
स्युष्टे सत्या इहाशिषः ॥२३॥

23. O Fire, if I wert thou and thou wert I, then would thy longings here become true.

वसुर्वसुपतिर्हि कमस्यग्ने विभावसुः ।
स्याम ते सुमतावपि ॥२४॥

24. O Fire, thou art the shining one, shining with thy lustres, lord of the shining riches; may we abide in thy right thinking.[1]

अग्ने धृतव्रताय ते समुद्रायेव सिन्धवः ।
गिरो वाश्रास ईरते ॥२५॥

25. O Fire, to thee holding firmly the law of thy workings, move my words like lowing cattle, as rivers move towards the sea.

युवानं विश्पतिं कविं विश्वादं पुरुवेपसम् ।
अग्निं शुम्भामि मन्मभिः ॥२६॥

---

[1] Or, thy grace.

26. Fire the youth, the lord of the peoples, the seer, the all-consuming, Fire of the many illuminations I glorify with my thoughts.

यज्ञानां रथ्ये वयं तिग्मजम्भाय वीळवे ।
स्तोमैरिषेमाग्नये ॥२७॥

27. May we strive towards the Fire by our lauds, the charioteer of the sacrifices, Fire with his solid strength, his sharp tusks of flame.

अयमग्ने त्वे अपि जरिता भूतु सन्त्य ।
तस्मै पावक मृळय ॥२८॥

28 May this thy worshipper, O Fire, abide in thee; on him have grace, O Right and True, O purifying Flame.

धीरो ह्यस्यग्रसद् विप्रो न जागृविः सदा ।
अग्ने दीदयसि द्यवि ॥२९॥

29. For thou art the wise thinker seated in the house, like an illumined sage ever awake; O Fire, thou shinest out in heaven.

पुराग्ने दुरितेभ्यः पुरा मृधेभ्यः कवे ।
प्र ण आयुर्वसो तिर ॥३०॥

30. Before the stumblings come, O Fire, before the spoilers arrive, O seer, carry forward our life, O Shining One.

BHARGA PRAGATHA

SUKTA 60

अग्न आ याह्यग्निभिर्होतारं त्वा वृणीमहे ।
आ त्वामनक्तु प्रयता हविष्मती यजिष्ठं बर्हिरासदे ॥१॥

1. Come, O Fire, with thy fires, we choose thee as the Priest of
the call, may the ladles extended, full of the offering anoint
thee, strongest for sacrifice when thou sittest on the sacrificial seat.

अच्छा हि त्वा सहसः सुनो अङगिरः स्रुचश्चरन्त्यध्वरे ।
ऊर्जो नपातं घृतकेशमीमहेऽग्निं यज्ञेषु पूर्व्यम् ॥२॥

2. For, towards thee, O Son of force, O Angiras, the ladles
move in the rite of the path; we seek the child of Energy
with his hair of light, the supreme fire in the sacrifices.

अग्ने कविर्वेधा असि होता पावक यक्ष्यः ।
मन्द्रो यजिष्ठो अध्वरेष्वीडचो विप्रेभिः शुक्र मन्मभिः ॥३॥

3. O Fire, thou art the seer and the ordainer, the Priest of the
call, the purifier to whom must be given sacrifice, rapturous,
strong for sacrifice, one to be prayed in the pilgrim-rites
with illumined thoughts, O brilliant Flame!

अद्रोघमा वहोशतो यविष्ठच देवाँ अजस्र वीतये ।
अभि प्रयांसि सुधिता वसो गहि मन्द्स्व धीतिभिर्हितः ॥४॥

4. Bring to me who betray not, O youngest, O unceasing
Flame, the gods that desire for the advent; come to our
well-founded pleasant things, O shining One, rejoice established by our thinkings.

त्वमित् सप्रथा अस्यग्ने त्रातर्ऋतस्कविः ।
त्वां विप्रासः समिधान दीदिव आ विवासन्ति वेधसः ॥५॥

5. O Fire, O deliverer, thou art very wide, the true, the seer,
thou who shinest out, O high-kindled Fire, thee the sages,
the ordainers illumine.

शोचा शोचिष्ठ दीदिहि विश्वे मयो रास्व स्तोत्रे महाँ असि ।
देवानां शर्मन् मम सन्तु सूरयः शत्रूषाहः स्वग्नयः ॥६॥

6. Flame out, O most luminous Flame, shine out for man, give to him who lauds thee the bliss, for thou art great; may my luminous seers abide in the peace of the gods, high in fire may they overcome the foe.

यथा चिद् वृद्धमतसमग्ने संजूर्वसि क्षमि ।
एवा दह मित्रमहो यो अस्मध्रुग् दुर्मन्मा कश्च वेनति ॥७॥

7. As, O Fire, thou consumest old dry wood on the earth so burn, O friendly Light, whosoever comes with evil mind, our hurter.

मा नो मर्ताय रिपवे रक्षस्विने माघशंसाय रीरधः ।
अस्रेधद्भिस्तरणिभिर्यविष्ठच शिवेभिः पाहि पायुभिः ॥८॥

8. Deliver us not to the mortal foe, to the demoniac, to him who gives expression to evil; guard us with thy unfailing and benignant, guardian and rescuer fires, O ever-youthful Flame!

पाहि नो अग्न एकया पाह्युत द्वितीयया ।
पाहि गीर्भिस्तिसृभिरूर्जां पते पाहि चतसृभिर्वसो ॥९॥

9. Guard, O Fire, with the single word, guard with the second, guard with the words that are three, O master of Energies; O shining One, guard with the fourth.

पाहि विश्वस्माद्रक्षसो अराव्णः प्र स्म वाजेषु नोऽव ।
त्वामिद्धि नेदिष्ठं देवतातय आपि नक्षामहे वृषे ॥१०॥

10. Guard us from every hostile demon, protect us in the plenitudes; for we come to thee as the closest of the gods and our ally for our increase.

आ नो अग्ने वयोवृधं रयिं पावक शंस्यम् ।
रास्वा च न उपमाते पुरुस्पृहं सुनीती स्वयशस्तरम् ॥११॥

11. O purifying Fire, bring to us and give a wealth that increases our growth, the wealth that has to be expressed in us, O measurer of our formations, by thy right leading a wealth full of many longed-for things and very great in its self-glory, —

येन वंसाम पृतनासु शर्धतस्तरन्तो अर्यं आदिशः ।
स त्वं नो वर्धं प्रयसा शचीवसो जिन्वा धियो वसुविदः ॥१२॥

12. by which we may conquer those who challenge us in our battles, breaking through the designs of the foe; so do thou increase us with thy delight, O luminous in might, speed on their way the thoughts that find the treasure.

शिशानो वृषभो यथाग्निः शृङ्गे दविध्वत् ।
तिग्मा अस्य हनवो न प्रतिधृषे सुजम्भः सहसो यहुः ॥१३॥

13. Fire is like a bull that sharpens its horns and tosses its head, his flaming jaws are too bright and keen to gaze at; strong-tusked is the Son of force.

नहि ते अग्ने वृषभ प्रतिधृषे जम्भासो यद्वितिष्ठसे ।
स त्वं नो होतः सुहुतं हविष्कृधि वंस्वा नो वार्या पुरु ॥१४॥

14. O Fire, O Bull, thy tusks of flame cannot be challenged by the gaze when thou rangest abroad; so do thou, O Priest of the call, make that our offering is well cast, conquer for us many desirable things.

शेषे वनेषु मात्रोः सं त्वा मर्तास इन्धते ।
अतन्द्रो हव्या वहसि हविष्कृत आ दिव् देवेषु राजसि ॥१५॥

15. In the forest thou sleepest in the two mothers, mortals kindle thee into a blaze; then sleepless thou carriest the offerings of the giver of the oblation and now thou shinest in the gods.

सप्त होतारस्तमिदीळते त्वाऽग्ने सुत्यजमह्वयम् ।
भिनत्स्यद्रि तपसा वि शोचिषा प्राग्ने तिष्ठ जनाँ अति ॥१६॥

16. Thee pray the seven priests of the call, thee the unhesitant,
shooting well thy shafts; thou breakest asunder the hill
with thy heat and thy light: O Fire, go forth beyond men.

अग्निमग्निं वो अध्रिगुं हुवेम वृक्तबर्हिषः ।
अग्निं हितप्रयसः शश्वतीष्वाऽऽहोतारं चर्षणीनाम् ॥१७॥

17. The Fire, the fire, let us call for you having placed the sacred
grass and placed the gifts of our pleasure, on day after day,
Fire of the unseizable ray, Priest of the call of seeing men.

केतेन शर्मन् त्सचते सुषामण्यग्ने तुभ्यं चिकित्वना ।
इषण्यया नः पुरूरूपमा भर वाजं नेदिष्ठमूतये ॥१८॥

18. O Fire, to thee constant in the peace of a deep calm I come
with the intuition that awakes to knowledge; by our impulsion bring to us for our protection wealth of many forms
that is most close.

अग्ने जरितर्विश्पतिस्तेपानो देव रक्षसः ।
अप्रोषिवान् गृहपतिर्महाँ असि दिवस्पायुर्दुरोणयुः ॥१९॥

19. O Fire, O god, for thy adorer thou art the lord of creatures,
thou art the master of his house who departs not from him,
afflicting the demons; great art thou, the guardian of heaven
who comes to his gated home.

मा नो रक्ष आ वेशीदाघृणीवसो मा यातुर्यातुमावताम् ।
परोगव्यूत्यनिरामप क्षुधमग्ने सेध रक्षस्विनः ॥२०॥

20. O blazing light, let not the demon enter into us; let not the
witchcraft of the goblin sorcerers take possession; O Fire,
push calamity and hunger far beyond the pastures of our
herds, ward the demon-possessed away from us.

SUKTA 71

त्वं नो अग्ने महोभिः पाहि विश्वस्या अरातेः ।
उत द्विषो मर्त्यस्य ॥१॥

1. O Fire, guard us by thy lights[1] from every hostile force and from mortal foe.

नहि मन्युः पौरुषेय ईशे हि वः प्रियजात ।
त्वमिदसि क्षपावान् ॥२॥

2. O beloved in thy birth, mortal wrath has no power over you: thou art master of the nights.

स नो विश्वेभिर्देवेभिरूर्जो नपाद् भद्रशोचे ।
रयिं देहि विश्ववारम् ॥३॥

3. So do thou with all the gods, O child of Energy, O happy light, give us the wealth in which are all boons.

न तमग्ने अरातयो मर्तं युवन्त रायः ।
यं त्रायसे दाश्वांसम् ॥४॥

4. The hostile forces, O Fire, cannot divorce from the Riches the mortal giver whom thou rescuest.

यं त्वं विप्र मेधसाताव्यग्ने हिनोषि धनाय ।
स तवोती गोषु गन्ता ॥५॥

5. O Fire, O illumined seer, he whom thou in the winning of the purity speedest towards the Riches, by thy protection reaches among the Ray-Cows.

त्वं रयिं पुरुवीरमग्ने दाशुषे मर्ताय ।
प्र णो नय वस्यो अच्छ ॥६॥

---

[1] Or, by thy greatnesses

6. Thou bringest, O Fire, the wealth in which are the many
   strengths to the mortal giver; lead us towards greater riches.

उरुष्या णो मा परा वा अघायते जातवेदः ।
दुराध्ये मर्तय ॥७॥

7. Protect us, deliver us not, O knower of all things born, to
   the mortal, the evil-thoughted who would bring on us
   calamity.

अग्ने माकिष्टे देवस्य रातिमदेवो युयोत ।
त्वमीशिषे वसूनाम् ॥८॥

8. O Fire, let none undivine take away from us what was given
   by thee, the divine; thou hast power over the riches.

स नो वस्व उप मास्यूर्जो नपान्माहिनस्य ।
सखे वसो जरितृभ्यः ॥९॥

9. Thou art the measurer to us, thy adorers of a mighty wealth,
   O child of Energy, O Friend, O shining One.

अच्छा नः शीरशोचिषम् गिरो यन्तु दर्शतम् ।
अच्छा यज्ञासो नमसा पुरूवसुं पुरुप्रशस्तमूतये ॥१०॥

10. May our words go towards thee with thy keen light and thy
    vision, our sacrifice to thee with surrender for our protection,
    thee the widely proclaimed, the master of many riches, —

अग्निं सूनुं सहसो जातवेदसं दानाय वार्याणाम् ।
द्विता यो भूवमृतो मर्त्येष्वा होता मन्द्रतमो विशि ॥११॥

11. to the Fire, the Son of force, the knower of all things born,
    for the gift of our desirable things; twofold he becomes the
    immortal in the mortals, the rapturous Priest of the call in
    man.

अग्निं वो देवयज्ययाग्निं प्रयत्यध्वरे ।
अग्निं धीषु प्रथममग्निमर्वत्यग्निं क्षेत्राय साधसे ॥१२॥

12. Fire for you by the worship to the gods, Fire in the journeying of the pilgrim-sacrifice, Fire in the thoughts first and
chief, Fire in the war-horse, Fire for perfection in our field.

अग्निरिषां सख्ये ददातु न ईशे यो वार्याणाम् ।
अग्निं तोके तनये शश्वदीमहे वसुं सन्तं तनूपाम् ॥१३॥

13. May the Fire give us force in his comradeship, he who has
power for the desirable things; Fire we seek continually
in the son of our begettings as the shining one and the guardian of the body.

अग्निमीळिष्वावसे गाथाभिः शीरशोचिषम् ।
अग्निं राये पुरुमीळ्ह श्रुतं नरोऽग्निं सुदीतये छर्दिः ॥१४॥

14. Pray with your chants Fire of the keen flame for the protection, O Purumilha! Fire for the Treasure, — the Fire men
pray for the inspired knowledge, a house for a splendid
light.

अग्निं द्वेषो योतवं नो गृणीमस्यग्निं शं योश्च दातवे ।
विश्वासु विश्ववितेव हव्यो भुवद्वस्तुर्ऋंषूणाम् ॥१५॥

15. Fire we hymn with our words that he may remove from us
the hostile power, Fire to give to us the peace and the movement; he is in all men like a protector to whom they may
call, he is the daylight of the wise.

HARYATA PRAGATHA

Sukta 72

हविष्कृणुध्वमा गमदध्वर्युर्वनते पुनः ।
विद्वाँ अस्य प्रशासनम् ॥१॥

1. Do you make the offering, the Priest of the pilgrim-rite has come and he conquers again, for he knows the commandment of the Fire.

नि तिग्ममभ्यंशुं सीदद्धोता मनावधि ।

जुषाणो अस्य सख्यम् ॥२॥

2. Let him sit within close to the keen burning ray the Priest of the call in thinking man accepting the comradeship of the Fire.

अन्तरिच्छन्ति तं जने रुद्रं परो मनीषया ।

गृभ्णन्ति जिह्वया ससम् ॥३॥

3. Within they wish him to be in a man the "terrible one", beyond the thinking mind; by his tongue they seize the peace.

जाम्यतीतपे धनुर्वंयोधा अरुह्द्वनम् ।

दृषवं जिह्वयावधीत् ॥४॥

4. High burnt the companion bow, a founder of the growth he climbed to woodland, he smote the rock with his tongue.

चरन् वत्सो रशन्मिह् निदातारं न विन्दते ।

वेति स्तोतव अम्ब्यम् ॥५॥

5. He is the shining calf who wanders and finds none to bind him here, to one who lauds him he manifests the mother.[1]

उतो न्वस्य यन्महदश्वावद्योजनं बृहत् ।

दामा रथस्य ददृशे ॥६॥

6. And now is the great and vast yoking as if of the Horse, the rope of the chariot is seen.

---

[1] Or, for one who lauds him he goes to the mother.

दुहन्ति सप्तैकामुप द्वा पञ्च सृजतः ।
तीर्थे सिन्धोरधि स्वरे ॥७॥

7. Seven milk the one, two let loose the five at the ford of the River upon the cry of the waters.

आ दशभिर्विवस्वत इन्द्रः कोशमचुच्यवीत् ।
खेदया त्रिवृता दिवः ॥८॥

8. By the ten of the sun Indra made fall the covering sheath of heaven with his triple mallet.

परि त्रिधातुरध्वरं जूर्णिरेति नवीयसी ।
मध्वा होतारो अञ्जते ॥९॥

9. A new adoration moves round the triple pilgrim-sacrifice, the priests of the call anoint with the honey-wine.

सिञ्चन्ति नमसावतमुच्चाचक्रं परिज्मानम् ।
नीचीनबारमक्षितम् ॥१०॥

10. With surrender they pour out the inexhaustible pervading well whose wheel is on high and its opening below.

अभ्यारमिद्द्रयो निषिक्तं पुष्करे मधु ।
अवतस्य विसर्जने ॥११॥

11. Close by are the stones and the honey-wine is poured in the lotus in the discharging of the well.

गाव उपावतावतं मही यज्ञस्य रप्सुदा ।
उभा कर्णा हिरण्यया ॥१२॥

12. O Ray-Cows, come to the well; here is the great wine-jar of the sacrifice, here are both the golden handles.

आ सुते सिञ्चत श्रियं रोदस्योरभिश्रियम् ।
रसा दधीत वृषभम् ॥१३॥

13.   Pour into the wine that is pressed, a joining splendour, the
glory of earth and heaven; by the juice of the wine sustain
the Bull.

ते जानत स्वमोक्यं सं वत्सासो न मातृभिः ।
मिथो नसन्त जामिभिः ॥१४॥

14.   They know their own home; like calves with their mothers
they met with each other as companions.

उप स्रक्वेषु बप्सतः कृण्वते धरुणं दिवि ।
इन्द्रे अग्ना नमः स्वः ॥१५॥

15.   In the jaws of the eater they made their foundation in
heaven, their prostrations of surrender to Indra and the
Fire made the Sun-world.

अधुक्षत् पिप्युषीमिषमूर्जं सप्तपदीमरिः ।
सूर्यस्य सप्त रश्मिभिः ॥१६॥

16.   The warrior milked out the seven-planed nourishing force
and energy by the seven rays of the sun.

सोमस्य मित्रावरुणोदिता सूर आ ददे ।
तदातुरस्य भेषजम् ॥१७॥

17.   O Mitra and Varuna, in the rising of the moon he received
it on the sun; it is the healing draught for him who suffers.

उतो न्वस्य यत् पदं हर्यतस्य निधान्यम् ।
परि द्यां जिह्वयातनत् ॥१८॥

18.   And now let him stretch out[1] with his tongue of flame
around heaven that plane of him in his full delight which is
to be laid as a foundation.

---
[1] Or, form

GOPAVANA ATREYA

SUKTA 74

विशोविशो वो अतिथिं वाजयन्तः पुरुप्रियम् ।
अग्निं वो दुर्यं वचः स्तुषे शूषस्य मन्मभिः ॥१॥

1. All kinds of beings replenish the guest domiciled in your
   house in whom are the many pleasant things; I laud
   him with my thoughts with the word of bliss.

यं जनासो हविष्मन्तो मित्रं न सर्पिरासुतिम् ।
प्रशंसन्ति प्रशस्तिभिः ॥२॥

2. He to whom men bringing the offering pour the stream of
   the libation and by their words that give expression to him
   proclaim as the friend, —

पन्यांसं जातवेदसं यो देवतात्युद्यता ।
हव्यान्यैरयद्दिवि ॥३॥

3. the wonderful,[1] the knower of all things born, who in the
   formation of the godheads sends up the offerings uplifted in
   heaven, —

आगन्म वृत्रहन्तमं ज्येष्ठमग्निमानवम् ।
यस्य श्रुतर्वा बृहन्नार्क्षो अनीक एधते ॥४॥

4. we have come to the Fire, strongest to slay the Coverers,
   eldest and ever new in whose force of flame Shrutarvana,
   son of Riksha, grows to vastness.

अमृतं जातवेदसं तिरस्तमांसि दर्शतम् ।
घृताहवनमीड्यम् ॥५॥

5. The immortal, the knower of all things born who is seen[2]
   across the darkness, one to be prayed to, one to whom are
   offered the clarities.

---

[1] Or, the great doer,   [2] Or, who sees

सबाधो यं जना इमेऽग्निं हव्येभिरीळते ।
जुह्वानासो यतस्रुचः ॥६॥

6. The Fire whom men here oppressed pray with their offerings casting their libations with the ladles at work.[1]

इयं ते नव्यसी मतिरग्ने अधाय्यस्मदा ।
मन्द्र सुजात सुक्रतोऽमूर दस्मातिथे ॥७॥

7. Thine, O Fire, is the new thought founded in us, O rapturous and well-born guest, strong of will, wise and powerful for action.

सा ते अग्ने शंतमा चनिष्ठा भवतु प्रिया ।
तया वर्धस्व सुष्टुतः ॥८॥

8. May that thought, O Fire, become pleasant and full of peace and gladness; grow by it, well-affirmed by our lauds.

सा द्युम्नैर्द्युम्निनी बृहदुपोप श्रवसि श्रवः ।
दधीत वृत्रतूर्ये ॥९॥

9. May it be luminous with many lights, and uphold in its inspiration a vast inspired knowledge in the piercing of the Coverers.

अश्वमिद् गां रथप्रां त्वेषमिन्द्रं न सत्पतिम् ।
यस्य श्रवांसि तूर्वथ पन्यंपन्यं च कृष्टयः ॥१०॥

10. He is the Horse of power and the Cow of light, it is he who fills our chariots, he is brilliant and like Indra the lord of beings; you shall cross through his inspiration, O men! and find each wonderful.

यं त्वा गोपवनो गिरा चनिष्ठदग्ने अङ्गिरः ।
स पावक श्रुधी हवम् ॥११॥

11. Thou whom Gopavana gladdens with his word, O Fire, O Angiras, O purifying Flame, hear his call.

---

[1] Or, with outstretched ladles.

यं त्वा जनास ईळते सबाधो वाजसातये ।
स बोधि वृत्रतूर्ये ॥१२॥

12. Thou whom men oppressed pray for the winning of the plenitudes, awake in the piercing of the Coverers.

अहं हुवान आर्क्षे श्रुतर्वणि मदच्युति ।
शर्धांसीव स्तुकाविनां मृक्षा शीर्षा चतुर्णाम् ॥१३॥

13. As if calling armed forces in Shrutarvan, son of Riksha, from whom drips the rapturous inspiration, I comb the shaggy-maned head of the four.

मां चत्वार आशवः शविष्ठस्य द्रविल्नवः ।
सुरथासो अभि प्रयो वक्षन् वयो न तुग्रचम् ॥१४॥

14. Me the swift and galloping four of that most strong one, well-charioted, bore[1] towards the delight as if birds flying to water.[2]

सत्यमित् त्वा महेनदि परुष्ण्यव देदिशम् ।
नेमापो अश्वदातरः शविष्ठादस्ति मर्त्यः ॥१५॥

15. O great river Parushni, I have marked out (with them) thy true course. O waters, than this most strong one no mortal man is a greater giver of the Horses of power.[3]

VIRUPA ANGIRASA

SUKTA 75

युक्ष्वा हि देवहूतमां अश्वां अग्ने रथीरिव ।
नि होता पूर्व्यः सदः ॥१॥

1. O Fire, yoke like a charioteer the horses most powerful for

---

[1] Or, let them bear me   [2] Or, as the birds carried Tugrya.
[3] Note on Riks 13, 14 and 15:
As is shown by the "Shravansi", "Turvatha" and the name "Shrutarvan" — the Rishi is giving a symbolic turn to the name as well as to the horses and the waters.

the calling of the gods; take thy seat, O ancient Priest of the call!

उत नो देव देवाँ अच्छा वोचो विदुष्टरः ।
श्रद्विश्वा वार्या कृधि ॥२॥

2. And now, since thou hast the knowledge, speak for us towards the gods, make true to our aspiration all desirable things.

त्वं ह यद्याविष्ठ्य सहसः सूनवाहुत ।
ऋतावा यज्ञियो भुवः ॥३॥

3. For thou, O Fire, O most youthful son of force, thou in whom are cast the offerings, art the possessor of the Truth to be worshipped with sacrifice.

अयमग्निः सहस्रिणो वाजस्य शतिनस्पतिः ।
मूर्धा कवी रयीणाम् ॥४॥

4. This Fire is the lord of the hundredfold and thousandfold plenitude, the seer who is the head of the treasures.

तं नेमिमृभवो यथाऽऽनमस्व सहूतिभिः ।
नेदीयो यज्ञमङ्गिरः ॥५॥

5. O Angiras, by words which bear in them the invocation, bring down nearer that sacrifice as the heaven's craftsmen brought down the rim of the wheel.

तस्मै नूनमभिद्यवे वाचा विरूप नित्यया ।
वृष्णे चोदस्व सुष्टुतिम् ॥६॥

6. To him now, O Virupa, by the eternal word give the impulse of the high laud to the luminous Bull.

कमु ष्विदस्य सेनयाऽग्नेरपाकचक्षसः ।
पणिं गोषु स्तरामहे ॥७॥

7. By the army of the Fire who has the eye that sees from afar[1] may we lay low whatever miser Trafficker and enter among the shining herds.

मा नो देवानां विश: प्रस्नातीरिवोल्ला: ।
कृशं न हासुरुघ्न्या: ॥८॥

8. May the peoples of the gods abandon us not, even as the unslayable luminous herds full of milk leave not a calf that is lean.

मा न: समस्य दूढघ: परिद्वेषसो अंहति: ।
ऊर्मिनं नावमा वधीत् ॥९॥

9. Let not calamity from every evil-thoughted hostile around smite us like a billow smiting a ship.

नमस्ते अग्न ओजसे गृणन्ति देव कृष्टय: ।
अमैरमित्रमर्वंय ॥१०॥

10. O divine Fire, men declare their prostration of surrender to thee that they may have force; crush by thy might the foe.

कुवित् सु नो गविष्टयेऽग्ने संवेषिषो रयिम् ।
उरुकृदुरु णस्कृधि ॥११॥

11. Once and again for our search for the Ray-Cow thou hast entered wholly into the riches, O Fire; O maker of wideness, make for us a wideness.

मा नो अस्मिन् महाधने परा वर्भारभूर्भया ।
संवर्गं सं रयिं जय ॥१२॥

12. Abandon us not in the winning of this great wealth as if one who bears a heavy burden; conquer this massed treasure.

---

[1] Or, who has the eye of wisdom

अन्यमस्मद्दिया इयमग्ने सिषक्तु दुच्छुना ।
वर्धा नो अमवच्छवः ॥१३॥

13. O Fire, may this mischief cling to another than us for his
terror; increase for us a forceful might.

यस्याजुषन्नमस्विनः शमीमदुर्मखस्य वा ।
तं घेदग्निर्वृधावति ॥१४॥

14. The man in whose work he takes pleasure, one who offers
the prostration of surrender and is not poor in sacrifice, him
the Fire protects with increase.

परस्या अधि संवतोऽवराँ अभ्या तर ।
यत्राहमस्मि ताँ अव ॥१५॥

15. From thy place in the supreme region break through[1] to
those who are below; here where I am, them protect.

विद्या हि ते पुरा वयमग्ने पितुर्यथावसः ।
अधा ते सुम्नमीमहे ॥१६॥

16. For we know from of old of thy protection like a father's,
O Fire, now we seek thy bliss.

USHANAS KAVYA

SUKTA 84

प्रेष्ठं वो अतिथिं स्तुषे मित्रमिव प्रियम् ।
अग्निं रथं न वेद्यम् ॥१॥

1. Your guest most beloved I laud who is like a beloved friend,
Fire who is as if the chariot of our journey, the one whom we
must know.

---

[1] Or, descend

कविमिव प्रचेतसं यं देवासो अध द्विता ।
नि मर्त्येष्वादधुः ॥२॥

2. He whom as the seer and thinker the gods have now set within twofold in mortals.

त्वं यविष्ठ दाशुषो नॄँः पाहि शृणुधी गिरः ।
रक्षा तोकमुत त्मना ॥३॥

3. O thou ever-young, guard men who give, hear our words;
protect the son by the Self.

कया ते अग्ने अङ्गिर ऊर्जो नपादुपस्तुतिम् ।
वराय देव मन्यवे ॥४॥

4. O divine Fire, O Angiras, O child of energy, by what word,
the laud, for thy supreme thinking?

दाशेम कस्य मनसा यज्ञस्य सहसो यहो ।
कदु वोच इदं नमः ॥५॥

5. By the mind of what master of sacrifice shall we give, O son
of force; how shall I word this prostration of my surrender?

अधा त्वं हि नस्करो विश्वा अस्मभ्यं सुक्षितीः ।
वाजद्रविणसो गिरः ॥६॥

6. Mayst thou thyself create for us all worlds of a happy dwelling, make our words a source of the plenitude and the
riches.

कस्य नूनं परीणसो धियो जिन्वसि दंपते ।
गोषाता यस्य ते गिरः ॥७॥

7. In whose wide-moving thought dost thou take delight, O
master of the house; thou from whom come our words in
the conquest of the Light?

तं मर्जयन्त सुक्रतुं पुरोयावानमाजिषु ।
स्वेषु क्षयेषु वाजिनम् ॥८॥

8. Him they make bright the strong of will and he goes in front in the race;[1] he is a master of plenitude in his own abodes.

क्षेति क्षेमेभिः साधुभिर्नकिर्यं घ्नन्ति हन्ति यः ।
अग्ने सुवीर एधते ॥९॥

9. He dwells safe on perfect foundations and there are none to slay him, it is he who slays; O Fire, he is a mighty hero and prosperous.

PRAYOGA BHARGAVA

SUKTA 102

त्वमग्ने बृहद्वयो दधासि देव दाशुषे ।
कविर्गृहपतिर्युवा ॥१॥

1. Thou, O divine Fire, foundest a vast expansion for the giver, thou art the seer, the youth, the master of the house.

स न ईळानया सह देवाँ अग्ने दुवस्युवा ।
चिकिद्विभानवा वह ॥२॥

2. Do thou, O Fire of the wide light, who art awake to know-ledge, go with our word of prayer and of works and call the gods.

त्वया ह स्विद्युजा वयं चोदिष्ठेन यविष्ठय ।
अभि ष्मो वाजसातये ॥३॥

3. With thee indeed as an ally, most strong in thy urge, we over-come for the conquest of the plenitude.

---

[1] Or, in the contests;

और्वभृगुवच्छुचिमप्नवानवदा हुवे ।
अग्निं समुद्रवाससम् ॥४॥

4. Even as the Flame-Seer, Son of the Wideness, even as the
   Doer of Works I invoke the pure ocean-dwelling Fire.

हुवे वातस्वनं कविं पर्जन्यक्रन्द्यं सहः ।
अग्निं समुद्रवाससम् ॥५॥

5. I call the force which has the sound of the wind and the cry
   of the rain, the ocean-dwelling Fire.

आ सवं सवितुर्यथा भगस्येव भुजिं हुवे ।
अग्निं समुद्रवाससम् ॥६॥

6. I call like the creation of the Creator-Sun, like the delight
   of the Lord of Delight, the ocean-dwelling Fire.

अग्निं वो वृधन्तमध्वराणां पुरूतमम् ।
अच्छा नप्त्रे सहस्वते ॥७॥

7. For the forceful offspring of the pilgrim-sacrifices towards
   Fire as he grows in his multitudes, —

अयं यथा न आभुवत् त्वष्टा रूपेव तक्ष्या ।
अस्य क्रत्वा यशस्वतः ॥८॥

8. so that he may come to be with us like the Form-Maker
   coming to the forms he has to carve, us made glorious by his
   will at work.

अयं विश्वा अभि श्रियोऽग्निर्देवेषु पत्यते ।
आ वाजैरुप नो गमत् ॥९॥

9. This Fire travels in the gods towards all glories; may he
   come to us with the plenitudes.

विश्वेषामिह स्तुहि होतृणां यशस्तमम् ।
अग्निं यज्ञेषु पूर्व्यम् ॥१०॥

10.   Laud here the most glorious of priests of the call, the supreme[1] Fire in the sacrifices.

शीरं पावकशोचिषं ज्येष्ठो यो दमेष्वा ।
वीदाय वीर्घश्रुत्तमः ॥११॥

11.   The intense Fire with its purifying light who dwells eldest in our homes, shines out as one who hears from afar.

तमर्वन्तं न सानसिं गृणीहि विप्र शुष्मिणम् ।
मित्रं न यातयज्जनम् ॥१२॥

12.   Declare him, O illumined sage, as the powerful and conquering war-horse, as the friend who takes man to the goal of his journey.

उप त्वा जामयो गिरो देदिशतीर्हविष्कृतः ।
वायोरनीके अस्थिरन् ॥१३॥

13.   Towards thee come the words of the giver of the offerings marking thee out and stand firm as companions in the might of the wind.

यस्य त्रिधात्ववृतं बर्हिस्तस्थावसंदिनम् ।
आपश्चिन्नि दधा पदम् ॥१४॥

14.   Thou whose triple-seat of sacrifice is untied and unconfined and the waters also have established thy abode, —

पदं देवस्य मीळ्हुषोऽनावृष्टाभिरूतिभिः ।
भद्रा सूर्य इवोपवृक् ॥१५॥

15.   the abode of the bounteous godhead with its inviolate safeties, like a happy regard of the Sun.

अग्ने घृतस्य धीतिभिस्तेपानो देव शोचिषा ।
आ देवान् वक्षि यक्षि च ॥१६॥

---

[1] Or, the ancient

16. O divine Fire, by our thinkings of the light, burning with thy flame, bring to us the gods and do them sacrifice.

तं त्वाजनन्त मातरः कविं देवासो अङ्गिरः ।
हव्यवाहममर्त्यम् ॥१७॥

17. The mothers bore thee, the gods brought thee to birth as the seer, the immortal, the carrier of offering, O Angiras.

प्रचेतसं त्वा कवेऽग्ने दूतं वरेण्यम् ।
हव्यवाहं नि षेदिरे ॥१८॥

18. O Fire, O seer, they set thee within as the thinker, the desirable messenger, carrier of the offerings.

नहि मे अस्त्यघ्न्या न स्वधितिर्वनन्वति ।
अथैतादृग्भरामि ते ॥१९॥

19. Mine is not the cow unslayable, I have no axe at hand, so I bring to thee this little that I have.

यदग्ने कानि कानि चिदा ते दारूणि दध्मसि ।
ता जुषस्व यविष्ठ्य ॥२०॥

20. What we place for thee, a few chance logs, them accept, O ever-young Fire.

यदत्त्युपजिह्विका यद्वम्रो अतिसर्पति ।
सर्वं तदस्तु ते घृतम् ॥२१॥

21. What is eaten by the ant, what the white ant overruns, let all that be to thee as if thy food of light.[1]

अग्निमिन्धानो मनसा धियं सचेत मर्त्यः ।
अग्निमीधे विवस्वभिः ॥२२॥

22. Kindling the Fire let mortal man cleave with his mind to the Thought; by things luminous[2] I kindle the Fire.

---

[1] Or, as if clarified butter.   [2] Or, by the shining ones

SOBHARI KANWA

SUKTA 103

अदर्शि गातुवित्तमो यस्मिन् व्रतान्यादधुः ।
उपो षु जातमार्यस्य वर्धनमग्निं नक्षन्त नो गिरः ॥१॥

1. He is seen, the great path-finder in whom they have founded
the laws of our action; to the Fire well-born, increaser of the
Aryan, go our words.

प्र दैवोदासो अग्निर्देवाँ अच्छा न मज्मना ।
अनु मातरं पृथिवीं वि वावृते तस्यौ नाकस्य सानवि ॥२॥

2. Fire lit by the Servant of Heaven travels in his might towards
the gods along our mother earth and on heaven's peak he
takes his stand.

यस्माद्रेजन्त कृष्टयश्चकृत्यानि कृण्वतः ।
सहस्रसां मेधसाताविव तमनाग्निं धीभिः सपर्यत ॥३॥

3. Fire because of whom men doing the works that have to be
done, grow luminous, him conqueror of the thousands as if
in the winning of the purities they serve by the self,[1] by
their thoughts.

प्र यं राये निनीषसि मर्तो यस्ते वसो दाशत् ।
स वीरं धत्ते अग्न उक्थशंसिनं त्मना सहस्रपोषिणम् ॥४॥

4. He whom thou willst to lead to the Riches, the mortal who
gives to thee, O shining One, he holds in himself, O Fire,
the hero, who utters the word, who increases the thousands.

स दृळ्हे चिदभि तृणत्ति वाजमर्वता स धत्ते अक्षिति श्रवः ।
त्वे देवत्रा सदा पुरूवसो विश्वा वामानि धीमहि ॥५॥

5. He rends open the plenitude even in the strong place by the

---

[1] Or, of themselves,

war-horse, he founds an imperishable inspired knowledge;
O thou of the many riches, in thee we ever hold in the godheads all beautiful things.

यो विश्वा दयते वसु होता मन्द्रो जनानाम् ।
मधोनं पात्रा प्रथमान्यस्मे प्र स्तोमा यन्त्यग्नये ॥६॥

6. He who gives to us all treasures, men's rapturous Priest of
the call, to him our lauds go forth as if supreme vessels of
the honey-wine.

अश्वं न गीर्भी रथ्यं सुदानवो मर्मृज्यन्ते देवयवः ।
उभे तोके तनये दस्म विश्पते पर्षि राधो मघोनाम् ॥७॥

7. The lavish givers, the seekers of the godhead, make him
bright by their words as if currying a chariot-horse. O
powerful for action, O lord of peoples, in the son of our begettings thou carriest achievement of the possessors of riches
beyond both the firmaments.

प्र संहिष्ठाय गायत ऋताव्ने बृहते शुक्रशोचिषे ।
उपस्तुतासो अग्नये ॥८॥

8. Chant to the most bounteous, the possessor of the Truth,
the brilliant in light, coming with the laud, to the Fire.

आ वंसते मघवा वीरवद्यशः समिद्धो द्युम्न्याहुतः ।
कुविन्नो अस्य सुमतिर्नवीयस्यच्छा वाजेभिरागमत् ॥९॥

9. High-kindled, fed with the offering full of light, the lord of
riches conquers a heroic glory; often may his new right-
thinking come towards us with the plenitudes, —

प्रेष्ठमु प्रियाणां स्तुह्यासावातिथिम् ।
अग्निं रथानां यमम् ॥१०॥

10. O thou who pressest the wine, laud the Fire, the guest most
beloved of the beloved, the controller of the chariots, —

उदिता यो निदिता वेदिता वस्वा यज्ञियो ववर्तति ।
दुष्टरा यस्य प्रवणे नोर्मयो धिया वाजं सिषासतः ॥११॥

11. the master of sacrifice who turns towards us the hidden
treasures now risen and known, he in whose downward
descent is a rush as of waves hard to cross, when he conquers
by the thought the plenitudes.

मा नो हृणीताम्मतिथिर्वसुरग्निः पुरुप्रशस्त एषः ।
यः सुहोता स्वध्वरः ॥१२॥

12. May not Fire, the guest, the shining One widely proclaimed,
be wroth with us; this is he who is the perfect Priest of the
call perfect in the pilgrim-rite.

मो ते रिषण्ये अच्छोक्तिभिर्वसोऽग्ने केभिश्चिदेवैः ।
कीरिश्चिद्धि त्वामीट्टे दूत्याय रातहव्यः स्वध्वरः ॥१३॥

13. May they not come to harm by any of their movements who
approach thee with invocation, O Fire, O shining One;
for the singer of the hymn[1] who has given the offering and
does well the pilgrim-rite demands of thee the office of the
messenger.

आग्ने याहि मरुत्सखा रुद्रेभिः सोमपीतये ।
सोभर्या उप सुष्टुतिं मादयस्व स्वर्णरे ॥१४॥

14. Come, O Fire, with the Rudras, comrade of the life-gods,
for the drinking of the Soma-wine, to the laud of Sobhari
and take thy rapture in the godhead of the Sun-world.

---

[1] Or, the doer of works

MANDALA TEN

TRITA APTYA

SUKTA 1

अग्रे बृहन्नुषसामूर्ध्वो अस्थान्निर्जगन्वान् तमसो ज्योतिषागात् ।
अग्निर्भानुना रुशता स्वङ्ग आ जातो विश्वा सद्मान्यप्राः ॥१॥

1. High and vast the Fire stood in front of the dawns; issuing
   out of the darkness he came with the Light: Fire, a perfect
   body of brilliant lustre, filled out at his very birth all the
   worlds.

स जातो गर्भो असि रोदस्योरग्ने चार्विभृत ओषधीषु ।
चित्रः शिशुः परि तमांस्यक्तून् प्र मातृभ्यो अधि कनिक्रदद् गाः ॥२॥

2. Thou art the child born from earth and heaven, the child
   beautiful carried in the growths of earth; an infant many-
   hued, thou goest forth crying aloud from the mothers around
   the nights and the darknesses.

विष्णुरित्था परमस्य विद्वाञ्जातो बृह्न्नभि पाति तृतीयम् ।
आसा यदस्य पयो अक्रत स्वं सचेतसो अभ्यर्चन्त्यत्र ॥३॥

3. Vishnu knowing rightly the supreme plane of this Fire,
   born in his vastness, guards the third (plane); when in his
   mouth they have poured the milk (of the cow), conscious
   they shine here towards his own home.

अत उ त्वा पितुभृतो जनित्रीरन्नावृधं प्रति चरन्त्यन्नैः ।
ता ई प्रत्येषि पुनरन्यरूपा असि त्वं विक्षु मानुषीषु होता ॥४॥

4. Hence the mothers who bear that draught come with their
   food to thee, and thou growest by the food: to them the
   same, but other in their forms, thou comest (returnest)
   again, then art thou Priest of the call in human beings.

होतारं चित्ररथमध्वरस्य यज्ञस्ययज्ञस्य केतुं रुशन्तम् ।
प्रत्यर्धि देवस्यदेवस्य मह्ना श्रिया त्वाग्निमर्तितिथिं जनानाम् ॥५॥

5. The Priest of the call of the pilgrim-rite with his many-hued
    chariot, in the brilliant ray of intuition of sacrifice on sacri-
    fice, Fire the guest of man who takes to himself the half of
    each god in might and glory.

स तु वस्त्राण्यध पेशनानि वसानो अग्निर्नाभा पृथिव्याः ।
अरुषो जातः पद इळायाः पुरोहितो राजन् यक्षीह देवान् ॥६॥

6. Putting on robes, putting on forms, Fire in the navel-centre
    of the earth is born a ruddy flame, in the seat of Revelation.
    O King, as the Priest set in front sacrifice to the gods.

आ हि द्यावापृथिवी अग्न उभे सदा पुत्रो न मातरा ततन्थ ।
प्र याह्यच्छोशतो यविष्ठाऽथा वह सहस्येह देवान् ॥७॥

7. Ever, O Fire, thou hast stretched out earth and heaven, as
    their son thou hast built up thy father and mother: O ever
    young, journey towards the gods who desire thee; then
    bring them to us, O forceful Flame!

SUKTA 2

पिप्रीहि देवाँ उशतो यविष्ठ विद्वाँ ¹ऋतूँ॒रृ॒॑तुपते यजेह ।
ये दैव्या ऋत्विजस्तेभिरग्ने त्वं होतृणामस्यायजिष्ठः ॥१॥

1. Satisfy the desire of the gods, O thou ever young, do sacrifice
    here, a knower of its order and its times, O master of the
    order and time of things; with those who are divine priests
    of the order of the work thou, O Fire, art the strongest for
    sacrifice.

वेषि होत्रमुत पोत्रं जनानां मन्धातासि द्रविणोदा ऋतावा ।
स्वाहा वयं कृणवामा हवींषि देवो देवान् यजत्वग्निरर्हन् ॥२॥

---

¹ In the exoteric sense, "*rtu*" seems to mean the rites of the sacrifice.

2. Thou comest to men's invocation, thou comest to the purification, thou art the thinker, the giver of the riches, the
possessor of the Truth: may we make the offerings with
svāhā; may Fire, availing, do the sacrifice, a god to the gods.

आ देवानामपि पन्थामगन्म यच्छक्नवाम तदनु प्रवोळ्हुम् ।
अग्निर्विद्वान् त्स यजात् सेदु होता सो अध्वरान् त्स ऋतून् कल्पयाति ॥३॥

3. We have come to the path of the gods, may we have power
to tread it, to drive forward along that road. The Fire is the
knower, let him do sacrifice; he verily is the Priest of the
call, he makes effective the pilgrim-sacrifices and the order
of our works.

यद्वो वयं प्रमिनाम व्रतानि विदुषां देवा अविदुष्टरासः ।
अग्निष्टद्विश्वमा पृणाति विद्वान् येभिर्देवाँ ऋतुभिः कल्पयाति ॥४॥

4. Whatever we may impair of the laws of your workings, O
gods, we in our ignorance maiming your workings who
know, all that may the Fire who is a knower make full by
that order in time with which he makes effective the gods.

यत् पाकत्रा मनसा दीनदक्षा न यज्ञस्य मन्वते मर्त्यासः ।
अग्निष्टद्धोता ऋतुविद्विजानन् यजिष्ठो देवाँ ऋतुशो यजाति ॥५॥

5. What in thee sacrifice mortals in the ignorance of their
minds, poor in discernment, cannot think out, that the
Fire knows, the Priest of the call, the finder of the right-will,
strongest of sacrificants and does the sacrifice to the gods
in the order and times of the truth.

विड्वेषां ह्याध्वराणामनीकं चित्रं केतुं जनिता त्वा जजान ।
स आ यजस्व नृवतीरनु क्षाः स्पार्हा इषः क्षुमतीर्विश्वजन्याः ॥६॥

6. The father brought thee to birth, the force of all pilgrim-
sacrifices, the many-hued ray of intuition; so do thou win
for us by sacrifice in the line of the planes with their god-

heads, their desirable and opulent universal forces.

यं त्वा द्यावापृथिवी यं त्वापस्त्वष्टा यं त्वा सुजनिमा जजान ।
पन्थामनु प्रविद्वान् पितृयाणं द्युमदग्ने समिधानो वि भाहि ॥७॥

7. Thou whom heaven and earth, thou whom the waters, thou
    whom the form-maker, creator of perfect births, have
    brought into being; O Fire, luminously along the path of
    the journey of the Fathers, knowing it beforehand, high-
    kindled blaze.

SUKTA 3

इनो राजन्नरतिः समिद्धो रौद्रो दक्षाय सुषुमाँ अदर्शि ।
चिकिद्धि भाति भासा बृहताऽसिक्नीमेति रुशतीमपाजन् ॥१॥

1. He is seen high-kindled, the master ruling all, the traveller,
    the terrible, he who creates perfectly right understanding,
    awake to knowledge he shines wide with a vast lustre; dri-
    ving the ruddy bright cow he comes to the dark one.

कृष्णां यदेनीमभि वर्पसा भूज्जनयन् योषां बृहतः पितुर्जाम् ।
ऊर्ध्वं भानुं सूर्यस्य स्तभायन् दिवो वसुभिररतिर्वि भाति ॥२॥

2. When he overspread with his body the black night and the
    dappled dawn bringing to birth the young maiden born from
    the great Father, pillaring the high-lifted light of the sun,
    the traveller shines out with the riches[1] of heaven.

भद्रो भद्रया सचमान आगात् स्वसारं जारो अभ्येति पश्चात् ।
सुप्रकेतेर्द्युभिरग्निर्नवतिष्ठन् रुशद्भिर्वर्णैरभि राममस्थात् ॥३॥

3. He has come closely companioning her, happy with her
    happy, a lover he follows behind his sister; Fire spreading
    out with his lights full of conscious knowledge overlays her
    beauty with his ruddy shining hues.

[1] Or, the shining ones

अस्य यामासो बृहतो न वग्नूनिन्धाना अग्नेः सख्युः शिवस्य ।
ईडयस्य वृष्णो बृहतः स्वासो भामासो यामन्नक्तवश्चिकित्रे ॥४॥

4. His movements flaming send forth as if vast callings of Fire
   the beneficent comrade in the march of this mighty and
   adorable flame, the vast and beautiful his radiances blazing
   have waked to knowledge.

स्वना न यस्य भामासः पवन्ते रोचमानस्य बृहतः सुदिवः ।
ज्येष्ठेभिर्यस्तेजिष्ठैः क्रीळुमद्भिर्वर्षिष्ठेभिर्भानुभिर्नक्षति द्याम् ॥५॥

5. His blazings as he shines stream like sounds of bright heaven
   in its vastness; with his greatest, most splendid and opulent
   lights at play he travels to heaven.

अस्य शुष्मासो दद्रशानपवेजहमानस्य स्वनयन् नियुद्भिः ।
प्रत्नेभिर्यो रुशद्भिर्देवतमो वि रेभद्भिररतिर्भाति विभ्वा ॥६॥

6. His strengths are those of a thunderbolt seen in the hurling,
   they neigh aloud in their teams; he, the traveller, most
   divine, shines wide-pervading with his ancient ruddy chanting fires.

स आ वक्षि महि न आ च सत्सि दिवस्पृथिव्योररतिर्युवत्योः ।
अग्निः सुतुकः सुतुकेभिरश्वै रभस्वद्भी रभस्वाँ एह गम्याः ॥७॥

7. So carry for us, so take thy seat, the mighty traveller of the
   young earth and heaven, Fire the swift and vehement with
   his swift and vehement horses, — so mayst thou come to us
   here.

SUKTA 4

प्र ते यक्षि प्र त इयर्मि मन्म भुवो यथा वन्द्यो नो हवेषु ।
धन्वन्निव प्रपा असि त्वमग्न इयक्षवे पूरवे प्रत्न राजन् ॥१॥

1. To thee I sacrifice, to thee I send forth my thought so that
   thou mayst manifest thyself adorable at our call; thou art

like a fountain in the desert to longing men, O ancient king,
O Fire.

यं त्वा जनासो अभि संचरन्ति गाव उष्णमिव व्रजं यविष्ठ ।
दूतो देवानामसि मर्त्यानामन्तर्महाँश्चरसि रोचनेन ॥२॥

2. O ever-young flame, towards thee men move, like herds that
    go to a warm pen; thou art the messenger of gods and mor-
    tals, thou movest between them vast through the luminous
    world.

शिशुं न त्वा जेन्यं वर्धयन्ती माता बिभर्ति सचनस्यमाना ।
धनोरधि प्रवता यासि हर्यंञ्जिगीषसे पशुरिवावसृष्टः ॥३॥

3. The mother bears thee like an infant child clinging cherish-
    ingly to thee, increasing thee to be a conqueror; headlong
    down over the dry land he goes rejoicing, he is fain to go like
    an animal let loose.

मूरा अमूर न वयं चिकित्वो महित्वमग्ने त्वमङ्ग वित्से ।
शये वव्रिश्चरति जिह्वयादन् रेरिह्यते युवतिं विश्पतिः सन् ॥४॥

4. O thou who art conscious and free from ignorance, igno-
    rant are we and we know not thy greatness, thou only know-
    est. Covert he lies, he ranges devouring with his tongue
    of flame, he licks the young earth and is the master of her
    creatures.

कुचिञ्जायते सनयासु नव्यो वने तस्थौ पलितो धूमकेतुः ।
अस्नातापो वृषभो न प्र वेति सचेतसो यं प्रणयन्त मर्ताः ॥५॥

5. Anywhere he is born new in eternal wombs; he stands in the
    forest hoary-old with smoke for his banner: a bull unbathed
    he journeys to the waters and mortals who are conscious
    lead him on his way.

तनूत्यजेव तस्करा वनर्गू रशनाभिर्दशभिरभ्यधीताम् ।
यं ते अग्ने नव्यसी मनीषा युक्त्वा रथं न शुचयन्द्रिरङ्गैः ॥६॥

6. Two robbers abandoning their bodies, rangers of the forest, have planted him in his place with ten cords. This is thy new thinking, O Fire, yoke thyself to it with thy illumining limbs like a chariot.

ब्रह्म च ते जातवेदो नमश्चेयं च गी: सदमिद्वर्धनी भूत् ।
रक्षा णो अग्ने तनयानि तोका रक्षोत नस्तन्वो अप्रयुच्छन् ॥७॥

7. Thine is this wisdom-word, O knower of all things born, and this prostration, this utterance is thine; may it have ever the power to make thee grow. Guard all that are off-spring of our begetting, guard undeviatingly our bodies.

SUKTA 5

एक: समुद्रो धरुणो रयीणामस्मद्धृदो भूरिजन्मा वि चष्टे ।
सिषक्त्यूधर्निण्योरुपस्थ उत्सस्य मध्ये निहितं पदं वे: ॥१॥

1. One sole ocean holding all the riches, born in manifold births from our heart it sees all; there cleaves to the teat in the lap of the two secret ones in the midst of the fountain-source the hidden seat of the being.

समानं नीळं वृषणो वसाना: सं जग्मिरे महिषा अर्वतीभि: ।
ऋतस्य पदं कवयो नि पान्ति गुहा नामानि दधिरे परारणि ॥२॥

2. The stallions inhabiting a common abode, the great stallions have met with the mares. The seers guard the seat of the Truth, they hold in the secrecy the supreme Names.

ऋतायिनी मायिनी सं दधाते मित्वा शिशुं जज्ञतुर्वर्धयन्ती ।
विश्वस्य नाभि चरतो ध्रुवस्य कवेश्चित् तन्तुं मनसा वियन्त: ॥३॥

3. The two mothers in whom is the Truth, in whom is the mage-wisdom, formed him and brought to birth like an infant child, they have put him firm in his place and make him grow.

Men found in him the navel-centre of all that is moving and
stable and they weave by the mind the weft of the seer.

ऋतस्य हि वर्तनयः सुजातमिषो वाजाय प्रदिवः सचन्ते ।
अधीवासं रोदसी वावसाने घृतैरन्नैर्वावृधाते मधूनाम् ॥४॥

4. Him well-born the routes of the Truth and its ancient im-
    pulsions close companion for the plenitude. Heaven and
    earth give lodging to him whose dwelling is above them,[1]
    they make him grow by the lights and foods of their sweet-
    nesses.

सप्त स्वसॄररुषीर्वावशानो विद्वान् मध्व उज्जभारा दृशे कम् ।
अन्तर्येमे अन्तरिक्षे पुराजा इच्छन् वव्रिमवदत् पूषणस्य ॥५॥

5. Desiring the seven shining sisters, the knower bore on high
    their sweetnesses that he might have vision; he who was born
    from of old laboured within in the mid-world, he wished for
    and found the covering of the all-fostering sun.

सप्त मर्यादाः कवयस्ततक्षुस्तासामेकामिदभ्यंहुरो गात् ।
आयोर्ह स्कम्भ उपमस्य नीळे पथां विसर्गे धरुणेषु तस्थौ ॥६॥

6. The seers fashioned the seven goals,[2] towards one of them
    alone goes the narrow and difficult road. A pillar of the
    supreme being in its abode, he stands at the starting-out of
    the ways, in the upholding laws.

असच्च सच्च परमे व्योमन् दक्षस्य जन्मन्नदितेरुपस्थे ।
अग्निर्ह नः प्रथमजा ऋतस्य पूर्व आयुनि वृषभश्च धेनुः ॥७॥

7. He is the being and non-being in the supreme ether, in the
    birth of the Understanding in the lap of the indivisible
    mother. Fire comes to us as the first-born of the Truth, he
    is the Bull and milch-Cow in the original existence.

---

[1] Or, as their inhabitant,   [2] Or, the seven frontiers,

Sukta 6

अयं स यस्य शर्मन्नवोभिरग्नेरेधते जरिताभिष्टौ ।
ज्येष्ठेभिर्यो भानुभिर्ऋतुषूणां पर्येति परिवीतो विभावा ॥१॥

1. This is he in whose peace,[1] and in his approach to it grows
   by his guardings the worshipper of the Fire, who encompas-
   ses all and is spread everywhere luminous with the largest
   lights of the wise.[2]

यो भानुभिर्विभावा विभात्यग्निर्देवेभिर्ऋतावाजस्रः ।
आ यो विवाय सख्या सखिभ्योऽपरिह्वृतो अत्यो न सप्तिः ॥२॥

2. Fire, who shines perpetual, possessor of the Truth, luminous
   with divine lights, he who follows out the works of a comrade for his comrades like a courser running straight to his
   goal.

ईशे यो विश्वस्या देववीतेरीशे विश्वायुरुषसो व्युष्टौ ।
आ यस्मिन् मना हवींष्यग्नावरिष्टरथः स्कभ्नाति शूषः ॥३॥

3. He who has power for every advent of godhead, who has
   power for the outbreak of the dawn and is the life of all,
   Fire in whom our thinkings are cast as offerings, his chariot
   goes unhurt and he supports all his strengths.

शूषेभिर्वृधो जुषाणो अर्केर्देवाँ अच्छा रघुपत्वा जिगाति ।
मन्द्रो होता स जुह्वा यजिष्ठः संमिश्लो अग्निरा जिघर्ति देवान् ॥४॥

4. Increasing by his strengths, rejoicing in his illuminations he
   goes a swift galloper towards the gods; he is the rapturous
   Priest of the call, strong to sacrifice with his tongue of flame,
   inseparable from the gods the Fire sheds on them his light.

तमुस्रामिन्द्रं न रेजमानमग्निं गीर्भिर्नमोभिरा कृणुध्वम् ।
आ यं विप्रासो मतिभिर्गृणन्ति जातवेदसं जुह्वं सहानाम् ॥५॥

---

[1] Or, house of refuge,   [2] Or, with his largest lights for the wise.

5.   Him fashion for you with your words and your obeisances
as if Indra quivering at the dawn-ray, him whom illumined
sages voice with their thoughts, the knower of all things
born, the overpowering Flame.

सं यस्मिन् विश्वा वसूनि जग्मुर्वाजे नाश्वाः सप्तीवन्त एवैः ।
अस्मे ऊतीरिन्द्रवाततमा अर्वाचीना अग्न आ कृणुष्व ॥६॥

6.   Thou in whom all the Riches meet together in the plenitude
like horses by their gallopings in their speed towards the
goal, the protections most desired by Indra to us make
close, O Fire.

अधा ह्यग्ने मह्ना निषद्या सद्यो जज्ञानो हव्यो बभूथ ।
तं ते देवासो अनु केतमायन्नधावर्धन्त प्रथमास ऊमाः ॥७॥

7.   Now, indeed, taking thy seat in thy greatness, O Fire, in thy
very birth thou hast become the one to whom we must call;
the gods walked by the ray of thy intuition, then they grew
and were the first and supreme helpers.

SUKTA 7

स्वस्ति नो दिवे अग्ने पृथिव्या विश्वायुर्धेहि यजथाय देव ।
सचेमहि तव दस्म प्रकेतैरुरुष्या ण उरुभिर्देव शंसैः ॥१॥

1.   Found for us felicity of earth and heaven and universal life
that we may worship thee with sacrifice, O god; O doer of
works, may we keep close to thy perceptions of knowledge;
guard us, O god, with thy wide utterances.

इमा अग्ने मतयस्तुभ्यं जाता गोभिरश्वैरभि गृणन्ति राधः ।
यदा ते मर्तो अनु भोगमानड् वसो दधानो मतिभिः सुजात ॥२॥

2.   For thee these thoughts are born, O Fire, towards thee they
voice our achievement of riches with its horses of power and

herds of light when the mortal upheld by his thoughts following thee attains to thy enjoyment, O Fire, perfectly born, O shining One.

अग्निं मन्ये पितरमग्निमापिमर्गिन भ्रातरं सदमित् सखायम् ।
अग्नेरनीकं बृहतः सपर्यं दिवि शुक्रं यजतं सूर्यस्य ॥३॥

3. I think of the Fire as my father, my ally, my brother, ever my comrade; I serve the force of vast Fire, his bright and worshipped force of the Sun in heaven.

सिध्रा अग्ने धियो अस्मे सनुत्रीर्यं त्रायसे दम आ नित्यहोता ।
ऋतावा स रोहिदश्वः पुरुक्षुर्द्युभिरस्मा अहर्भिर्वाममस्तु ॥४॥

4. O Fire, effective in us are thy thoughts and conquerors of our aims: he whom thou deliverest, thou the eternal Priest of the call in the house, who art that driver of the red horses, possessed of the Truth, possessor of the much store of riches, may happiness be his through the shining days.

शुभिर्हितं मित्रमिव प्रयोगं प्रत्नमृत्विजमध्वरस्य जारम् ।
बाहुभ्यामग्निमायवोऽजनन्त विक्षु होतारं न्यसादयन्त ॥५॥

5. The Fire founded by the heavens[1] as our friend and the means for our works, the ancient Priest of the pilgrim-rites, the lover men brought into being by the strength of their two arms and seated within as the Priest of the call in beings.

स्वयं यजस्व दिवि देव देवान् किं ते पाकः कृणवदप्रचेताः ।
यथायज ऋतुभिर्देव देवानेवा यजस्व तन्वं सुजात ॥६॥

6. Thyself sacrifice in heaven to the gods, for what shall man immature in thought and unconscious of the knowledge do of thy work? Even as thou didst sacrifice in the order and times of the Truth, a god to the gods, O perfectly born Fire, so sacrifice to thy body.

[1] Or, with his lights

भवा नो अग्नेऽवितोत गोपा भवा वयस्कृदुत नो वयोधाः ।
रास्वा च नः सुमहो हव्यदातिं त्रास्वोत नस्तन्वो अप्रयुच्छन् ॥७॥

7. O Fire, become our guardian and protector, become the
creator of our growth and of our growth the upholder, O
mighty One, give to us what we shall give as offerings to the
gods, and unfailing our bodies deliver.

TRISHIRAS TWASHTRA

SUKTA 8

प्र केतुना बृहता यात्यग्निरा रोदसी वृषभो रोरवीति ।
दिवश्चिदन्ताँ उपमाँ उदानळपामुपस्थे महिषो ववर्ध ॥१॥

1. The Fire journeys on with his vast ray of intuition, the Bull
bellows to earth and heaven; he has reached up to the highest extremities of heaven, the mighty one has grown in the
lap of the waters.

मुमोद गर्भो वृषभः ककुद्मानस्त्रेमा वत्सः शिमीवाँ अरावीत् ।
स देवतात्युद्यतानि कृण्वन् त्स्वेषु क्षयेषु प्रथमो जिगाति ॥२॥

2. The Bull of the heights,[1] the new-born rejoiced, the unfailing child worker rejoiced and shouted aloud; in the
formation of the gods he does his exalted works and comes
the first in his own abodes.

आ यो मूर्धानं पित्रोररब्ध न्यध्वरे दधिरे सूरो अर्णः ।
अस्य पत्मन्नरुषीरश्वबुध्ना ऋतस्य योनौ तन्वो जुषन्त ॥३॥

3. He who grasps the head of the father and mother they set
within in the pilgrim-sacrifice, a sea from the Sun-world; in
his path are the shining rays that are the foundations of the
Horse of Power and they accept embodiment in the native
seat of the Truth.

[1] Or, the humped-Bull,

उषउषो हि वसो अग्रमेषि त्वं यमयोरभवो विभावा ।
ऋताय सप्त दधिषे पदानि जनयन् मित्रं तन्वे स्वायं ॥४॥

4. O shining One, thou comest to the front of dawn after dawn,
thou hast become luminous in the Twins; thou holdest the
seven planes for the Truth bringing Mitra to birth for thy
own body.

भुवश्चक्षुर्महं ऋतस्य गोपा भुवो वरुणो यदृताय वेषि ।
भुवो अपां नपाज्जातवेदो भुवो दूतो यस्य हव्यं जुजोषः ॥५॥

5. Thou becomest the eye of the vast Truth; when thou journeyest to the Truth thou becomest Varuna, its guardian;
thou becomest the child of the waters, O knower of all
things born, thou becomest the messenger of the man in
whose offering thou hast taken pleasure.

भुवो यज्ञस्य रजसश्च नेता यत्रा नियुद्भिः सचसे शिवाभिः ।
दिवि मूर्धानं दधिषे स्वर्षां जिह्वामग्ने चकृषे हव्यवाहम् ॥६॥

6. Thou art the leader of the sacrifice and leader to the mid-
world to which thou resortest constantly with thy helpful
team of mares; thou upholdest in heaven thy head that
conquers the Sun-world, thy tongue thou makest, O Fire,
the carrier of our offerings.

अस्य त्रितः क्रतुना वत्रे अन्तरिच्छन् धीतिं पितुरेवैः परस्य ।
सचस्यमानः पित्रोरुपस्थे जामि ब्रुवाण आयुधानि वेति ॥७॥

7. By his will Trita in the secret cave desiring by his movements the thinking of the supreme Father cherished in the
lap of the Father and Mother, speaking the companion-
word, seeks his weapons.

स पित्र्याण्यायुधानि विद्वानिन्द्रेषित आप्त्यो अभ्ययुध्यत् ।
त्रिशीर्षाणं सप्तरश्मिं जघन्वान् त्वाष्ट्रस्य चिन्निः ससृजे त्रितो गाः ॥८॥

8. Trita Aptya discovered the weapons of the Father and
missioned by Indra went to the battle; he smote the Three-

headed, the seven-rayed and let loose the ray-cows of the son of Twashtri the form-maker.

भूरीदिन्द्र उदिनक्षन्तमोजोऽवाभिनत् सत्पतिर्मन्यमानम् ।
त्वाष्ट्रस्य चिद्विश्वरूपस्य गोनामाचक्राणस्त्रीणि शीर्षा परा वर्क् ॥९॥

9. Indra, the master of beings, broke that great upstriving meditating force and cast it downward and making his own the ray-cows of Twashtri's son of the universal forms he took away from him his three heads.

HAVIRDHANA ANGI

SUKTA 11

वृषा वृष्णे दुदुहे दोहसा दिवः पयांसि यह्वो अदितेरदाभ्यः ।
विश्वं स वेद वरुणो यथा धिया स यज्ञियो यजतु यज्ञियाँ ऋतून् ॥१॥

1. Mighty from the mighty, strong and inviolable, he milked by the milking of heaven the streams of the Indivisible; Varuna knew all by his right thought. A lord of sacrifice, may he perform the order of the rites of the sacrifice.

रपद्गन्धर्वीरप्या च योषणा नदस्य नादे परि पातु मे मनः ।
इष्टस्य मध्ये अदितिर्नि धातु नो भ्राता नो ज्येष्ठः प्रथमो वि बोचति ॥२॥

2. May the Gandharvi speak to me and the Woman born from the Waters, may her protection be around my mind midst the roar of the river; may the indivisible mother establish us in the heart of our desire: my brother the greatest[1] and first declares it to me.

सो चिन्नु भद्रा क्षुमती यशस्वत्युषा उवास मनवे स्ववंती ।
यदीमुशन्तमुशतामनु ऋतुमग्निं होतारं विदथाय जीजनन् ॥३॥

3. She the happy, and opulent and glorious, dawn has shone

---
[1] Or, the eldest

out for man bringing the Sun-world with her. When they
gave birth to this Fire, an aspirant doing the will of the
aspirants for the discovery of knowledge.

अध त्यं द्रप्सं विभ्वं विचक्षणं विराभरदिदिषितः श्येनो अध्वरे ।
यदी विशो वृणते दस्ममार्या अग्निं होतारमध धीरजायत ॥४॥

4. Now the Bird, the missioned Hawk, has brought the draught
of the great and seeing wine to the pilgrim-sacrifice. When
the Aryan peoples chose the doer of works, Fire the Priest
of the call, then the thought was born.

सदासि रण्वो यवसेव पुष्यते होत्राभिरग्ने मनुषः स्वध्वरः ।
विप्रस्य वा यच्छशमान उक्थ्यं वाजं ससवाँ उपयासि भूरिभिः ॥५॥

5. Ever art thou delightful like grasses to that which feeds on
them, O Fire, doing well with thy voices of invocation the
pilgrim-sacrifice for man when thou givest utterance to the
plenitude of the word of the illumined sage, as one who has
conquered, thou comest with thy multitude.

उदीरय पितरा जार आ भगमियक्षति हर्यतो हृत्त इष्यति ।
विवक्ति वह्निः स्वपस्यते मखस्तविष्यते असुरो वेपते मती ॥६॥

6. Upward lift the Father and Mother; the lover aspires to his
enjoyment, rejoicing he obeys the urgings from his heart:
a bearer of the word he speaks and jocund longs for the good
work, the Mighty One puts forth his strength and is illumined by the Thought.

यस्ते अग्ने सुमतिं मर्तो अक्षत् सहसः सूनो अति स प्र शृण्वे ।
इषं दधानो वहमानो अश्वैरा स द्युमाँ अमवान् भूषति द्यून् ॥७॥

7. O Fire, O son of Force, the mortal who attains to thy right
thinking goes forward and hears the truth beyond; holding
the impelling force, borne by the horses of power, luminous
and mighty he seeks to possess the heavens.

26

यदग्ने एषा समितिर्भवाति देवी देवेषु यजता यजत्र ।
रत्ना च यद्विभजासि स्वधावो भागं नो अत्र वसुमन्तं वीतात् ॥८॥

8. When, O Fire, takes place that sacrificial assembly, O master
    of sacrifice, the assembly divine among the gods, when thou
    distributest the ecstasies, O lord of nature, an opulent por-
    tion bring to us.

श्रुधी नो अग्ने सदने सधस्थे युक्ष्वा रथममृतस्य द्रविल्लुम् ।
आ नो वह रोदसी देवपुत्रे माकिर्देवानामप भूरिह स्याः ॥९॥

9. Hear us, O Fire, in thy house, in the hall of thy session, yoke
    the galloping car of the Immortal; bring to us heaven and
    earth, parents of the gods; let none of the gods be away
    from us and mayst thou be here.

SUKTA 12

द्यावा ह क्षामा प्रथमे ऋतेनाऽभिश्रावे भवतः सत्यवाचा ।
देवो यन्मर्तान् यजयाय कृण्वन् त्सीदद्धोता प्रत्यङ्ख् स्वमसुं यन् ॥१॥

1. Heaven and earth are the first to hear and by the Truth
    become possessed of the true speech when the god fashioning
    the mortal for the sacrificial act takes his seat as his Priest
    of the call and turned towards its own force moves towards
    it.

देवो देवान् परिभूर्ऋतेन वहा नो हव्यं प्रथमश्चिकित्वान् ।
धूमकेतुः समिधा भाऋजीको मन्द्रो होता नित्यो वाचा यजीयान् ॥२॥

2. A god encompassing the gods with the Truth, carry our
    offering, the first to awake to the knowledge; erect, thy light
    rises by the kindling with smoke for thy banner; thou art
    the rapturous eternal Priest of the call strong by speech for
    the sacrifice.

स्वावृग्देवस्यामृतं यदी गोरतो जातासो धारयन्त उर्वी ।
विश्वे देवा अनु तत् ते यजुर्गुर्दुहे यदेनी दिव्यं घृतं वाः ॥३॥

3. When perfectly achieved is the immortality of the godhead, the immortality of the Light, men born in this world
hold wide earth and heaven; all the gods follow in the track
of that sacrificial act[1] of thine when the white cow is milked
of her stream of divine Light.

अर्चामि वां वर्धयापो घृतस्नू द्यावाभूमी शृणुतं रोदसी मे।
अहा यद् द्यावोऽसुनीतिमयन् मध्वा नो अत्र पितरा शिशीताम् ॥४॥

4. O earth and heaven, I sing to you the word of illumination,
pouring your light make my work grow, may the two firmaments hear me; when the days and the heavens have come
by the guidance of the force, may the Father and Mother
quicken us here with the sweetness of the wine.

किं स्विन्नो राजा जगृहे कदस्याऽति व्रतं चक्रमा को वि वेद।
मित्रश्चिद्धि ष्मा जुहुराणो देवाञ्छ्लोको न यातामपि वाजो अस्ति ॥५॥

5. On something in us the king has laid hold; what have we
done that transgresses his law who can know? Even if the
Friend is dealing crookedly with the gods there is as if a call
to us as we go, there is upon us a plenitude.

दुरन्त्वत्रामृतस्य नाम सलक्ष्मा यद्विषुरूपा भवाति।
यमस्य यो मनवते सुमन्त्वग्ने तमृष्व पाह्याप्रयुच्छन् ॥६॥

6. Hard to seize by the mind in this world is the name of the
immortal because he puts on features and becomes divergent
forms; he who grasps perfectly with his mind and his
thought seizes its controlling law, him, O Fire, O mighty
One, undeviatingly protect.

यस्मिन् देवा विदथे मादयन्ते विवस्वतः सदने धारयन्ते।
सूर्ये ज्योतिरदधुर्मास्यक्तून् परि द्योतनि चरतो अजस्रा ॥७॥

7. The discovery of knowledge in which the gods find their
rapture they hold in the house of the radiant sun; they have

---

[1] Or, sacrificial word

set in the sun its light, in the moon its rays and both circle unceasingly around its illumination.

यस्मिन् देवा मन्मनि संचरन्त्यपीच्ये न वयमस्य विद्म ।
मित्रो नो अत्रादितिरनागान् त्सविता देवो वरुणाय वोचत् ॥८॥

8. The thought in which the gods meet together, when it is occult we know not of it. May Mitra and the indivisible mother and the godhead of the creative sun declare us sin-less to Varuna.

श्रुधी नो अग्ने सदने सधस्ये युक्ष्वा रथममृतस्य द्रवित्नुम् ।
आ नो वह रोदसी देवपुत्रे माकिर्देवानामप भूरिह स्याः ॥९॥

9. Hear us, O Fire, in thy house, in the hall of thy session, yoke the galloping car of the Immortal; bring to us heaven and earth, parents of the gods; let none of the gods be away from us and mayst thou be here.

VIMADA AINDRA OR PRAJAPATYA
OR VASUKRIT VASUKRA

SUKTA 20

भद्रं नो अपि वातय मनः ॥१॥

1. Bring to us a happy mind.

अग्निमीळे भुजां यविष्ठं शासा मित्रं दुर्धरीतुम् ।
यस्य धर्मन् त्स्वरेनीः सपर्यन्ति मातुरूधः ॥२॥

2. I pray the Fire, the friend who is irresistible in his own com-mand, in whose law the white rays attend on the Sun-world, serve the teat of the mother.

यमासा कृपनीळं भासाकेतुं वर्धयन्ति ।
भ्राजते श्रेणिदन् ॥३॥

3. Fire whom face to face a home of light, one who brings the ray of intuition by his lustre they increase; he blazes with his row of flaming tusks.

अर्यो विशां गातुरेति प्र यदानड् दिवो अन्तान् ।
कविरभ्रं दीद्यानः ॥४॥

4. He comes to us as a noble path for men when he travels to the ends of heaven; he is the seer and he lights up the sky.[1]

जुषद्ध्या मानुषस्योर्ध्वस्तस्थावृभ्वा यज्ञे ।
भिन्वन् त्सद्य पुर एति ॥५॥

5. Accepting the oblation of man he stands high exalted in the sacrifice, a skilful craftsman; he goes in our front building our home.

स हि क्षेमो हविर्यज्ञः श्रुष्टीदस्य गातुरेति ।
अग्निं देवा वाशीमन्तम् ॥६॥

6. He is our secure foundation, he is our offering, he is the sacrifice; his path goes swiftly to its goal: the gods call Fire with its adze.

यज्ञासाहं दुव इषेऽग्निं पूर्वस्य शेवस्य ।
अद्रेः सूनुमायुमाहुः ॥७॥

7. I desire from the Fire, powerful for the sacrifice the work of the supreme bliss;[2] they speak of him as the living son of the stone.[3]

नरो ये के चास्मदा विश्वेत् ते वाम आ स्युः ।
अग्निं हविषा वर्धन्तः ॥८॥

8. Whatever men are with us may they in all ways abide in happiness making the Fire to grow by the offerings.

---

[1] Or, the cloud.   [2] Or, the work that brings the supreme bliss;
[3] Or, of the Rock, or the Peak.

कृष्णः श्वेतोऽरुषो यामो अस्य ब्रध्न ऋज्र उत शोणो यशस्वान् ।
हिरण्यरूपं जनिता जजान ॥९॥

9.   Black is his movement and white and luminous and crimson-
     red, it is large and straight and glorious; golden of form
     the father brought into being.

एवा ते अग्ने विमदो मनीषामूर्जो नपादमृतेभिः सजोषाः ।
गिर आ वक्षत् सुमतीरियान इषमूर्जं सुक्षिति विश्वमाभाः ॥१०॥

10. So, O Fire, rapturous thou bearest thy thinking mind, O
     son of energy, companioning the immortals, coming to us
     thou bearest thy words and thy right thinkings, thou bringest
     impelling force, energy, happy worlds of habitation, all.[1]

Sukta 21

अग्निं न स्ववृक्तिभिर्होतारं त्वा वृणीमहे ।
यज्ञाय स्तीर्णबर्हिषे वि वो मदे शीरं पावकशोचिषं विवक्षसे ॥१॥

1.   By our self-purifications we elect thee, the Fire as our Priest
     of the call, for the sacrifice where strewn is the grass, — in
     the intoxication of your rapture, — intense with thy purifying
     light of flame, — and thou growest to greatness.

त्वामु ते स्वाभुवः शुम्भन्त्यश्वराधसः ।
वेति त्वामुपसेचनी वि वो मद ऋजीतिरग्न आहुतिर्विवक्षसे ॥२॥

2.   Those who have achieved possession of the Horse, are very
     close to thee and glorify thee; the ladle goes to thee, —
     in the intoxication of your rapture, — direct, carrying the
     oblation, O Fire, — and thou growest to greatness.

त्वे धर्माण आसते जुह्वभिः सिञ्चतीरिव ।
कृष्णा रूपाण्यर्जुना वि वो मदे विश्वा अधि श्रियो धिषे विवक्षसे ॥३॥

---

[1] Or, Vimada, the rapturous one, coming carries to thee, O Fire, his thinking mind, to thee
his words and his right thinkings, brings etc.

3. In thee the upholding laws reside; sprinkling out their contents as with ladle black forms and white — in the intoxication of your rapture — all glories thou holdest — and thou
   growest to greatness.

यमग्ने मन्यसे रयिं सहसावन्नमर्त्यं ।
तमा नो वाजसातये वि वो मदे यज्ञेषु चित्रमा भरा विवक्षसे ॥४॥

4. O forceful and immortal Fire, whatever wealth thou deemest
   fit, that for the winning of the plenitudes, — in the intoxication of your rapture, — bring to us a wealth of various lights
   in the sacrifices, — and thou growest to greatness.

अग्निर्जातो अथर्वणा विदद्विश्वानि काव्या ।
भुवद् दूतो विवस्वतो वि वो मदे प्रियो यमस्य काम्यो विवक्षसे ॥५॥

5. The Fire born from Atharvan knows all seer-wisdoms, he
   becomes the messenger of the luminous sun, — in the intoxication of your rapture, — dear and desirable to the lord of
   the law, — and thou growest to greatness.

त्वां यज्ञेष्वीळतेऽग्ने प्रयत्यध्वरे ।
त्वं वसूनि काम्या वि वो मदे विश्वा दधासि दाशुषे विवक्षसे ॥६॥

6. Thee they pray in the sacrifices, O Fire, as the pilgrim-
   sacrifice goes on its way; all desirable treasures — in the
   intoxication of your rapture — thou foundest for the giver,
   and thou growest to greatness.

त्वां यज्ञेष्वृत्विजं चारुमग्ने नि षेदिरे ।
घृतप्रतीकं मनुषो वि वो मदे शुक्रं चेतिष्ठमक्षभिर्विवक्षसे ॥७॥

7. Thee as the Priest of the rite in the sacrifices men have seated,
   O Fire, beautiful, luminous of front, — in the intoxication
   of your rapture, — bright and, with thy eyes, most conscious
   of knowledge, — and thou growest to greatness.

अग्ने शुक्रेण शोचिषोरु प्रथयसे बृहत् ।
अभिक्रन्दन् वृषायसे वि वो मदे गर्भं दधासि जामिषु विवक्षसे ॥८॥

8. O Fire, with thy bright light of flame thou spreadest the wide
Vast, clamouring thou becomest the bull, — in the intoxication of your rapture, — and settest the child of the womb in
the sisters, — and thou growest to greatness.

VATSAPRI BHALANDANA

SUKTA 45

दिवस्परि प्रथमं जज्ञे अग्निरस्मद् द्वितीयं परि जातवेदाः ।
तृतीयमप्सु नृमणा अजस्रमिन्धान एनं जरते स्वाधीः ॥१॥

1. Above heaven was the first birth of the Fire, over us was
his second birth as the knower of all things born, his third
birth was in the waters, a god-mind; him continuously one
kindles and with one's thought perfectly fixed on him adores.

विद्मो ते अग्ने त्रेधा त्रयाणि विद्मा ते धाम विभृता पुरुत्रा ।
विद्मा ते नाम परमं गुहा यद्विद्मा तमुत्सं यत आजगन्थ ॥२॥

2. O Fire, we know the triple three of thee, we know thy seats
borne widely in many planes, we know thy supreme Name
which is in the secrecy, we know that fount of things whence
thou camest.

समुद्रे त्वा नृमणा अप्स्वन्तनृंचक्षा ईधे दिवो अग्न ऊधन् ।
तृतीये त्वा रजसि तस्थिवांसमपामुपस्थे महिषा अवर्धन् ॥३॥

3. He of the god-mind kindled thee in the Ocean, within the
Waters, he of the divine vision kindled thee, O Fire, in the
teat of heaven; the mighty ones made thee to grow where
thou stoodest in the third kingdom, in the lap of the waters.

अक्रन्ददग्निः स्तनयन्निव द्यौः क्षामा रेरिहद्वीरुधः समञ्जन् ।
सद्यो जज्ञानो वि हीमिद्धो अख्यदा रोदसी भानुना भात्यन्तः ॥४॥

4. Fire cried aloud like heaven thundering, he licked the earth revealing its growths: when kindled and born, at once he saw all this that is; he shines out with his light between earth and heaven.

श्रीणामुदारो धरुणो रयीणां मनीषाणां प्रार्पणः सोमगोपाः ।
वसुः सूनुः सहसो अप्सु राजा वि भात्यग्र उषसामिधानः ॥५॥

5. An exalter of glories, a holder of the riches, a manifester of thinking mind, a guardian of the wine of delight, a shining One, the son of force, the king in the Waters, he grows luminous as he burns up in the front of the dawns

विश्वस्य केतुर्भुवनस्य गर्भ आ रोदसी अपृणाज्जायमानः ।
वीळुं चिदद्रिमभिनत् परायञ्जना यदग्निमयजन्त पञ्च ॥६॥

6. The ray of intuition of the universe, the child in the womb of the world, in his coming to birth he filled earth and heaven; going beyond them he rent even the strong mountain when the peoples of the five births sacrificed to the fire.

उशिक् पावको अरतिः सुमेधा मर्तेष्वग्निरमृतो नि धायि ।
इयर्ति धूममरुषं भरिभ्रदुच्छुक्रेण शोचिषा द्यामिनक्षन् ॥७॥

7. An aspirant and traveller and wise of mind, a purifying flame, the Fire who is set within as the immortal in mortals, he sends forth and carries a ruddy smoke striving with his bright flame of light to reach heaven.

दृशानो रुक्म उर्विया व्यद्यौद् दुर्मर्षमायुः श्रिये रुचानः ।
अग्निरमृतो अभवद्वयोभिर्यदेनं द्यौर्जनयत् सुरेताः ॥८॥

8. Visible, golden of light, widely he shone; resplendent in his glory he is life hard to violate: the Fire by his expandings became immortal when heaven with its strong seed had brought him to birth.

यस्ते अद्य कृणवद् भद्रशोचेऽपूपं देव घृतवन्तमग्ने ।
प्र तं नय प्रतरं वस्यो अच्छाऽभि सुम्नं देवभक्तं यविष्ठ ॥९॥

9. O god, O happy light, O Fire, he who has prepared for thee
    the luminous honeycomb[1] him lead forward towards a more
    opulent state, O youthful godhead, even to the bliss enjoyed
    by the gods.

आ तं भज सौश्रवसेष्वग्न उक्थउक्थ आ भज शस्यमाने ।
प्रियः सूर्ये प्रियो अग्ना भवात्युज्जातेन भिनदद्जुज्जनित्वैः ॥१०॥

10. O Fire, bestow on him his share in the things of inspired
    knowledge, in word upon word as it is spoken: he becomes
    dear to the sun, dear to Fire; upward he breaks with what is
    born in him, upward with the things that are to be born.

त्वामग्ने यजमाना अनु द्यून् विश्वा वसु दधिरे वार्याणि ।
त्वया सह द्रविणमिच्छमाना व्रजं गोमन्तमुशिजो वि वव्रुः ॥११॥

11. O Fire, men who sacrifice to thee day after day hold in
    themselves all desirable riches; desiring the treasure in thy
    companionship, aspiring, they burst open the covered pen
    of the Ray-Cows.

अस्ताव्यग्निर्नरां सुशेवो वैश्वानर ऋषिभिः सोमगोपाः ।
अद्वेषे द्यावापृथिवी हुवेम देवा धत्त रयिमस्मे सुवीरम् ॥१२॥

12. The Fire has been affirmed in their lauds by the sages, he who
    is full of bliss for men, the Universal Godhead, guardian of
    the wine of delight. Let us invoke earth and heaven free
    from hostile powers; found in us, O gods, a wealth full of
    hero-mights.

SUKTA 46

प्र होता जातो महान् नभोविन्नृषद्वा सीददपामुपस्थे ।
दधिर्यो धायि स ते वयांसि यन्ता वसूनि विघते तनूपाः ॥१॥

---

[1] Or, the cake of light

1. The great Priest of the call has been born; the knower of the
   heavens, he who is seated in man, may he take his seat in the
   lap of the waters: he who upholds us and who is held in
   us, rules for thee his worshipper thy expandings and thy
   riches and is the protector of thy body.

इमं विधन्तो अपां सधस्थे पशुं न नष्टं पदैरनु ग्मन् ।
गुहा चतन्तमुशिजो नमोभिरिच्छन्तो धीरा भृगवोऽविन्दन् ॥२॥

2. They worshipped him in the session of the waters, as if the
   cow of vision lost they followed him by his tracks; where he
   hid in the secret cavern, aspiring with obeisance the Flame-
   Seers, the wise thinkers desired and found him.

इमं त्रितो भूर्यविन्ददिच्छन् वैभूवसो मूर्धन्यघ्न्यायाः ।
स शेवृधो जात आ हर्म्येषु नाभिर्युवा भवति रोचनस्य ॥३॥

3. Him greatly desiring Trita, son of the master of wide riches,[1]
   found on the head of the light unslayable; he is born the
   youth who increases the felicity in our mansions and becomes the navel-centre of the luminous world.

मन्द्रं होतारमुशिजो नमोभिः प्राञ्चं यज्ञं नेतारमध्वराणाम् ।
विशामकृण्वन्नरतिं पावकं हव्यवाहं दधतो मानुषेषु ॥४॥

4. In their aspiration they created him by their obeisance and
   set him in men as the rapturous Priest of the call, the sacrificer ever-moving forward, the leader of the pilgrim-sacrifices, the traveller, the carrier of the offering, the purifying
   Flame.

प्र भूर्जयन्तं महां विपोधां मूरा अमूरं पुरां दर्माणम् ।
नयन्तो गर्भं वनां धियं धुर्हिरिश्मश्रुं नार्वाणं धनर्चम् ॥५॥

5. He has come into being and leading him like a golden-maned
   war-horse, the great, the victorious, the founder of the Light,
   men ignorant, one who is free from ignorance, the render

---

[1] Trita the triple born from the All-pervading Substance,

of the cities, the child of the forests, whose wealth is the illumined word[1] — they established the thought.

नि पस्त्यासु त्रितः स्तभूयन् परिवीतो योनौ सीददन्तः ।
अतः संगृभ्या विशां दमूना विधर्मणायन्त्रैरीयते नॄन् ॥६॥

6. May Trita in the homesteads holding all firmly[2] take his session in his native seat within and all-encompassing; thence, a dweller in man's home, taking all into his grasp, by a wide law of his action, by unrestrained movements he journeys to the gods.

अस्याजरासो दमामरित्रा अर्चद्धूमासो अग्नयः पावकाः ।
शिवतीचयः श्वात्रासो भुरण्यवो वनर्षदो वायवो न सोमाः ॥७॥

7. His ageless and purifying fires are the defenders of our homes, lifting their luminous smoke; white-flaming, dwellers in the Tree, they are our strengtheners and supporters and like winds and like wine.

प्र जिह्वया भरते वेपो अग्निः प्र वयुनानि चेतसा पृथिव्याः ।
तमायवः शुचयन्तं पावकं मन्द्रं होतारं दधिरे यजिष्ठम् ॥८॥

8. Fire carries with his tongue the illumination of wisdom, he carries in his consciousness earth's discoveries of knowledge; him men hold the illuminating and purifying rapturous Priest of the call most strong for sacrifice.

द्यावा यमग्निं पृथिवी जनिष्टामापस्त्वष्टा भृगवो यं सहोभिः ।
ईळेन्यं प्रथमं मातरिश्वा देवास्ततक्षुर्मनवे यजत्रम् ॥९॥

9. This is the Fire to whom earth and heaven gave birth; and the waters, the form-maker and the Flame-Seers by their strengths, and life that grows in the mother and the gods have fashioned for man desirable, first and supreme, a master of sacrifice.

---

[1] Or, the illumination   [2] Or, setting himself firmly

यं त्वा देवा दधिरे हृव्यवाहं पुरुस्पृहो मानुषासो यजत्रम् ।
स यामन्नग्ने स्तुवते वयो धाः प्र देवयन् यशसः सं हि पूर्वीः ॥१०॥

10. Thou art he whom the gods have set as the carrier of the
offerings and men with their many desires as the lord of
sacrifice; so do thou, O Fire, found in thy journeying wide
expansion for him who lauds thee and making him divine
gather in him many glorious things.

DEVAS AND AGNI SAUCHIKA

SUKTA 51

महत् तदुल्बं स्थविरं तदासीद्येनाविष्टितः प्रविवेशिथापः ।
विश्वा अपश्यद्बहुधा ते अग्ने जातवेदस्तन्वो देव एकः ॥१॥

1. Large was the covering and it was dense in which thou wert
wrapped when thou didst enter into the waters; one was the
god who saw thee but many and manifold were thy bodies
which he saw, O Fire, O knower of all things born.

को मा ददर्श कतमः स देवो यो मे तन्वो बहुधा पर्यपश्यत् ।
क्वाह मित्रावरुणा क्षियन्त्यग्नेर्विश्वाः समिधो देवयानीः ॥२॥

2. Which of the gods was he who saw everywhere my bodies
in many forms? O Mitra and Varuna, where then dwell all
the blazings of the Fire which are paths of the gods?

ऐच्छाम त्वा बहुधा जातवेदः प्रविष्टमग्ने अप्स्वोषधीषु ।
तं त्वा यमो अचिकेच्चित्रभानो दशान्तरुष्यादतिरोचमानम् ॥३॥

3. We desire thee, O Fire, O knower of all things born, when
thou hast entered manifoldly into the growths of the earth
and into the waters; there the lord of the law grew aware
of thee, O thou of the many diverse lights, shining luminous
beyond the ten inner dwelling-places.

होत्रादहं वरुण बिभ्यदायं नेदेव मा युनजन्नत्र देवाः ।
तस्य मे तन्वो बहुधा निविष्टा एतमर्थं न चिकेताहमग्निः ॥४॥

4. O Varuna, fearing the sacrificants' office that so the gods
might not yoke me to that work; so my bodies entered
manifoldly, for I, Fire, was not conscious of this goal of the
movement.

एहि मनुर्देवयुर्यज्ञकामोऽरंकृत्या तमसि क्षेष्यग्ने ।
सुगान् पथः कृणुहि देवयानान् वह हव्यानि सुमनस्यमानः ॥५॥

5. Come to us; the human being, god-seeking, is desirous of
sacrifice, he has made all ready but thou dwellest in the
darkness, O Fire. Make the paths of the journeying of the
gods easy to travel, let thy mind be at ease, carry the
offerings.

अग्नेः पूर्वे भ्रातरो अर्थमेतं रथीवाध्वानमन्वावरीवुः ।
तस्माद्भिया वरुण दूरमायं गौरो न क्षेप्नोरविजे ज्यायाः ॥६॥

6. The ancient brothers of the Fire chose this goal to be reached
as charioteers follow a path; therefore in fear I came far
away, O Varuna. I started back as a *gaur* from the bow-
string of the archer.

कुर्मस्त आयुरजरं यदग्ने यथा युक्तो जातवेदो न रिष्याः ।
अथा वहासि सुमनस्यमानो भागं देवेभ्यो हविषः सुजात ॥७॥

7. Since we make thy life imperishable, O Fire, O knower of all
things born, so that yoked with it thou shalt not come to
harm, then with thy mind at ease thou canst carry their share
of the offering to the gods, O high-born Fire.

प्रयाजान् मे अनुयाजांश्च केवलानूर्जस्वन्तं हविषो दत्त भागम् ।
घृतं चापां पुरुषं चौषधीनामग्नेश्च दीर्घमायुरस्तु देवाः ॥८॥

8. Give me the absolutes that precede and follow the sacrifice
as my share of the oblation packed with the energy; give
me the light from the waters and the soul from the plants
and let there be long life for the Fire, O gods.

तव प्रयाजा अनुयाजाश्च केवल ऊर्जस्वन्तो हविषः सन्तु भागाः ।
तवाग्ने यज्ञोऽयमस्तु सर्वस्तुभ्यं नमन्तां प्रदिशश्चतस्रः ॥९॥

9. Thine be the absolute precedents and consequents of the
sacrifice, the portions packed with energy of the oblation;
thine, O Fire, be all this sacrifice; may the four regions bow
down to thee.

SUMITRA VADHRYASHWA

SUKTA 69

भद्रा अग्ने बंध्रघश्वस्य संदृशो वामी प्रणीतिः सुरणा उपेतयः ।
यदीं सुमित्रा विशो अग्र इन्धते घृतेनाहुतो जरते वविद्युतत् ॥१॥

1. Happy are the seeings of the Fire of the gelded Horse, plea-
surable his guidance, delightful his approaches; when the
friendly peoples set him ablaze in their front, fed with the
oblations of the Light he flames up for his worshipper.

घृतमग्ने बंध्रघश्वस्य वर्धनं घृतमन्नं घृतम्वस्य मेदनम् ।
घृतेनाहुत उर्विया वि पप्रथे सूर्य इव रोचते सर्पिरासुतिः ॥२॥

2. The Light is the increasing of the Fire of the gelded Horse,
Light is his food, Light is his fattening: fed with the oblation of the Light wide he spread; he shines as the Sun when
there is poured on him its running stream.

यत् ते मनुर्यदनीकं सुमित्रः समीधे अग्ने तदिदं नवीयः ।
स रेवच्छोच स गिरो जुषस्व स वाजं दर्षि स इह श्रवो धाः ॥३॥

3. The force of flame which thinking man, which the friendly
one, set ablaze, this is that new force, O Fire; so opulently
shine, so accept our words, so take the plenitude by violence,
so found here the inspired knowledge.

यं त्वा पूर्वमीळितो वध्रघश्वः समीधे अग्ने स इदं जुषस्व ।
स नः स्तिपा उत भवा तनूपा दात्रं रक्षस्व यदिदं ते अस्मे ॥४॥

4. That flame of thine of old which the gelded Horse, when prayed, set blazing high, O Fire who art that flame, this too accept; as that flame, become the protector of our stable erections and the protector of our bodies, guard this giving of thine which is here in us.

भवा द्युम्नी वाध्रयश्वोत गोपा मा त्वा तारीदभिमातिर्जनानाम् ।
शूर इव धृष्णुश्च्यवनः सुमित्रः प्र नु वोचं वाध्रयश्वस्य नाम ॥५॥

5. Become full of light, O gelded Horse, and become our protector, let not the assault of men pierce thee; thou art like a hero, a violent overthrower and the good Friend: lo, I have uttered the names of the Fire of the gelded Horse.

समज्यघा पर्वत्या वसूनि दासा वृत्राण्यार्या जिगेथ ।
शूर इव धृष्णुश्च्यवनो जनानां त्वमग्ने पृतनायूँरभि ष्याः ॥६॥

6. Thou hast conquered the riches of the plains and the riches of the mountain, the destroyer foemen, and the Aryan freemen: like a hero art thou, a violent overthrower of men, O Fire, mayst thou overcome those who battle against us.

दीर्घंतन्तुर्बृहदुक्षायमग्निः सहस्रस्तरीः शतनीथ ऋग्भवा ।
द्युमान् द्युमत्सु नृभिमृज्यमानः सुमित्रेषु दीदयो देवयत्सु ॥७॥

7. This Fire is the long Thread, the vast Bull, one with a thousand layers and a hundred leadings, he is the Craftsman; luminous in men luminous, made bright by the hands of men, may he flame out in the strivers after godhead, in the friendly people.[1]

त्वे धेनुः सुदुघा जातवेदोऽसश्चतेव समना सबर्धुक् ।
त्वं नृभिर्दक्षिणावद्भिररने सुमित्रेभिरिध्यसे देवयद्भुः ॥८॥

8. In thee is the good milch-cow, O knower of all things born, as if unstayingly equal in its yield, giving its nectar-milk.

---

[1] In the Sumitras, the name of the Rishi; but throughout the hymn there is a double or symbolic meaning in the names.

O Fire, thou art set alight by men who have the intuitive judgment, strivers after godhead, the friendly people.

देवाश्चित् ते अमृता जातवेदो महिमानं वाध्रचश्व प्र वोचन् ।
यत् संपृच्छं मानुषीर्विश आयन् त्वं नृभिरजयस्त्वावृषेभिः ॥९॥

9. Even the immortal gods proclaim thy greatness, O knower of all things born, O Fire of the gelded Horse. That which I sought by questioning, coming to the human peoples, thou hast conquered by men who grow by thee.[1]

पितेव पुत्रमबिभरुपस्थे त्वामग्ने वध्रचश्वः सपर्यन् ।
जुषाणो अस्य समिधं यविष्ठोत पूर्वाँ अवनोर्वाधतश्चित् ॥१०॥

10. Thee, as the father carries his son in his lap so the gelded Horse carried and tended thee, O Fire; O youthful god, accepting his fuel thou didst conquer even the supreme and mighty.

शश्वदग्निर्वध्रचश्वस्य शत्रून् नृभिर्जिगाय सुतसोमवद्भिः ।
समनं चिददहश्चित्रभानोऽव व्राधन्तमभिनद्वृधश्चित् ॥११॥

11. Fire has ever conquered the enemies of the gelded Horse by men who have pressed the Soma-wine; O thou of the bright diverse lights, thou hast broken and cast down the foe that was equal and the foe that was mighty and thou hast given him increase.

अयमग्निर्वध्रचश्वस्य वृत्रहा सनकात् प्रेद्धो नमसोपवाक्यः ।
स नो अजामीँरुत वा विजामीनभि तिष्ठ शर्धतो वाध्रचश्व ॥१२॥

12. This Fire is the slayer of the enemies of the gelded Horse, lit from of old and to be invoked with obeisance; so do thou assail those who attack him, both the uncompanioned and the one with many companions, O Fire of the gelded Horse.

---

[1] Or, who make thee grow in them.

27

SUKTA 70

इमां मे अग्ने समिधं जुषस्वेळस्पदे प्रति हर्या घृताचीम् ।
वर्ष्मन् पृथिव्याः सुदिनत्वे अह्नामूर्ध्वो भव सुक्रतो देवयज्या ॥१॥

1. O Fire, accept the fuel I give thee; in the seat of revelation
    take joy in the luminous Thought: on the high top of earth,
    in the brightness of the days, become high uplifted by wor-
    ship of sacrifice to the gods, O strong of will!

आ देवानामप्रयावेह यातु नराशंसो विश्वरूपेभिरश्वैः ।
ऋतस्य पथा नमसा मियेधो देवेभ्यो देवतमः सुषवत् ॥२॥

2. May he who travels in front of the gods, he who voices the
    godhead, come here with his horses of universal forms; pure
    and most divine, may he hasten with our obeisance on the
    path of the Truth to the gods.

शश्वत्तममीळते दूत्याय हविष्मन्तो मनुष्यासो अग्निम् ।
वहिष्ठैरश्वैः सुवृता रथेनादेवान् वक्षि नि षदेह होता ॥३॥

3. Men bringing their offerings ask for the Fire everlasting to
    be their envoy: so do thou with thy horses strong to bear
    and thy swiftly moving car bring to us the gods; take here
    thy seat as the Priest of the call.

वि प्रथतां देवजुष्टं तिरश्चा दीर्घं द्राघ्मा सुरभि भूत्वस्मे ।
अहेळता मनसा देव बर्हिरिन्द्रज्येष्ठाँ उशतो यक्षि देवान् ॥४॥

4. May the seat acceptable to the gods spread wide in us and
    all its long horizontal length become fragrant. Occupy that
    seat, O god, with a mind not inclining to wrath, and to the
    gods with Indra for their greatest offer sacrifice.

दिवो वा सानु स्पृशता वरीयः पृथिव्या वा मात्रया वि श्रयध्वम् ।
उशतीर्द्वारो महिना महद्भिर्देवं रथं रथयुर्धारयध्वम् ॥५॥

5. Touch either heaven's superior peak or swing wide open with all the extent of earth, O doors of aspiration, who desire the chariot of the gods, hold in your greatness and by the great the divine car.

देवी दिवो दुहितरा सुशिल्पे उषासानक्ता सदतां नि योनौ ।
आ वां देवास उशती उशन्त उरौ सीदन्तु सुभगे उपस्थे ॥६॥

6. Let the two divine daughters of heaven, formed beautifully, dawn and night, sit in their native seat; O dawn and night, O you who aspire, may the gods aspiring sit on your wide lap, O blissful ones.

ऊर्ध्वो ग्रावा बृहदग्निः समिद्धः प्रिया धामान्यदितेरुपस्थे ।
पुरोहितावृत्विजा यज्ञे अस्मिन् विदुष्टरा द्रविणमा यजेथाम् ॥७॥

7. High stands up the stone of the pressing, high the Fire is kindled, may it touch the vast and the seats dear to us in the lap of the infinite mother; O you who are vicars and ordinants of the rite in this sacrifice, you twain who have greater knowledge, may you win for us by sacrifice the Treasure.

तिस्रो देवीर्बर्हिरिदं वरीय आ सीदत चक्रमा वः स्योनम् ।
मनुष्वद्यज्ञं सुधिता हवींषीळा देवी घृतपदी जुषन्त ॥८॥

8. O ye three goddesses, sit on the superior seat which we have made delightful for you; may the mother of Revelation and the two goddesses with the luminous feet accept our firmly placed offerings and our human worship of sacrifice.

देव त्वष्टर्यद्ध चारुत्वमानड् यदङ्गिरसामभवः सचाभूः ।
स देवानां पाथ उप प्र विद्वानुशन् यक्षि द्रविणोदः सुरत्नः ॥९॥

9. O divine maker of forms, since thou hast reached beauty in thy works, since thou hast become companion in thy being to the Angiras seers, forward then to the goal of the journeyings of the gods, for thou knowest it! Aspiring, perfect in ecstasy, sacrifice to the gods, O giver of the treasure.

वनस्पते रशनया नियूया देवानां पाथ उप वक्षि विद्वान् ।
स्वदाति देवः कृणवद्धवींष्यवतां द्यावापृथिवी हवं मे ॥१०॥

10   O Tree, knowing the goal of the journeying of the gods,
bear us to it binding with the radiant cord. May the godhead fashion the offerings in which he takes pleasure : may
heaven and earth protect our call.

आग्ने वह वरुणमिष्टये न इन्द्रं दिवो मरुतो अन्तरिक्षात् ।
सीदन्तु बर्हिविश्व आ यजत्राः स्वाहा देवा अमृता मादयन्ताम् ॥११॥

11.   O Fire, bring Varuna to our sacrifice, Indra from heaven,
the Life-Gods from mid-air; may all the lords of sacrifice
sit on our sacred seat, may the immortal gods take rapture
in the *svāhā.*

AGNI SAUCHIKA OR VAISHWANARA
OR SAPTI VAJAMBHARA

SUKTA 79

अपश्यमस्य महतो महित्वममर्त्यस्य मर्त्यासु विक्षु ।
नाना हनू विभृते सं भरेते असिन्वती बप्सती भूयंत्तः ॥१॥

1.   I have seen the greatness of this great one, the Immortal in
the mortal peoples. The jaws of this abundant eater, separate and held apart, are brought close together, devouring,
insatiable.

गुहा शिरो निहितमृधगक्षी असिन्वन्नत्ति जिह्वया वनानि ।
अत्राण्यस्मे पड्भिः सं भरन्त्युत्तानहस्ता नमसाधि विक्षु ॥२॥

2.   His head is in the secrecy, his eyes wide apart, insatiable he
eats up the forest with his tongue of flame. They bring together his foods for him with the pacings of their feet, their
hands of obeisance are outstretched in the peoples.

प्र मातुः प्रतरं गुह्यमिच्छन् कुमारो न वीरुधः सर्पदुर्वीः ।
ससं न पक्वमविदच्छुचन्तं रिरिह्वांसं रिप उपस्थे अन्तः ॥३॥

3. Desiring the secret place of the mother farther beyond he
crawls like a child over the wide growths of earth. One finds
him shining like ripe corn, licking away the hurts, within in
her lap.

तद्वामृतं रोदसी प्र ब्रवीमि जायमानो मातरा गर्भो अत्ति ।
नाहं देवस्य मर्त्यश्चिकेताऽग्निरङ्ग विचेताः स प्रचेताः ॥४॥

4. O heaven and earth, I declare to you that Truth of you, —
in his very birth the child of your womb devours his parents.
I am mortal and know not of the godhead; Fire is the
all-conscious knower and he is the thinker.

यो अस्मा अन्नं तृष्वादधात्याज्यैर्घृतैर्जुहोति पुष्यति ।
तस्मै सहस्रमक्षभिर्वि चक्षेऽग्ने विश्वतः प्रत्यङ्ङसि त्वम् ॥५॥

5. He who sets swiftly for him his food casts on him the outpourings of light by which he is nourished, for him he sees
with a thousand eyes: O Fire, thou frontest us on every side.

किं देवेषु त्यज एनश्चकर्थाऽग्ने पृच्छामि नु त्वामविद्वान् ।
अक्रीळन् क्रीळन् हरिरत्तवेऽद्न् वि पर्वशश्चकर्तं गामिवासिः ॥६॥

6. What omission or sin hast thou done before the gods, I ask
thee, O Fire, for I know not. In his play unplaying a tawny
lion, eating only to devour, he has cut all asunder limb by
limb, as a knife cuts the cow.

विषूचो अश्वान् युयुजे वनेजा ऋजीतिभी रशनाभिर्गृभीतान् ।
चक्षदे मित्रो वसुभिः सुजातः समानृधे पर्वभिर्वावृधानः ॥७॥

7. He who is born in the forests has yoked his horses tending
all ways but caught back by straight-held reins. Mitra, well-
born, has distributed to him the treasures and he has grown
to completeness increasing in every member.

SUKTA 80

अग्निः सर्पि वाजंभरं ददात्यग्निर्वीरं श्रुत्यं कर्मनिःष्ठाम् ।
अग्नी रोदसी वि चरत् समञ्जन्नग्निर्नारीं वीरकुक्षिं पुरंधिम् ॥१॥

1. Fire gives to us the Horse that carries the plenitude, Fire
    gives the Hero who has the inspired hearing and stands firm
    in the work; Fire ranges through earth and heaven reveal-
    ing all things, Fire gives the Woman, the tenant of the city,[1]
    from whose womb is born the hero.

अग्नेरप्नसः समिदस्तु भद्राऽग्निर्महीं रोदसी आ विवेश ।
अग्निरेकं चोदयत् समत्स्वग्निर्वृत्राणि दयते पुरूणि ॥२॥

2. May there be a happy fuel for Fire at his labour, Fire enters
    into the great earth and heaven: Fire urges on one who is all
    alone in his battles, Fire cleaves asunder the multitude of
    the enemy.

अग्निर्हं त्यं जरतः कर्णमावाऽग्निरद्भूधो निरदहज्जरूथम् ।
अग्निरत्रिं घर्मं उरुष्यदन्तरग्निर्नृमेधं प्रजयासृजत् सम् ॥३॥

3. Fire has protected the ear[2] of the worshipper,[3] Fire burnt out
    the Waster[4] from the waters; Fire delivered Atri within the
    blaze,[5] Fire united man's sacrifice with its progeny.[6]

अग्निर्ददद् द्रविणं वीरपेशा अग्निर्ऋषिं यः सहस्रा सनोति ।
अग्निर्दिवि हव्यमा ततानाऽग्निर्धर्मानि विभृता पुरुत्रा ॥४॥

4. May Fire in the hero's shape give us the Treasure, may Fire
    give us the sage who wins the thousands; Fire has extended
    the offering in heaven, his are the planes upheld separately
    in many spaces.

---

[1] Or, the many-thoughted,

[2] "*Tyam*", "that other" ear, the inner ear which listens to inspired knowledge.

[3] Sayana takes the two words "*jarataḥ*", "*karṇam*" as if they were one indicating the name
of the Rishi "Jaratkarna".

[4] Sayana renders "*jarūtha*" "a demon".

[5] Sayana renders "in the hot cauldron in the earth".

[6] Sayana renders "gave progeny to the Rishi Nrimedha".

अग्निमुक्थैरृषयो वि ह्वयन्तेऽग्निं नरो यामनि बाधितासः ।
अग्निं वयो अन्तरिक्षे पतन्तोऽग्निः सहस्रा परि याति गोनाम् ॥५॥

5. Fire the sages with their utterances call to every side, to Fire
   men call who are opposed in their march, to Fire the Birds
   flying in mid-air; Fire encircles the thousands of the Ray-
   Cows.

अग्निं विश ईळते मानुषीर्या अग्निं मनुषो नहुषो वि जाताः ।
अग्निर्गन्धर्वीं पथ्यामृतस्याऽग्नेर्गव्यूतिर्घृत आ निषत्ता ॥६॥

6. Fire the peoples pray who are human, Fire men of different
   birth who dwell as neighbours, Fire brings the Gandharvi to
   the path of the Truth, the Fire's path of the ray-cows is
   settled in the Light.

अग्नये ब्रह्म ऋभवस्ततक्षुरग्निं महामवोचामा सुवृक्तिम् ।
अग्ने प्राव जरितारं यविष्ठाऽग्ने महि द्रविणमा यजस्व ॥७॥

7. The divine craftsmen have fashioned the Wisdom-Word for
   the Fire, the Fire we have declared as a vast purification.
   O ever-youthful Fire, protect thy worshipper; O Fire, win
   for him by sacrifice the great Treasure.

PAYU BHARADWAJA

Sukta 87

रक्षोहणं वाजिनमा जिघर्मि मित्रं प्रथिष्ठमुप यामि शर्म ।
शिशानो अग्निः क्रतुभिः समिद्धः स नो दिवा स रिषः पातु नक्तम् ॥१॥

1. I set ablaze Fire of the plenitude, the slayer of the Rakshasas, I approach him as a friend and the widest house of refuge;[1] the Fire has been kindled and grows intense by the
   workings of the will, may he protect us from the doer of
   hurt, by the day and by the night.

---

[1] Or, a widest peace;

अयोदंष्ट्रो अर्चिषा यातुधानानुप स्पृश जातवेदः समिद्धः ।
आ जिह्वया मूरदेवान् रभस्व क्रव्यादो वृक्त्व्यपि धत्स्वासन् ॥२॥

2. O knower of all things born, high-kindled, iron-tusked,
   touch with thy ray the demon-sorcerers; do violence to him
   with thy tongue of flame, the gods who kill,[1] the eaters of
   flesh, putting them off from us shut them into thy mouth.

उभोभयाविष्वप् धेहि दंष्ट्रा हिंस्रः शिशानोज्वरं परं च ।
उतान्तरिक्षे परि याहि राजञ्जम्भैः सं धेह्याभि यातुधानान् ॥३॥

3. Destruction, whetting set upon them both thy tusks, the
   higher and the lower, O thou who art of both worlds,[2] thou
   circle in the mid-air, O king, and snap up in thy jaws the
   demon-sorcerers.

यज्ञैरिषूः संनममानो अग्ने वाचा शल्याँ अशनिभिर्दिहानः ।
ताभिर्विध्य हृदये यातुधानान् प्रतीचो बाहून् प्रति भङ्ध्येषाम् ॥४॥

4. Turning on them by our sacrifices thy arrows, O Fire, by our
   speech thy javelins, plastering them with thy thunderbolts
   pierce with these in their hearts the demon-sorcerers who
   confront us, break their arms.

अग्ने त्वचं यातुधानस्य भिन्धि हिंस्राशनिर्हरसा हन्त्वेनम् ।
प्र पर्वाणि जातवेदः शृणीहि क्रव्यात् क्रविष्णुर्वि चिनोतु वृक्णम् ॥५॥

5. O Fire, tear the skin of the demon-sorcerer; let the cruel
   thunderbolt slay him in its wrath; rend his limbs, O knower
   of all things born; hungry for its flesh let the carrion-eater
   pick asunder his mangled body.

यत्रेदानीं पश्यसि जातवेदस्तिष्ठन्तमग्न उत वा चरन्तम् ।
यद्वान्तरिक्षे पथिभिः पतन्तं तमस्ता विध्य शर्वा शिशानः ॥६॥

6. Wherever now thou seest him, O knower of all things born,
   whether standing or walking, or flying on the paths in the

---

[1] Or, the gods of ignorance,   [2] Or, O thou who hast both,

mid-air, a shooter sharpening his weapon, pierce him with
thy arrow.

उतालब्धं स्पृणुहि जातवेद आलेभानादृष्टिभिर्यातुधानात् ।
अग्ने पूर्वो नि जहि शोशुचान आमादः क्ष्विङ्क्रास्तमदन्त्वेनीः ॥७॥

7. Rescue from the assault of the demon-sorcerer with his
spears the man touched by his grasp, O knower of all things
born, O Fire, blazing supreme slay these devourers of the
flesh; let the brilliant birds of prey eat him up.

इह प्र ब्रूहि यतमः सो अग्ने यो यातुधानो य इदं कृणोति ।
तमा रभस्व समिधा यविष्ठ नृचक्षसश्चक्षुषे रन्धयैनम् ॥८॥

8. Here proclaim which is he, O Fire, what demon-sorcerer,
who is the doer of this deed? To him do violence with thy
blaze, O youthful god, subject him to the eye of thy divine
vision.

तीक्ष्णेनाग्ने चक्षुषा रक्ष यज्ञं प्राञ्चं वसुभ्यः प्र णय प्रचेतः ।
हिंस्रं रक्षांस्यभि शोशुचानं मा त्वा दभन् यातुधाना नृचक्षः ॥९॥

9. O Fire, guard with thy keen eye the sacrifice, lead it moving
forward to the Shining Ones, O conscious thinker; O thou of
the divine vision, when thou blazest fierce against the Rakshasas let not the demon-sorcerers overcome thee.

नृचक्षा रक्षः परि पश्य विक्षु तस्य त्रीणि प्रति शृणीह्यग्रा ।
तस्याग्ने पृष्टीर्हरसा शृणीहि त्रेधा मूलं यातुधानस्य वृश्च ॥१०॥

10. Divine of vision, see everywhere the Rakshasa in the peoples, cleave the three peaks of him; his flanks, O Fire, cleave
with thy wrath, rend asunder the triple root of the demon-
sorcerer.

त्रिर्यातुधानः प्रसितिं त एत्वृतं यो अग्ने अनृतेन हन्ति ।
तमर्चिषा स्फूर्जयञ्जातवेदः समक्षमेनं गृणते नि वृङ्धि ॥११॥

11.   Triply may the demon-sorcerer undergo thy onrush, he who
      slays the Truth by falsehood; him overspreading with thy
      ray, O knower of all things born, fell down in front of him
      who hymns thee.

तदग्ने चक्षुः प्रति धेहि रेभे शफारुजं येन पश्यसि यातुधानम् ।
अथर्ववज्ज्योतिषा दैव्येन सत्यं धूर्वन्तमचितं न्योष ॥१२॥

12.   Set in thy singer, O Fire, the eye with which thou seest the
      trampler with his hooves, the demon-sorcerer; even as did
      Atharvan, burn with the divine Light this being without
      knowledge who does hurt to the Truth.

यदग्ने अद्य मिथुना शपातो यद्वाचस्तृष्टं जनयन्त रेभाः ।
मन्योर्मनसः शरव्या जायते या तया विध्य हृदये यातुधानान् ॥१३॥

13.   The cursing with which today couples revile each other,
      the curses which are born in the imprecations of the singers,
      the arrow which is born from the mind of wrath, with that
      pierce through the heart the demon-sorcerers.

परा शृणीहि तपसा यातुधानान् पराग्ने रक्षो हरसा शृणीहि ।
परार्चिषा मूरदेवाञ्छृणीहि परासुतृपो अभि शोशुचानः ॥१४॥

14.   Away from us cleave by thy burning energy the demon-
      sorcerers, away from us cleave by the heat of thy wrath the
      Rakshasa, O Fire, away from us cleave by thy ray these
      slayer gods,[1] blazing away from us cleave these who glut
      themselves with men's lives.

पराद्य देवा वृजिनं शृणन्तु प्रत्यगेनं शपथा यन्तु तृष्टाः ।
वाचास्तेनं शरव ऋच्छन्तु मर्मन् विश्वस्यैतु प्रसिति यातुधानः ॥१५॥

15.   May the gods cleave away today the crooked one, may harsh
      curses come to confront him, may the shafts enter into the
      vital part of one who thieves by speech, may he undergo the

---

[1] Or, the gods of ignorance,

onset of each and every one, the demon-sorcerer.

यः पौरुषेयेण क्रविषा समङ्क्ते यो अश्व्येन पशुना यातुधानः ।
यो अघ्न्याया भरति क्षीरमग्ने तेषां शीर्षाणि हरसापि वृश्च ॥१६॥

16. The demon-sorcerer who feeds on the flesh of human beings, who feeds on horses and on cattle, the one who carries away the milk of the Cow unslayable, cut asunder their necks with the flame of thy anger, O Fire.

संवत्सरीणं पय उस्त्रियायास्तस्य माशीद्धातुधानो नृचक्षः ।
पीयूषमग्ने यतमस्तितृप्सात् तं प्रत्यञ्चमर्चिषा विध्य मर्मन् ॥१७॥

17. O thou who hast the divine vision, let not the demon-sorcerer partake of the yearly milk of the shining cow; O Fire, whichever of them would glut himself on the nectar him pierce in front in his vital part with thy ray of light.

विषं गवां यातुधानाः पिबन्त्वा वृश्च्यन्तामदितये दुरेवाः ।
परैनान् देवः सविता ददातु परा भागमोषधीनां जयन्ताम् ॥१८॥

18. May the demon-sorcerers drink poison from the Ray-Cows, may they be cloven asunder who are of evil impulse before the infinite mother, may the divine sun betray them to thee, may they be deprived of their share of the growths of earth.

सनादग्ने मृणसि यातुधानान् न त्वा रक्षांसि पृतनासु जिग्युः ।
अनु दह सहमूरान् क्रव्यादो मा ते हेत्या मुक्षत दैव्यायाः ॥१९॥

19. Ever dost thou crush the demon-sorcerer, O Fire, never have the Rakshasas conquered thee in the battles; burn one by one from their roots the eaters of raw flesh, may they find no release from thy divine missile.

त्वं नो अग्ने अधरादुद्वक्तात् त्वं पश्चादुत रक्षा पुरस्तात् ।
प्रति ते ते अजरासस्तपिष्ठा अघशंसं शोशुचतो दहन्तु ॥२०॥

20. O Fire, do thou guard us from above and from below, thou

from behind and from the front; may those most burning
ageless flames of thine blazing burn one who is a voice of
evil.

पश्चात् पुरस्तादधरादुदक्तात् कविः काव्येन परि पाहि राजन् ।
सखे सखायमजरो जरिम्णेऽग्ने मर्तां अमर्त्यस्त्वं नः ॥२१॥

21. From behind and from in front, from below and from above,
a seer by thy seer-wisdom protect us, O king; a friend protect
thy friend, ageless protect from old age, immortal protect
us who are mortals, O Fire.

परि त्वाग्ने पुरं वयं विप्रं सहस्य धीमहि ।
धृषद्वर्णं दिवेदिवे हन्तारं भङ्गुरावताम् ॥२२॥

22. O forceful Fire, let us think of thee, the illumined sage as a
fortress around us, one violent of aspect, slayer from day to
day of the crooked ones.

विषेण भङ्गुरावतः प्रति ष्म रक्षसो दह ।
अग्ने तिग्मेन शोचिषा तपुरग्राभिर्ऋष्टिभिः ॥२३॥

23. Consume with poison the crooked Rakshasas; O Fire, burn
them with thy keen flame, with thy fiery-pointed spears.

प्रत्यग्ने मिथुना दह यातुधाना किमीदिना ।
सं त्वा शिशामि जागृह्यद्बुधं विप्र मन्मभिः ॥२४॥

24. Burn the bewildered demon-sorcerer couples; I thee whet to
sharpness, inviolate, with my thoughts, O illumined sage;
awake.

प्रत्यग्ने हरसा हरः शृणीहि विश्वतः प्रति ।
यातुधानस्य रक्षसो बलं वि रुज वीर्यम् ॥२५॥

25. O Fire, cleave asunder their wrath with thy flame of wrath
to every side; break utterly the strength, the energy of the
Rakshasa, of the demon-sorcerer.

ARUNA VAITAHAVYA

SUKTA 91

सं जागृवद्भिर्जरमाण इध्यते दमे दमूना इषयन्निळस्पदे ।
विश्वस्य होता हविषो वरेण्यो विभुर्विभावा सुषखा सखीयते ॥१॥

1. Adored by those who are wakeful, the dweller in the house
   is kindled in the house aspiring in the seat of revelation, the
   sacrificant of every offering, one Supreme,[1] wide of being,
   wide in light, a perfect friend to the man who seeks his
   friendship.

स दर्शतश्रीरतिथिर्गृहेगृहे वनेवने शिश्रिये तक्ववीरिव ।
जनंजनं जन्यो नाति मन्यते विश आ क्षेति विश्यो विशंविशम् ॥२॥

2. In his visioned glory he lodges as the guest in every house,
   as a bird in forest and forest; he disdains not the peoples,
   universal he dwells in being and being, common to all he
   dwells in man and man.

सुदक्षो दक्षैः ऋतुनासि सुऋतुरग्ने कविः काव्येनासि विश्ववित् ।
वसुर्वसूनां क्षयसि त्वमेक इद् द्यावा च यानि पृथिवी च पुष्यतः ॥३॥

3. Thou art discerning in thy judgments, strong of will in thy
   workings of will, O Fire, an omniscient seer in thy seer-
   wisdoms; a possessor of riches thou rulest sole over all the
   riches nourished by earth and by heaven.

प्रजानन्नग्ने तव योनिमृत्वियमिळायास्पदे घृतवन्तमासदः ।
आ ते चिकित्र उषसामिवेतयोऽरेपसः सूर्यस्येव रश्मयः ॥४॥

4. Thou hast known and reached thy luminous native seat
   where is the order of the Truth in the plane of revelation;
   free from stain of evil have come thy perceptions of knowledge like the white brilliances of the dawns,[2] like rays of the
   sun.

---

[1] Or, one desirable,   [2] Or, like the advents of the dawns,

तव श्रियो वर्ष्यस्येव विद्युतश्चित्राश्चिकित्र उषसां न केतवः ।
यदोषधीरभिसृष्टो वनानि च परि स्वयं चिनुषे अन्नमास्ये ॥५॥

5. Thy glories like lightnings from a storm cloud break into
    light of knowledge brilliant like the rays of intuition of the
    dawns; when loosed on the growths of earths and woods
    of pleasaunce thou seekest out thyself the food for thy
    mouth.[1]

तमोषधीर्दधिरे गर्भमृत्वियं तमापो अग्निं जनयन्त मातरः ।
तमित् समानं वनिनश्च वीरुधोऽन्तर्वतीश्च सुवते च विश्वहा ॥६॥

6. Him the growths of earth held as a child in the womb in
    whom was the order of the Truth, the Waters become the
    mothers of that Fire who gave him birth; he is the common
    child with whom the pleasaunce-woods and the plants of
    earth are pregnant and they are delivered of him always.

वातोपधूत इषितो वशाँ अनु तृषु यदन्ना वेविषद्विति्ष्ठसे ।
आ ते यतन्ते रथ्यो यथा पृथक् शर्धांस्यग्ने अजराणि धक्षतः ॥७॥

7. Missioned, fanned by the wind when swiftly entering into
    thy food thou spreadest wide after thy desire, thy ageless
    hosts, as thou becomest, toil like chariot-warriors far apart.

मेघाकारं विदथस्य प्रसाधनमग्निं होतारं परिभूतमं मतिम् ।
तमिद्रर्भं हविष्या समानमित् तमिन्महे वृणते नान्यं त्वत् ॥८॥

8. Fire the creator of wisdom, the accomplisher of the disco-
    very of knowledge, Fire the Priest of the call, the all-embra-
    cing thinker, him they choose universal in the little offering,
    him in the great, — not another, O Fire, than thou.

त्वामिदत्र वृणते त्वायवो होतारमग्ने विदथेषु वेधसः ।
यद्देवयन्तो दधति प्रयांसि ते हविष्मन्तो मनवो वृक्तबर्हिषः ॥९॥

9. The ordainers of the work, they who desire thee, choose thee
    as Priest of the call in their discoveries of knowledge when

---

[1] Or, heapest food in thy mouth.

the seekers of the godhead hold thy delight,[1] human beings
who have plucked for thee the sacred grass of thy seat and
have brought their offerings.

तवाग्ने होत्रं तव पोत्रमृत्वियं तव नेष्ट्रं त्वमग्निदृतायतः ।
तव प्रशास्त्रं त्वमध्वरीयसि ब्रह्मा चासि गृहपतिश्च नो दमे ॥१०॥

10. O Fire, thine are the call and the offering, thine the purification and the order of the sacrifice, thine the lustration;
thou art the fire-bringer for the seeker of the Truth. The
annunciation is thine, thou becomest the pilgrim-rite:[2] thou
art the Priest of the Word and the master of the house in
our home.

यस्तुभ्यमग्ने अमृताय मर्त्यः समिधा दाशदुत वा हविष्कृति ।
तस्य होता भवसि यासि दूत्यमुप ब्रूषे यजस्यध्वरीयसि ॥११॥

11.*

इमा अस्मे मतयो वाचो अस्मद्रा ऋचो गिरः सुष्टुतयः समग्मत ।
वसूयवो वसवे जातवेदसे वृद्धासु चिद्वर्धनो यासु चाकनत् ॥१२॥

12. For him these thoughts and utterances go forth from us,
these words high and hymns of illumination and these high
lauds and meet together seeking the riches for the master of
riches, for the knower of all things born, and his desire is
towards them.

इमां प्रत्नाय सुष्टुतिं नवीयसीं वोचेयमस्मा उशते शृणोतु नः ।
भूया अन्तरा हृदस्य निस्पृशे जायेव पत्य उशती सुवासाः ॥१३॥

13. I would speak to the ancient One a laud new to his desire,
may he hear us; may it avail to touch his heart deep within
like a wife beautifully robed for her lord's desire.

---

[1] Or, set before thee the things of thy delight,
[2] Or, thou art the priest of the pilgrim-rite: * Translation not found in MSS.

यस्मिन्नश्वास ऋषभास उक्षणो वशा मेषा अवसृष्टास आहुताः ।
कीलाल्पे सोमपृष्ठाय वेधसे हृदा मतिं जनये चारुमग्नये ॥१४॥

14. Fire to whom are loosed and offered our horses, our bulls
    and oxen and heifers and our rams, to Fire the nectar-
    drinker who bears on his beak the Soma-wine, to the
    ordainer of things, I beget a thinking full of beauty from
    my heart.

अहाव्यग्ने हविरास्ये ते स्रुचीव घृतं चम्वीव सोमः ।
वाजसनिं रयिमस्मे सुवीरं प्रशस्तं धेहि यशसं बृहन्तम् ॥१५॥

15. An oblation has been offered into thy mouth, O Fire, as if
    clarified butter in a ladle, as if Soma-wine in a bowl. Found
    in us the treasure in which are the heroes and which wins for
    us the plenitudes, — the treasure excellent[1] and glorious
    and vast.

JAMADAGNI BHARGAVA OR RAMA JAMADAGNYA

SUKTA 110

समिद्धो अद्य मनुषो दुरोणे देवो देवान् यजसि जातवेदः ।
आ च वह मित्रमहश्चिकित्वान् त्वं दूतः कविरसि प्रचेताः ॥१॥

1. High-kindled today in the house of the human being, thou
   doest sacrifice a god to the gods, O knower of all things
   born; bring them to us as one who has knowledge, O friendly
   Light; for thou art the messenger, the seer, the thinker.

तनूनपात् पथ ऋतस्य यानान् मध्वा समञ्जन्त्स्वदया सुजिह्व ।
मन्मानि धीभिरुत यज्ञमृन्धन् देवत्रा च कृणुह्यध्वरं नः ॥२॥

2. O son of the body, revealing the paths of our journeyings to
   the Truth make them sweet with the Wine of Delight, O thou
   with thy high tongue of flame; enriching with our thoughts

---

[1] Or, high-proclaimed

the mantras and the sacrifice set our pilgrim-sacrifice in the gods.

आजुह्वान ईड्यो वन्द्यश्चाऽऽयाह्याग्ने वसुभिः सजोषाः ।
त्वं देवानामसि यह्व होता स एनान् यक्षीषितो यजीयान् ॥३॥

3. One prayed and adored, O Fire, calling them to us arrive, companioned by the Shining Ones, O mighty One, thou art the summoner of the gods, so, missioned, strong to sacrifice, do them sacrifice.

प्राचीनं बर्हिः प्रदिशा पृथिव्या वस्तोरस्या वृज्यते अग्रे अह्नाम् ।
व्यु प्रथते वितरं वरीयो देवेभ्यो अदितये स्योनम् ॥४॥

4. An ancient seat of sacred grass is plucked this morn, in the direction of this earth, in front of the days, wide it spreads beyond a supernal seat of happy ease for the gods and the mother infinite.

व्यचस्वतीरुर्विया वि श्रयन्तां पतिभ्यो न जनयः शुम्भमानाः ।
देवीर्द्वारो बृहतीर्विश्वमिन्वा देवेभ्यो भवत सुप्रायणाः ॥५॥

5. Widely expanding may they spring apart making themselves beautiful for us as wives for their lords; O divine doors, vast and all-pervading, be easy of approach to the gods.

आ सुष्वयन्ती यजते उपाके उषासानक्ता सदतां नि योनौ ।
दिव्ये योषणे बृहती सुरुक्मे अधि श्रियं शुक्रपिशं दधाने ॥६॥

6. Let night and day come gliding to us and queens of sacrifice, sit close together in their place of session, the two divine women, great and golden, holding a supreme glory of brilliant form, —

दैव्या होतारा प्रथमा सुवाचा मिमाना यज्ञं मनुषो यजध्यै ।
प्रचोदयन्ता विदथेषु कारू प्राचीनं ज्योतिः प्रदिशा दिशन्ता ॥७॥

7. the two divine priests of the call, also, the first and perfect

in speech building the sacrifice of man that he may do worship, doers of the work impelling to the discoveries of knowledge, pointing by their direction to the ancient Light.

आ नो यज्ञं भारती तूयमेत्विळा मनुष्वदिह चेतयन्ती ।
तिस्रो देवीर्बर्हिरेदं स्योनं सरस्वती स्वपसः सदन्तु ॥८॥

8. May Bharati come swiftly to our sacrifice, Ila awakening to
    knowledge here like a human thinker, and Saraswati, the
    three goddesses, — may they sit, perfect in their works, on
    this sacred seat of happy ease.

य इमे द्यावापृथिवी जनित्री रूपैरपिंशद् भुवनानि विश्वा ।
तमद्य होतरिषितो यजीयान् देवं त्वष्टारमिह यक्षि विद्वान् ॥९॥

9. He who fashioned in their forms this earth and heaven, the
    Parents, and fashioned all the worlds, him today and here,
    O missioned Priest of the call, do thou worship, strong for
    sacrifice, having the knowledge, even the divine maker of
    forms.

उपावसृज त्मन्या समञ्जन् देवानां पाथ ऋतुथा हवींषि ।
वनस्पतिः शमिता देवो अग्निः स्वदन्तु हव्यं मधुना घृतेन ॥१०॥

10. Revealing by thy self-power the goal of the gods, release
    towards it in the order of the Truth our offerings. Let the
    tree and the divine accomplisher of the work and the Fire
    take the taste of the offering with the sweetness and the light.

सद्यो जातो व्यमिमीत यज्ञमग्निर्देवानामभवत् पुरोगाः ।
अस्य होतुः प्रदिश्यृतस्य वाचि स्वाहाकृतं हविरदन्तु देवाः ॥११॥

11. As soon as he was born Fire measured out the shape of the
    sacrifice and became the leader who goes in front of the gods.
    In the speech of this Priest of the call which points out by its
    direction the Truth, may the gods partake of the oblation
    made *svāhā*.

UPASTUTA VARSHTIHAVYA

SUKTA 115

चित्र इच्छिशोस्तरुणस्य वक्षथो न यो मातरावप्येति धातवे ।
अनूधा यदि जीजनदघा च नु ववक्ष सद्यो महि दूत्यं चरन् ॥१॥

1. Marvellous is the power to upbear of this young, this infant god, for he goes not to his two mothers to drink their milk, even though one without teats of plenty brought him to birth then as now, from the first he did his carrying, performing his mighty embassy.

अग्निहं नाम धायि वम्रपस्तमः सं यो वना युवते भस्मना वता ।
अभिप्रमुरा जुह्वा स्वध्वर इनो न प्रोथमानो यवसे वृषा ॥२॥

2 Fire, verily, is established, a giver and mighty doer of works, he clings to the trees with his blazing tusks achieving the pilgrim-sacrifice with his besieging tongue of flame, he is like a snorting bull, master in his pasturage.

तं वो वि न वृषवं देवमन्धस इन्दुं प्रोथन्तं प्रवपन्तमर्णवम् ।
आसा वह्नि न शोचिषा विरप्शिनं महिव्रतं न सरजन्तमध्वनः ॥३॥

3. He is to you like a bird settled on a tree, like the divine moon-flow of the Soma-plant, like a clamorous spreading ocean; he is as one who carries in his mouth of flame, exuberant in strength, mighty in the way of his works, rushing on his paths.

वि यस्य ते ज्रयसानस्याजर धक्षोनं वाताः परि सन्त्यच्युताः ।
आ रण्वासो युयुधयो न सत्वनं त्रितं नशन्त प्र शिषन्त इष्टये ॥४॥

4. O ageless Fire, when thou rangest the spaces in thy will to burn, there are all around thee as if unsinking winds like joyful fighters, having the command for the seeking they march towards the warrior of the triple world.[1]

[1] Or, Trita the warrior.

स इदग्निः कण्वतमः कण्वसखार्यः परस्यान्तरस्य तरुषः ।
अग्निः पातु गृणतो अग्निः सूरीनग्निर्ददातु तेषामवो नः ॥५॥

5. This is the Fire, friend of the seer, himself the greatest of
seers, who delivers from the inner foe; may Fire guard the
speakers of the word, Fire the illumined seers, may he give
his protection to them and to us.

वाजिन्तमाय सह्वसे सुपित्र्य तृषु च्यवानो अनु जातवेदसे ।
अनुद्रे चिद्यो धृषता वरं सते महिन्तमाय धन्वनेदविष्यते ॥६॥

6. O high-born, thou art he who moves swiftly in the wake of
the knower of all things born, the Fire forceful and most full
of the plenitude and even in the waterless desert for him who
is there and desires it and is full of greatness, winnest by the
violence of thy bow that which is supreme.

एवाग्निमंतँ सह सूरिरिभर्वंसुः ष्ट्वे सहसः सूनरो नृभिः ।
मित्रासो न ये सुधिता ऋतायवो द्यावो न द्युम्नैरभि सन्ति मानुषान् ॥७॥

7. This is the Fire who is lauded accompanied by mortal illumined seers, the Shining One,[1] strong and glad by men, they
who are seekers of the Truth, and like well-established
friends, like the heavens with their lights have power on
human beings.

ऊर्जो नपात् सहसावन्निति त्वोपस्तुतस्य वन्दते वृषा वाक् ।
त्वां स्तोषाम त्वया सुवीरा द्राघीय आयुः प्रतरं दधानाः ॥८॥

8. "O son of energy, O forceful One", so adores thee the mighty
speech of Upastuta, thee let us laud, by thee may we be
armed with the heroes, holding more and more an ever
longer life.

इति त्वाग्ने वृष्टिहव्यस्य पुत्रा उपस्तुतास ऋषयोऽवोचन् ।
ताँश्च पाहि गृणतश्च सूरीन् वषड्वषट्‌लित्यूर्ध्वासो अनक्षन्
नमो नम इत्यूर्ध्वासो अनक्षन् ॥९॥

---

[1] Or, the master of riches,

9. Thus have extolled thee, O Fire, the sons of Vrishtihavya, the
   Upastuta Rishis;[1] protect them and the illuminates who
   speak the word, rising on high they have attained with the
   cry of *vaṣaṭ, vaṣaṭ*, with the cry of obeisance.

CHITRAMAHAS VASISHTHA

SUKTA 122

वसुं न चित्रमहसं गृणीषे वामं शेवमतिथिमद्विषेण्यम् ।
स रासते शुरुधो विश्वधायसोऽग्निर्होता गृहपतिः सुवीर्यम् ॥१॥

1. I voice the Shining One with its richly varied lights,[2] the
   fair and happy, the guest in whom is nothing hostile; Fire,
   the Priest of the call, the master of the house gives the
   healing forces that sustain the world, he gives us the hero-
   energy.

जुषाणो अग्ने प्रति हर्यं मे वचो विश्वानि विद्वान् वयुनानि सुक्रतो ।
घृतनिर्णिग्ब्रह्मणे गातुमेरय तव देवा अजनयन्नु व्रतम् ॥२॥

2. O Fire, take pleasure in my word, let thy joy respond to it,
   for thou knowest all discoveries of knowledge, O strong
   will! Robed in light, put out a path for the Word, the gods
   have begotten all according to thy law of works.

सप्त धामानि परियन्नमर्त्यो दाशद्दाशुषे सुकृते मामहस्व ।
सुवीरेण रयिणाग्ने स्वाभुवा यस्त आनट् समिधा तं जुषस्व ॥३॥

3. Encompassing the seven planes, O immortal, giving to the
   giver, to the doer of good deeds, grow great;[3] O Fire, with
   riches full of hero-strength crowding on him, accept the
   man who has come to thee with the fuel.

यज्ञस्य केतुं प्रथमं पुरोहितं हविष्मन्त ईळते सप्त वाजिनम् ।
शृण्वन्तमग्निं घृतपृष्ठमुक्षणं पृणन्तं देवं पृणते सुवीर्यम् ॥४॥

----
[1] Or, sages, extolled; [2] Or, greatnesses, [3] Or, exalt him;

4. The seven givers of the offering pray the lord of plenitudes,
the supreme Ray of intuition, the vicar of the sacrifice, Fire,
the Bull with the luminous back who hears our words, the
god who on him who satisfies him with gifts bestows fullness
of heroic might.

त्वं दूतः प्रथमो वरेण्यः स हूयमानो अमृताय मत्स्व ।

त्वां मर्जयन् मरुतो दाशुषो गृहे त्वां स्तोमेभिर्भृगवो वि रुरुचुः ॥५॥

5. Thou art the first and supreme messenger, as such when
thou art called be rapturous for immortality: thee the life-
powers make resplendent in the house of the giver, thee
with their lauds the flame-seers made to shine out wide.

इषं दुहन्त्सुदुघां विश्वधायसं यज्ञप्रिये यजमानाय सुक्रतो ।

अग्ने घृतस्नुस्त्रिरृंतानि दीद्यद्वर्तिर्यज्ञं परियन्त्सुक्रतूयसे ॥६॥

6. In one to whom sacrifice is dear, for the giver of sacrifice,
milking the force that is a good milch-cow, the force that
founds all, O strong will, O Fire, thrice pouring light, illumining the Truths, circling round our house and our sacrifice thou puttest forth thy strength of will.

त्वामिदस्या उषसो व्युष्टिषु दूतं कृण्वाना अयजन्त मानुषाः ।

त्वां देवा महयाय्याय वावृधुराज्यमग्ने निमृजन्तो अध्वरे ॥७॥

7. Thee, O Fire, making their messenger men have offered
sacrifice in the outshining of this dawn; thee the gods have
increased for their growing to greatness making bright the
oblation of light in the pilgrim-sacrifice.

नि त्वा वसिष्ठा अह्वन्त वाजिनं गृणन्तो अग्ने विदथेषु वेधसः ।

रायस्पोषं यजमानेषु धारय यूयं पात स्वस्तिभिः सदा नः ॥८॥

8. The Vasishthas called thee within them; full of plenitude,
voicing the Fire, ordainers of works in the discoverings of
knowledge; uphold the increasing of the riches in the doers
of the sacrifice, do you ever guard us with all kinds of weal.

AGNI PAVAKA

SUKTA 140

अग्ने तव श्रवो वयो महि भ्राजन्ते अर्चयो विभावसो ।
बृहद्भ्रानो शवसा वाजमुक्थ्यं दधासि दाशुषे कवे ॥१॥

1. O Fire, thy inspiration and thy growth and thy lights blaze
   in their greatness, O thou who shinest out with thy lustres;
   O great luminousness, O seer, thou foundest by thy strength
   for the giver a plenitude of utterance.

पावकवर्चाः शुक्रवर्चा अनूनवर्चा उदियर्षि भानुना ।
पुत्रो मातरा विचरन्नुपावसि पृणक्षि रोदसी उभे ॥२॥

2. Purifying is thy flaming energy, bright is thy energy, indefi-
   cient is thy energy as thou ascendest with thy light — a son
   thou rangest and protectest the Parents and thou joinest
   together earth and heaven.

ऊर्जो नपाज्जातवेदः सुशस्तिभिर्मन्दस्व धीतिभिर्हितः ।
त्वे इषः सं दधुर्भूरिवर्पसश्चित्रोतयो वामजाताः ॥३॥

3. O son of energy, O knower of all things born, well-founded
   rejoice in our perfect utterances and our thinkings; in thee
   they have joined together impelling forces of many forms,
   richly varied in their prospering, born to charm and beauty.

इरज्यन्नग्ने प्रयत्यस्व जन्तुभिरस्मे रायो अमर्त्य ।
स दर्शतस्य वपुषो वि राजसि पृणक्षि सानसि क्रतुम् ॥४॥

4. O immortal Fire, ruling over creatures born, spread in us
   thy Riches; thou art master of[1] thy body of vision and thou
   satest thy conquering will.

इष्कर्तारमध्वरस्य प्रचेतसं क्षयन्तं राधसो महः ।
रातिं वामस्य सुभगां महीमिषं दधासि सानसि रयिम् ॥५॥

---
[1] Or, thou shinest out from

5. A thinker, an arranger of sacrifice, a master of great achievement thou foundest a bounty of delight and a great and fortunate impulsion and conquering Riches.

ऋतावानं महिषं विश्वदर्शतमग्निं सुम्नाय दधिरे पुरो जनाः ।
श्रुत्कर्णं सप्रथस्तमं त्वा गिरा दैव्यं मानुषा युगा ॥६॥

6. Men have set in front this great Truth-possessing and all-seeing Fire for the bliss; thee who hast the ear that hears our words voice, wide-extended, one divine throughout the human generations.

MRIDIKA VASISHTHA

SUKTA 150

समिद्धश्चित् समिध्यसे देवेभ्यो हव्यवाहन ।
आदित्यै रुद्रैर्वसुभिर्न आ गहि मृळीकाय न आ गहि ॥१॥

1. Already kindled thou art kindled again for the gods, O carrier of the offering, come along with the sons of Aditi and with the Rudras and with the Shining Ones, come to us for grace.

इमं यज्ञमिदं वचो जुजुषाण उपागहि ।
मर्तासस्त्वा समिधान हवामहे मृळीकाय हवामहे ॥२॥

2. Accepting this sacrifice, this word come to us, we who are mortals call thee, O high-kindled Fire, we call thee for grace.

त्वामु जातवेदसं विश्ववारं गृणे धिया ।
अग्ने देवाँ आ वह नः प्रियव्रतान् मृळीकाय प्रियव्रतान् ॥३॥

3. Thee I voice with my thought, the knower of all things born, in whom are all desirable things, O Fire, bring to us the gods whose law of working is dear to us, dear to us for their grace.

अग्निर्देवो देवानामभवत् पुरोहितोऽग्निं मनुष्या ऋषयः समीधिरे ।
अग्निं महो धनसातावहं हुवे मृळीकं धनसातये ॥४॥

4. Fire, the god, became the vicar priest of the gods, Fire the
human Rishis have kindled, Fire I call in the conquest of the
riches of the vast, gracious for the conquest of the riches.

अग्निररात्रि भरद्वाजं गविष्ठिरं प्रावत्रः कण्वं त्रसदस्युमाहवे ।
अग्निं वसिष्ठो हवते पुरोहितो मृळीकाय पुरोहितः ॥५॥

5. Fire protected Atri and Bharadwaja and Gavishthira, protected for us Kanwa and Trasadasyu in the battle, Fire
Vasishtha the vicar priest calls, the vicar priest calls him for
grace.

KETU AGNEYA

SUKTA 156

अग्निं हिन्वन्तु नो धियः सप्तिमाशुमिवाजिषु ।
तेन जेष्म धनंधनम् ॥१॥

1. May our thoughts speed the Fire on his way like a swift
galloper in the battles, by him may we conquer every kind
of wealth.

यया गा आकरामहे सेनयाग्ने तवोत्या ।
तां नो हिन्व मघत्तये ॥२॥

2. The army by which we may make ours the Ray-Cows under
thy guard, that army send to us[1] for the getting of plenty.

आग्ने स्थूरं रयिं भर पृथुं गोमन्तमश्विनम् ।
अङ्धि खं वर्तया पणिम् ॥३॥

3. Bring to us, O Fire, a stable wealth of the Ray-Cows and the

---
[1] Or, speed for us

horses of power, reveal heaven, turn away from us the evil
Trafficker.

अग्ने नक्षत्रमजरमा सूर्यं रोहयो दिवि ।
दधज्ज्योतिर्जनेभ्यः ॥४॥

4.　O Fire, make to ascend the ageless traveller-star, the sun in
heaven upholding the Light for me.

अग्ने केतुर्विशामसि प्रेष्ठः श्रेष्ठ उपस्थसत् ।
बोधा स्तोत्रे वयो दधत् ॥५॥

5.　O Fire, thou art the ray of intuition in creatures, most dear,
most glorious, seated in the centre.[1] Awake, founding his
expansion who lauds thee.

VATSA AGNEYA

SUKTA 187

प्राग्नये वाचमीरय वृषभाय क्षितीनाम् ।
स नः पर्षदति द्विषः ॥१॥

1.　Send forth the word to the Fire, the bull of the worlds,[2] may
he carry us through beyond the hostile forces.

यः परस्याः परावतस्तिरो धन्वातिरोचते ।
स नः पर्षदति द्विषः ॥२॥

2.　He who shines beyond the desert across the supreme Beyond,
may he carry us through beyond the hostile forces.

यो रक्षांसि निजूर्वति वृषा शुक्रेण शोचिषा ।
स नः पर्षदति द्विषः ॥३॥

3.　He who destroys the Rakshasas, the bull with the brilliant

---

[1] Or, in the lap of the mother.　[2] Or, of the peoples,

light, may he carry us through beyond the hostile forces.

यो विश्वाभि विपश्यति भुवना सं च पश्यति ।
स नः पर्षदति द्विषः ॥४॥

4. He who looks upon all the worlds and sees them wholly, may he carry us through beyond the hostile forces.

यो अस्य पारे रजसः शुक्रो अग्निरजायत ।
स नः पर्षदति द्विषः ॥५॥

5. Fire who is born brilliant on the further shore of this world, may he carry us through beyond the hostile forces.

SAMVANANA ANGIRASA

SUKTA 191

संसमिद्युवसे वृषन्नग्ने विश्वान्यर्य आ ।
इळस्पदे समिध्यसे स नो वसून्या भर ॥१॥

1. O Fire, O strong one, as master thou unitest us with all things and art kindled high in the seat of revelation; do thou bring to us the Riches.

सं गच्छध्वं सं वदध्वं सं वो मनांसि जानताम् ।
देवा भागं यथा पूर्वे संजानाना उपासते ॥२॥

2. Join together, speak one word, let your minds arrive at one knowledge even as the ancient gods arriving at one knowledge partake each of his own portion.

समानो मन्त्रः समितिः समानी समानं मनः सह चित्तमेषाम् ।
समानं मन्त्रमभि मन्त्रये वः समानेन वो हविषा जुहोमि ॥३॥

3. Common Mantra have all these, a common gathering to union, one mind common to all, they are together in one

knowledge; I pronounce for you a common Mantra, I do sacrifice for you with a common offering.

समानी व आकूति: समाना हृदयानि व: ।
समानमस्तु वो मनो यथा व: सुसहासति ॥४॥

4. One and common be your aspiration, united your hearts, common to you be your mind, — so that close companionship may be yours.

SUPPLEMENT

The following notes and studies found among Sri Aurobindo's early manuscripts, evidently unrevised, are printed here for their intrinsic value.

The First Rik of the Rig-veda

Madhuchchhandas Vaishwamitra's Hymn to Agni written in the Gayatri metre in which the first verse runs in the *devabhāṣā*,

अग्निमीळे पुरोहितं यज्ञस्य देवमृत्विजम् ।
होतारं रत्नधातमम् ॥१॥

*Agnimiḷe purohitam yajñasya devamṛtvijam,
hotāram ratnadhātamam.*

and in English,

"Agni I adore, who stands before the Lord, the god who seeth Truth, the warrior, strong disposer of delight."

So the Rig-veda begins with an invocation to Agni, with the adoration of the pure, mighty and brilliant God. "Agni (he who excels and is mighty)," cries the Seer, "him I adore." Why Agni before all the other gods? Because it is he that stands before Yajna, the Divine Master of things; because he is the god whose burning eyes can gaze straight at Truth, at the *satyam*, the *vijñānam*, which is the Seer's own aim and desire and on which all Veda is based; because he is the warrior who wars down and removes all the crooked attractions of ignorance and limitation (*asmajjuhurāṇam enaḥ*) that stand persistently in the way of the Yogin; because as the vehicle of Tapas, the pure divine superconscious energy which flows from the concealed higher hemisphere of existence, (*avyakta parārdha*), he more than any develops and arranges Ananda, the divine delight. This is the signification of the verse.

Who is this Yajna and what is this Agni? Yajna, the Master of the Universe, is the universal living Intelligence who possesses and controls His world; Yajna is God. Agni also is a living intelligence that has gone forth, is *sṛṣṭa* from that Personality to do His work and represent His power; Agni is a God. The material sense sees neither God nor gods, neither Yajna nor Agni; it sees only the elements and the formations of the elements, material appearances and the movements in or of those appearances. It does not see Agni, it sees a fire; it does not see God, it sees the earth green and the sun flaming in heaven and is aware of the wind that blows and the waters that roll. So too it sees the body or appearance of a man, not the man himself; it sees the look or the gesture, but of the thought behind look or gesture it is not aware. Yet the man exists in the body and thought exists in the look or the gesture. So too Agni exists in the fire and God exists in the world. They also live outside of as well as in the fire and outside of as well as in the world.

How do they live in the fire or in the world? As the man lives in his body and as thought lives in the look or the gesture. The body is not the man in himself and the gesture is not the thought in itself; it is only the man in manifestation or the thought in manifestation. So too the fire is not Agni in himself but Agni in manifestation and the world is not God in Himself but God in manifestation. The man is not manifested only by his body, but also and much more perfectly by his work and action. Thought is not manifested only by look and gesture, but also and much more perfectly by action and speech. So too, Agni is not manifested only by fire, but also and much more perfectly by all workings in the world, — subtle as well as gross material, — of the principle of heat and brilliance and force; God is not manifested only by this material world, but also and much more perfectly by all movements and harmonies of the action of consciousness supporting and informing material appearances.

What then is Yajna in Himself and what is Agni in himself? Yajna is Being, Awareness and Bliss; He is Sat with Chit and Ananda, because Chit and Ananda are inevitable in Sat. When in His Being, Awareness and Bliss He conceals Guna or quality, He is *nirguṇa sat*, impersonal being with Awareness and Bliss either gathered up in Himself and passive, they *nivṛtta*, He also *nivṛtta* or working as a detached activity in His impersonal existence, they *pravṛtta*, He *nivṛtta*. Then He should not be called Yajna, because He is then aware of himself as the Watcher and not as the Lord of activity. But when in His being, He manifests Guna or quality He is *saguṇa sat*, personal being. Even then He may be *nivṛtta*, not related to His active awareness and bliss except as a Watcher of its detached activity; but He may also by His Shakti enter into their activity and possess and inform His universe (*praviśya, adhiṣṭhita*), He *pravṛtta*, they *pravṛtta*. It is then that He knows Himself as the Lord and is properly called Yajna. Not only is He called Yajna, but all action is called Yajna, and Yoga, by which alone the process of any action is possible, is also called Yajna. The material sacrifice of action is only one form of Yajna which, when man began to grow again material, took first a primary and then a unique importance and for the man of men stood for all action and all Yajna. But the Lord is the master of all our actions; for Him they are, to Him they are devoted, with or without knowledge (*avidhipūrvakam*) we are always offering our works to their Creator. Every action is, therefore, an offering to Him and the world is the altar of our life-long session of sacrifice. In this world-wide Karmakanda the mantras of the Veda are the teachers of right action (*ṛtam*) and it is therefore that the Veda speaks of Him as Yajna and not by another name.

This Yajna, who is the Saguna Sat, does not do works Himself, (that is by Sat), but He works in Himself, in Sat by His power of Chit, — by His Awareness. It is because He becomes aware of things in Himself by some process of Chit that things are created, brought out, that is to say, brought from His all-containing non-manifest Being into His manifest Self. Power and awareness, Chit and Shakti are one, and though we speak for convenience' sake of the Power of Chit, and call it Chichchhakti, yet the expression should really be understood not as the Power of Chit, but Chit that is Power. All awareness is power and all power conceals awareness. When Chit that is Power begins to work, then She manifests Herself as kinetic force, Tapas, and makes it the basis of all activity. For, because all power is Chit subjectively, therefore all power is objectively attended with light; but there are different kinds of light, because there are different manifestations of Chit. Seven rays have cast out this apparent world from the Eternal Luminousness which dwells like a Sun of ultimate being beyond its final annihilation, *ādityavat tamasaḥ parastāt*, and by these seven rays in their subjectivity the subjective world and by these seven rays in their objectivity the phenomenal world is manifested. Sat, Chit, Ananda, Vijnana, Manas, Prana, Annam are the sevenfold subjectivity of the Jyotirmaya Brahman. Prakasha, Agni, Vidyut, Jyoti, Tejas, Dosha and Chhaya are His sevenfold objectivity. Agni is the Master of the vehicle of Tapas. What is this vehicle of Tapas of which Agni is the master? It is fiery light. Agni is the light of Tapas, its vehicle and continent. The Master is known by the name of his kingdom. Strength, heat, brilliance, purity, mastery of knowledge and impartiality are his attributes. He is Yajna manifest as the Master of the light of Tapas, through whom all kinetic energy of consciousness, thought, feeling or action is manifested in this world which Yajna has made out of His own being. It is for this reason that he is said to stand before Yajna. He or Vidyut or Surya full of him is the blaze of light in which the Yogins see God with the divine vision. He is the instrument of that universal activity in which Yajna at once reveals and conceals His being.

Agni is a god — He is of the Devas, the shining ones, the Masters of light — the great cosmic gamesters, the lesser lords of the Lila, of which Yajna is the Maheshwara, our Almighty Lord. He is fire and unbound or binds himself only in play. He is inherently pure and he is not touched nor soiled by the impurities on which he feeds. He enjoys the play of good and evil and leads, raises or forces the evil towards goodness. He burns in order to purify. He destroys in order to save. When the body of the Sadhaka is burned up with the heat of the Tapas, it is Agni that is roaring and devouring and burning up in him the impurity and the obstructions. He is a dreadful, mighty, blissful, merciless and loving God, the kind and fierce helper of all who take refuge in his friendship.

Knowledge was born to Agni with his birth — therefore he is called Jatavedas.

ANALYSIS

अग्निम् (*agnim*)

Agni is a Devata, one of the most brilliant and powerful of the masters of the intelligent mind. Man, according to Vedic psychology, consists of seven principles, in which the Atman cases itself, — *annam*, gross matter; *prāṇa*, vital energy; *manas*, intelligent mind; *vijñānam*, ideal mind; *ānanda*, pure or essential bliss; *cit*, pure or essential awareness; *sat*, pure or essential being. In the present stage of our evolution ordinary humanity has developed *annam, prāṇa* and *manas* for habitual use; and well-developed men are able to use with power the *vijñānam* acting not in its own habitation, स्वे दमे (*sve dame*), nor in its own *rūpa*, but *vijñānam* in the mind and as reasoning faculty, *buddhi*; extraordinary men are able to aid the action of *manas* and *buddhi* proper by the *vijñānam* acting in the intelligent mind indeed and so out of its proper sphere, but in its own form as ideal consciousness — the combination of *mānasika* and *vaijñānika* action making what is called genius, *pratibhānam*, a reflection or luminous response in the mind to higher ideation; the Yogin goes beyond to the *vijñānam* itself or, if he is one of the greatest Rishis, like Yajnavalkya, to the *ānanda*. None in ordinary times go beyond the *ānanda* in the waking state, for the *cit* and *sat* are only attainable in *suṣupti*, because only the first five sheaths or *pañcakoṣas* are yet sufficiently developed to be visible except to the men of the Satya Yuga and even by them the two others are not perfectly seen. From the *vijñānam* to the *annam* is the *aparārdha* or lower part of Existence where Vidya is dominated by Avidya; from the *ānanda* to the *sat* is the *parārdha* or higher half in which Avidya is dominated by Vidya and there is no ignorance, pain or limitation.

In man as he is at present developed, the intelligent mind is the most important psychological faculty and it is with a view to the development of the intelligent mind to its highest purity and capacity that the hymns of the Veda are written. In this mind there are successively the following principles; *sūkṣma anna*, refinement of the gross *anna* out of which the physical part of the *manaḥkoṣa* or *sūkṣma deha* is made; *sūkṣma prāṇa*, the vital energy in the mind which acts in the *nāḍis* or nervous system of the *sūkṣma deha* and which is the agent of desire; *citta* or receptive consciousness, which receives all the impressions from without and within by *tāmasika* reaction, but, being *tāmasika*, does not make them evident to the *sāttvika* consciousness or intelligent awareness which we call knowledge, so that we remember with the *citta* everything noticed or unnoticed, but that knowledge is useless for our life owing to its lying enveloped in *tamas*; *hṛt* or the *rājasika* reaction to impressions which we call feeling or emotion, or, when it is habitual, character; *manas* or active definite sensational consciousness rendering impressions of all kinds into percept or concept by a *sāttvika* reaction called intelligence or thought which men share with the animals; *buddhi* or rational, imaginative and intellectually mnemonic faculty, observing, retaining, comparing, reasoning, comprehending, combining and creating, the amalgam of which functions we call intellect; *mānasa ānanda* or the pure bliss of existence manifesting through the impure mind, body and *prāṇa* impurely, i.e. mixed with pain of various kinds, but in itself pure, because disinterested, *ahaituka*; *mānasa tapas* or the pure will-power acting towards knowledge, feeling and deed, impurely through the impure mind, body and *prāṇa*, i.e. mixed with weakness, dull inertia and ignorance or error; but in itself pure because *ahaituka*, disinterested, without any ulterior purpose or preference that can interfere with truth of thought, act and emotion; *ahaituka sat* or pure realisation of existence, operating through the impure organs as *ahaṅkāra* and *bheda*, egoism and limitation, but in itself pure and aware of unity in difference, because disinterested, not attached to any particular form or name in manifestation; and finally, Atma or Self seated in mind. This Atman is Sat and Asat, positive and negative, *sadbrahman* and Shunyam Brahma; both positive and negative are contained in the *saḥ* or Vasudeva and *tat* or Parabrahman, and *saḥ* and *tat* are both the same. The *buddhi* again is divided into understanding (*medhā*), which merely uses the knowledge given by sensation and, like *manas, citta, hṛt* and *prāṇa*, is *adhīna, aniśa*, subject to sensation; reason or *buddhi* proper, (*smṛti* or *dhī*, also called *prajñā*), which is superior to sensation and contradicts it in the divided light of a higher knowledge; and direct *jñānam*, *satyam* or *sattvam* which is itself that light of higher knowledge. All these faculties have their own *devatās*, one or many, each with his *gaṇas* or subordinate ministers. The *jīva* or spirit using these faculties is called the *hansa*, he who flies or evolves upward; when he leaves the lower and rises to the *saccidānanda* in the mind, using *sat-cit* and *ānanda* only, and reposing in the *sadātman* or in Vasudeva, then he is called the Parabrahma, one who has gone or evolved to the highest in that stage of evolution. This is the fundamental knowledge underlying the Veda, the loss of which, aided by the corruption of the Nirukta, has led to the present confusion and degradation of its meaning.

Chandra is the devata of the *smṛti* or *prajñā*; Surya of the *satyam*; Indra of the understanding and *manas*; Vayu of the *sūkṣma prāṇa*; Mitra, Varuna, Aryama and Bhaga are the four masters of the emotional mind or character; Brihaspati of the *sahaituka cit* or Tapas of knowledge; Brahma of the *sahaituka sat*; Agni of the *sahaituka tapas* etc. This is only an indication. The various characteristics and energies of the gods are best developed by an examination of the Veda itself. The Gods strive to function perfectly for the Lord or Yajna, the Isha, Master of the *ādhāra* or sevenfold medium of manifestation; the Titans or Daityas, equally divine, try to upset this perfect functioning. Their office is to disturb that which is established in order to push man below or give him an opportunity of rising higher by breaking that which was good and harmonious in itself but imperfect, and in any case to render him dissatisfied with anything short of perfection and drive him continually to the Infinite, either by the *uttama gati* to Vasudeva or, if he will not have that, by the *adhama gati* to Prakriti. The Vedic Aryans sought to overcome the Daityas or Dasyus by the aid of the gods; afterwards the gods had themselves to be overcome in order that man might reach his goal.

Agni in the sphere of material energies is the master of *tejas*, the third and central material principle in the five known to Vedic science. Tejas itself is of seven kinds, *chāyā* or negative luminosity which is the principle of *annakoṣa*; twilight or *doṣa*, the basis of the *prāṇakoṣa* being *tejas* modified by *chāyā*; *tejas* proper or simple clarity and effulgence, dry light, which is the basis of the *manaḥkoṣa*; *jyotis* or solar light, brilliance which is the basis of the *vijñānakoṣa*; Agni or fiery light, which is the basis of the *citkoṣa*; *vidyut* or electrical illumination which is the basis of the *ānandakoṣa*; and *prakāśa* which is the basis of the *satkoṣa*. Each of the seven has its own appropriate energy; for the energy is the essential reality and the light only a characteristic accompaniment of the energy. Of all these Agni is the greatest in the world, greater even than *vidyut* — although the God of the Vaidyuta energy is Vishnu himself who is the Lord of the Ananda, the *vaidyuto mānavaḥ*, Electrical Man, of the Upanishads. In the *vijñāna*, Surya as well as Vishnu, is greater than Agni, but here he and Vishnu both work under the dominant energy of Agni and for the satisfaction of Indra, — Vishnu in the Upanishads being younger than Indra, — Upendra. Translated into the language of physics, this means that Agni, commanding as he does heat and cold, is the fundamental active energy behind all phenomenon of light and heat; the Sun is merely a reservoir of light and heat, the peculiar luminous blaze of the sun being only one form of *tejas* and what we call sunlight is composed of the static energy of *prakāśa* or essential light which is the basis of the *satkoṣa*, the electrical energy or *vaidyutam*, and the *tejas* of Agni modified by the nature of Surya and determining all other forms of light. The *prakāśa* and *vaidyutam* can only become active when they enter into Agni and work under the conditions of his being and Agni himself is the supplier of Surya; he creates *jyotis*, he creates *tejas*, he creates, negatively, *chāyā*. Right or wrong, this is the physics of the Veda. Translated into the language of psychology, it means that in the intelligent mind, which now predominates, neither *jñānam* nor *ananda* can be fully developed, though essentially superior to mind; not even Soma, the rational *buddhi*, can really govern; but it is Indra full of Soma, the understanding based on the senses and strengthened by the *buddhi*, who is supreme and for whose satisfaction Soma, Surya, Agni and even the supreme Vishnu work. The reason on which man prides himself, is merely a link in evolution from the *manas* to the *vijñānam* and must serve either the senses or the ideal cognition; if it has to work for itself it only leads to universal agnosticism, philosophic doubt and the arrest of all knowledge. It must not be thought that the Veda uses these names merely as personifications of psychological and physical forces; it regards these gods as realities standing behind the psychological and physical operations, since no energy can conduct itself, but all need some conscious centre or centres from or through which they proceed. A doubt will naturally arise, how Vishnu, the supreme Lord, can be the Upendra of the Vedas. The answer is that, whatever energy is of supreme importance at a particular stage of the evolution, is taken up by Vishnu-Virat as his especial care. We have seen that the Ananda is now highest in the developed evolution. Vishnu is therefore now pre-eminently the Lord of the Ananda and when he comes down into the material world he stands in the Sun as the supreme electrical force involved in Agni and evolving out of him, which is the physical counterpart of Ananda and without which no action in the world can proceed. He is not inferior, he only subordinates himself, pretending to serve, while really by service he commands. But *upendratva* is not the highest plane of Vishnu's manifestation, the *param dhāma*; rather it is a special function here of the lowest *dhāma*. *Upendratva* is not *viṣṇutva* but only one of its workings.

Agni, therefore, is master of *tejas*, especially fiery *tejas*, and the agent of the *sahaituka tapas* in the mind. In the language of modern psychology, this *sahaituka tapas* is Will in action, — not desire, but Will embracing desire and exceeding it. It is not even choice, wish or intention. Will, in the Vedic idea, is essentially knowledge taking the form of force. Agni, therefore, is purely mental force, necessary to all concentration. Once we perceive this Vedic conception, we realise the immense importance of Agni and are in a position to understand the hymn we are studying.

The word Agni is formed from the root अग् (*ag*) with the nominal addition नि (*ni*). The root अग् (*ag*) is itself a derivative root from the primitive अ (*a*), meaning "to be", of which traces are found in many languages. The ग् (*g*) gives an idea of force and अग् (*ag*), therefore, means to exist in force, pre-eminently — to be splendid, strong, excellent and Agni means mighty, supreme, splendid, forceful, bright. We find the same root in the Greek *agathos*, good, meaning originally, strong, noble, brave;

agan, excessively; *agō*, I lead; Latin *ago*, *age*; *aglaos* (Gr.), bright, the names, *Agis*, *Agamemnōn*, and in the Sanskrit अग्र (*agra*), अगस्ति (*agasti*). It is interchangeable with its brother root अज् (*aj*), from which some of the meanings of *agō* (Gr.) are derived. It seems also to have meant to love, from the idea of embracing, cf. Greek *agapē*, but in this sense the old Sanskrit preferred अङ्ग् (*aṅg*). For the connection between the two roots, अग्, अङ्ग् (*ag*, *aṅg*), cf. अङ्गति (*aṅgati*), in the sense of fire, अङ्गिराः (*aṅgirāḥ*), as a name of Agni, अङ्गारः (*aṅgāraḥ*), a live coal.

ईळे (*iḷe*)

The root like all simple Sanskrit roots has two forms ईळ् (*iḷ*) and ईळ् (*il*). The original root was इल् (*il*) to love, embrace, flatter, praise, adore; the cerebral ळ् (*ḷ*) is a later form, — a dialectical peculiarity belonging to some of the dominant races of the Dwapara Yuga, which established itself for a time but could not hold its own and either resolved itself back into ल् (*l*) or was farther transformed into the soft cerebral ड् (*ḍ*) with which it was interchangeable. So we have the form ईड् (*iḍ*) in precisely the same sense. There is no idea necessarily involved of adoration to a superior, the dominant ideas being love, praise and desire. The meaning here is not "praise" or "worship", but "desire", "yearn for".

पुरोहितम् (*purohitam*)

The words are two and not one. The sense of "priest, purohita", put on the compound word in the later ceremonial interpretation of the Veda, is entirely absent in this hymn. The word पुरः (*puraḥ*) was originally the genitive of पुर् (*pur*) used adverbially. पुर् (*pur*) meant door, gate, front, wall; afterwards, house or city; cf. the Greek *pulē*, a gate, *pulos*, a walled city or fort, *polis*, a city; so in front. हितम् (*hitam*) is the participial adjective from the root हि (*hi*) in the sense of to cast down, throw down, plant, place, which appears in Greek as *cheō*, I pour; हयाः (*hayāḥ*), पुरोहितम् (*purohitam*) means therefore set or planted before.

यज्ञस्य (*yajñasya*)

The word यज्ञ (*yajña*) is of supreme importance in the Veda.

In the ceremonial interpretation यज्ञ (*yajña*) is always understood as sacrifice and no other conception admitted. The Veda cannot be understood as the source of all Indian spirituality and divine knowledge, if this materialistic interpretation is accepted. In reality यज्ञ (*yajña*) is the name of the supreme Lord Vishnu himself; it also means धर्म (*dharma*) or योग (*yoga*) and by a later preference of meaning it came to signify sacrifice, because sacrifice in the later Dwapara Yuga became the one dharma and yoga which dominated and more and more tended to replace all others. It is necessary to recover the proper meaning of this important word by Nirukta, and, in order to do it, to lay down briefly the principle of Nirukta.

The Sanskrit language is the *devabhāṣā* or original language spoken by men in Uttara Meru at the beginning of the Manwantara; but in its purity it is not the Sanskrit of the Dwapara or the Kali, it is the language of the Satya Yuga based on the true and perfect relation of *vāk* and *artha*. Everyone of its vowels and consonants has a particular and inalienable force which exists by the nature of things and not by development or human choice; these are the fundamental sounds which lie at the basis of the Tantric *bījamantras* and constitute the efficacy of the mantra itself. Every vowel and every consonant in the original language had certain primary meanings which arose out of this essential Shakti or force and were the basis of other derivative meanings. By combination with the vowels, the consonants, and, without any combination, the vowels themselves formed a number of primary roots, out of which secondary roots were developed by the addition of other consonants. All words were formed from these roots, simple words by the addition again of pure or mixed vowel and consonant terminations with or without modification of the root and more complex words by the principle of composition. This language increasingly corrupted in sense and sound becomes the later Sanskrit of the Treta, Dwapara and Kali Yuga, being sometimes partly purified and again corrupted and again partly purified so that it never loses all apparent relation to its original form and structure. Every other language, however remote, is a corruption formed by detrition and perversion of the original language into a Prakrit or the Prakrit of a Prakrit and so on to

increasing stages of impurity. The superior purity of the Indian
language is the reason of its being called the Sanskrit and not
given any local name, its basis being universal and eternal; and it
is always a rediscovery of the Sanskrit tongue as the primary
language that prepares first for a true understanding of human
language and, secondly, for a fresh purification of Sanskrit
itself.

This particular root यज् (*yaj*) from which यज्ञ (*yajña*) is formed
is a secondary root on the base of the consonant य् (*y*), the Gunas
of which are strength and tenderness applied to action, motion,
formation and contact. The primary roots are य (*ya*), यि (*yi*)
and यु (*yu*) with their lengthened forms या (*yā*), यी (*yī*) and यू (*yū*)
— the original *devabhāṣā* recognising only three pure vowels,
the rest being either modified or mixed vowels. The primary
root of यज् (*yaj*) is य (*ya*) which means essentially to go quietly
and persistently, to act or apply oneself quietly and with force
and persistence, to master (knowledge or anything or person)
by steady application, to come or bring into contact with gently
or lovingly and effectively, to form or express clearly etc. The first
sense appears, with its colour rubbed out, in the lengthened form
या (*yā*), in यक्ष् (*yakṣ*), in one of the meanings of यम् (*yam*) etc.;
the second in यत् (*yat*) and यश् (*yaś*), the third in यज् (*yaj*), यम् (*yam*)
and यन्त्र् (*yantr*); the fourth in यज् (*yaj*) and याच् (*yāc*) which is
originally a causal of यच् (*yac*) to give, now lost except in certain
conjugational forms of यम् (*yam*), the fifth in one of the meanings
of यम् (*yam*) to show, etc. Besides यच् (*yac*), there are other lost
roots यल् (*yal*) to seek after, love, desire (Greek *iallō*), यश् (*yaś*)
with a similar meaning, from which we have यशः (*yaśaḥ*) which
was originally an adjective meaning lovely, charming, and a
noun meaning sometimes an object of love or pursuit, sometimes
beauty, ambition, fame etc., or love itself, favour, partiality.
This is a brief example of the method followed by the original
tongue as it can now be observed with its distinctions and shades
confused and the colours of the words expunged.

In the root यज् (*yaj*) the force of the consonant ज् (*j*) determines the meaning. Its essential nature is swiftness, decisiveness,
rapid brilliance, and restlessness. It has therefore a frequentative
and intensive force. It means to love habitually and fervently,

so to worship, to adore. It means to give freely, wholly or continuously; from these shades comes the meaning of sacrifice. It
means to master thoroughly, habitually, with a continual repetition of the act of mastery; the word यत् (*yat*) means endeavour,
but यज् (*yaj*) can never have meant endeavour, it is too decisive
and triumphant and must imply possession or mastery, action
sense of its result. It means therefore to rule, govern, order,
possess. That is why यज्ञ (*yajña*) is Vishnu, in the sense of the
Almighty Ruler, the Master of man's action, body, thought,
the supreme Lord ruling from the higher faculty in man, the
parārdha or Sachchidananda.

यज्ञ (*yajña*) is formed by the addition of न (*na*), a nominal
suffix which has the sense of action. It may be adjectival or nominal. It may convey the actor, the instrument, the manner or
the sufferer of the action. यज्ञ: (*yajñaḥ*) therefore came to mean,
he who rules, the governor or master; loving, adoring, also he
who is loved; the means of mastery and so Yoga, in its processes,
not in its realisations; the manner of mastery and so dharma, a
rule of action or self-government; adoration or an act of worship, though this sense was usually kept for यजु: (*yajuḥ*), giving,
offering, sacrifice. As the name of Vishnu it meant, predomi-
nantly, the Master who directs, compels and governs; but the
idea of the Lover and Beloved, the Giver and the object of all
actions, ritual and worship of all Karma also entered into it
in the associations of the worshipper and sometimes became
prominent.

The Vishnu Purana tells us that Vishnu in the Satya Yuga
incarnates as Yajna, in the Treta as the conqueror and king, in
the Dwapara as Vyasa, the compiler, codifier and law-giver. It
is not meant that He incarnates as sacrifice. The Satya Yuga is
the age of human perfection when a harmonious order is established, the perfect or *catuṣpād dharma* whose maintenance de-
pends on the full and universal possession of Yoga or direct relation to God and that again on the continual presence of incarnate Vishnu as the Adored, the Master and centre of Dharma
and Yoga. The *catuṣpād dharma* is the perfect harmony of the four
Dharmas, Brahmanyam, Kshatram, Vaishyam and Shaudram;
for this reason separate castes do not exist in the Satya Yuga. In

the Treta the Brahmanyam begins to fail, but remains as a subordinate force to help the Kshatram which then governs humanity. Mankind is maintained no longer by *vīryam* or Tapas easily sustained by inherent *brahmajñānam*, but by *vīryam* or Tapas sustaining the *brahmajñānam* with some difficulty and preventing its collapse. Vishnu incarnates as the Kshatriya, the incarnate centre of *vīryam* and Tapas. In the Dwapara, the Brahmanyam farther fails and turns into mere knowledge or intellectuality, the Kshatram becomes a subordinate force supporting the Vaishyam which has its turn of supremacy. The main qualities of the Vaishya are *kauśalam*, order and method, and therefore the Dwapara is the age of codification, ritual, Shastra, external appliances to maintain the failing internal spirituality; *dānam*, and therefore hospitality, liberality, the sacrifice and *dakṣinā* begin to swallow up other Dharmas — it is the *Yuga Yajñiya,* — the age of sacrifice; *bhoga*, and therefore the Veda is used for procuring enjoyment, in this world and the next, *bhogaiśvaryagatim prati*. Vishnu incarnates as the law-giver, ritualist and *śāstrakāra* to preserve the knowledge and practice of the Dharma by the aid of the intellect and *abhyāsa*, customary practice based on intellectual knowledge. In the Kali all breaks down except love and service, the Dharma of the Shudra by which humanity is maintained and from time to time purified; for the *jñānam* breaks down and is replaced by worldly, practical reason, the *vīryam* breaks down and is replaced by lazy mechanical appliances for getting things done lifelessly with the least trouble, *dāna*, *yajña* and *śastra* break down and are replaced by calculated liberality, empty ritual and tamasic social forms and etiquette. Love is brought in by the Avatars to break down these dead forms in order that the world may be rejuvenated and a new order and a new Satya Yuga emerge, when the Lord will again incarnate as Yajna, the supreme Vishnu in full manifestation of the *catuṣpād dharma*, knowledge, power, enjoyment and love.

It has been said that Vishnu in our present stage of evolution is pre-eminently the Lord of Ananda, but he is also the *sanmaya brahman* and the *tapomaya*. It is as the *sanmaya* that He is Yajna — Sat containing in it the Chit or Tapas and the Ananda. It must be remembered that while in the *aparārdha* we envisage

Brahman through thought, feeling, action etc., in the *parārdha* we envisage him through essential realisation superior to thought, feeling and action. In the Ananda we realise essential delight; in the Chit, essential energy, intelligence and will; in the Sat, essential truth or be-ness. The Sat is therefore called the *mahā-satyam* and *mahābrahman*, the highest truth in the manifestation, out of which everything proceeds. It is by this *mahāsatyam* — distinguished from ordinary *satyam* or *kāraṇam* called objectively *mahat* and subjectively *vijñānam*, the fourth of the seven *bhūmis*, — that Vishnu as Yajna supports the dharma and yoga in the Satya Yuga. He is the *sadbrahman* in manifestation. We shall see when we deal with the word ऋत्विजम् (*ṛtvijam*), in what sense Agni stands before the Lord.

देवम् (*devam*)

A god — from the secondary root दिव् (*div*) to flash, gleam, vibrate, play. On the basis of the consonant द् (*d*) of which the Gunas are force, heavy violence, density, dense penetration, dense movement, we get दा (*dā*) to cut, दि (*di*) to vibrate and दु (*du*) to trouble and from दि (*di*) we get द्यु (*dyu*) and दिव् (*div*) or दीव् (*dīv*) meaning to vibrate shiningly, gleam, scintillate or play. The Devas are those who play in light, — their proper home is in the *vijñānam*, महर्लोक (*maharloka*), *kāraṇa jagat*, where matter is *jyotirmaya* and all things luminous, स्वेन धाम्ना (*svena dhāmnā*), by their own inherent lustre, and where life is an ordered Lila or play. Therefore when the Bhagawata speaks of the power of seeing the life of the Gods in Swarga, it calls that particular siddhi देवक्रीडानुदर्शनम् (*devakrīḍānudarśanam*), watching the sports of the gods, because all life is to them a sport or Lila. The Gods, however, dwell for us in the lower Swarloka, i.e., Chandraloka of which the summit is Kailasa and the basis Swarga with Pitriloka just above Swarga. Nevertheless even there they keep their *jyotirmaya* and *līlāmaya* nature, their luminous bodies and worlds of self-existent bliss free from death and care.

ऋत्विजम् (*ṛtvijam*)

This word is taken in the ceremonial interpretation of the

Veda in the later sense of Ritwik, a sacrificial priest, and it is explained by separating as ऋतु+इज् (*rtu+ij*), one who sacrifices seasonably. In reality, ऋत्विज् (*rtvij*) is a very old word compounded in ancient Sanskrit before the creation of the modern rules of Sandhi, and is composed of ऋत् (*rt*), truth, and विज् (*vij*), ecstasy or ecstatic. It means one who has the ecstasy of the truth or सत्यम् (*satyam*).

ऋत् (*rt*) is an abstract noun formed from the root ऋ (*r*) whose essential meaning was to vibrate, shake, dart, go straight; and its derivate meanings to reach, acquire, or else attack, hurt, injure, or to be erect, rise or raise; to shine; to think, realise truth, etc. From the sense of going straight in the secondary verb ऋज् (*rj*) with its adjective ऋजु (*rju*), straight, cf. Latin *rego, rectus*; ऋत (*rta*) straight, right, true; ऋतम् (*rtam*), truth, right, established law or custom; — सत्यम् (*satyam*) applied to the Supreme Brahman as the *satyam* or *mahākāraṇam*; — ऋतु (*rtu*), rule, fixed order, fixed time or season; ऋषि (*rṣi*), a thinker, direct seer of truth, cf. Latin *reor*, I think, *ratio*, method, order, reason, proposition, etc. The obsolete word ऋत् (*rt*) meant directness, truth, law, rule, thought, सत्यम् (*satyam*).

विज् (*vij*) is noun or adjective from the verb विज् (*vij*) meaning to shake, be troubled, excited, tremble, to be ecstatic, joyous, full of rapture, felicity or ecstatic energy, cf. Latin *vigeo* and *vigor*, from which comes the English vigour. ऋत्विज् (*rtvij*) is therefore one who is ecstatic with the fullness of the truth or सत्यम् (*satyam*). Agni, it has been pointed out, is the god of the Tapas or energy at work disinterestedly on the intellectual plane, one of the higher gods working on the lower level in the service of the lower deity Indra. He proceeds straight from the *cit*, which, when active, is known as *mahātapas* or *cicchakti*, the energy of the essential intelligence in the *sadbrahman*, Yajna or Vishnu. The Shakti begins creation by *kṣobha* or ecstatic vibration in the calm *sadātman* and this ecstatic vibration or विज् (*vij*), वेग: (*vegaḥ*), goes out as speed, force, heat, तप: (*tapaḥ*), or अग्नि (*agni*), the basis of life and existence. This Tapas born of the *cicchakti*, (Shakti, Devi, Kali, Prakriti) is full of the ecstatic movement of the *sat* or *mahāsatyam* manifesting itself. For this reason Agni is called ऋत्विज् (*rtvij*), vibrating ecstatic with the सत्यम् (*satyam*).

For the same reason he is called जातवेदाः (*jātavedāḥ*), he from whom the higher knowledge is born, because he holds in himself the Veda or *satyam* and manifests it; Tapas is the basis of all concentration of Chit, awareness (the *samyama* of Patanjali) and it is by *samyama* or concentration of awareness either on the object of the awareness (*rājayoga*) or on itself (*jñānayoga* and *adhyātmayoga*) that *satyam* and *veda* become directly self-manifest and luminous to the Yogin. Without the *samyama* no Yoga is possible, no effective action of any kind is possible. When Brahma turned his mind to creation, it was the cry of "Tapas, Tapas" that was heard on the waters of the *kāraṇa samudra* (*mahākāraṇam* or *sadbrahman*). The immense importance of Agni as the *ṛtvij* to the Yogin, therefore, becomes manifest; and it is also clear why he is पुरोहितं यज्ञस्य (*purohitaṁ yajñasya*) for it is the Tapas which stands before the *satyam*, which we reach before we can get the Sat. It is the *cicchakti* which takes us to the Sat, — the Devi, Shakti or Kali who brings us to Brahman, to Vasudeva, and Agni, her especial agent for Tapas in the mind, is therefore a special intermediary between us and Yajna, who, as has been seen, is Vishnu, Vasudeva or Brahman, in the Sachchidananda or *parārdha* on the intellectual plane, which is all man in the average has yet reached. This is the reason why Agni was so great a god to the Rishi. To mere sacrificers and ritualists he was great only as the god of fire indispensable in all their ritual, but to the Yogin he has a much greater importance, as great as that of Surya, the lord of illumination, and Soma, the lord of Amrita. He was one of the most indispensable helpers in the processes which the Veda illumines and assists.

होतारम् (*hotāram*)

Here is another word of great importance in the Veda. In all existing interpretations of the Veda *hotā* is interpreted as the priest who offers the libation, हविः (*haviḥ*) as the libation and हु (*hu*) in the sense of pouring the offering. So fixed is this notion born of the predomination through several millenniums of the ceremonial meanings attached to all the important words of the Veda, that any other rendering would be deemed impossible.

But in the original Veda होता (*hotā*) did not mean a sacrificial priest, nor हविः (*haviḥ*) an offering. Agni may by a metaphorical figure be called a *purohita* of the sacrifice though the figure will not have any very great Sanskritic exactness, but he can in no sense be the one who pours the libation. He devours the libation, he does not offer or pour it. Hota, therefore, must have some other signification which, without outraging fact and commonsense, can be applied to Agni.

The root हु (*hu*), like the roots हा (*hā*) and हि (*hi*), is based on the consonant ह् (*h*), the essential Gunas of which are aggression, violent action, impetuosity, loud breathing and so challenge, summons etc. This verb हु (*hu*) originally like ह (*ha*), हा (*hā*) and हि (*hi*) meant to strike or throw down, attack, slay, the vowel उ (*u*) adding a sense of pervasiveness which easily brought the idea of battle. We find, therefore, that this root meant to attack, fight, as in आहवः (*āhavaḥ*), battle; to call, shout, summons, as in ह्वे (*hve*), originally हवे (*have*) etc.; to throw, overthrow, destroy; to throw, pour, offer. From the last sense it came to have its more modern meaning. The transference from the sense of battle to the sense of sacrifice is paralleled by the Greek word *machē*, battle, which is certainly the same as the Sanskrit मखः (*makhaḥ*), sacrifice. It must be remembered that the Yoga was to the old Aryans a battle between the Devas and Daityas, the gods being the warriors who fought the Daityas for man and were made strong and victorious by the क्रिया (*kriyā*) or effective practices of Yoga; the Daityas being the Dasyus or enemies of Yajna and Yoga. This will become clearer and clearer as we proceed. This view of life as well as Yoga, which is only the sublimation of life, as a struggle between the Devas and Daityas is one of the most fundamental ideas of Veda, Purana, Tantra and every practical system in Hinduism. Agni is *par excellence* the warrior whom the Daityas must dread, because he is full of the *ahaituka tapas*, against which, if properly used and supported by the Yajamana, the Yogin, no evil force can prevail. The *ahaituka tapas* destroys them all. It is the mighty, effective and fighting force which once called in prepares perfect *siddhi* and an almost omnipotent control over our nature and our surroundings. Even when *aśuddha*, impure, Tapas fights the enemy, *tamas*, when *śuddha,* when the very action of Agni, it brings *vīryam,* it brings *jñānam,* it brings *ānanda,* it brings *mukti.* होतारम् *(hotāram)* means therefore the warrior, the destroyer of the Daityas, *agni jātavedas; havis* and *hava* mean battle or strength in violent action, हु *(hu)* to fight.

रत्नधातमम् *(ratnadhātamam)*

Superlative of रत्नधा *(ratnadhā),* joy-giving, the disposer of delight. We have the root रत् *(rat)* as a derivative from the primary root र *(ra).* Three roots र *(ra),* रि *(ri),* रु *(ru)* are themselves variations of the elemental *śabda* र् *(r),* whose essential significance is tremulous continual vibration. र *(ra)* means essentially to vibrate, shake, quiver abroad, the vowel अ *(a)* conveying essentially absoluteness, wideness, want of limitation as opposed to the vowel इ *(i)* which gives a sense of relation and direction to a given point. From this essential sense come the derivative meanings, to play, to shine; as in रतम् *(ratam),* रत्न *(ratna)* a jewel, रति: *(ratiḥ),* रम् *(ram),* रञ्ज् *(rañj),* रजतम् *(rajatam)* silver, रज: *(rajaḥ)* dust, रजनी *(rajanī),* रात्रि *(rātri)* night etc. From the former meaning there comes the sense, to please, delight, love, adore, etc., as in रामा *(rāmā),* रामः *(rāmaḥ),* राध् *(rādh),* रज् *(raj),* रज: *(rajaḥ),* रजोगुण *(rajoguṇa),* etc. The word रत्न *(ratna)* in ancient Sanskrit from the root रत् *(rat),* had two sets of senses, delight, Ananda, pleasure, play, sexual intercourse, a thing of delight, mistress, etc., and splendour, light, lustre, brilliance, a brilliant, a jewel, — the modern sense. At first sight it would seem that lustre, brilliance is more appropriate to Agni, and it would apply well to the warrior who destroys the darkness of the mind, but the central idea of the hymn is not Agni as the master of light, — that is Surya, — but as the master of force, Tapas, which is the source out of which comes delight. The three terms of the *parārdha* are *sat, cit,* and *ānanda.* In *sat cit* abides and emerges from *sat.* As soon as it emerges, it generates the energy of *cicchakti* which plays throughout the universe; this play, रत्न *(ratna),* is *ānanda* in *cit* and it emerges from *cit.* All Tapas therefore generates *ānanda,* and the pure *sahaituka tapas* generates pure *sahaituka ānanda* which being universal, self-existent and by its nature incapable of any admixture of sorrow, is the most sure, wide and intense. Therefore Agni is most joy-giving, a great disposer of delight. The word घा (*dhā*) means to set, create, give, arrange; here it is the old Aryan substantive expressing the agent and often used adjectivally.

Riks of Madhuchchhandas

TRANSLATION AND NOTES : I.1.1-5

अग्निमीळे पुरोहितं यज्ञस्य देवमृत्विजम् ।
होतारं रत्नधातमम् ॥१॥

Agnimīḷe purohitam yajñasya devamṛtvijam,
hotāram ratnadhātamam.

Rik 1. ईळे (*iḷe*): to praise, in the ritualistic sense; but as a
secondary root of ई (*ī*) ईळ् (*iḷ*) meant to seek, go towards, attain,
desire, adore, pray, ask for (cf. मातरमन्नमैट्ट, *mātaramannamaiṭṭa,*
III. 48. 3). The former senses have been lost and only "to desire",
"pray" or "ask for" are left in later Sanskrit; but the other
senses must have existed, as the idea of desiring, asking is never
a primary sense of any root, but derived figuratively from
the physical sense "to go, seek, approach". We may therefore
render ईळे (*iḷe*), either "seek", "desire", "adore" or "pray to".

पुरोहितम् (*purohitam*): Sayana — "Purohita", or else "placed
in the front of the sacrifice as the *āhavanīya* fire". The Purohita
of the Veda is the representative power in the sacrifice who stands
in front of the consciousness and the action and conducts it.
This is always the force of the "placing in front" which is so
common an idea in the hymns. Normally, this place belongs to
Agni who leads the sacrifice.

देवम् (*devam*): Sayana — दानादिगुणयुक्तम् (*dānādiguṇayuktam*).
Sayana's dealing with the word Deva is peculiar. Sometimes
he renders it simply "god", sometimes he gives it some root
values, दान (*dāna*), देवन (*devana*), sometimes he makes it mean
the priest. There is not a single passage in the Veda where the
ordinary sense "god", "divine being" does not give a clear and
sufficient and the best sense. No doubt, the Vedic poets never
left out of sight its root meaning: the gods are the Shining Ones,
the Lords of Light as are the Dasyus the Dark or Black Ones, the
sons of Darkness.

ऋत्विजम् (*ṛtvijam*): "He who sacrifices at the right season" is the outward or ritualistic sense; but ऋतु (*ṛtu*), in the Veda, as we shall see, is the order of the truth, its arranged law, time, circumstance. Agni is the representative priest who sacrifices according to the law, order, season of the Ritam.

होतारम् (*hotāram*): Sayana — "because he utters the Mantra" and he quotes अहं होता स्तौमि (*aham hotā staumi*); but he renders it sometimes आह्वाता (*āhvātā*), sometimes होमनिष्पादकः (*homaniṣpādakaḥ*), sometimes gives us the choice. Undoubtedly, होता (*hotā*) is the priest of the oblation, who gives the offering, हु (*hu*) to offer, and not हू (*hū*) to call. The hymn was an attendant circumstance of the offering, therefore the invocation or praise might also fall to the part of the होता (*hotā*); but in the system of the Rig-veda the proper name for the reciter of the Mantra is ब्रह्मा (*brahmā*). Agni is the होतृ (*hotṛ*), Brihaspati the ब्रह्मा (*brahmā*).

रत्न (*ratna*): Sayana — यागफलरूपाणां रत्नानामतिशयेन धारयितारं पोषयितारं वा (*yāgaphalarūpāṇām ratnānāmatiśayena dhārayitāram poṣayitāram vā*). धा (*dhā*) to hold and to nourish (cf. धात्री, *dhātrī*, nurse). But in other passages he takes रत्नं=रमणीयं धनं (*ratnam =ramaṇīyam dhanam*) which shows that he took it to mean literally "that which is delightful" and made it=wealth, as he makes द्युम्न (*dyumna*)=that which is shining, and renders it "wealth". We need not follow him. रत्नं (*ratnam*) means "delight" or Ananda (cf. रम्, रतिः, रण्, रण्व, राध्, रञ्ज्, *ram, ratiḥ, raṇ, raṇva, rādh, rañj*, etc.), just as द्युम्नम् (*dyumnam*) means "light". धा (*dhā*) is to hold or else to place.

Translation: RITUALISTIC

I praise Agni, the Purohita[1] of the sacrifice, the god,[2] the Ritwik, the Hota who holds very much wealth.

Translation: PSYCHOLOGICAL

I seek the God-Will, the Priest set in front of our sacrifice, the divine offerer who sacrifices in the order of the truth, who disposes utterly the delight.

[1] Or, who is set in front   [2] Or, bountiful,

अग्निः पूर्वेभिर्ऋषिभिरीड्यो नूतनैरुत ।
स देवाँ एह वक्षति ॥२॥

Agniḥ pūrvebhirṛṣibhirīḍyo nūtanairuta,
sa devān eha vakṣati.

Rik 2. ऋषिः (*ṛṣiḥ*): lit. "seeker, attainer", so "knower", from ऋष् (*ṛṣ*) to go. इह देवान् (*iha devān*): the divine powers into the mortal life and mortal being. वक्षति (*vakṣati*)=वह्+स+ति (*vah+sa +ti*). This स (*sa*) seems to have been either frequentative in force, "he constantly or habitually bears", or intensive, "he entirely bears", or desiderative, "he wills or intends to bear". From the latter sense we have the use of स् (*s*) for the future, cf. नी (*nī*), नेष्यामि (*neṣyāmi*), Gr. *luō*, I loose, *lusō*, I shall loose, and English, I will go, where the desiderative "will=wish, intend" has acquired the sense of a simple future.

Translation:

The God-Will is desirable as to the ancient sages, so to the new, for it is he that bringeth here the gods.

अग्निना रयिमश्नवत् पोषमेव दिवेदिवे ।
यशसं वीरवत्तमम् ॥३॥

Agninā rayimaśnavat poṣameva divedive,
yaśasam vīravattamam.

Rik 3. अश्नवत् (*aśnavat*): Sayana — प्राप्नोति (*prāpnoti*), but the form gives a certain semi-imperative sense or the idea of a rule of action or law of occurrence. "He shall attain." अश् (*aś*) to possess, have, obtain, enjoy; Greek *echō*, I have.

यशसं (*yaśasam*): Sayana — दानादिना यशोयुक्तं (*dānādinā yaśoyuk-tam*), so "famous"; but "a famous and men-fullest wealth" seems an absurd way of talking. यश् (*yaś*) is literally to go, strive towards, attain; here it means success, fame; also from another sense "to shine"="splendour"; it is connected in sense with या (*yā*), यत्

(*yat*), यस् (*yas*). We have in the Veda रयि (*rayi*), wealth or felicity, often described as expansive, pervading, breaking down
obstacles on the way. There is therefore no inappropriateness
or violence in rendering it "enjoyment that attains" or "victorious riches".

बीरवत्तमम् (*vīravattamam*): Sayana — अतिशयेन पुत्रभृत्यादिबीरपुरुषोपेतम्
(*atiśayena putrabhṛtyādivīrapuruṣopetam*). It is absurd to take
बीर=पुत्र (*vīra=putra*) as Sayana does; it means "men, heroes,
strengths" and is often the equivalent of नृ (*nṛ*) which is never
used for servants in the Rig-veda.

रयिम् (*rayim*): There are two words, रयि (*rayi*) from रि (*ri*)
to go and रयि (rayi) from रि (*ri*) to attain, enjoy. The latter means
"enjoyment" or the things enjoyed, "felicity, prosperity, riches".
The former sense is found in the Upanishad where रयि (*rayi*),
movement or matter is opposed to प्राण (*prāṇa*), life.

Translation: RITUALISTIC

By Agni one attains a wealth daily increasing, famous and
most full of men.

Translation: PSYCHOLOGICAL

By the God-Will one shall enjoy a felicity that shall increase
day by day, victorious, fullest of hero-powers.

अग्ने यं यज्ञमध्वरं विश्वतः परिभूरसि ।
स इद् देवेषु गच्छति ॥४॥

Agne yam yajñamadhvaram viśvataḥ paribhūrasi,
sa id deveṣu gacchati.

Rik 4. अध्वरम् (*adhvaram*): Sayana —हिंसारहितम् (*himsārahitam*),
because it is not destroyed by the Rakshasas, from अ (*a*) priva-
tive+dhvara (ध्वृ, *dhvṛ* to hurt). But अध्वर (*adhvara*) is used by
itself to mean sacrifice and it is quite impossible that the word
"unhurt" used by itself can have come to mean sacrifice. It must

express some essential quality of the sacrifice or it could not thus
have been singled out. It is a notable fact that अध्वर (*adhvara*)
is continually used for the sacrifice when there is a question of
the sacrifice travelling or moving on the path towards the gods,
as here. I therefore take अध्वर (*adhvara*) from an original root अध्
(*adh*) to move and connect it with अध्वन् (*adhvan*), path; it means
the moving or travelling sacrifice, the sacrifice regarded as a
pilgrimage of the soul or its gifts towards the gods.

Translation: RITUALISTIC

O Agni, the unhurt sacrifice that thou encompassest on all
sides, that goes to the gods.

Translation: PSYCHOLOGICAL

O God-Will, whatsoever sacrifice in the path thou encompassest with thy being on every side, that indeed arrives to
the gods.

अग्निर्होता कविक्रतुः सत्यश्चित्रश्रवस्तमः ।
देवो देवेभिरा गमत् ॥५॥

Agnirhotā kavikratuḥ satyaścitraśravastamaḥ,
devo devebhirā gamat.

Rik 5. कविक्रतुः (*kavikratuḥ*): Sayana takes कवि (*kavi*) here=
क्रान्त (*krānta*) and क्रतुः (*kratuḥ*)=either knowledge or work.
It means then the priest whose work or whose knowledge
moves. But there is absolutely no reason to take कवि (*kavi*)
in any other than its natural and invariable sense. कवि (*kavi*) is
the seer, the one who has the divine or supramental knowledge.
क्रतु (*kratu*): from कृ (*kṛ*) or rather old root क्र (*kra*) to divide,
to do, make, shape, work. From the sense "divide" comes that
of the discerning mind, Sayana's प्रज्ञान (*prajñāna*); cf. Greek
kritos, judge etc.; and this is the sense of *karuthi* in Tamil which
means mind. But from the sense "to do" क्रतु (*kratu*) means (1)

work, (2) power of work, strength, cf. Greek *kratos*, strength, (3) will or working force of the mind. For this last sense cf. Isha Upanishad क्रतो कृतम् स्मर (*krato kṛtam smara*) where the collocation क्रतो कृतम् (*krato kṛtam*) shows that that power of the mind is meant which conducts or dictates the work or action. Agni is the divine Seer-Will that works with the perfect supramental knowledge.

सत्यः (*satyaḥ*): Sayana explains "true in its fruits"; but the collocation of "seer-will" and श्रवस् (*śravas*), inspired knowledge, indicates rather the sense "true in his being" and therefore "true in knowledge", श्रवस् (*śravas*), and "in will" क्रतुः (*kratuḥ*). श्रवस् (*śravas*) is the supramental knowledge called the Truth, ऋतम् (*ṛtam*), the Vijnana of the Upanishads. कविक्रतुः (*kavikratuḥ*) means having the will that is full of that knowledge, the *vijñānamaya* will, the divine *ājñāna*, सत्यः (*satyaḥ*) means "*vijñānamaya* in his substance".

चित्रश्रवस्तमः (*citraśravastamaḥ*): Sayana — 'having most varied kinds of fame', — an insipid and meaningless epithet for a god. श्रवस् (*śravas*) is used like श्रुति (*śruti*) to indicate the inspired hymn; it must therefore be capable of meaning inspired knowledge. There are two kinds of supramental knowledge, दृष्टि (*dṛṣṭi*) and श्रुति (*śruti*), sight and hearing, revelation and inspiration, but श्रवस् (*śravas*) is usually used to indicate the knowledge gained by the supramental faculties.

Translation: RITUALISTIC

Agni, the priest, who sets in motion the knowledge (or work), true in his fruit, very varied in his fame, may he come with the gods.

Translation: PSYCHOLOGICAL

The God-Will, Priest of our offering, true in his being, with the will of the seer, with richest variety of inspired knowledge, may he come to us divine with the powers divine.

The Vamadeva Hymns to Agni

INTRODUCTION

THE interpretation of the Rig-veda is per-
haps the most difficult and disputed question with which the
scholarship of today has to deal. This difficulty and dispute are
not the creation of present-day criticism; it has existed in different forms since very early times. To what is this incertitude due?
Partly, no doubt, it arises from the archaic character of a language in which many of the words were obsolete when ancient
Indian scholars tried to systematise the traditional learning about
the Veda, and especially the great number of different meanings
of which the old Sanskrit words are capable. But there is another
and more vital difficulty and problem. The Vedic hymns are full
of figures and symbols, — of that there can be no least doubt,
— and the question is, what do these symbols represent, what is
their religious or other significance? Are they simply mythological figures with no depth of meaning behind them? Are they the
poetic images of an old Nature-worship, mythological, astrono-
mical, naturalistic, symbols of the action of physical phenomena
represented as the action of the gods? Or have they another and
more mystic significance? If this question could be solved with
any indubitable certitude, the difficulty of language would be no
great obstacle; certain hymns and verses might remain obscure,
but the general sense, drift, purport of the ancient hymns could
be made clear. But the singular feature of the Veda is that none
of these solutions, at least as they have been hitherto applied,
gives a firm and satisfactory outcome. The hymns remain confused, bizarre, incoherent, and the scholars are obliged to take
refuge in the gratuitous assumption that this incoherence is
a native character of the text and does not arise from their
own ignorance of its central meaning. But so long as we can
get no farther than this point, the doubt, the debate must
continue.

A few years ago I wrote a series of articles in which I suggested an explanation of the ambiguous character of the Veda. My suggestion hinged on this central idea that these hymns were written in a stage of religious culture which answered to a similar period in Greece and other ancient countries, — I do not suggest that they were contemporary or identical in cult and idea, — a stage in which there was a double face to the current religion, an outer for the people, *profanum vulgus*, an inner for the initiates, the early period of the Mysteries. The Vedic Rishis were mystics who reserved their inner knowledge for the initiates; they shielded them from the vulgar by the use of an alphabet of symbols which could not readily be understood without the initiation, but were perfectly clear and systematic when the signs were once known. These symbols centred around the idea and forms of the sacrifice; for the sacrifice was the universal and central institution of the prevailing cult. The hymns were written round this institution and were understood by the vulgar as ritual chants in praise of the Nature-gods, Indra, Agni, Surya Savitri, Varuna, Mitra and Bhaga, the Ashwins, Ribhus, Maruts, Rudra, Vishnu, Saraswati, with the object of provoking by the sacrifice the gifts of the gods, — cows, horses, gold and other forms of wealth of a pastoral people, victory over enemies, safety in travel, sons, servants, prosperity, every kind of material good fortune. But behind this mask of primitive and materialistic naturalism, lay another and esoteric cult which would reveal itself if we once penetrated the meaning of the Vedic symbols. That once caught and rightly read, the whole Rig-veda would become clear, consequent, a finely woven, yet straightforward tissue.

According to my theory the outer sacrifice represented in these esoteric terms an inner sacrifice of self-giving and communion with the gods. These gods are powers, outwardly of physical, inwardly of psychical nature. Thus Agni outwardly is the physical principle of fire, but inwardly the god of the psychic godward flame, force, will, Tapas; Surya outwardly the solar light, inwardly the god of the illuminating revelatory knowledge; Soma outwardly the moon and the Soma-wine or nectarous moon-plant, inwardly the god of the spiritual ecstasy, Ananda. The principal psychical conception of this inner Vedic cult was the idea of the Satyam, Ritam, Brihat, the Truth, the Law, the

Vast. Earth, Air and Heaven symbolised the physical, vital and mental being, but this Truth was situated in the greater Heaven, base of a triple Infinity actually and explicitly mentioned in the Vedic Riks, and it meant therefore a state of spiritual and supramental illumination. To get beyond earth and sky to Swar, the Sun-world, seat of this illumination, home of the gods, foundation and seat of the Truth, was the achievement of the early Fathers, *pūrve pitaraḥ*, and of the seven Angiras Rishis who founded the Vedic religion. The solar gods, children of Infinity, Adityas, were born in the Truth and the Truth was their home, but they descended into the lower planes and had in each plane their appropriate functions, their mental, vital and physical cosmic motions. They were the guardians and increasers of the Truth in man and by the Truth, *ṛtasya pathāḥ*, led him to felicity and immortality. They had to be called into the human being and increased in their functioning, formed in him, brought in or born, *devavīti*, extended, *devatāti*, united in their universality, *vaiśvadevya*.

The sacrifice was represented at once as a giving and worship, a battle and a journey. It was the centre of a battle between the Gods aided by Aryan men on one side and the Titans or destroyers on the opposite faction, Dasyus, Vritras, Panis, Rakshasas, later called Daityas and Asuras, between the powers of the Truth or Light and the powers of falsehood, division, darkness. It was a journey, because the sacrifice travelled from earth to the gods in their heaven, but also because it made ready the path by which man himself travelled to the Home of the Truth. This journey opposed by the Dasyus, thieves, robbers, tearers, besiegers (Vritras) was itself a battle. The giving was an inner giving. All the offerings of the outer sacrifice, the cow and its yield, the horse, the Soma were symbols of the dedication of inner powers and experiences to the Lords of Truth. The divine gifts, resul tof the outer sacrifice, were also symbols of inner divine gifts, the cows of the divine light symbolised by the herds of the sun, the horse of strength and power, the son of the inner godhead or divine man created by the sacrifice, and so through the whole list. This symbolic duplication was facilitated by the double meaning of the Vedic words; *go*, for instance, means both cow and ray; the cows of the dawn and the sun, Heaven's *boes Helioi*, are the rays of the sun-god, Lord of Revelation, even as in Greek mythology Apollo the sun-god is also the Master of poetry and of prophecy. *Ghṛta* means clarified butter, but also the bright thing; *soma* means the wine of the moon-plant, but also delight, honey, sweetness, *madhu*. This is the conception, all other features are subsidiary to this central idea. The suggestion seems to me a perfectly simple one, neither out of the way and recondite, nor unnatural to the mentality of the early human peoples.

There are certain *a priori* objections which can be brought against this theory. One may be urged against it from the side of Western scholarship. It may be objected that there is no need for all this mystification, that there is no sign of it in the Veda unless we choose to read it into the primitive mythology, that it is not justified by the history of religion or of the Vedic religion, that it was a refinement impossible to an ancient and barbaric mind. None of these objections can really stand. The Mysteries in Egypt and Greece and elsewhere were of a very ancient standing and they proceeded precisely on this symbolic principle, by which outward myth and ceremony and cult-objects stood for secrets of an inward life or knowledge. It cannot therefore be argued that this mentality was non-existent, impossible in antique times or any more impossible or improbable in India, the country of the Upanishads, than in Egypt and Greece. The history of ancient religion does show a transmutation of physical Nature-gods into representatives of psychical powers or rather an addition of psychical to physical functions; but the latter in some instances gave place to the less external significance. I have given the example of Helios replaced in later times by Apollo; just so in the Vedic religion Surya undoubtedly becomes a god of inner light, the famous Gayatri verse and its esoteric interpretation are there to prove it as well as the constant appeal of the Upanishads to Vedic Riks or Vedic symbols taken in a psychological and spiritual sense, e.g. the four closing verses of the Isha Upanishad. Hermes, Athena represent in classical mythology psychical functions, but were originally Nature-gods, Athena probably a dawn-goddess. I contend that Usha in the

Veda shows us this transmutation in its commencement. Dionysus the wine-god was intimately connected with the Mysteries; he was given a similar role to Soma, the wine-god of the Vedas.

But the question is whether there is anything to show that there was actually such a doubling of functions in the Veda. Now, in the first place, how was the transition effected from the alleged purely materialistic Nature-worship of the Vedas to the extraordinary psychological and spiritual knowledge of the Upanishads unsurpassed in their subtlety and sublimity in ancient times? There are three possible explanations. First, this sudden spirituality may have been brought in from outside; it is hastily suggested by some scholars that it was taken from an alleged highly spiritual non-Aryan southern culture; but this is an assumption, a baseless hypothesis for which no proof has been advanced; it rests as a surmise in the air without foundation. Secondly, it may have developed from within by some such transmutation as I have suggested, but subsequent to the composition of all but the latest Vedic hymns. Still, even then, it was effected on the basis of the Vedic hymns; the Upanishads claim to be a development from the Vedic knowledge, Vedanta, repeatedly appeal to Vedic texts, regard Veda as a book of knowledge. The men who gave the Vedantic knowledge are everywhere represented as teachers of the Veda. Why then should we rigidly assume that this development took place subsequent to the composition of the bulk of the Vedic mantras? For the third possibility is that the whole ground had already been prepared consciently by the Vedic mystics. I do not say that the inner Vedic knowledge was identical with the Brahmavada. Its terms were different, its substance was greatly developed, much lost or rejected, much added, old ideas shed, new interpretation made, the symbolic element reduced to a minimum and replaced by clear and open philosophic phrases and conceptions. Certainly, the Vedic mantras had already become obscure and ill-understood at the time of the Brahmanas. And still the ground work may have been there from the beginning. It is, of course, in the end a question of fact; but my present contention is only that there is no *a priori* impossibility, but rather a considerable probability or at least strong possibility in favour of my suggestion. I will put my argument in this way. The later hymns undoubtedly contain a beginning of the Brahmavada; how did it begin, had it no root origins in the earlier mantras? It is certain that some of the gods, Varuna, Saraswati, had a psychological as well as a physical function. I go further and say that this double function can everywhere be traced in the Veda with regard to other gods, as for instance, Agni and even the Maruts. Why not then pursue the inquiry on these lines and see how far it will go? There is at least a *prima facie* ground for consideration, and to begin with, I demand no more. An examination of the actual text of the hymns can alone show how far the inquiry will be justified or produce results of a high importance.

Another *a priori* objection comes from the side of orthodox tradition. What it amounts to is an objection to go behind the authority of Sayana, who belongs to an age at least two or three thousand years later than the Veda, and of Yaska, the ancient lexicographer. Besides, the Veda is currently regarded as *karmakāṇḍa*, a book of ritual works, the Vedanta only as *jñānakāṇḍa*, a book of knowledge. In an extreme orthodox standpoint it is objected that reason, the critical faculty, the historical argument have nothing to do with the question; the Vedas are beyond such tests, in form and substance eternal, in interpretation only to be explained by traditional authority. That attitude is one with which I am not concerned; I am seeking for the truth of this matter and I cannot be stopped by a denial of my right to seek for any truth contrary to tradition. But if in a more moderate form the argument be that when there is an unbroken and consistent ancient tradition, there is no justification in going behind it, then the obvious reply is that there is no such thing. Sayana moves amidst a constant uncertainty, gives various possibilities, fluctuates in his interpretations. Not only so, but though usually faithful to the ritualistic and external sense he distinguishes and quotes occasionally various ancient schools of interpretation, one of which is spiritual and philosophic and finds the sense of the Upanishads in the Veda. Even he feels himself obliged sometimes, though very rarely, to follow its suggestions. And if we go back to the earliest times we

see that the Brahmanas give a mystically ritualistic interpretation
of the Veda, the Upanishads treat the Riks as a book not of
ritual, but of spiritual knowledge. There is therefore nothing
fantastically new or revolutionary in an attempt to fix the psychological and spiritual purport of the Rig-veda.

A last objection remains that the interpretation of the Veda
has been a field for the exercise of the most extraordinary ingenuity, each attempt arriving at widely different results, and
mine is only one ingenuity the more. If it were so, then I stand in
good company. The interpretations of Sayana are packed with
the most strained and far-fetched ingenuities, which not unoften
light-heartedly do violence to grammar, syntax, order, connection, on the idea that the Rishis were in no way restrained by
these things. Yaska is full of etymological and other ingenuities, some of them of a most astonishing kind. The scholarship
of Europe has built up by a system of ingenious guesses and de-
ductions a new version and evolved the history, true or imaginative, of an Aryan invasion and a struggle between Aryan and
Dravidian which was never before suspected in the long history
of Vedic interpretation. The same charge has been brought
against Swami Dayananda's commentary. Nevertheless, the universality of the method does not make it valid, nor have I any
need to take refuge in this excuse, which is not a justification. If
my or any interpretation is got by a straining of the text, a licen-
tious or fantastic rendering or a foreign importation, then it can
have no real value. The present volume, which I hope to make
the first of a series, is intended to show my method actually at
work and dispel this objection by showing the grounds and
justification.

I hold that three processes are necessary for a valid interpretation of the Veda. First, there must be a straightforward rendering word by word of the text which shall stick to a plain and
simple sense at once suggested by the actual words, no matter
what the result may be. Then, this result has to be taken and it
has to be seen what is its actual purport and significance. That
meaning must be consistent, coherent with itself; it must show
each hymn as a whole in itself proceeding from idea to idea,
linked together in sequence, as any literary creation of the human

mind must be linked which has not been written by lunatics or is not merely a string of disconnected cries. It is impossible to suppose that these Rishis, competent metrists, possessed of a style of great power and mobility, composed without the sequence of ideas which is the mark of all adequate literary creation. And if we suppose them to be divinely inspired, mouthpieces of Brahman or the Eternal, there is no ground for supposing that the divine wisdom is more incoherent in its word than the human mind, it should rather be more luminous and satisfying in its totality. Finally, if a symbolic interpretation is put on any part of the text, it must arise directly and clearly from suggestions and language of the Veda itself and must not be brought in from outside.

A few words may be useful on each of these points. The first rule I follow is to try to get at the simplest and straightforward sense to which the Rik is open, not to strain, twist and involve. The Vedic style is terse, but natural, it has its strong brevities and some ellipses, but all the same it is essentially simple and goes straight to its object. Where it seems obscure, it is because we do not know the meaning of the words or miss the clue to the idea. Even if at one or two places, it seems to be tortured, that is no reason why we should put the whole Veda on the rack or even in these places torture it still worse in the effort to get at a sense. Where the meaning of a word has to be fixed, this difficulty comes either because we have no clue to the true meaning or because it is capable in the language of several meanings. In the latter case I follow certain fixed canons. First, if the word is one of the standing terms of the Veda intimately bound up with its religious system, then I must first find one single meaning which attaches to it wherever it occurs; I am not at liberty to vary its sense from the beginning according to my pleasure or fancy or sense of immediate fitness. If I interpret a book of obscure Christian theology, I am not at liberty to interpret freely the constantly recurring word *grace* sometimes as the influx of the divine favour, sometimes as one of the three Graces, sometimes as charm of beauty, sometimes as grace marks in an examination, sometimes as the name of a girl. If in one it evidently bears this or that sense and can have no other, if it has no reference to the ordinary meaning, then indeed it is different; but I must not put in one of these other meanings where the normal sense fits the context. In other cases I may have greater freedom, but this freedom must not degenerate into licence. Thus the word *ṛtam* may signify, we are told, truth, sacrifice, water, motion and a number of other things. Sayana interprets freely without obvious rule or reason according to any of them and sometimes gives us no alternative; not only does he interpret it variously in different hymns, but in three different senses in the same hymn or even in the same line. I hold this to be quite illegitimate. Ritam is a standing term of the Veda and I must take it consistently. If I find truth to be its sense in that standing significance, I must so interpret it always, unless in any given passage it evidently means water or sacrifice or the man who has gone and cannot mean truth. To translate so striking a phrase as *ṛtasya panthāḥ* in one passage as the "path of truth", in another "the path of sacrifice", in another "the path of water", in another "the path of the one who has gone" is a sheer licence, and if we follow such a method, there can be no sense for the Veda except the sense of our own individual caprice. Then again we have the word Deva, which undoubtedly means in ninety-nine places out of a hundred, one of the shining ones, a god. Even though this is not so vital a term as *ṛtam*, still I must not take it in the sense of a priest or intelligent man or any other significance, where the word 'god' gives a good and sufficient meaning unless it can be shown that it is undoubtedly capable of another sense in the mouth of the Rishis. On the other hand, a word like *ari* means sometimes a fighter, one's own champion, sometimes a hostile fighter, assailant, enemy, sometimes it is an adjective and seems almost equivalent to *arya* or even *ārya*. But mark that these are all well-connected senses. Dayananda insists on a greater freedom of interpretation to suit the context. *Saindhava*, he says, means a horse or rock-salt; where it is a question of eating we must interpret as salt, where it is a question of riding, as horse. That is quite obvious; but the whole question in the Veda is, what is the bearing of the context, what are its connections? If we interpret according to our individual sense of what the context ought to mean, we are building on quicksands. The only safe rule is to fix the sense usually current in the

Veda and admit variations only where they are evident from the
context. Where the ordinary sense makes a good meaning, I
ought to accept it; it does not at all matter that that is not the
meaning I should like it to have or the one suitable to my theory
of the Veda. But how to fix the meaning? We can evidently do it
only on the totality or balance of the evidence of all the passages
in which the word occurs and, after that, on its suitability to the
general sense of the Veda. If I show that *ṛtam* in all passages can
mean truth, in a great number of passages, but not by any means
all, sacrifice, in only a few water, and in hardly any, motion, and
this sense, truth, fits in with the general sense of the Veda then I
consider I have made out an unanswerable case for taking it in
that significance. In the cases of many words this can be done;
in others we have to strike a balance. There remain the words of
which frankly we do not know the meaning. Here we have to
use the clue of etymology and then to test the meaning or possible
meanings we arrive at by application to the passages in which the
word occurs, taking into consideration where necessary not only
the isolated Riks, but the context around, and even the general
sense of Veda. In a few cases the word is so rare and obscure that
only a quite conjectural meaning can be attached to it.

When we have got the rendering of the text, we have to see to
what it amounts. Here what we have to do is to see the connections of the ideas in the verse itself, next its connection if any,
with the ideas in the verses that precede and follow and with the
general sense of the hymn; next parallel passages and ideas and
hymns and finally the place of the whole in the scheme of ideas
of the Veda. Thus in IV.7 we have the line अग्ने कदा त आनुषग् भुवद्
देवस्य चेतनम्, and I render it, "O Flame, when shall there be
in uninterrupted sequence the awakening (to knowledge or consciousness) of thee the god (the shining or luminous One)?" But
the question I have to put is this, "Does this mean the constant
burning of the physical fire on the altar and the ordered sequence
of the physical sacrifice, or does it mean the awakening to
constant developing knowledge or ordered conscious action of
knowledge of the divine Flame in man?" I note that in the next
Rik (3) Agni is described as the possessor of truth (or of
sacrifice?), the entirely wise, ऋतावानं विचेतसम्, (in 4) as the vision or

knowledge, the perception shining for each creature, केतुं ... भृगवाणं विशेविशे, (in 5) as the Priest who knows, होतारं ... चिकित्वांसम्, (in 6) as the bright one in the secrecy who has perfect knowledge, चित्रं ... गुहा हितम् सुवेदम्, (in 7 and 8) as coming possessed of the truth for the sacrifice when the gods rejoice in the seat of the Truth, as the messenger, ऋतस्य धामन् रणयन्त देवाः ... वेरध्वराय सदमिदृतावा .... दूत ईयसे. All this is ample warrant for taking Agni not merely as the physical flame on the altar, but as a flame of divine knowledge guiding the sacrifice and mediating between man and the gods. The balance is also, though not indisputably, in favour of taking it as a reference to the inner sacrifice under the cover of the outer symbols; for why should there be so much stress on divine knowledge if the question were only of a physical sacrifice for physical fruits? I know that he is the priest, sage, messenger, eater, swift traveller and warrior. How are these ideas, both successive and interwoven in the Veda, connected together? Is it the physical sacred flame that is all these things or the inner sacred flame? There is sufficient warrant even in provisionally taking it for the inner flame; but to be sure I cannot rely on this one Rik. I have to note the evolution of the same ideas in other hymns, to study all the hymns dedicated to Agni or in which he is mentioned, to see whether there are passages in which he is undoubtedly the inner flame and what light they shed on his whole physiognomy. Only then shall I be in a position to judge certainly the significance of the Vedic Fire.

This example will show the method I follow in regard to the third question, the interpretation of the Vedic symbols. That there are a mass of figures and symbols in the hymns, there can be no doubt. The instances in this 7th hymn of the Fourth Mandala are sufficient by themselves to show how large a part they play. In the absence of any contemporary evidence of the sense which the Rishis attached to them, we have to seek for their meaning in the Veda itself. Obviously, where we do not know we cannot do without a hypothesis, and my hypothesis is that of the outer material form as a significant symbol of an inner spiritual meaning. But this or any hypothesis can have no real value if it is brought in from outside, if it is not suggested by the words and indications of the Veda itself. The Brahmanas are too full of ingenuities; they read too much and too much at random into the text. The Upanishads give a better light and we may get hints from later work and even from Sayana and Yaska, but it would be dangerous at once to read back literally the ideas of a later mentality into this exceedingly ancient scripture. We must start from and rely on the Veda to interpret the Veda. We have to see, first, whether there are any plain and evident psychological and spiritual conceptions, what they are, what clue they give us, secondly, whether there are any indications of psychological meanings for physical symbols and how the outer physical is related to the inner psychological side. Why, for instance, is the Flame Agni called the seer and knower? Why are the rivers called the waters that have knowledge? Why are they said to ascend or get on the mind? And a host of other similar questions. The answer again must be found by a minute comparative study of the Vedic hymns themselves. In this volume I proceed by development. I take each hymn, get at its first meaning; I see whether there are any psychological indications and what is their force and what their interweaving and relation to the other surrounding ideas. I proceed thus from hymn to hymn linking them together by their identical or similar ideas, figures, expressions. In this way it may be possible to arrive at a clear and connected interpretation of the Veda.

This method supposes that the hymns of the Rig-veda are one whole composed by different Rishis, but on the basis of a substantially identical and always similar knowledge and one system of figures and symbols. This, I think, is evident on the very surface of the Veda. The only apparent exceptions are certain hymns, mostly in the tenth Mandala, which seem to belong to a later development, some almost purely ritualistic, others more complex and developed in symbol than the body of the Riks, others clearly announcing philosophical ideas with a modicum of symbol, the first voices which announce the coming of the Upanishads. Some hymns are highly archaic, others of a more clear and relatively modern type. But for the most part throughout we find the same substance, the same images, ideas, standing terms, the same phrases and expressions. Otherwise the problem would be insoluble; as it is, the Veda itself gives a key to the Veda.

The hymns I have chosen for a beginning are the fifteen hymns of Vamadeva to Agni. I take them in the order that suits me, for the first few are highly charged with symbol and therefore to us obscure and recondite. It is better to proceed from the simple to the difficult, for so we shall get better the preliminary clue which may help us through the obscurity of the earlier hymns.

Agni, the Lord of Fire, is physically the god of the sacrificial flame, the fire found in the tinders, in the plants, in the waters, the lightning, the fire of the sun, the fiery principle of heat and light, *tapas, tejas*, wherever it is found. The question is whether he is also the same principle in the psychical world. If he is, then he must be that psychological principle called Tapas in the later terminology. The Vedic Agni has two characteristics, knowledge and a blazing power, light and fiery force. This suggests that he is the force of the universal Godhead, a conscious force or Will instinct with knowledge, — that is the nature of Tapas, — which pervades the world and is behind all its workings. Agni then in the psychical and spiritual sense of his functions would be the fire of a Will doing the works of its own inherent and innate knowledge. He is the seer, कवि:, the supreme mover of thought, प्रथमो मनोता, the mover too of speech and the Word, उपवक्ता जनानाम्, the power in the heart that works, हृदिस्पृशं ऋतुम्, the impeller of action and movement, the divine guide of man in the act of sacrifice. He is the Priest of the sacrifice, Hotri, he who calls and brings the gods and gives to them the offering, the Ritwik, who sacrifices in right order and right season, the purifying priest, Potri, the Purohita, he who stands in front as the representative of the sacrificer, the conductor of the sacrifice, Adhwaryu; he combines all the sacred offices. It is evident that these functions all belong to the divine Will or conscient power in man which awakes in the inner sacrifice. This Fire has built all the worlds; this creative Power, Agni Jatavedas, knows all the births, all that is in the worlds; he is the messenger who knows earth, knows how to ascend the difficult slope of heaven, *ārodhanaṁ divaḥ*, आरोधनं दिव:, knows the way to the home of the Truth; he mediates between God and man. These things apply

only with difficulty to the god of physical fire; they are of a striking appropriateness if we take a larger view of the divine nature
and functions of the god Agni. He is a god of the earth, a force
of material being, अवमः; but he seems to be a vital (Pranic) force
of will in desire, devouring, burning through his own smoke;
and again he is a mental power. Men see him like heaven with
stars द्यामिव स्तृभिः; heaven and the mid-world and earth are his
portion. But again he is a god of Swar, one of the solar deities;
he manifests himself as Surya; he is born in the Truth, a master
of Truth, a guardian of Truth and Immortality, a getter and
keeper of the shining herds, the eternal Youth, and he renews
the youth of these mystic cattle. He is triply extended in the
Infinite. All these functions cannot be predicated of the god of
physical fire; but they are all just attributes of the conscient
divine Will in man and the universe. He is the horse of battle and
the horse of swiftness and again he gives the white horse; he is
the son and he creates for man the son. He is the warrior and he
brings to man the heroes of his battle. He destroys by his flame
the Dasyu and the Rakshasa; he is a Vritra-slayer. Are we to see
here the slayer only of mortal Dravidians or of the demons who
oppose the sacrifice? He is born in a hundred ways; from the
plants, from the tinder, from the waters. His parents are the
two Aranis, but again his parents are Earth and Heaven, and
there is a word which seems to combine both meanings. Are not
the two Aranis then a symbol of Earth and Heaven, Agni
born for mortals from the action of the diviner mental on
the material being? The ten sisters are his mothers, — the ten
fingers, says the scholiast; yes, but the Veda describes them as
the ten thoughts or thought-powers, दश धियः . The seven rivers,
the mighty ones of heaven, the waters that have knowledge, the
waters of Swar are also his mothers. What is the significance of
this symbolism, and can we really interpret it as only and solely
a figurative account of natural phenomena, of the physical principle or works of Fire? There is at least here, to put the thing in
its lowest terms, a strong possibility of a deeper psychological
functioning of Agni. These are the main points for solution.
Let us see then how the physiognomy of Agni evolves in the Riks;
keeping our minds open, let us examine whether the hypothesis

of Agni as one of the Gods of the Vedic Mysteries is tenable or untenable. And that means, whether the Veda is a semi-barbaric book of ritual hymns, the book of a primitive Nature-worship or a scripture of the seers and mystics.

MANDALA IV SUKTA 7 MANTRAS 1-3

अयमिह प्रथमो धायि धातृभिर्होता, यजिष्ठो अध्वरेष्वीड्यः ।
यमप्नवानो भृगवो विरुरुचुर्वनेषु चित्रं विभ्वं विशोविशे ॥१॥

अयं this (before you) होता Hotri, प्रथमः first or supreme, यजिष्ठः (यष्टृतमः) most strong for sacrifice, अध्वरेषु ईड्यः adorable in the (pilgrim) sacrifices इह धायि has here been set धातृभिः by the Ordainers (of things), यं he whom अप्नवानः भृगवः Apnavana and the Bhrigus विरुरुचुः made to shine, वनेषु चित्रं luminous (or variegated) in the woods (or in the logs), विभ्वं pervading, विशे-विशे for creature and creature or for each (human) being.

CRITICAL NOTES

धातृभिः : : Sayana explains धातृ as one who does action for the sacrifice, therefore a priest. But धातारः here would more naturally signify the gods, creators and ordainers of things, though it is possible to take it as the arrangers of the sacrificial action. The close collocation धायि धातृभिः can hardly be void of all significance. The gods are those who place or arrange the order of creation, set each thing in its place, to its law and its function; they have set Agni here, इह. 'Here' may mean in the sacrifice, but more generally it would mean here on earth.

होता : Sayana takes sometimes as "the summoner of the gods", sometimes "the performer of the Homa, the burned offering". In fact it contains both significances. Agni as Hotri calls the gods to the sacrifice by the Mantra and, on their coming, gives to them the offering.

अध्वरेषु : the word अध्वर is explained by the Nirukta as meaning literally अहिंस्रः, "unhurting", अ+ध्वर from ध्वृ, and so, the unhurt sacrifice, and so simply sacrifice. Certainly, it is used as an adjective qualifying यज्ञ, अध्वरो यज्ञः. It must therefore express some characteristic so inherent in the sacrifice as to be able to convey by itself that significance. But how can the "unhurting" come to mean by itself the sacrifice? I suggest that as in अमुर it is a mistake to take the अ as preventive, अमुर comes from अमु (not अस्) and means strong, forceful, mighty, अध्वर is similarly formed from अध्वन्, path, journey. It means the pilgrim-sacrifice, the sacrifice which travels from earth to heaven, led by Agni along the path of the gods. If we must take the word from ध्वृ, it is better to take the ordinary sense of ध्वृ, not crooked, straight, and then it would still mean the sacrifice which goes straight undeviating by the straight path to the gods, ऋजु, पन्था अनृक्षरः.

ईड्यः : Sayana: "who is praised or hymned" by the Ritwiks. But it must then mean "worthy to be hymned". ईळ्, ईड् must have meant originally to go, approach; it came to mean to pray to, ask for, desire, याचामहे. I take it in the sense of "desirable" or "adorable".

वनेषु : वन means in the Veda tree, wood, but also log, timber. चित्रं : Sayana takes चित्र sometimes चायनीयं=पूज्यं, sometimes विचित्र, varied or wonderful. Here "variedly beautiful". It is in this last sense of varied light or beauty that I take it in all passages in the Veda as in इन्द्र चित्रभानो. I can see no reason for taking it anywhere as पूजनीय.

विभ्वं : Sayana: "lord". But विभु in Rig-veda means certainly "widely becoming" or "wide in being" or "pervading, abundant, opulent". I find no passage in which it must mean lord, the later classical sense. विभ्व must bear the same sense as विभु.

Translation:

"Lo, here has been set by the Ordainer, the Priest of the offering, the supreme, the most mighty in sacrifice, one to be adored in the pilgrim-sacrifices, whom Apnavana and the Bhrigus made to shine out all-pervading, rich in hues, in the woods, for each human creature."

This is the first Rik; it contains nothing of an undoubtedly psychological significance. In the external sense it is a statement of the qualities of Agni as priest of the sacrifice. He is pointed to in his body of the sacrificial fire kindled, put there in his place

or sent by the priests. It amounts to an obvious statement that
this sacred flame is a great power for the sacrifice; that he is the
chief of the gods who has to be hymned or adored, that Apnavana and other Bhrigus first discovered the (sacrificial?) use of
the fire and caused it to be used by all men. The description here
of the forest fire seems inappropriate unless it is meant that they
got the idea by seeing Agni burning widely and beautifully as a
forest fire or that they discovered it by seeing the fire produced
by the clashing of boughs or that they first lit it in the shape of a
forest fire. Otherwise it is an ornamental and otiose description.

But if we assume for the moment that behind this image
Agni is hinted at as the Hotri of the inner sacrifice, then it is
worth seeing what these images mean. The first words tell us
that this flame of conscient Will, this great thing within us,
अयमिह, has been set here in man by the Gods, the creators of the
order of the world, to be the power by which he aspires and calls
the other divine Forces into his being and consecrates his knowledge, will, joy, and all the wealth of his inner life as a sacrificial
action to the Lords of the Truth. These first words then amount
for the initiate to a statement of the fundamental idea of the
Vedic mysteries, the meaning of the sacrifice, the idea of a God-
will in man, the Immortal in mortals, अमर्त्यं...मर्त्येषु. This flame is
spoken of as the supreme or first power. The godward will leads
all the other godward powers; its presence is the beginning of the
movement to the Truth and Immortality and the head too of the
march. It is the greatest power in the conduct of the mystic
discipline, यजिष्ठ, the most mighty for sacrifice. Man's sacrifice
is a pilgrimage and the divine Will its leader; therefore it is that
which we must adore or pray to or ask for its presence in each
sacrificial action.

The second line of the Rik gives us a statement of the first
discovery or birth of this Flame among men. For the spirit is
there concealed in man, *guhā hita*, as it is said in Veda and
Upanishad, in the inner cave of our being; and his will is a spiritual will, hidden there in the spirit, present indeed in all our
outward being and action; for all being and action are of the
spirit, but still its real nature, its native action is concealed,
altered, not manifest in the material life in its true nature of a

spiritual force. This is a fundamental idea of Vedic thinking; and if we keep it well in mind, we shall be able to understand the peculiar imagery of the Veda. Earth is the image of the material being; material being, delight, action, etc. are the growths of Earth; therefore their image is the forests, the trees, plants, all vegetation, वन, वनस्पति, ओषधि. Agni is hidden in the trees and plants, he is the secret heat and fire in everything that grows on earth, वनेषु. All that we take pleasure in in the material life, could not be or grow without the presence of the secret flame of the spirit. The awakening of the fire by the friction of the Aranis, the rubbing together of the two pieces of tinder-wood is one way of making Agni to shine out in his own form, रूपे, but this is said elsewhere to have been the work of the Angiras Rishis. Here the making of Agni so to shine is attributed to Apnavana and the Bhrigus and there is no indication of the method. It is simply indicated that they made him to shine out so that he burned with a beauty of varied light in the woodlands, a pervading presence, वनेषु चित्रं विभ्वम्. This must mean in the esoteric symbolism a rich and varied manifestation of the flame of divine will and knowledge in the physical life of man, seizing on its growths, all its being, action, pleasure, making it its food, अन्नम्, and devouring and turning it into material for the spiritual existence. But this manifestation of the spirit in the physical life of man was made available by the Bhrigus to each human creature विशे-विशे — we must presume, by the order of the sacrifice. This Agni, this general flame of the divine Will-force, was turned by them into the Hotri of the sacrifice.

The question remains, who are the Bhrigus of whom we may suppose that Apnavana is in this action at least the head or chief? Is it simply meant to preserve a historical tradition that the Bhrigus like the Angiras Rishis were founders of the esoteric Vedic knowledge and discipline? But this supposition, possible in itself, is contradicted by the epithet भृगवाणम् in verse 4 which evidently refers back to this first Rik. Sayana interprets there, "acting like Bhrigu" and to act like Bhrigu is to shine. We find this significant fact emerge, admitted even by the ritualistic commentator in spite of his attachment to a rational matter of fact, that some at least of the traditional Rishis and their families are symbolic in their character. The Bhrigus in the Veda (भृज् to burn) are evidently burning powers of the Sun, the Lord of Knowledge, just as the Angiras Rishis are very evidently the seven lustres of Agni, सप्त धामानि, — Sayana says the live coals of the fire, but that is a mere etymological ingenuity — the hints are everywhere in the Veda, but it is made quite clear in the tenth Mandala. The whole idea, then, comes out with convincing luminosity. It is the powers of the revelatory knowledge, the powers of the seer-wisdom, represented by the Bhrigus who make this great discovery of the spiritual will-force and make it available to every human creature. Apnavana means he who acts or he who attains and acquires. It is the seer-wisdom that scales and attains in the light of the revelation which leads the Bhrigus to the discovery. This completes the sense of the Rik.

It will be at once said that this is an immense deal to read into this single Rik, and that there is here no actual clue to any such meaning. No actual clue, indeed, only covert hints, which it is easy to pass over and ignore, — that was what the Mystics intended the *profanum vulgus*, not excluding the uninitiated Pundit, should do. I bring in these meanings from the indications of the rest of the Veda. But in the hymn itself so far as this first Rik goes, it might well be a purely ritualistic verse. But only if it is taken by itself. The moment we pass on, we land full into a mass of clear psychological suggestions. This will begin to be apparent even as early as the second verse.

अग्ने कदा त आनुषग् भुवद्देवस्य चेतनम् ।
अधा हि त्वा जगृभिरे मर्तासो विक्ष्वीड्यम् ॥२॥

अग्ने O Agni, कदा when ते देवस्य चेतनं the awakening to knowledge (consciousness) of thee the god आनुषग् भुवत् may it be continuously (in uninterrupted sequence). अधा हि for then (or, now indeed) मर्तासः mortals त्वा जगृभिरे have seized (taken and held) thee विक्षु ईड्यं adorable in (human) beings (or among the peoples).

CRITICAL NOTES

देवस्य: Sayana takes देव sometimes in the sense of "god", sometimes as equivalent simply to an epithet "shining". The Gods are called देवाः because they are the Shining Ones, the Children of Light; and the word may well have recalled always that idea to the Rishis; but I do not think देव is ever in the Veda merely a colourless epithet; in all passages the sense "god" or "divine" gives excellent sense and I see no good reason for taking it otherwise.

चेतनं: Sayana takes=तेजः, but चित् does not mean to shine, it means always, "to be conscious, aware, know", चेतति, चेतयति= knows, causes to know, चेतस्=heart, mind, knowledge, चेतन्यं, चेतना =consciousness, चित्तं=heart, consciousness, mind. To take it here=light, except by figure, is deliberately to dodge without any justification the plain psychological suggestion.

अधा: अ-धा=in this or that way, thus, but also then or now. Sayana takes it=therefore with भुवत् preparing for हि=because, for this reason : why thy light should be continuous? because... (a very forced structure absolutely unnatural and contrary to order, movement and the plain sequence of sense).

जगृभिरे: a Vedic form, taken by the grammarians as derived from ग्रह् to seize, by change of ह् to भ्, more probably an old root गृभ् and a peculiar archaic formation. If the force is "for him they seize", the perfect (tense) giving the sense of an already completed action, in English one would (say) "will have seized", i.e. "when thou knowest continuously". Or take अधा=now, "now indeed they have seized but have not yet the आनुषग् चेतनम्". But this does not make so good a sense and brings in besides an awkward inversion and ellipse.

Translation:

"O Flame, when shall thy awakening to knowledge be a continuous sequence? For then shall men have seized on thee as one to be adored in creatures."

Here we get the first plain psychological suggestion in the

word चेतनम्. But what is the sense of this continuous knowing or awakening to knowledge of Agni? First, we may try to get rid of the psychological suggestion, take चेतनं=consciousness, and the consciousness of the fire as simply a poetic figure for its burning. But against this we have the repetition of the phrase in the आनुषक् चेतनं in the अग्निर्देवस्य आनुषक् चिकित्वांसं of Rik 5 which certainly means conscious knowledge and not merely burning; the next verse (3) in which the idea of चेतनं is taken up and the word itself echoed in the two opening words ऋतावानं विचेतसं, possessed of truth, complete in knowledge (wisdom), applied to the god. To shut one's eyes to this emphatic indication and take चेतनं= merely ज्वलनं would be a mere dodge. Does it then mean the continuous burning of the flame of the physical sacrifice, but with this idea that the flame is the body of the god and indicates the presence of the conscious deity? But in what then does the knowledge or wisdom of Agni consist? It may be said that he is wise only as the होता, a seer, कविः, who knows the way to heaven (Verse 8). But what then of the ऋतावानं विचेतसम्? That must surely refer to some greater knowledge, some great Truth which Agni possesses. Does it at all refer to a god of physical Fire alone or to the knowledge and wisdom of an inner Fire, the flame of the God-Force or God-Will in man and the world, देवस्य, the shining One, the Guest, the Seer, अतिथिः कविः?

I take it in this sense. The Rishi cries to this inner Flame, "When wilt thou shine in me continuously, on the altar of my sacrifice; when wilt thou be a constant force of knowledge to give all the uninterrupted sequence, relation, order, completeness of the revelations of wisdom, speaking always and wholly its words, काव्यानि?" If it refers at all to the inner flame, this must be the sense. We must remember that in the Vedic symbolism it was by the continuous sacrifice all round the symbolic year, the nine or the ten months of the sacrifice of the Angirasas, that the Sun, Master of the Truth, the Wisdom, was recovered from the cave of darkness. The repeated single sacrifice is only a preparation for this continuity of the revealing Flame. It is only then that men not only awake Agni from time to time, by repeated pressure, but have and hold continuously the inner flame of will and knowledge, a present godhead, the one whom we then see and adore in all conscious thinking beings. Or we may take the last two *padas* in the sense "now indeed they seize" etc. and we will have to take it in the opposite sense, i.e., that for the present men do not have this continuous flame, but only lay hold of him for the actual duration in the effort of sacrifice. This is possible, but does not make so natural a sense; it arises less simply and directly from the actual words. It is in the next two Riks (3, 4) that the present action of Agni before his आनुषक् चेतनं is described, while in Rik 5 the Rishi returns to the idea of the greater continuous flame of knowledge, repeating the आनुषक् चेतनं still more significantly in the आनुषक् चिकित्वांसं of that verse. This seems to me the evident natural order of the thought in the Sukta.

ऋतावानं विचेतसं पश्यन्तो द्यामिव स्तृभिः ।
विश्वेषामध्वराणां हस्कर्तारं दमेदमे ॥३॥

पश्यन्तः they see him ऋतावानं (ऋतवन्तम्) having the truth, विचेतसं completely wise द्यामिव स्तृभिः like heaven with stars, हस्कर्तारं the maker to shine विश्वेषामध्वराणां of all (pilgrim) sacrifice दमे-दमे (गृहे गृहे) in house and house.

CRITICAL NOTES

ऋतावानम्, ऋत + वन् = ऋतावान्
The Vedic suffix वन् has the same force as the classical वत्, ऋतावा = ऋतवान्, ऋत from root ऋ to go. Hence the sense 'water'. The sense 'truth' may = what is learned, literally, what we go in search of and attain or what we go over and so learn (of ऋषि), but it may also come from the idea of straightness, latin *rectum*, ऋजु. How it comes to mean sacrifice is not so clear, perhaps from the idea of rite, observance, rule, विधि, or a line followed, cf. Latin *regula*, rule; or again action, कर्म, and so the sacrificial action; verbs of motion often bear also the sense of action, cf. चरितं, वृत्तम्. ऋतावा, says Sayana, often may mean possessed of truth or possessed of sacrifice. But here he takes it = truthful, free from deceit,

अमायिनम्. Elsewhere he takes सत्य used as an epithet of Agni, सत्यफल, giving a true fruit of the sacrifice. Oftenest he takes ऋत=यज्ञ. But it is perfectly evident here that ऋतावानं must mean truth-having, in whatever sense we may take the truth of Agni.

विचेतसं: Sayana: विशिष्टज्ञानं, having a special, a great knowledge; in Veda प्रचेता: and विचेता: are distinguished very much as प्रज्ञान and विज्ञान in the Upanishads and later Sanskrit; चेत: or चित्ति stands for ज्ञान, the latter word being classical and not Vedic. प्र gives the idea of knowledge directed towards an object, प्रचेता:=intelligent, wise in a general sense (thus Sayana takes प्रकृष्टज्ञान: and makes no distinction between the words). वि means widely, pervadingly or else in high degree; विचेता: means then having a complete or great or perfect knowledge, knowledge of the whole and the parts.

हस्कर्तारं: from हस् to shine, shining (from which comes the sense, to smile) and कृ to make. Sayana says प्रकाशकम्; illuminer of the sacrifices.

दमे-दमे: the Vedic word (Greek *domos*, Latin *domus*) means always "house"; it is not used in the later classical sense of "subduing, control", etc.

Translation:

"They see the master of truth, the complete in wisdom like a heaven with stars, the illuminer of all pilgrim-sacrifices in house and house."

In this Rik the word विचेतसं evidently takes up the चेतनं of the last Rik; it means complete in knowledge and is coupled with ऋतावानं, truth-having, possessed of truth; it is the god Agni, not the physical fire who is described by these epithets. Therefore ते चेतनं in the last Rik must mean Agni "awakening to knowledge" or Agni's awakening of man to knowledge, — for चेतयति means letting to know or to cause to know, and cannot mean the burning of the physical flame. But what is this truth and knowledge of Agni? It is associated again in the next verse with his function of illumining the sacrifice, अध्वराणां हस्कर्तारम्. What is the illumination he gives to the sacrifice? And what is meant by saying that he is seen "like a heaven with stars". Sayana with much scholastic ingenuity, but in characteristic disregard of all good taste and literary judgment, says that the scattering sparks of the fire are like stars, therefore Agni is like heaven, — though there is no reason to suppose that the स्तृभिः here are shooting stars; I cannot imagine any poet with eyes in his head and a judgment and sense of proportion in his brain so describing a fire burning on an altar. But if it does not mean that, then we have here a purely ornamental description and very bad, exaggerated and vicious ornament at that. All that the verse will then mean is that men see this wise and truthful Agni in the physical form of the sacrificial fire shedding light by its flames on the whole business of the sacrifice. The two epithets are also then otiose ornament; there is then absolutely no connection between the idea of Agni's wisdom and the image of the heaven with stars or the illumination of the sacrifice which is the main idea of the verse.

I go on the hypothesis, not, I think, an unfair one, that the Vedic Rishi Vamadeva like other poets wrote with some closer connection than that between their ideas. We must remember that in the last verse he has desired, what he has not got, the continuous knowledge of Agni and said that then indeed men hold and possess him. But how do they see him before that continuously, though after the Bhrigus have found him for the utility of each human being? They see him as the master of truth, the complete in knowledge, but as we must suppose, — they do not yet possess him in all his truth or his complete knowledge; for he is seen only as a heaven with stars and as an illuminer of their sacrifices. A heaven with stars is heaven at night without the light of the sun. Agni in the Veda is described as shining even in the night, giving light in the night, burning through the nights till there comes the dawn, — which too is brought by him aiding Indra and the Angirasas. If the meaning of Agni is the inner flame, this gets a striking, appropriate and profound meaning. In the Veda darkness or night is the symbol of the ignorant mentality, as is the day and its sunlight of the illumined mentality. But before there is the day or the continuous knowledge, the illuminations of Agni are like stars in the nocturnal heavens. Heaven is the mental as Earth is the physical being; all the truth and knowledge of Agni is there, but hidden only by the darkness of night. Men know that this Light is there pervading the skies but see only the stars which Agni has kindled as his fires of illumination in these heavens.

A Great God has been Released

1. Agni by the fuel heaped by the peoples has awakened towards the coming Dawn as towards the sun-cow coming; like the waters spouting up for wide flowing, his flames move towards the heaven.

2. The Priest of the offering awoke for sacrifice to the gods; Agni stood up high in the dawn and perfect-minded; the gathered force of him was seen reddening when he was entirely kindled; a great god has been released out of the darkness.

3. When so he has put forth the tongue of his multitude, pure is the activity of Agni with the pure herd of his rays; then is the goddess discerning yoked to her works in a growing plenty; she upward-straining, he high-uplifted, he feeds on her with his flaming activities.

4. Towards Agni move the minds of the seekers after the God-head, as their eyes move in the Surya; when the two unlike Dawns bring him forth, he is born a white steed of being in the van of the days.[1]

5. He is born full of delight at the head of the days helpful in the helpful gods, active in those that take their joy; in each of our homes establishing his seven ecstasies Agni, Priest of the offering, takes seat in his might for the sacrifice.

6. Mighty for sacrifice Agni of the offerings takes his seat in the lap of the Mother, in that rapturous middle world, young and a seer, seated in many homes of his dwelling, full of the

---

* For the original text refer to pp. 201-203.   [1] Or, at the head of our forces.

Truth, upholding our actions and therefore kindled in the mid-spaces.

7. Verily, it is this Agni, the illumined seer who perfects us in these lower activities, the master of offering, that they adore with obeisances and submission; who stretched out the double firmament by the force of the Truth, him they strengthen[1] with the rich droppings, the eternal master of substance.

8. Strong ever, he grows stronger housed in his own seat in us, and home, our guest auspicious to us; master-bull with the thousand horses of thy flame, strong with that Strength, O Agni, by thy might thou art in front of all others.

9. At once, O Agni, thou passest beyond all others in him to whom thou makest thyself manifest in thy splendid beauty, adorable and full of body and widely luminous, the beloved guest of the human peoples.

10. To thee, O vigorous Agni, the continents[2] bring their oblation from near and bring from afar; perceive the perfected mind in one most happy, for wide and mighty is the blessed peace of thee, O Agni.

11. O luminous Agni, mount today thy perfect and luminous chariot with the masters of the sacrifice; thou knowest those paths, bring then hither through the wide mid-world the gods to eat of our offerings.

12. Utterance have we given to the word of our delight for the seer who hath understanding, for the lord who is mighty; firm in the light one by submission to him reaches in Agni a fixity, even as in heaven, so here golden bright and vast-expanding.

[1] Or, brighten   [2] Or, the peoples

EXPLANATION

The awakening of the divine Force and its action in a man is in this hymn rather indicated than described. The Sukta is purely lyric in its character, *vaco vandāru*, an expression of delight and adoration, a stoma, or stabilising Mantra intended to fix in the soul the sevenfold delight of Agni, *damedame sapta ratnā* (Rik 5), and assure that state of perfected and happy mentality, pure in perception, light and calm in the emotional parts, *bhandiṣṭhasya*, the summation of the truth which the divine force dwelling in us abidingly assures to our conscious being. The image of the physical morning sacrifice is maintained throughout the first two Riks, but from its closing phrase, *mahān devastamaso niramoci* the Rishi departs from the ritualisitic symbol and confines himself to the purely psychological substance of his thought, returning occasionally to the physical aspects of Agni but only as a loose poetical imagery. There is nothing of the close symbolic parallelism which is to be found in some hymns of the Veda.

अबोध्यग्निः समिधा जनानां प्रति धेनुमिवायतीमुषासम् ।
यह्वा इव प्र वयामुज्जिहानाः प्र भानवः सिस्रते नाकमच्छ ॥१॥

Abodhi agniḥ samidhā janānām
        prati dhenum iva āyatīm uṣāsam;
Yahvā iva pra vayām ujjihānāḥ
        pra bhānavaḥ sisrate nākam accha.

Force, pure, supreme and universal, has in man awakened; divine power is acting, revealed, in the consciousness of the creature born into matter, *janānām*. It wakes when the fuel has been perfectly heaped, *abodhi samidhā*, — that power, plenty and richness of being on which this cosmic force in us is fed and which minister to intensity and brightness. It wakes towards the coming dawn of illumination, as to the Sun-cow, the cow of Surya, the illumination of the ideal life and the ideal vision entering the soul that works imprisoned in the darkness of Matter. The flames of the divine activity in us are pointing upwards towards heaven, mounting up from the lower levels of our being to the heights of the pure mind, *sisrate nākam accha*, and their rising is like the wide gushing up into manifestation of waters that have been hidden. For it is a great god that has been released out of the darkness, *mahān devastamaso niramoci*.

The two familiar images in *dhenu* and in *yahvā* are intended to convey directly in one, suggest obliquely by the simile in the other, the inseparable companionship of divine power with the divine light and the divine being. All the gods are indeed *uṣarbudhaḥ*; with the morning of the revelation all divine faculties in us arise out of the night in which they have slept. But the figure here is that of awakening towards the coming dawn. The illumination has not touched the mortal mind, it is on its way, approaching, *āyatīm*, like a cow coming from a distance to its pasture; it is then that the power divine stirs in its receptacle, seizes upon all that is available in the waking consciousness of the creature and, kindled, streams up towards the altitudes of the pure mind in the face of the coming divine knowledge which it rises to meet. Divine knowledge, revealing, inspiring, suggesting, discerning, calls up the godlike ideal activity in us which exceeds man's ordinary motions, — wakes it even before it actually occupies this mortal system by its far-off touch and glimmer on the horizon; so too divine, inspired and faultless activity in us rises heavenward and calls down God's dawn on His creature.

This great uprush of force is in its nature a great uprush of divine being; for force is nothing but the power of being in motion. It is the secret waters in us that, released, gush up openly and widely from their prison and their secrecy in our mortal natures; for in vitalised matter, in mind enmeshed in material vitality, the ideal and spiritual self are always concealed and await release and manifestation; in this mortal that immortal is covered and curtained in and lives and works behind the veil, *martyeṣu devam amartyam.* Therefore is the uprush of divine force in the great release felt to be the wide uprush of divine being and consciousness, *yahvā iva pra vayām ujjihānāḥ.*

अबोधि होता यजथाय देवानूर्ध्वो अग्निः सुमनाः प्रातरस्थात् ।
समिद्धस्य रुशदर्दशि पाजो महान् देवस्तमसो निरमोचि ॥२॥

Abodhi hotā yajathāya devān
ūrdhvo agniḥ sumanāḥ prātar asthāt;
Samiddhasya ruśad adarśi pājaḥ
mahān devastamaso niramoci.

The purpose of the waking is next emphasised. It is for divine action in man that God's force awakes in us. It is the divine priest of the offering who stands up in the dawn of the illumination to offer to the gods, to each great god his portion, to Indra a pure and deified mentality, to Vayu a pure and divine vital joy and action, to the four great Vasus, Varuna, Mitra, Bhaga and Aryaman the greatnesses, felicities, enjoyments and strengths of perfected being, to the Ashwins the youth of the soul and its raptures and swiftnesses, to Daksha and Saraswati, Ila, Sarama and Mahi the activities of the Truth and Right, to the Rudras, Maruts and Adityas the play of physical, vital, mental and ideative activities. Agni has stood up in the dawning illumination high uplifted in the pure mentality, *ūrdhva*, with a perfected mind, *sumanāḥ*. He purifies in his rising the temperament and fixes on it the seal of peace and joy; he purifies the intellectuality and makes it fit to receive the activity of the illuminating Truth and Infinite Rightness which is beyond intellect. Great is the god who has been released out of the darkness of this Avidya, out of this our blind bodily matter, out of this our smoke-enveloped vital energy, out of this our confused luminous murk of mortal mind and sense-enslaved intelligence. *Mahān devastamaso niramoci.* For now that he has been perfectly kindled, it is no longer God's occasional flamings that visit our nature, but His collected and perfect force, *pājaḥ*, that is seen reddening in our heavens.

The first verse is preoccupied with the idea of the self-illumination of Agni, the *bhānavaḥ*, the flames of Force manifesting Knowledge as its essential nature — for Force is nothing but Knowledge shaped into creative energy and the creations of energy, and veiled by its shape, as a man's soul is veiled by his mind and body which are themselves shapes of his soul. In the words *abodhi, vayām, nākam,* in the relation of Agni to Usha and the emphasis on the illuminative character of Usha as the Sun-

Cow, this aspect of illumination and manifestation is stressed and enlarged. In the second verse the native aspect of the divine Force as a mighty power of action consummating and purifying is brought out with an equal force and insistence. It is as the Hota that Agni awakes; in this illumination of the dawn that comes with him to man, *prātaḥ*, he stands up with the intellect and emotional temperament perfected and purified, sun for the great offering of man's whole internal and external life and activity to God in the gods, *yajathāya devān*, fulfilling the upward impulse, *ūrdhva*, which raises matter towards life, life towards mind, mind towards ideality and spirit, and thus consummating God's intention in the creature. In the next verse the nature of this human uplifting, this upward straining of the mind through heart and intellect to ideal Truth and Love and Right, is indicated and particularised in an image of great poetical force and sublimity.

यदीं गणस्य रशनामजीगः शुचिरङ्क्ते शुचिभिर्गोभिरग्निः ।
आद् दक्षिणा युज्यते वाजयन्त्युत्तानामूर्ध्वो अधयज्जुहूभिः ॥३॥

Yadīm gaṇasya raśanām ajīgaḥ
śucir aṅkte śucibhir gobhir agniḥ;
Ād dakṣiṇā yujyate vājayantī
uttānām ūrdhvo adhayat juhūbhiḥ.

When so he has put forth the tongue of enjoyment of his host, *yadīm gaṇasya raśanām ajīgaḥ*, Agni has put forth his powers for an uplifted and perfect activity, *ruśad adarśi pājaḥ*, — for redness is always the symbolic colour of action and enjoyment. This *pājas*, Agni's force or massed army, is again described in the *gaṇasya raśanām*, but while the idea in the second verse is that of their indistinctive mass, here the *gaṇaḥ* or host of Agni's powers, the Devatas of his nature who apply themselves to his particular works, are represented as brought out in their individuality collected in a mass, — for this is always the fire of *gaṇaḥ*, — each with his tongue of flame licking the mid-air, (*surabhā u loke — madhye iddhaḥ* in Verse 6), enjoying that is to say the vital energies and vital pleasure (*aśva* and *ghṛta*), which support this higher action. Supported by this vital joy and force Agni acts, *ankte agniḥ*; but the enjoyment is not impure and unilluminated enjoyment of the unuplifted creature, — he is *śuciḥ*, purely bright, not smoky with unpurified Pranic impulses, and his flames of action are in their nature pure flames of illumination, *śucibhiḥ gobhiḥ*. In modern diction, when the divine force has so far purified us, our activities and enjoyments are not darkened and troubled with striving and clouded vital desires which strain dimly towards a goal, but, not being *ṛtajā*, know not what they should seek, how they should seek it, in what force and by what methods and stages, our action becomes a pure illumination, our enjoyment a pure illumination; by the divine illuminations as their motive force, essence and instrument, our actions and enjoyments are effected. We see just the curious and delicate literary art of the Vedic style in its symbolism, by this selection of the great word, *go*, in this context, in preference to any other, to describe the flames of Agni. In the next line, with an equally just delicacy of selection *juhū* is used for the same flames instead of *bhānu* or *go*.

It is in this state of pure activity and enjoyment that the characteristic uplifting action of Agni is exercised, for then, *āt*, the discriminative intellect, *dakṣiṇā*, growing in the substance of its content and havings, *vājayantī*, is yoked or applied to its work under these new conditions. Dakshina, the discriminative intellect is the energy of *dakṣa*, master of the works or unerring right discernment but unerring in the ideality, in *mahas* or *vijñāna*, his and her own home, not unerring in the intellect, but only straining towards hidden truth and right out of the mental dualities of right and wrong, truth and falsehood. This deputy and messenger of the Ritam Brihat seated in *manas* as reason, discernment, intellect, can only attain its end and fulfill its mission when Agni, the divine Force, manifests in the Prana and Manas and uplifts her to the ideal plane of consciousness. Therefore in this new activity she is described as straining and extending herself upwards, *uttānām*, to follow and reach Agni where are his topmost planes, *ūrdhva*, in the ideal being. From there he leans down and feeds on her, *adhayat*, through the flames of the divine activity, *juhūbhiḥ*, burning in the purified and upward aspiring activities of the intellectual mind. This essential relation of the divine force and the purified mind is brought out in a more general thought and figure in the first line of the succeeding Rik.

अग्निमच्छा देवयतां मनांसि चक्षूंषीव सूर्ये सं चरन्ति ।
यदीं सुवाते उषसा विरूपे श्वेतो वाजी जायते अग्रे अह्नाम् ॥४॥

Agnimacchā devayatām manāṁsi
   cakṣūṁṣīva sūrye saṁ caranti;
Yad īm suvāte uṣasā virūpe
   śveto vājī jāyate agre ahnām.

Iva in the Veda is not always a particle of similitude and comparison. Its essential meaning is truly, verily, so thus, and it is from this sense that it derives its conjunctive uses, sometimes meaning "and" or "also", sometimes "as", "like". Its force here is to distinguish between the proper activity of Agni and Surya, of *manas* and *cakṣus*, and to confine the latter to their proper sphere and thus by implication to confine the former also. When we are mortals content with our humanity, then we are confused in our functions; the *manas* or sense-mind attempts to do the work of the *mahas* or idea-mind, to effect original knowledge, to move in Surya, in the powerful concrete image of the Veda. The ideal also confuses itself with sense and moves in the sense-forces, the *indriyas*, instead of occupying itself in all purity with its own function. Hence the confusions of our intellect and the stumblings of our mental activity in its grappling with the contacts of the outer world. But when we rise from our mortal nature to the nature of godhead, *devayantaḥ, amṛtaṁ sapantaḥ*, then the first change is the passage from mortal impurity to immortal purity, and the very nature of purity is a clear brightness and rightness, in which all our members work perfectly in God and the gods, each doing its own function and preserving its right relation with its superior and inferior fellows. Therefore in those who are attaining this nature of godhead, *devayatām*, their sense-minds strain towards Agni, the divine force of Right Being and Right Action, *satyam ṛtam*, — they tend, that is to say, to have the right

state, *bhāva* or temperament, out of which the right action of the
indriyas spontaneously proceeds; the seeings of the Yogin who
attains, move in Surya, the god of the ideal powers, all that he
perceives, creates, distinguishes, is worked out by the pure ideal
mentality which then uses its four powers of self-revelation,
self-inspiration, self-intuition, self-discernment, without suffering obscuration by the clouds of vital desire and impulse or
deflection by the sense-impacts and sense-reactions. The sensational mind confines itself then to its proper work of receiving
passively the impacts of the vital and material and mental outer
world and the illuminations of Surya and of pouring out on the
world in its reaction to the impacts, not its own hasty and dis-
torted responses, but the pure force and action of Agni which
works in the world, pure, right and unerring, and seizes on it to
possess and enjoy it for God in the human being. This is the
goal towards which Dakshina is striving in her upward self-
extension which ends by her taking her place as *viveka* or right
discernment in the kingdom of Surya, and this she begins already
in her new activity by discerning the proper action of the mind
from the proper action of idea in the mind. The purified intellect liberates itself from the obscurations of desire, the slavery
to vital impulse, and the false reports and false values of the
matter-besieged sense-powers.

The essential nature of Agni's manifestation which is at the
root of this successful distinction, is then indicated. Night and
Dawn are the two unlike mothers who jointly give birth to Agni,
Night, the *avyakta*, unmanifest state of knowledge and being,
the power of Avidya, Dawn, the *vyakta*, manifest state of knowledge and being, the power of Vidya. They are the two dawns,
the two agencies which prepare the manifestation of God in us,
Night fostering Agni in secret on the activities of Avidya, the
activities of unillumined mind, life and body by which the god in
us grows out of matter towards spirit, out of earth up to heaven,
Dawn manifesting him again, more and more, until he is ready
here for his continuous, pure and perfect activity. When this
point of our journey towards perfection is reached he is born,
śveto vājī, in the van of the days. We have here one of those
great Vedic figures with a double sense in which the Rishis at

once revealed and concealed their high knowledge, revealed it
to the Aryan mind, concealed it from the un-Aryan. Agni is the
white horse which appears galloping in front of the days, — the
same image is used with a similar Vedantic sense in the opening
of the Brihadaranyaka Upanishad; but the horse here is not, as
in the Upanishad, *aśva*, the horse of vital and material being in
the state of life-force, but *vājī*, the horse of Being generally, Being
manifested in substance whether of mind, life, body or idea or
the three higher streams proper to our spiritual being. Agni
therefore manifests as the fullness, the infinity, the *bṛhat* of all this
sevenfold substantial being that is the world we are, but white,
the colour of illumined purity. He manifests therefore at this
stage primarily as that mighty wideness, purity and illumination
of our being which is the true basis of the complete and unassail-
able *siadhi* in the yoga, the only basis on which right knowledge,
right thinking, right living, right enjoyment can be firmly, vastly
and perpetually seated. He appears therefore in the van of the
days, the great increasing states of illuminated force and being,
— for that is the image of *ahan*, — which are the eternal future
of the mortal when he has attained immortality.

In the next Rik the idea is taken up, repeated and amplified
to its final issues in that movement of solemn but never otiose
repetition which is a feature of Vedic style.

जनिष्ट हि जेन्यो अग्रे अह्नां हितो हितेष्वरुषो वनेषु ।
दमेदमे सप्त रत्ना दधानोऽग्निर्होता नि षसादा यजीयान् ॥५॥

Janiṣṭa hi jenyo agre ahnām
hito hiteṣu aruṣo vaneṣu;
Dame-dame sapta ratnā dadhānaḥ
agnir hotā ni ṣasādā yajīyān.

This divine force is born victorious by its very purity and
infinity over all the hostile forces that prevent, obstruct, limit or
strive to destroy our accomplished freedoms, powers, illuminations and widenesses; by his victory he ushers in the wide days
of the *siddha*, for which these nights and dawns of our human
life are the preparatory movements. He is effective and helpful

in the effective powers that work out for our good the movements of this lower life towards immortal strength and power, he
is active and joyous, *aruṣaḥ*, in those that take the delight of these
movements and to prepare us for the immortal bliss and ecstasy
of the divine nature. Manifesting progressively that Ananda, he
the force of God establishes and maintains in each house of
our habitation, in each of our five bodies, in each of our seven
levels of conscious existence, the seven essential forms of Ananda,
the bliss of body, the bliss of life, the bliss of mind, the senses,
the bliss of ideal illumination, the bliss of pure divine universal
ecstasy, the bliss of cosmic Force, the bliss of cosmic being. For
although we tend upwards immediately to the pure Idea, yet
not that but Ananda is the goal of our journey; the manifestation in our lower members of the divine bliss reposing on the
divine force and being is the law of our perfection. Agni, whether
he raises us to live in pure mind or yet beyond to the high plateaus of the pure ideal existence, *adhi ṣṇunā bṛhatā vartamānam*,
establishes and supports as the divine force that divine bliss in
its seven forms in whatever houses of our being, whatever worlds
of our consciousness have been already possessed by our waking
existence, life, body and mind, or life, body, mind and idea,
dame-dame dadhānaḥ. Thus manifesting God's bliss in us he takes
his seat in those houses, domiciled, *damūnāḥ*, as we have it in
other Suktas, and in those worlds, to perform as the *hotā* in his
greater might for the sacrifice, greater than the might of other
gods or greater than he has hitherto possessed, the offering of
human life into the immortal being, *ā daivyam janam, yajathāya
devān*.

In a culminating Rik which at once completes the first half
of the Sukta and introduces a new movement, the Rishi once
more takes up the closing thought of this verse and carries it out
into a fuller conclusion.

अग्निर्होता न्यसीदद् यजीयानुपस्थे मातुः सुरभा उ लोके ।
युवा कविः पुरुनिःष्ठ ऋतावा कृष्टीनामुत मध्य इद्धः ॥६॥

Agnir hotā ni asīdad yajīyān
upasthe mātuḥ surabhā u loke;

*Yuvā kaviḥ puruniḥṣṭha ṛtāvā
dhartā kṛṣṭīnām uta madhya iddhaḥ.*

Agni thus takes his seat in us and because it is through human activity that he is to fulfil the sacrifice, because the ascending movement is not completed, he takes it in the lap of his mother in that rapturous middle world. For the middle world, the Bhuvah, including all those states of existence in which the mind and the life are interblended as the double medium through which the Purusha acts and connects Heaven and Earth, is the proper centre of all human action. Mind blended with the vital energies is our seat even here in the material world. The Bhuvah or middle regions are worlds of rapture and ecstasy because life-energy and the joy of life fulfil themselves there free from the restrictions of the material world in which it is an exile or invader seeking to dominate and use the rebellious earthly material for its purposes. Agni sits in the lap of the mother, on the principle of body in the material human being, occupying there the vitalised mind consciousness which is man's present centre of activity and bringing into it the mightier bliss of the rapturous middle world to support and enlarge even the vital and physical activities and enjoyments of our earthly existence. He sits there in the human sacrifice, full of eternal youth and vigour, *yuvā*, in possession of the ideal truth and knowledge, in possession of the unerring rightness of the liberated pure ideal life and consciousness, *kaviḥ ṛtāvā*, and releasing that truth and right in many purposes and activities, *puruniḥṣṭhaḥ*, for he works all these results as the upholder of men in their actions and efforts and labours, *dhartā kṛṣṭīnām*, — he is that in all his forms of force from the mere physical heat in earth and in our bodies to the divine Tapas in us and without us by which God affects and supports the existence of the cosmos; and because he is thus supremely the upholder of human life and activity, therefore he is kindled in the mid-space; the seat is on the fullness of the realised mind-consciousness in the microcosm, in the rapturous mid-world of fulfilled life-energy in the macrocosm. There kindled, awakened and manifested in man, *samidhā abodhi, samiddhaḥ*, he does his work for upward-climbing humanity. Thus by the return in *iddhaḥ* to the words and the idea with which he started, the Rishi marks the close of the first movement of thought.

WORD-FORMATION
from
Material for a full Philological Reconstruction of
the old Aryabhasha from which the Indo-Aryan
and Dravidian languages are derived.

Word-Formation

THE language of man is not framed on earth, but in heaven, as indeed are all things that the earth-soul uses in this mortal journey. By the threefold energy of eternal truth, manifesting force and sustaining delight everything is created as a type in the world of ideas, the *mahat* of the ancients, in the principle of self-manifest and perfectly arranged knowledge, it is diversely developed by the more discursive but less sure-footed agencies of intellectual mind. Imagination hunts after new variations, memory and association corrupt, analogy perverts, sensation, emotion, pleasure seize violent and partial satisfaction. Hence, change, decay, death, rebirth, — the law of the world. All this takes place in the descent into the world of mind and the world of matter. Therefore mankind has one original language based on certain eternal types of sound, developed by certain laws of rhythmic variation, perfectly harmonious and symmetrical in its structure and evolution. This is the *devabhāṣā* and is spoken in the Satyayuga. Then it suffers change, detrition, collapse. Innumerable languages, dialects, vernaculars are born. The guardians of the sacred language attempt always to bring back the early purity, but even they cannot do it; they reconstruct it from time to time, compromise with the new tendencies, preserve something of the skeleton, lose the flesh, blood, sinew, much of the force and spirit. This reconstructed language they call Sanskrit; all else Prakrit.

The backbone of the skeleton is composed of the roots of the original language that survive; the rest is the various principles of word-formation. Accordingly in the languages of the world which are nearest to the old secret language, the ancient Aryan languages, there is one common element, the roots, the elemental word-formations from the roots and so much of the original significance as survives variety of mental development playing on different lines and to different purposes. The object of this treatise is to provide a reasoned basis, built up on the facts of the old languages, Sanskrit, Greek, Latin, German, Celtic, Tamil, Persian, Arabic, for a partial reconstruction, not of the original *devabhāṣā*, but of the latest forms commonly original to the variations in these languages. I shall take the four languages, Sanskrit, Greek, Latin and Tamil first, to build up my scheme and then support it by the four other tongues. I omit all argument and handling of possible objections, because the object of this work is suggestive and constructive only, not apologetic. When the whole scheme is stated and has been worked out on a more comprehensive scale than is possible in the limits I have here set myself, the time will come for debate. Over an uncompleted exegesis, it would be premature.

I shall first indicate the principle on which the roots of the *devabhāṣā* were formed. All Shabda (*vāk*) as it manifests out of the *ākāśa* by the force of *mātariśvan*, the great active and creative energy, and is put in its place in the flux of formed things (*apas*) carries with it certain definite significances (*artha*). These are determined by the elements through which it has passed. *Śabda* appears in the *ākāśa*, travels through *vāyu*, the second element in which *sparśa* is the vibration; by the vibrations of *sparśa*, it creates in *tejas*, the third element, certain forms, and so arrives into being with these three characteristics, first, certain contactual vibrations, secondly, a particular kind of *tejas* or force, thirdly, a particular form. These determine the *bhāva* or general sensation it creates in the mind and from that sensation develop its various precise meanings according to the form which it is used to create.

BIBLIOGRAPHICAL NOTE

HYMNS TO THE MYSTIC FIRE, containing translations of hymns to Agni from Mandalas 1, 2 and 6 of the Rig-veda, was first published in 1946 with a Foreword by Sri Aurobindo.

An enlarged edition of HYMNS TO THE MYSTIC FIRE was issued in 1952 and contained the following additional material:

1) Revised translations of the "Hymns of the Atris" which had appeared originally in the *Arya* and subsequently had been published in ON THE VEDA.

2) Translations of other hymns to Agni which had hitherto remained unpublished. A few of these had been found in Sri Aurobindo's earlier manuscripts and included as they had stood.

Barring some forty hymns not translated, all the remaining Agni-Hymns of the Rig-veda were presented in this volume.

For the purposes of the Sri Aurobindo Birth Centenary Edition the 1952 enlarged edition has been used as "Copy". However, the entire text has been rechecked and several corrections are made. A few hymns to Agni and the article, "The Doctrine of the Mystics", have been shifted from ON THE VEDA to this volume. In the first two editions of HYMNS TO THE MYSTIC FIRE this article was only partly reproduced.

Certain notes and studies found among Sri Aurobindo's manuscripts dealing with the hymns to Agni and with "Word-formation" from his material for a full philological reconstruction of the old Aryabhasha, have been added here as a supplement.

OTHER TITLES BY SRI AUROBINDO

Sri Aurobindo
Secret of the Veda

SECRET OF THE VEDA by Sri Aurobindo

In this ground-breaking book, Sri Aurobindo has revealed the Secret of the Veda and illustrated his method with numerous translations of the ancient hymns. *Secret of the Veda* has been acclaimed by scholars and yogins as the ultimate key to revealing the hidden sense and secret inner meanings of the original spiritual revelation of the Veda. The Rig Veda provides an inner spiritual and psychological practice to achieve realization. It is the foundation upon which the Upanishads were later developed.
Now in its First U.S. Edition
LOTUS LIGHT PUBLICATIONS. ISBN 0-914955-19-5   581p $19.95

ESSAYS ON THE GITA by Sri Aurobindo

Sri Aurobindo
Essays on the Gita

The Bhagavad Gita stands alone in the spiritual tradition of humanity, by being at the same time a Scripture, a teaching, a poetic utterance and a practical guidebook to the problems of life in the world. For this reason, the Gita is a powerful aid to anyone who wants to integrate the life of the Spirit with the issues of life in the world. It does not "cut the knot" but systematically works to untie it. In so doing, it helps us clarify the issues alive within ourselves. Sri Aurobindo understood these issues and in his famous *Essays on the Gita* he was able to reveal many subtle and hidden aspects of the teaching of the Gita. He entered into the spirit of the original and created a commentary that has stood the test of time in its lucidity and value for anyone wishing to truly understand the Bhagavad Gita. *Essays on the Gita* has been widely acclaimed for opening up the deeper sense of the Bhagavad Gita.
Now in its First U.S. Edition LOTUS LIGHT PUBLICATIONS. ISBN 0-914955-18-7   588p $19.95

Sri Aurobindo
The Mother

THE MOTHER by Sri Aurobindo

Sri Aurobindo has created, in this small book, a powerful guide to the practice of spirituality in life. To discover this gem is to gain a constant companion whose guidance remains forever meaningful. Its power of expression and meaning are so concentrated and far reaching that many have called it "Matri Upanishad," the Upanishad of the Mother. Sri Aurobindo's Matri Upanishad is the text which reveals this power and energy of creation in its universal and personal sense, providing both truth of philosophy and truth of yogic experience at one and the same time.
Now in its First U.S. Edition
LOTUS LIGHT PUBLICATIONS. ISBN 0-941524-79-5   62p   pb $2.95

SAVITRI: A Legend and a Symbol by Sri Aurobindo

Sri Aurobindo
Savitri
A Legend and a Symbol

Savitri is an inner guidebook for the soul. These mantric verses imbue even the body with potent spiritual resonance. In this epic spiritual poem, Sri Aurobindo reveals his vision of mankind's destiny within the universal evolution. He sets forth the optimistic view that life on earth has a purpose, and he places our travail within the context of this purpose: to participate in the evolution of consciousness that represents the secret thread behind life on earth. Sri Aurobindo's verses describe the origin of the universe, the appearance of sentient beings, and the stages of evolution, as well as speak to many of mankind's unanswered questions concerning pain and death.
Now in its First U.S. Edition
LOTUS LIGHT PUBLICATIONS. ISBN 0-941524-80-9   816p   pb $24.95

available from your local bookseller or
LOTUS LIGHT PUBLICATIONS
PO Box 325, Twin Lakes, WI 53181
414/889-8561

REBIRTH AND KARMA

$9.95; 190 pp; pb ISBN 0-941524-63-9

Sri Aurobindo

Rebirth and Karma

In depth study of the concepts of rebirth, karma and the higher lines of karma. One of the best introductions to this area we've ever found.

LIFE DIVINE

By Sri Aurobindo

$29.95; 1113 pp; pb ISBN 0-941524-61-2
$39.95; 1113 pp; hb ISBN 0-941524-62-0

Sri Aurobindo

The Life Divine

The Life Divine is Sri Aurobindo's major philosophical exposition, spanning more than a thousand pages and integrating the major spiritual directions of mankind into a coherent picture of the growth of the spiritual essence of man through diverse methods, philosophies and spiritual practices.

THE INTEGRAL YOGA:
Sri Aurobindo's Teaching and Method of Practice
by Sri Aurobindo (compilation)

"These carefully selected excerpts from the writings of Sri Aurobindo provide a wonderfully accessible entre into the writings of one of the great masters of spiritual synthesis."
    Ram Dass
ISBN 0-941524-76-0   416 pp p $14.95

Sri Aurobindo

The Integral Yoga
Sri Aurobindo's Teaching and Method of Practice

available from your local bookseller or
LOTUS LIGHT PUBLICATIONS
PO Box 325, Twin Lakes, WI 53181
414/889-8561